GONZO MARKETING

ALSO BY CHRISTOPHER LOCKE

The Cluetrain Manifesto

(with Rick Levine, Doc Searls,
and David Weinberger)

GONZO MARKETING

Winning through Worst Practices

CHRISTOPHER LOCKE

PERSEUS
PUBLISHING

www.gonzomarkets.com

Cataloging-in-Publication Data is available from the Library of Congress
ISBN 0-7382-0408-0

Perseus Publishing is a member of the Perseus Books Group.
Find us on the World Wide Web at http://www.perseuspublishing.com
Perseus Publishing books are available at special discounts for bulk purchases in the U.S. by corporations, institutions, and other organizations. For more information, please contact the Special Markets Department at the Perseus Books Group, 11 Cambridge Center, Cambridge, MA 02142, or call (617) 252-5298.

Text design by Jeffrey P. Williams
Set in 11-point ITC Garamond by Perseus Publishing Services

First printing, October 2001

1 2 3 4 5 6 7 8 9 10—03 02 01

contents

Acknowledgements · · · ix

Introduction:
Participating in the Scene · · · 1

1 Eight Miles High: The View from 40,000 Feet · · · 19

2 The Value Proposition · · · 43

3 Code Blue in the Marketing Ward · · · 65

4 Stories as Strange Attractors · · · 103

5 Social Marketing and Public Journalism · · · 129

6 From Micromedia to Micromarkets · · · 165

7 The Gonzo Model · · · 183

8 Champions of the World · · · 203

Notes · · · 215

Index · · · 229

About the Author · · · 243

for

LAURIE DOCTOR

your mind my sky
your eyes my fire

www.lauriedoctor.com

ACKNOWLEDGEMENTS

BITS AND PIECES OF THIS BOOK FIRST APPEARED IN DIFFERENT FORM— they've since been sliced and diced through my gonzo Vegematic— in various hardcopy and online publications: *Agency* (the journal of the American Association of Advertising Agencies), *byte.com* (thanks to Daniel Dern), *Digitrends, Harvard Business Review* (thanks to John Landry), *Publish, sweetfancymoses.com* (thanks to Matt Herlihy), *Feed* (thanks to Steven Johnson), and *Release 1.0* (thanks to Kevin Werbach). I'd like to especially thank Esther Dyson for her support and inspiration over the past 15 years, even when she wasn't aware she was providing it. Esther, you're a brick.

Chris Anderson, formerly with *The Economist* and now at *Wired*, jousted with me over sundry issues surrounding e-commerce. His good natured yet insistent prodding led to the beginnings of *The Cluetrain Manifesto*, in which book I neglected to thank him. As those ideas are still operative in the present work, it's not too late to say thanks. So thanks.

I'd also like to thank my *Cluetrain* co-authors David Weinberger, Doc Searls, and Rick Levine for keeping the flame(s) alive, David at *JOHO* (hyperorg.com), Doc through his excellent blogging (doc.weblogs.com), and Rick at Word of Mouth (www.wom.com).

To my agent David Miller, I owe a great deal. And not just for the great deal he cut on this book. The outfit he cut it with, Perseus Publishing, is the best company I've ever worked with. David Goehring, Elizabeth Carduff, Lissa Warren, and my new editor Nick Philipson have all been wonderful: smart, understanding, and loads of fun. Jacqueline Murphy, who was my editor through the main construction phase, has since moved on. But in ways too numerous to catalog, this is her book.

Many thanks to Eric Norlin of The Titanic Deck Chair Rearrangement Corporation (tdcrc.com) for his thoughtful feedback on early drafts, and for sending the Everclear and Eminem CDs. Eric is beyond a doubt the world's most capable CEO.

J.P. Rangaswami (of Dresdner Kleinwort Wasserstein) and Fritz Gutbrodt (of Swiss Re) both make brief appearances here. Too brief. They were fabulous hosts in London and Zurich, respectively, and I learned much from our conversations.

My sister, Elizabeth Locke, gave me more suggestions than I knew what to do with; for instance, about arcane matters like reciprocal ethnography. Liz, you're a trip, but you already knew that. Selene, my 11 year old daughter, also provided innumerable cool ideas. I believe her insight into the current state of marketing practice remains unparalleled.

Though Laurie Doctor appears on the dedication page, what is not apparent to anyone but myself is *her* dedication, for which no amount of gratitude will ever be sufficient.

Finally, I'd like to thank the thousands of (valued) *EGR* readers, who have not only endured my abstruse prolixity and unwarranted abuse, but who continue to grant me the invaluable permission to publicly discover what I mean to say

Participating in the Scene

Only the insane take themselves quite seriously.

—SIR MAX BEERBOHM[1]

THIS IS A SERIOUS BOOK. NO FOOLING.

Now right off the bat that has to make you wonder, right? Because most books, especially business books, pretty much take it for granted that you believe that going in. Of course the book is serious. That's why you bought it. Either that, or you needed an over-the-counter alternative to your regular insomnia medication. Don't laugh. Recent studies show that seven out of ten business book buyers are really looking for semantic Sominex. And, as Harley Manning of Forrester Research points out in his insightful report—"The Snooze Factor: Sleepy Time in the Management Aisle"—these consumers find what they're looking for in 82% of all online book transactions.[2]

But seriously. In his seminal work, *Homo Ludens: A Study of the Play Element in Culture,* the Dutch cultural historian Johan Huizinga riffs on the perennial theme of wisdom, from the Latin *sapientia.* "A happier age than ours," he wrote, "once made bold to call our species by the name of Homo Sapiens." However, he wonders how appropriate this label remains today. "In the course of time we have come to realize that we are not so reasonable after all as the Eighteenth Century, with its worship of reason and its naive optimism, thought us." So someone came up with Homo Faber: Man the Maker. Better, Huizinga says, but still no cigar. Homo Ludens, he then proposes: Man the Player.[3]

While some will find the notion ludicrous, play is no less an important aspect of business than it is of life. This is probably because, contrary to widespread popular belief, commerce is a subset of life and not the other way around. Therefore, as Huizinga goes to great lengths to point out, play is serious business. Or something like that. I only read the foreword.

In 1962, the French anthropologist Claude Levi-Strauss wrote a book called *The Savage Mind*, in which he says "Language is a form of human reason and has its reasons which are unknown to man." Man, I don't even know why I quoted that, except that it sounds pretty cool.[4] More to the point, he talks about a concept for which English has no equivalent: *bricolage*.[5] In essence, bricolage is what tinkers do—collecting odd bits of stuff they think may be potentially useful, then using whatever bits seem to work in the context of some later repair job. Simple. And yet profound. Because the bits the bricoleur ends up using were not designed for the use they end up being put to. Figuring out which bits to collect and how to apply them to some task at hand requires a completely different kind of thinking than the procedural algorithmic thought processes business has become so dependent upon. While the Internet may have convinced some businesses to think "out of the box," most are still not even sure what box they're in, much less which way to turn for emergency egress. If some unprincipled individual were to yell "fire!" right about now, the entire edifice of global commerce might suddenly collapse.

Fire! Fire!

What the hell. Because, while few corporations seem to realize it, the entire edifice of global commerce is collapsing already—under its own top-heavy weight. And this is happening at the very moment business is crowing loudest about its own gross tonnage: the biggest media mergers, biggest advertising budgets, biggest aggregation of eyeballs. Yuck, what an image. In short, the messiest, massiest mass-marketing morass the world has ever seen. It's ironic.

In a wonderful *Newsweek* article titled "Will We Ever Get Over Irony?" David Gates writes about the postmodern inclination to rip (off) ideas from a broad range of historical contexts and recombine them in odd and often glaring ways. "Such juxtapositional ironies flourish in the 20th century's most characteristic artistic mode: call it collage, assemblage, bricolage, pastiche or (to be less Frenchified and more *au courant*) sampling."[6] Aha! Now we're getting somewhere—though these equivalents make the overall effect no less odd. The glare produced is still a kind of cognitive dissonance. Things that don't fit together in expected ways can make your head hurt. However, under the right conditions, this pain can also produce insight. It can illuminate not only the box, but the EXIT sign as well.

I can see already that you're skeptical, gentle reader. This isn't sounding entirely level-headed, is it? Doesn't quite have that grim-visaged wrinkle-browed aura of unassailable fact. Hmmm, must be time for a quote from *Harvard Business Review*. "Pragmatic managers. . . know what resources are available and how to round up more on short notice," write a couple of bona fide Ph.D.s, doubtless recalling how they managed to scrape by on assistant professor salaries. "We call this aspect of pragmatism bricolage . . . Effective managers are bricoleurs . . . They play with possibilities. . . They tinker. . . ."[7]

Now you believe me? Well, good. Oh yeah and by the way, Levi-Strauss says bricolage is analogous to the mythical thinking typical of primitive peoples. Savages. You know, the kind of uncivilized barbarians you get in places like Harvard, Borneo, New Guinea and the World Wide Web.[8] So, taking all the above into account (along with a grain of salt and two aspirins), think of this book as playful bricolage involving serious matters. As sampling. As a hip-hop cover of boring old best practices played backwards and burned into a bad-ass MP3 dance remix download. At times, the recombinant results may strike you as freakish, as frivolous. Feel free to sue me. However, you'll get far more satisfaction by thinking of yourself as I do: as a Raider of the Lost Arc. To sample once again the comedy stylings of Johan Huizinga. . .

The reader of these pages should not look for detailed documentation of every word. In treating of the general problems of culture one is constantly obliged to undertake predatory incursions into provinces not sufficiently explored by the raider himself. To fill in all the gaps in my knowledge beforehand was out of the question for me. I had to write now, or not at all. And I wanted to write.[9]

As Lou Gerstner, chairman and CEO of IBM once said, "Hey, I can dig it."[10] The concept of gonzo marketing would never have come together at all if I'd had to rigorously research every damn thread we're about to touch on. Will some of these lead us into curious intellectual culs-de-sac? Yeah, probably. Are you likely to encounter grievous gaffes and disquieting half truths? Sure, but what else is new? By screwing up royally here, I hope to provide a new kind of model demonstrating to business that it not only can, but *must* move beyond its unhealthy fear of error and imprecision. Today, it is certainty that is not an option. Failure is almost guaranteed.

In addition to being a sort of indie-Indy, I also think of myself as An Amateur and a Dilettante. The caps are there to echo the title of the movie, *An Officer and a Gentleman*—though as you're already finding out, I'm neither. At its heart, gonzo is animated by an attitude of deeply principled anti-professionalism in the best sense. And there is a best sense. Historian and former Librarian of Congress Daniel J. Boorstin once wrote: "Democracy is government by amateurs. . . . The survival of our society depends on the vitality of the amateur spirit. . . . The representative of the people . . . must be wary of becoming a professional politician."[11]

Here, amateur clearly doesn't mean incompetent or unskilled. It doesn't mean unprofessional. But professional-*ism* is something altogether else. Over time, any functional specialization tends to forget its relationship to the larger social context it was created to work within and serve. Instead, it concentrates on developing an inner sanctum of specialists who talk among themselves in a private language inaccessible to outsiders. Almost without exception, such professionals despise amateurs. Or worse, accord them a patronizing form of faux eye-rolling patience.

Related to "amateur" is the even more pejorative term *"dilettante"*—someone who practices a craft or studies a field of knowledge in which he or she is not a "recognized professional." But the etymological roots of these words tell a different story. Amateurs do what they do for love (from the Latin *amare*), while dilettantes are not mere casual dabblers, but instead are inspired by delight (from the Italian *dilettare* by way of the Latin *delectare*). But delight and passion for the work are precisely the qualities professionals tend to lose first. The opposite of professionalism is what Zen master Shunryu Suzuki called *"beginner's mind"*—an ability to look at the world with fresh eyes and an open spirit.[12]

Boorstin's observation can be equally applied to the commercial sphere. In marketing, just as in government, professionalism tends to hew unimaginatively to its own timid orthodoxy. It does not provide leadership, enthusiasm or the kind of impassioned personal engagement that has come to be called gonzo. In stark contrast, business professionalism tends to be arid and passionless, narrowly focused, self-involved. However, this doesn't mean that everyone in business fits this damning characterization. Far from it. In my own experience, there are many more lively intellects at work in the workplace than the misbegotten "corporate communications" coming out of those places would lead one to believe. There's often more going on in today's corporation than today's corporation would care to admit. New life is growing between the cracks in the corporate edifice, and it's spreading like a weed.

In the past year or so, I've had the opportunity to test many of the ideas in this book before *very* live business audiences from Maui to Bangalore. At places like Peoplesoft, Gartner Group, Sun Microsystems, SAP, First Union Bank, the Direct Marketing Association, and Andersen Consulting—now, for their sins, renamed Accenture. To be fair, my Accenture-nee-Andersen audience was great. It was clear they'd been around the block. They'd seen it all. They laughed in all the right places. On the other hand, the Direct Marketing crowd was thoroughly unamused. Understandable. The rending of garments and gnashing of teeth would have been appropriate responses.

The day before I spoke at Swiss Re (the Re is for reinsurance, a hugely lucrative niche), my hosts opened an impressive mucho-multimillion-dollar conference facility called Rüschlikon. The festivities included a Chinese dancer performing on a rooftop in the snow to piano music piped to her wireless headset and further accompanied by nocturnal animal cries taped in some Southeast Asian jungle. In addition, there was an extremely Zen-looking Japanese guy playing a 2000-year-old stone flute that appeared to be nearly as ancient as himself, and a terrorist-looking dude with his face weirdly painted in striking primary colors, who read long strings of numbers in German, timed to a strobe light. "Acht hundert neun und zwanzig, sieben hundert vier und dreizig. . ." Yeah, just another day of business as usual. The center's director, Fritz Gutbrodt, told me over a wonderfully animated dinner that he still teaches literature at the University of Zürich.

The investment banking firm of Dresdner, Kleinwort, Benson was a slightly different story. IT director J. P. Rangaswami runs offsite swat teams that take a real problem, break it down, come up with a solution, code it, and integrate the results into the corporate computing infrastructure—all within a week. In an industry where this sort of thing is usually measured in months, quarters or years, such results are astounding. Everyone on the team is expected to drink copious amounts of beer, liberally provided, between the impossibly long, often round-the-clock, hacking sessions. J. P. is working on a book about certain structural and management challenges facing large corporations. Working title: *Fossil Fools*. We had many deep exchanges about what's truly important in this industry at the moment. He turned me on to a Dire Straits bootleg. I convinced him to buy a pricey but totally kickass Roland guitar synth. "Damn you," he wrote later in email, "you are starting to cost me real money!"

The Dresdner gang isn't cheap, though. They gleefully fete me with sumptuous dinners in Mayfair, theater tickets, limousines. Would I care to take in The Tate? They put me up in the Docklands, an outrageous suite overlooking the Thames. I drop some laundry off with the valet and it comes back wrapped in rich brocade, my socks and underwear not only *ironed*—what were they thinking?— but also tied into little bundles with red ribbons that say "Four Seasons Hotel—Canary Wharf." It's totally over the top. I love it. But finally I have to get out, get real again. I give my talk on gonzo marketing, then ditch the chauffer. I take a train, then a bus. I get lost. London is better at eye level. . .

Waiting for History

"There was a demon that lived in the air. They said whoever challenged him would die. Their controls would freeze up,

> their planes would buffet wildly, and they would
> disintegrate. The demon lived at Mach 1. . .
> They called it the sound barrier."
>
> —FROM THE MOVIE *THE RIGHT STUFF*

> "We're never gonna survive unless we get a little crazy . . . "
>
> —SEAL

I round the corner in Covent Garden and hear what sounds like Coltrane wafting up the block. Bent into his horn as if in fervent prayer, a musician is laying down fat splashy bop notes in the rain, punctuating the oblivious crowds of pre-Christmas shoppers. His saxophone case is open for donations and I drop in a ten pound note. He's surprisingly good to be playing in the street. Seeing the denomination, he jumps up and presses a compact disc into my hand. I turn it over. Karlsax Online it says.

The rain forests of the world constitute a cauldron of biological ferment and co-evolutionary experimentation, a living ecosystem where few parts exist independent of the whole. Lianas and mahoganies, primates and insect colonies, jaguars and bromeliads, slow-moving sloths and dazzling butterflies, intermittent light and impenetrable darkness, the endless cycle of rain and evaporation, transpiration and erosion, all weave together to produce a tapestry of nearly unimaginable color and complexity. The human world is no less complex, and the Internet reflects a similarly rich interweaving, the customs and experience of myriad diverse societies and cultures. The net is a planet-spanning virtual ecosystem, a cognitive rain forest teeming with new concepts and connections, issues and inquiries, studies and speculations, proposals, predictions and unlimited potential.

Something's shaking, something's up. But we're none of us quite sure what it is, what it all adds up to. How long will we have to wait for the history books that explain this amazing period we're living through? Fifty years? A hundred? I don't know about you, but I don't have that long. As you may recall, we die. My dates are the same as Jackson Browne's. "In '65 I was 17," he sang in "Running on Empty." Plus: "gotta do what you can just to keep your love

alive"—immediately thereafter warning of the dangers of confusing
that with whatever you need to do to survive, to "make a living" as
we say. And now you're wondering again: *Jackson Browne?* Hey,
when you write these sorts of penetrating and insightful business
books for busy executive types, you take your inspiration wherever
you find it.

In the meantime, the time of our lives, all we have is intuition and
stories to try to make sense of the world, to provide some sort of
vision of where we're at and where we may be headed. But that's
not so bad. As a species, it's all we've ever had.

Gonzo marketing is the shorthand I use for the work I do—work
I fell into almost accidentally, rather than as a path I set out on
knowing in advance where it would lead. At first, I looked for models, guidelines, some sort of framework that would make sense of
the business world I suddenly found myself inhabiting. But what I
found seemed oddly broken, or ill-conceived from the outset. Perhaps because I came to the computer industry from such a contrasting set of experiences—brain surgery (yes, really), railroad
braking, goat husbandry, boat carpentry, pharmaceutical, uh. . .
mergers and acquisitions—most of what I saw passing for best practice seemed naïve to the point of being ridiculous. Even from the
inside, it felt demeaning.

At first I thought I'd get the hang of it with time. But I never did.
Along the way, I've become less and less professional. To make a
living, I had to find something I could do that actually worked. And
to work for my company or client, first it had to work for me. Call
it a character defect, but I'm no good at anything I can't put my
heart into. So I explored. I followed my heart. And I began to discover that many of the things that worked were the diametric opposite of what was normal and expected in business. In fact, the
more diametrically opposed, the more contrarian the approach, the
more effective it tended to be. I began calling these directions, attitudes and informal rules-of-thumb "worst practices."

They aren't algorithms or recipes. They're not procedures.
They're inclinations and actions that flow from a particular state of
mind. And states of mind don't lend themselves very well to bullet
points. However, they can sometimes be transmitted through stories. Stories don't deal in definitions and formulas. Instead, they

convey impressions, colors, connotations. Their effect is cumulative. The whole encompasses more than the sum of the parts, suggesting new ways to look at problems. And sometimes, imaginative new approaches to solving them.

I once heard a talk on aircraft design in which the speaker explained the aerodynamic basis for a scene in a movie I saw as a kid. I can't recall the name of the film, but I've often used this scenario as an analogy for solving critical problems by going against "the rules" dictated by the sort of sanity and logic that would apply under normal conditions. In the movie, various test pilots attempt to fly an experimental plane capable of supersonic speed. As the plane approaches Mach 1, something strange happens to the controls. Instead of causing the plane to climb, pulling back on the stick puts it into a dive, with terminal consequences for both plane and pilot. Finally, our hero, Chuck Yeager, breaks the sound barrier and lives to tell about it by reversing the normal procedure. As the plane begins to bore in, he pushes forward on the stick instead of pulling it back. The story may be apocryphal, but the point is that the pilot never would have survived unless he did something that was— according to all available evidence up until that time—a little crazy.

This story was retold by Tom Wolfe in *The Right Stuff*, the 1979 book from which the movie was made four years later. Wolfe was fascinated by people who did the wrong thing at the right time— like Ken Kesey and the Merry Pranksters dropping way too much LSD in *The Electric Kool-Aid Acid Test*. But that was later. In 1973, six years before *The Right Stuff*, Wolfe wrote another book called *The New Journalism*, in which he included Hunter S. Thompson's story "The Kentucky Derby is Decadent and Depraved." Here Thompson answers a worried question from his illustrator, Ralph Steadman:

"Is it safe out there? Will we *ever* come back?"

"Sure," I said. "We'll just have to be careful not to step on anybody's stomach and start a fight." I shrugged. "Hell, this clubhouse scene right below us will be almost as bad as the infield. Thousands of raving, stumbling drunks, getting angrier and angrier as they lose more and more money. By midafternoon they'll be guzzling mint juleps with both hands and vomiting on each other between races.

The whole place will be jammed with bodies, shoulder to shoulder. It's hard to move around. The aisles will be slick with vomit; people falling down and grabbing at your legs to keep from being stomped. Drunks pissing on themselves in the betting lines. Dropping handfuls of money and fighting to stoop over and pick it up."

He looked so nervous that I laughed. "I'm just kidding," I said. "Don't worry. At the first hint of trouble I'll start Macing everybody I can reach."[13]

And Dr. Thompson has been Macing everybody he could reach ever since. He's reached quite a few. Merriam-Webster defines *gonzo* as "idiosyncratically subjective but engagé." As dictionary definitions go, this one's delicious. A bit fruity perhaps, but a great nose and a nice finish. It also means "bizarre" the lexicographers add rather woodenly, ruining the whole effect.

Thompson created gonzo journalism, a genre in which high humor meets bad taste. *Fear and Loathing in Las Vegas* burst onto the literary scene with tsunami force in 1971. It was shocking, electrifying. He was simultaneously writing for *Rolling Stone* magazine, and the rock-and-roll connection was no accident. There's a clue here the size of Everest that, to this day, remains invisible in plain sight. Around the same time, the Temptations were singing "Papa Was a Rolling Stone," the Rolling Stones were singing "I bet your mama was a tent show queen," and Thompson was writing: "Moments after we picked up the car, my attorney went into a drug coma and ran a red light on Main Street. . . "[14] It makes the historian's task a real bitch when everything is connected and nothing is what is seems.

But gonzo is far more than the shock tactics it employs. *"The writer must be a participant in the scene while he's writing it,"* Thompson said. Being a full participant in events, having a point of view, a deeply personal perspective: gonzo is about being *engaged*. It's not distanced, impartial or "objective"—it cares about outcomes. When Hunter Thompson wrote about Nixon, he wasn't just writing about one of two presidential candidates. He was writing about someone he hated—hated to the point of intimacy, so much that he almost loved the man. When Thompson got done with Nixon, Nixon wasn't an abstraction. He was as real as a hurricane hitting into the Keys. As concrete as a head-on train wreck.

Gonzo journalism represented a significant shift in news reporting, or at least the option of a new direction. It granted other writers the permission to be human, to stop pretending they were automatic cameras recording events about which they had no opinion, in which they had no personal stake. And it granted this permission even to writers who *didn't* sprinkle acid on their morning cornflakes.

While the so-called legitimate press (where does *that* come from?) has not exactly risen to the occasion in overwhelming numbers, plenty of net-heads have. In the next X years, billions of dollars worth of news, information, entertainment and what I like to call "The Artist Formerly Known As Advertising" are going to do a full 180. That is, a very large proportion of these media functions will no longer be delivered top-down, as in the broadcast model, but will be coming bottom-up from creative individuals on the Internet. X may be two years or five years or ten—the question is not if but when. These changes are inevitable for reasons the balance of this book will explore more deeply.

Business created mass markets through broadcast advertising, the same stentorian voice of command-and-control it used on workers, but in this case applied to the marketplace. "Shut up and do what you're told" is not that much different a proposition from "shut up and buy our product." The "shut up" part was built in to broadcast, as there was never any back-channel—never a way to ask questions. The 30-second jive-and-jingle TV spot was never an invitation to converse.

The Internet brings something different into the world. It has connected people person-to-person, and the people so connected are today talking among each other about things they truly value. People are telling stories. From the dawn of human society, people have been drawn together by storytellers who not only shared their interests but also had a special quality of speech—let's call it *voice*. True voice is not just the ability to speak, but the ability to speak effectively. The best measure of this effectiveness is whether a particular voice can attract and hold an audience. This is as true today as it was in Neolithic times.

Tom and Ray Magliozzi are Click and Clack, the self-styled Tappet Brothers of National Public Radio's "Car Talk" show. They're funny, engaging, and they know their stuff cold. I don't know what a carburetor even looks like, but I could listen to these guys for hours.

While "Car Talk" is an offline phenomenon—and as NPR's largest non-news program it is a phenomenon—another critical factor comes into play when the Internet is involved. Because the barriers to entry are so low, storytelling and voice do not necessarily have much to do with what business usually cares most about: the size of the audience. An online audience can be microscopic by mass-media standards. Nonetheless, the micro audiences just now taking shape on the net are also potential micro *markets*. web-based micromarkets are currently coalescing in real-time around articulate, entertaining, knowledgeable voices.

Take Motley Fool, which began as a minuscule dot in the petri dish of AOL's greenhouse incubator.[15] Today, these "fools" touch millions of personal investors. Micromarkets needn't remain micro. Internet communities have always been self-selecting—audiences gather around content of high personal interest. In this natural aggregation, online is far more efficient than conventional media. People find what they want not as much through advertising as through far more credible word-of-mouth from friends and colleagues.

The mass markets traditionally served by broadcast media have been steadily fragmenting for decades as a result of global competition. Evidence of this erosion are market segmentation and targeting techniques, which attempt to track the detritus of once-mass markets the way an astronomer tracks the remnants of a burnt-out supernova. As competition for even tiny niches has intensified, market segments have become smaller and more refined, to the point that business is currently in hot pursuit of concepts like personalization and one-to-one marketing. However, many of these "mass customization" approaches still rely on analytic tools developed for conventional market segmentation, which in turn require some sort of historical market data—e.g., left-handed red-headed 18–25 year old males tend to buy more Snickers bars than right-handed blond 25–32 year old females.

But what happens when such historical data does not exist? Entirely new micromarkets are emerging on the web today. The real challenge lies not in predicting the behavior of markets this small, but in determining their existence. Because they are currently much smaller than existing market segments, they don't show up on conventional market radar screens. Because they have no history and don't behave like the markets that grew up around broadcast media, demographic segmentation is of little use in determining who constitutes these new micromarkets.

These new realities are presented above as seen from a corporate vantage point. From an Internet perspective, web micromarkets don't think of themselves as markets at all, but rather as nascent communities of interest. They tend to gravitate around articulate, knowledgeable, entertaining voices—individuals or small groups driven by a passion to communicate their views. Because entry costs require high returns on investment, broadcast media rarely offer such emergent voices a hearing. However, the Internet reverses this trend, providing many low-cost vectors for small-scale publishing—Usenet newsgroups, email lists, weblogs, web pages. Think of these as "*micromedia*" as opposed to mass media.

Such micromedia will replace a great deal of current advertising. They will quickly become the best source of user-supplied news about products and services (Amazon.com broke new ground along these lines by inviting customer reviews). Potential buyers will not have to hunt down this information, but will find it in the online venues to which they naturally gravitate according to their interests. Companies that engage in this type of dialogue will forge powerful relationships with micromarkets that will soon—continuing a trend toward market fragmentation that's been in effect for many decades—become their major source of revenues.

The Internet constitutes a market for ideas—real ideas that interest real people, not just the feel-good fantasies of product vendors. What's missing today is an effective method of *marketing* those ideas undistorted by hype and hucksterism. Mass production, whether of goods or information, has always depended on broadcast marketing in which markets are viewed as top-down targets from the lofty vantage point of long-established power and control. The Internet has destroyed that vantage. Wave after wave of new arrivals have eroded the cliffs it's built upon and the castle is crumbling into the sea.

It's about time.

Net markets are micromarkets, reflecting not the mass of humanity, but rather the voluntary alliance of individuals around deeply shared interests. Because such communities are still growing bottom-up, they have don't have the sort of demographic profiles companies have always depended on to identify new business. These micromarkets are just emerging. They hardly exist yet. Invisible to the lens of traditional marketing, they are ignored.

But don't be fooled. Micromarkets aren't insignificant markets, and given the speed of propagation the net enables, their emergence will be faster than the emergence of the Internet itself. This book describes how billions of dollars of advertising, news, information and entertainment are about to shift out of corporate control forever.

The resulting landscape will not be a neat and orderly world, any more than a rain forest, or any physical ecosystem, is neat and orderly. Rather, it will be wild in many of the senses poet Gary Snyder lists in his book *The Practice of the Wild*:[16]

> free, self-propagating, self-maintaining, flourishing in accord with innate qualities, pristine, ordered from within and maintained by the force of consensus and custom rather than explicit legislation, populated with original and eternal inhabitants, resisting economic and political domination, unintimidated, self-reliant, independent, proud, far-out, outrageous, "bad," admirable, artless, spontaneous, unconditioned, expressive and ecstatic.

Of course, artlessness and ecstatic badness don't always come in such a poetic package. The quality of wildness most lacking in commerce is play. Yet play, once again, is serious business. To the rollicking delight of online audiences everywhere, corporations seem to get easily confused trying to balance their overly earnest brand personas with their All-New SuperCool E-Brand Avatars that plead, "hey look, we're just one of the gang!" The resulting display is a little like watching baboons dress up in Barbie doll outfits: amusing for a while, but ultimately unconvincing. Play is serious stuff, profound even. While it's hard to describe, we all know it when we see it, flourishing as it tends to do, in accord with innate qualities. Even when those qualities are coming at you right straight off the wall. . .

Difficulty At The Beginning[17]

". . . you can go up on a steep hill in Las Vegas and look West, and with the right kind of eyes you can almost see the high-water mark—that place where the wave finally broke and rolled back."

—HUNTER S. THOMPSON, *FEAR AND LOATHING IN LAS VEGAS*[18]

How many days have I been racked out on this couch? Three? Four? I got back from London last week and immediately came down with the flu. Influenza the ancients called it. An evil influence from the stars. Between hits of Alka Seltzer Plus and fitful bouts of restless, fevered sleep, I've been reading Elmore Leonard's novel, *The Hunted*. Maybe that's what did it.

Somebody's banging on my door and bellowing. "Locke! Come out here you bottom-feeding scum sucker! I know you're in there. Come out or I'm coming in!" Something much harder than a fist hits the door with a sickening thud. A window shatters. I'm waking up now. More like coming to. What was I just dreaming? Something about the book. Something terrible. You know those dreams that keep repeating, won't let you go? One of those. I won't be able to finish it on time. I don't know what I'm doing, what to write. What if my publisher wants the money back? But this is worse. I stumble to the door, undo the bolt.

And find myself eye-to-eye with the uncompromising orifice of a shotgun barrel. Look how round it is. Nasty. I am definitely not ready for this. "Look," I croak, my voice breaking, "I've got a mother of a cold going on here. Could you maybe come back later?"

A rough hand reaches through the door and grabs me by the shirt, yanking me out into the cold, then hurling me back against the long bank of entryway windows. It's not the Fed-Ex guy. Not UPS or the mailman. Nobody else ever comes here. "Who are you?" I manage, "and why are you doing this?" The man looks crazed. He looks as if he's been drinking. Maybe even on drugs.

Then I notice the cigarette holder. Oh dear God. My worst nightmare come true. It's Hunter S. Thompson. In that case, definitely on drugs. "I wish I had something to offer you," I say, thinking as fast as I can, which isn't very, "but I quit drinking 17 years ago." He jacks a shell into the pump. Uh-oh, wrong approach. However, he sees that I've recognized him. Sees the confusion lifting, the fear dawning in my face.

"I understand you're writing a book," he drawls. And just lets it hang there, the whole scene suddenly framed in tableaux. I should have seen this coming. I should have called it Seven something. Or something about Simplicity or Cheese. "Look," I say . . . but that's as far as I get because the shotgun is now jammed between my teeth. "Mrphh rmble xltrig forqwad!" I protest.

"A book about gonzo," he says with towering contempt. "A book about gonzo *marketing*," he says, and spits—an ugly gesture at the best of times, and I'm thinking this isn't one of them. But at least he's pulled the gun back some, so I can talk.

"Hunter, man! It's not what you think! You're gonna love it, actually. See, the reason it's gonzo is what you said about the writer needing to be engaged in what he's writing." I compulsively add ". . . well, he or she." Big mistake. He rams the barrel into my sternum, pinning me against the window. "Yeah sure, so it's a business book, OK. But not *that* kind of business book. You know?" It doesn't look like he knows. "Listen . . ." I try again.

But he says "No, you listen to this!" And suddenly there's a blinding light and a very loud noise that I'm hearing with every auditory synapse as I watch myself, fascinated, tumbling backwards in slow motion through the glass, which has shattered into a rainbow catching the morning light, fractal, delicate, heartbreakingly beautiful.

I slam into the Sony XBR TV, my head crashing through the largest tube job on today's consumer electronics market. Circuits spark and leap. The current streams into my brain. I realize as consciousness fades that the damn thing is trying to mate with me. Artificial intelligence attempting to spawn itself on the far and fading shores of broadcast. Predictably, the attempt fails.

The phone rings.

"Hello?" Tentative. Thinking maybe this is what comes after. You get some kind of call. But it's David Weinberger. You remember him from *Cluetrain*, right? "So how's the book coming?" he wants to know, all rested and cheery. At this moment I hate him. "I've decided not to write it," I hear myself saying. "I'm afraid people won't. . . you know, they just won't *get it*." Even though it's dawning on me it was all a dream. Still . . .

"What do you mean you're not writing it!" Weinberger thunders. I can tell he's secretly pleased, though. He just signed a contract for his own book and, really, the guy is more competitive than Larry Ellison. Also, he senses something deeply neurotic with strong psychoanalytic potential. But I head him off before he can get into it. "I just realized it was too complex," I say. "These business types haven't evolved enough yet. Maybe if I live another thousand years. . . "

I don't want to tell him the truth. That Woody Creek, Colorado, is only a few hundred miles into the mountains west of here and it's all too clear that that fearful loathsome Dr. Thompson is still up there somewhere. Alive and kicking.

CHAPTER 1

Eight Miles High:
The View from 40,000 Feet

"All your base are belong to us."

—*ZERO WING*[1]

MARKET RESEARCH IS DEAD. LET'S HOPE SO ANYWAY, BECAUSE ALL IT does is predict we'll want the same things tomorrow that we wanted yesterday. As practiced in most of the 20th century, market research works against creativity and the kind of risk taking that's crucially prerequisite to innovative products and services. Today, there's a counter-phenomenon at work, beginning in the realm of ideas. If they're any good, ideas propagate well over networks. And ideas create new markets.

The outcome hinges on that little word *if*. *If* they're any good. Market research takes an idea and asks what proof there is of an audience. Will the idea fly? And if so, with whom? To start a new cable channel today, it's necessary to prove an audience of 30 million viewers. That's a lot of eyeballs. And terms like *eyeballs* are what you get when you begin to think this way. How much can you know about individual tastes and interests among that many people? Not much. But all you really want to know is the chances of whether they'll tune in, because launching such a channel is going to take megabucks and whoever is putting up the cash is going to want pretty strong assurance of seeing those bucks back someday real soon, accompanied by a handsome return on the investment.

The return will come through advertising. Or so goes the formula. Aggregate enough eyeballs, show them whatever you think they want to see—which you hope market research will tell you—and slip in as much spam as you can between the "content" segments. The spam then cooks up into a tasty profit sandwich.

Traditionally, this approach has produced a lot of money. And little else. It has produced the kind of television programming where everything is nearly indistinguishable from everything else—where the women are always beautiful, the men are always tough, neither are any too bright and everybody wants to be a millionaire. Market research says that's what we want. So we get it by the bucketful, ad nauseam.

The same formula has produced "news" in which nothing is new. Watch CNN for a day and you'll hear the same stories repeated over and over in an endless loop. You think, how amazing that so little is happening in such a big world. If something really juicy is afoot—say a football advertising personality offs his wife, or some minor British royalty buys it in a car crash—you can watch the news for months at a time without hearing about much else. God help you if some cute little Cuban kid accidentally washes up in Florida.

But then, so much gets washed up in Florida. Two hundred years of American democracy, for instance. And again, it's the same market research formula at work behind the scenes. A presidential race run like a focus group, with a couple hundred million people expressing their poll-driven proclivities for the product features of Brand X or Brand Y. The U.S. election of 2000 reflected an almost beautiful, if totally twisted symmetry. Offered no real choice, the electorate returned no real decision. The only surprise is that anyone was surprised.

So what choice have we got? If everything we see and hear is beamed at us on the theory that what we want to see and hear is what we've *always* seen and heard, it seems we're inexorably condemned to some maddening media hell where it's always Groundhog Day. No wonder Eli Lilly sells so much Prozac. Who wouldn't go batshit under such conditions? Lab rats wouldn't just display neurotic behavior. They'd explode.

But we do have a choice: the Internet. Rather than explode with anger and frustration, a flood tide of humanity has immigrated to this temporary autonomous zone. The net is like a vast global city packed with displaced persons, refugees fleeing the insanity of mass media. "The sky above the port was the color of television tuned to a dead channel," wrote William Gibson in the opening salvo of *Neuromancer*,[2] the book that coined the word "*cyberspace*" in 1984 before anyone had ever been there. Artists are outsiders. But artists are also outriders. A dense and crowded matrix of rainy street corners, the net offers little shelter from the elements. But you can pick up your guitar and play. Just like yesterday. Or your sax or your word processor or your graphics or film editing software. Like tens of millions of disaffected kids with more time than money and more brains than most record company executives, you can crank up your MP3 encoder and your CD burner. As the music industry learned from Napster—just a few days late and a couple billion dollars short—you can change the rules.

Mass media works top-down. Like Aztec temples, they concentrate power and ownership atop steep pyramids based on command and control, using broadcast as a form of human sacrifice. To the teeming millions massing from the bottom up on the net today, this is not just an overburdened metaphor. Having been treated their entire lives only as eyeballs, as fodder for this impersonal, inhuman media mill, they have no allegiance to the gods of broadcast and their unholy rituals of content licensing and windfall profit. If you change the rules, you can change the world. And the only real question has become: why not?

But as predicted, this revolution is not being televised. Business depends for its intelligence on broadcast news and market research, both of which tell it what it wants to hear. Business has its ear to the wrong ground. Happily touting the wonders of e-commerce, it is tuned to a dead channel, deaf to the voices of the dispossessed.

At first, the world at large ignored the net, missed its significance, scoffed, then jumped in with both feet, thinking it was a bandwagon, asked the wrong questions about how to make money with it, got too excited when it seemed to be something it wasn't, too depressed when it turned out to be what it is: mirrored fractal nets within nets, the collective intelligence of the human race unfolding in real time—and for the first time, on its own terms. The Internet routes around obstacles; the bigger the obstacle, the more joyous the detour. The humorless power of the state, the iron-fisted control demanded by the corporation, the sexless desire insinuated by broadcast advertising—all are falling to networked imagination.[3]

And so far, we've just been playing. The flap over Napster is merely the toy of public opinion wound up and released—a plastic duck quacking its way through the mainstream media. It's right! It's wrong! The millennium has come! The end is nigh! But who cares? Most of this "debate" is looking backward, trying to salvage constructs that no longer matter. Whose property is intellect? Whose right the right to copy what has gone before? Human culture has always been the work of thieves, beginning with Prometheus. Kill Napster today, get the fire next time.

While the music industry wrings its hands over profits lost from catchy tunes it ensnared in the twentieth-century equivalent of bad-faith treaties with native tribes, the net is already dreaming about arts and music and literatures not yet composed. About how they will travel, whose eyes and ears, whose hearts they will arrive at. Business made an unholy pact with technology, and thought it had found the keys to the kingdom. But unlocking the gates, it imported a Trojan horse into the city of commerce. Within the code is a deeper code that business does not understand.

"Today I want to talk about piracy and music," said Courtney Love to the Digital Hollywood online entertainment conference in May 2000. "What is piracy?" she asked, then answered her own question. "Piracy is the act of stealing an artist's work without any intention of paying for it. I'm not talking about Napster-type software. I'm talking about major label recording contracts."[4]

Business goes into heat at the smell of teen spirit. It dreams of new and untapped Internet markets, actionable tips on viral marketing to the stupid-turned-contagious? Yeah well, here we are now. Entertain us.

Missing the darkly nuanced reference, business does indeed seek to entertain us. What it fails to realize is that, like Whitman, we are multiple. There is no "us" that can be entertained the way America was once entertained en masse by Norman Rockwell magazine covers. Nevertheless and notwithstanding that, nearly all business approaches to the Internet shoot for a mass market. "Let's see, it'll cost us a million-five for the site and another mil for the ad campaign, but think of all the ways we can monetize a billion clicks! We'll hit break-even inside 90 days. Cool! How soon can we IPO?"

Uh-huh. But it ends up costing three times as much—and no one shows. Meanwhile, some teenager puts up a page of dancing hamsters that pulls eighty-three bajillion hits in two weeks—so many that her ISP's server melts down. Total cost: twenty-nine dollars.

But does business make the correct inference from this? Does anyone in the boardroom say "Jeepers! They'd rather be looking at singing rodents than our zillion-dollar e-commerce site!" Generally speaking, this realization is strenuously deprecated. And though everyone in the organization knows it's true, giving voice to such a sentiment at any level *below* the boardroom constitutes seriously career-inhibiting behavior.

So, very few in the business scene seem to have learned much from the hamster gambit. Most companies kept on shooting for those imaginary mass markets on the web. Kept on, that is, until the dot.com bandwagon threw a wheel early in the year 2000. Too bad too, as it was during this period of Internet tulip mania that I was able to sell brooklynbridge.com. Seventeen times. And I don't even own it. But then the bottom fell out and, predictably, all these negative stories started appearing in the mainstream press. Is the Internet a Flop? Is There Any Money to be Made Online? Net Entrepreneurs Share Dumpster-Dining Tips. Etc. But the headline I kept looking for never appeared: E-commerce Exposed As Pathological Corporate Hallucination. The financial markets were worried, yes. There was deep concern on The Street. But what everyone seemed to take away from all this was what I like to call the e-berserker model. That online business plans needed to be even *more* Byzantine and grandiose. That only the super-huge and hyper-capitalized could possibly survive "the shakeout." Faster, faster, more hysteria, more hand-waving, more investment!

Among the top 10 most-visited websites as of this writing, Media Metrix lists AOL, Yahoo, Microsoft, Lycos, Excite, Go, and AltaVista. Microsoft has hit on a unique strategy for maintaining its position on this list: millions of customers trying to figure out why their computers suddenly stopped working. The rest are portals and search engines—places people go online on their way to going *somewhere else*. If you look at the most frequent queries submitted to these sites, you find an interesting pattern. Most people are looking for dirty pictures, jokes and—you already guessed it—the latest dancing-hamster equivalent. At the moment, that would be the single-page graphic of Al Gore and George W. Bush got up to look like Beavis and Butthead.

Back in there somewhere I wondered: is it a shakeout when you flush a toilet? However, not being privy to my private ruminations, the press continued to drool over the prospect of a big media mating season just ahead.

Let me propose a wager, gentle reader. I bet when you first heard about the merger of AOL and Time Warner, your reactions were . . . well, let's say a little mixed. On the one hand, impressive sums were mentioned, mountains of virtual money no one will ever see, numbers too large to count. On the other hand, you had no idea what any of it meant.[5]

The one thing you must at all costs *not* consider—it would be rude of you at best—is that it means nothing. Nada. Zero. Zip. But of course, we would never entertain such thoughts, so the rudeness issue is entirely moot. We all know it's a big deal. We all know it will shape our fortunes and our futures as surely as God made Edsels and Atari games.

You see, we now have this ultra-cool hyper-high-tech Internet, with which we must keep up. We must. And as we all know, it's moving fast—at warp 8 light speed. Faster than sliced bread moved off the shelves the day after it was invented. We're running just to stay in place. We're checking out equipment down at DigiMart. We're taking courses. We're reading manuals thicker than *War and Peace* that don't even have a basic plot. Pant-pant!

But the real problem—as you'll appreciate when you come to fully understand these things—is that the Internet is so darn slow.

Eh? Howzat?

Well, look: Sure you got your basic e-mail and your basic 100 billion kajillion web pages, but do you have true broadband? Are you fully hardwired to a 7 x 24 x 365 multiply redundant TCP/IP-enabled cable infrastructure? Because whether you know it or not, that's what you really want. It's what you need. Let's not mince words: it's what you'll fork out for. And it's been the American Dream for many years now. So much money has been spent already. Just for you.

Back around 1993, another mega-convergence deal was announced between TCI and Bell Atlantic (*"convergence"* is a technical term for hybrid—sort of like when you mate a horse with a donkey and get a mule). True, it fell apart before it came together, but you have to admit they tried. Then, just a few years later another world-class merger of media titans was announced to great fanfare—between MCI and Rupert Murdoch's News Corporation. The fact that it lasted less than a year should not blind us to its historic import, its brave and selfless attempt to bring us more precious bandwidth.

Bandwidth is an enormously complex concept, which you are probably not congenitally predisposed to understand. Here's the watered down Cliff Notes version. A word is worth one word. A picture is worth 1,000. We have the bandwidth to exchange these sorts of things online today, but they are embarrassingly low-tech. What can you really do with them? Draw some funny pictures for your home page? Write a letter to your granddaughter in China? Meet new people? Learn new things? Maybe explore another culture, or find a cure for cancer? Oh, puh-leease!

Be honest. Look your techno-fetishism in the face for once. You don't want e-mail. You don't want friends or conversations. You certainly don't want knowledge. What you want is user-selectable full-motion video-on-demand. You want golf clubs and cubic zirconiums, strange new forms of exercise equipment, otherworldly food processors. You want nonstop astrological advice and 24-hour wall-to-wall home shopping. What you really want is Jerry Springer!

And this is what AOL and Time Warner want too. It's what they want for you. Why? Because bandwidth this fat can deliver advertising like there's no tomorrow. And that, gentle reader, is worth considerably more than 1,000 words. Imagine this: It's worth a bucketful of bucks so big, so vast, so overwhelmingly impressive, that all those numbers you've seen up till now are nothing more than petty-cash chump change.

Now does it all make sense?

The AOL/Time Warner hookup represents the ultimate shared goals of mass media and mass marketing. Simply stated, the objective is to become as big as possible as fast as possible, to reach and lock in "the mass market." This sort of strategy made perfect sense at one time—when there *was* a mass market. But mass markets were fragmenting for many decades before the Internet came onstream, and since then, the net has enormously accelerated the fragmentation. I often refer to the new company resulting from the AOL/Time Warner merger as The Titanic Deck Chair Rearrangement Corporation (NASDAQ:TDCRC). Huge media empires with dreams of top-down mass market control are living in a past that's no longer relevant. No more can broadcast advertising shape the tastes and desires of some undifferentiated mass of humanity. In contrast to mass media, the net has liberated audiences and markets to seek out what *they* are interested in. And thereby hangs another tale entirely.

If they're any good, ideas propagate well over networks. And ideas create new markets. (Remember that bit? Just checking. . .) Unlike market research, the net provides another, more immediate way to find out if ideas are "any good." What you do is simply take the plunge. If a website or mailing list you create attracts an audience, you're off and running. If not, you crash and burn. Oh well. Of course, business never thinks "oh well." It wants to know out front and top down that success is assured. It wants risk reduction and dependable size-of-audience projections. It wants a guaranteed return on its investment. But this is usually because it invests way too much based on obsolete mass-market expectations.

Here's what's wrong with approaches based on this model: all they care about is making money for investors. And here's where many business readers will pull a full-body Keanu Reeves: "Whoa!" Because isn't that what business is all about? Yeah sure. But business is not what the Internet is all about. Never was, never will be. Mass media were created to serve the marketing requirements of corporations. The net had no such provenance. Companies that assume the net is there so they can sell more tend to forget why so many *people* are there: because business is *not*—at least not in the same intrusive and unavoidable way business is there on television. People are there because of their interest in other people and what those other people are interested in. The net never promised anyone a media empire. It never purported to be the Northwest Passage to enormous corporate profits. If it turns out not to work the same way as conventional mass media—and it doesn't—whose fault is that?

Companies have always correctly assumed that people are not naturally inclined to be interested in their products. Not sufficiently interested, at any rate. However, mass media provided a perfect cure for this inattention: advertising. Advertising was an effective way to "remind" people of how much they really wanted—how much they *needed*—that new car or insurance policy or washday miracle. Companies talk about branding products, but what mass marketing is really about is branding people—stamping product impressions onto as many forebrains as possible as many times a day as possible. The product is boring? No problem. Get a bigger hammer to drive the message home. This process is what most media mediate. Commercial sponsors are their lifeblood and reason for existing.

Not so with the net. It's possible to spend days and weeks online without ever seeing an ad—if you don't count the email spam (delete, delete). Many sites have no sponsors, yet are drawing an audience. How do they make money? They don't. They are labors of love, created on nights and weekends by people deeply, often obsessively interested in their subject matter. Think about it this way. You know those horses and bison on the cave walls in places like Lascaux and Altamira? Can you imagine this conversation with one of the Neolithic artists who created them?

"Nice execution, Gork, but who's bankrolling this site? I mean, have you lined up investors yet? Any backers? And what about sponsors? Do you have a business plan *at all?*"

"Duh. Gork not think of that. Gork guess he get busboy job down at Wooly Mammoth Burgers. . . "

Think about it this way. If the business notion of best practices had been applied from the dawn of human civilization, human beings never would have achieved civilization. Art history would focus on things like ancient Roman bas-reliefs of the current Tide and Cheer equivalents, the Sistine Chapel ceiling would say "Bank With Medici!" and instead of a torch, the Statue of Liberty would be brandishing a tube of Preparation H.

Fortunately for us, product placement is a relatively new idea. But hold the phone, some will indubitably say. Without making a profit for investors. . . why business wouldn't be. . . [sputter, choke, sputter] business! Well, one thing's for sure. It wouldn't be business as usual. Hmmm. . . interesting phrase, that. David Weinberger, Doc Searls, Rick Levine and myself used it in the name of a book we wrote together—*The Cluetrain Manifesto: The End of Business As Usual.* We were as serious about that subtitle as I am about Winning Through Worst Practices. There's even a connection.

Before *Cluetrain* was a book it was a website. But long before that, it was a set of tentative, half-formed ideas. Ideas, as it turned out, that propagated well over the Internet. Ideas that not only created a new market—for a highly unusual business book—but that also began to question the whole idea of business and to redefine the very notion of markets. Years before *Cluetrain* hit *Fast Company* and *The Industry Standard, The Wall Street Journal* and *The New York Times,* we had no conscious plan to make a nickel off any of the ideas we were kicking around. Perhaps I'd best speak for myself from here on out. What I thought *I* was doing was destroying my (hah!) professional career. What can I say? I was bored.

Very bored. From where I was sitting five years ago—IBM as it happens—business looked like a fetid swamp. All day I would watch as overgrown dinosaurs stumbled into the La Brea tar pits of their own bottomless ignorance. Fun for a while, to be sure. Godzilla Meets Gerstnera. Fortuna–500 vs. Earth. Et cetera. But it was all reruns after about the first 90 minutes.

Hocus Focus

So I started a market research project. An Internet focus group. Only I didn't call it that. I disguised my true intentions by calling it Entropy Gradient Reversals.[6] The name should be fair warning in itself. EGR was (and still is) a webzine and email list that, from the beginning, sought to answer one burning question: does intelligent life exist in online business?

But first, a word about shameless self-promotion. Media budget in the low three figures? Don't know how you'll ever make ends meet? As four out of five net-heads and zinesters have discovered, shameless self-promotion is just the ticket! And as your dentist will tell you, it's an important part of a regular program of bottom-up gonzo marketing. It's also an important part of our core theme, so try not to look too shocked as it dawns on you that, in this case, the bogus self-effacement so typical of business books went AWOL right from the outset in this one. We now return you to another exciting episode of Practice What You Preach, *already in progress. . .*

EGR is hard to characterize. Some would say impossible. From day one, it sought to rankle, to antagonize readers, drive them crazy. In fact, one of the site's primary objectives is to get curious viewers to go away. Needless to say, this was a major step in the evolution of gonzo marketing. However, nothing I've tried has worked. The number of hits on the site, while not exactly threatening to edge out Yahoo, has always grown, never diminished. What am I doing wrong?

Since May Day 1996, EGR has been pumping out an irreverent stream of over-the-top gonzo effluvia as insurance against my ever again accepting employment in a so-called Fortune-class company. In the agonizingly slow process of aggregating an audience bottom-up, without benefit of a mega-dollar-java-animated-web-banner-advertising budget, and depending solely on its readership's goodwill and word-of-mouth peer review to attract new subscribers, here are some of the editorial mandates to which the publication has hewed religiously:

- Assume that anyone who disagrees is a patent imbecile.
- Insult readers at every opportunity; impugn their motives; question their cognitive reach.
- Use profanity with licentious abandon.
- Use arcane vocabulary demanding recourse to out-of-print editions of unabridged dictionaries.

- Make pompous offhand allusions to literary works *no one* has ever read.
- Include interviews with fictitious media "personalities," farm animals and B-movie monsters.
- Encourage loyal subscribers to unsubscribe "to make room for others."
- Publish lurid personal confessions, often entailing wanton sex and the use of illegal pharmaceuticals.
- Drop gratuitous equal-opportunity racial, religious and gender slurs.
- Brutally mock potential sponsors.
- Threaten to hand over subscribers' personal information to spammers.
- Demand payment from readers for no apparent reason, then abruptly change tack and announce: "We wouldn't take your stinking money if you paid us!"
- Make endless lists about which no one in their right mind could reasonably be presumed to give a rat's ass.

. . . and so on; you catch the general drift. Or perhaps you don't. But either way, what did all this bombastic rant-and-raillery set out to accomplish? What could it possibly have hoped to prove?

EGR is largely written by spectral constellation of psychic flotsam who insists on calling himself RageBoy®. There are days I'd like to forget about him, believe me. He is the product of what Poe called the imp of the perverse, a certain inexplicable inclination to self-destruct just as everything is going well. You're standing at the edge of an abyss, Poe says—just taking in the scenery—and suddenly you feel this incredible urge to throw yourself off the edge. That's the imp of the perverse, the ultimate font of worst practices.

RageBoy is all my own worst qualities and character defects, somehow split out into a separate personality that, allowed free range on the web, has attained a disturbing measure of autonomy. He is my science-fiction monster run amok. My albatross. And probably my well-deserved karma for past offenses against various deities. But I can't get rid of him. He's also my cash cow. When new clients call up, do they want to talk to me? No way. "Is RB available?" they ask, as if I'm just the office boy. This is so unfair. Me,

I've worked really hard all my life to develop ideas that made some sort of logical sense. I've struggled to express them clearly and persuasively. I think I've even succeeded a few times. But nobody cared about that. It was so boring people fell asleep reading the stuff. Some even died.

RageBoy, on the other hand, is insane. I don't mean this metaphorically, you understand. The guy is certifiably nuts. When I think of all the times he's threatened to destroy my career, I cringe. When I was working at IBM, he published a lengthy interview with Mr. Ed. That's right, the talking horse. He pretended that Ed was secretly running the whole worldwide media scene—and intimated that he regularly overdosed on psychedelics. It was horrible. What if my employer had found out about this? As if that weren't bad enough, he started "interviewing" ranking individuals at IBM itself, including its chairman, Lou Gerstner. Jesus Christ!

I lived in terror of what he'd do next. I still do.

But it's weird. RageBoy also has this knack of getting it precisely right by following these whacked-out inclinations. At times, anyway. Plenty of people hate him—with just cause—but there are also plenty who love him dearly and, against all logic, go to great lengths to do his insalubrious bidding. One time he got email from this business guy in the UK. "You really don't give a shit, do you?" he wrote. "I am incredibly impressed." RB framed that one. I tell you, the guy's a total lunatic, but what can I do? He does all the writing and the interviews. He's now bringing all the income into this operation.

OK, so we're the same person in reality, or whatever passes for that around here. But you see how it is. To be generous, a bit confusing. I've learned to live with this fractured personality setup, however, because it has taught me something. Everyone needs an outlet for that part of themselves that usually isn't allowed to speak at all. Not always to be sure, but often, that part has something vital to say. It has a certain wisdom, but we repress it, thinking it's too weird, too untamed, too out of control.

This is one sense of gonzo. Whenever I've thought about *Gonzo Marketing* up till now (this book has been brewing for years), I've thought I would say that this *daemon*, this wild and somewhat dangerous element wasn't really essential. Yes, it's a dimension I've explored, I was going to say, but it isn't something you need to consider yourself. I thought I could get away with it. Hey, if I didn't have to spook anybody, bigger market for the book, right?

But I can't get away with it. As I write these paragraphs, I realize how wrong that separation sounds. While there are other, hugely important dimensions of gonzo (which we'll get to in due time), I now see that gonzo marketing can't possibly work without at least some measure of, well. . . call it fear and loathing. There has to be some sense of going over the edge, taking a leap into the unknown, going against all those internal alarms that pose as instincts but are really just paranoid defense mechanisms. There has to be some real sense that you're not only breaking the rules, but burning the bridge to boot. And that has to scare you. Otherwise, how would you become fearless?

To speak from the heart is to become who we truly are, and that's always risky, or at least surprising. If I strategize my speech, anticipate what I think you want me to say, things may go more smoothly on the surface. Certainly, there will be less confusion. Things will be simpler and more predictable. Fearful of exposure, we read from the expected social script. But we haven't really met. We haven't yet entered into that terra incognita where genuine communication becomes possible. Voice is far more than the sounds we make.

Noting that corporate notions of markets were not based on real people but on cardboard cutout models of customers so straight and so stupid it's hard to imagine anyone except maybe Ward and June Cleaver ever fit the mold, I wondered out loud (or RB wondered, I forget) what impact all this might have on current approaches to on-line marketing. Like maybe all the hysterical e-commerce hoopla was a crock. But no one was really listening anyway. Or so I thought.

In December 1999, under the heading "The wisdom of RageBoy," *The Economist* wrote:

> For the past four years, Mr. Locke has exorcised his demons with an irregular e-mail screed sent under the name of his one-man consultancy, Entropy Gradient Reversals. . . As often as not, he writes in the voice of his psychotic alter-ego, RageBoy, in a profanity-laced ramble that occasionally touches on the subject of Internet business strategy, ridiculing all it sees. There are plenty of nuts out there

firing off crazed e-mails, but what is extraordinary about Mr. Locke is that he has attracted some 3,500 devoted readers from some of the Internet's largest firms. After months of paging through his abuse, they eventually realise that it is all a subversive demonstration of his big idea, "gonzo marketing". . . [7]

Unfortunately, the magazine didn't quite grasp this big idea—assuming it was a way for "big companies to reach a new class of young, hip consumer with edgy, humorous and self-deprecating web content." Uh, no. . . not exactly. Though it would certainly be refreshing if companies could be less humorless and self-congratulatory—a style, you may have noted, that I've adopted as a subversive demonstration of ham-fisted irony. *The Economist* did hit the mark in one respect, however. "Being right," the article observed, "has not made Mr. Locke rich. . . "

Yes, my readers expressed sincere and deeply warped delight. They egged me on. They begged for more. But I asked myself why I was doing this. It seemed thoroughly insane. Over the past five years, I have invested an absurd amount of time in this zine. And for what? At the moment, EGR is up to about 5,000 subscribers. By online business standards, this doesn't even rank in the pathetic showing category. However, what they lack in numbers, these readers make up for in raw intelligence, boundless skepticism and massive net savvy. They're smart. They're unconvinced. They're wired to the eyes. Oddly enough, many do work in major corporations.[8]

In *The Cluetrain Manifesto* I wrote, "The word that's passing like a spark from keyboard to screen, from heart to mind, is the permission we're giving ourselves and each other: to be human and to speak as humans." And that's exactly what happened when the book hit. Before the publisher could launch its marketing campaign, *Cluetrain* was already climbing the charts. The sales rank figures on Amazon had to be a mistake. It started out way too high. But it stayed in the top 50 for months; in the top 100 for most of the year.

While much has been written about viral marketing, most of it is crap—carrot-dangling to corporate sales droids who desperately want to believe their lackluster product come-on will go platinum on the net. Not bloody likely. But *Cluetrain* did go platinum, did go viral. Why? Because it passed on that permission to be human. And it passed it on via gonzo marketing—which is *not* some slick new trick for corporations to manipulate the young, the hip, the edgy. Gonzo marketing is market advocacy, the marketplace speaking in its own behalf.

Cluetrain was hardly what you'd call a *nice* book. Not nice to business, at any rate. It railed, it ranted, it used bad words. It told corporations that everything they knew about the net was wrong. And not just wrong, but laughably deluded. Then, adding injury to insult, it refused to provide any sort of guidelines. You're on your own, it said. But suddenly, companies like BP Amoco, Citicorp, Conde Nast, Conoco, J. Walter Thompson, Nordstrom, Ogilvy & Mather, Reuters, Young & Rubicam were reading my harsh, implacable words. Buying them, in fact, in several senses. And making me rich as a result (it's always so nice to disprove the financial press). I almost began to feel guilty. *Almost*. The problem was this. Many companies seemed to agree with what I'd written in the manifesto: "Conversations among human beings *sound* human. They are conducted in a human voice. . . People recognize each other as such from the sound of this voice." And companies wanted to know, therefore, how they too could sound human. But I didn't think they could. And I still don't. I felt bad about it sure, especially with all those outfits purchasing *my* product for a change. But there it was. Bummer, dudes. Impasse. You just can't get here from there. *Cluetrain* said that a metaphorical Berlin Wall was separating the corporate conversations inside companies from the market conversations outside.

Ripping Out the Wall

". . . we don't need no thought control."

—PINK FLOYD, *THE WALL*

In February 2000 something extraordinary happened. One company—a very large one—ripped out the wall. Ford announced it was giving home PCs and Internet access to all 350,000 of its employees worldwide. The first sentence of the press release said: "Ford Motor Company is taking a step forward to reach its vision of being on the leading edge of technology and connect more closely with its customers."

This bold move was reported prominently on the front pages of *The Washington Post* and *The New York Times*. However, these articles focused on who would be supplying the computers, how much the program would cost, how the move was good for labor relations, and detailed specs of the hardware. The *Post* quoted Jac Nasser, Ford president and CEO as saying, "We're committed to serving consumers better by understanding how they think and act. Having a computer and Internet access in the home will accelerate the development of these skills, provide information across our business and offer opportunities to streamline our processes."

But other than this clip, neither paper said anything about the company connecting more closely with customers. And none of the coverage that I saw quoted Nasser's far more detailed remarks in making the actual announcement:

> . . . we want to be able to improve communications—two-way communications—and make sure that our employees—every one of us—is connected to what's going on in the marketplace, so that we know where consumers are heading, what's happening to market trends, what's happening to product trends, and make it easier for our employees to have a better understanding of the shift that's happening out there. . . .[9]

Maybe that doesn't make for a great sound bite on the six o'clock news, but it's the heart of the story—a story the mainstream press completely missed. The real deal here is that Ford has unleashed 350,000 independent—and genuinely intelligent—agents to fan out online and listen carefully.

But not just listen—"two-way communications," Nasser said. These computers and net connections will not be under corporate control. They will not be monitored in any way. Ford has unleashed 350,000 people to whom it has tacitly granted permission to speak on its behalf. Not in a legal sense, but in a much more powerful way. These are people who will tell their own stories, in their own voices, any way they see fit. Ford not only got out of their way, it provided the tools and the encouragement to use them. That's smart. Replacing paranoia and control with no-strings permission is always smart.

The next day, Delta Air Lines announced a similar offer to its 75,000 employees. American Airlines, Intel and Bertelsmann have since followed suit, and I expect we'll hear many more such announcements. This trend alone could revolutionize current notions of Internet marketing. I suspect it will pick up momentum as the attendant advantages accruing to these companies become obvious to competitors and industry analysts.

And Ford had even more strange news up its sleeve. In May, the company issued a "corporate citizenship report" in which it noted that sports utility vehicles—including its own Explorers and Expeditions—kill more people than tend to get killed in non-SUV crashes. Ford also said it wasn't too happy about the lousy gas mileage these vehicles get, as it's damaging the planet. When the media expressed surprise that the company would be so forthright on such potentially damning issues, Debbie Zemke, Ford's director of corporate governance, said "For heaven's sake, everybody else is talking about it, so why shouldn't we?"[10]

Perhaps Ford's willingness to tell the truth comes as even more of a surprise because, being digital and all, we've been conditioned by the simplistic wired/tired dichotomy of Nicholas Negroponte that bits are way cool but atoms are old hat. Ford is a very atomic company—a rustbelt NYSE discrete manufacturer, not a NASDAQ dot.com darling—so it must not "get it," right? Wrong. Companies like Ford were among the first to feel the fire of global competition, and it was no picnic. Ford was the first major U.S. company to bring in Deming and go through the Total Quality transformation. The company had to radically rethink its entire purpose. Perhaps most important, as Deming demanded, it had to drive out fear.

Fear masks arrogance, which in turn masks the kind of ignorance unable to admit it needs ideas that were "not invented here." Managers from CEO on down had to become humble enough to realize that workers they'd been bossing around for better than half a century often knew more than they did. Ford began listening to its workers. So did General Electric. Jack Welch got religion for self-directed teams and process mapping. The results spoke for themselves—not just competitive survival, but better products, greater profits, better places to work.

Now these "old-economy" corporations are listening again, extending the same attention to their markets via the Internet. This has nothing to do with facile tricks like "permission" or "viral" marketing. Instead, it's about what I have come to call *wide-area knowledge acquisition*. It's about the profound understanding that intellectual capital has little to do with ownership today, and everything to do with invitation, access and enthusiastic bottom-up community involvement. Is "open source marketing" an impossible oxymoron? Think about Linux and Napster. And reflect on how odd it is that sleepy old atomic tortoises like Ford and GE may turn out to be faster companies than digital hares like Intel, Microsoft and IBM.

In a clear reference to the infamous dictum that what's good for General Motors is good for America, Ford president and CEO Jac Nasser wrote:

> It was not so long ago that leading companies believed what was good for them was good for the world. Business leaders made decisions without scrutiny or accountability and assumed the world would accept the consequences of those choices—be they good or bad. At Ford, we believe exactly the opposite is true. What is good for the world is good for Ford Motor Company.[11]

This might easily come across as just more corporate hot air—sounds nice, means nothing—except that Ford is putting its money where its mouth is. More to the point, it is putting its many voices where its money comes from. By giving PCs and Internet connections to its entire workforce worldwide, Ford has opened itself to the marketplace as no company has ever dared. These workers will fan out online and tell their own stories, engage in their own conversations, not about Mustangs and Explorers and Tauruses, but about the kinds of things human beings tend to get excited about. You know: what kind of education their kids are getting, why government is so broken, how grandma won the chili cookoff at the state fair, where wireless technology is headed, and by the way, how much *would* it cost to start a chinchilla ranch in Tasmania?

Speak boldly and don't carry a big shtick. Most of the "thinking" in marketing these days is simply missing the boat. Mass markets have been steadily fragmenting many decades. They are being replaced by vibrant new micromarkets just now emerging from the web. These don't show up on corporate radars tuned to lock onto mass-market targets of opportunity—or the fragmented debris of former mass markets, which is what conventional market segmentation keeps desperately trying to salvage.

A Preview of the Gonzo Model

For nearly a century, companies like Ford have told workers to "check your brain at the door." Corporations broadcast work orders down a tiered bureaucracy driven by command-and-control management. Similarly, they broadcast orders to the marketplace in the form of advertising: buy our product! But imagine Ford today, releasing all those workers into a chaotic uncontrolled and uncontrollable market space. Suddenly, the company might very much like to know what's in their workers' brains—and not just the sorts of things they do on the job. Imagine the following scenario. While speculative, there is nothing preventing companies from exploring this model, and much to gain by testing its potential.

Suppose Ford discovers, through offering open web space to self-motivated employees, that one-tenth of one percent of its workforce are gung-ho organic gardeners. Why would a car company be interested in such an avocation? Two reasons. First, 350,000 people is a pretty fair sample of the population at large, so it's reasonable to guess that a similar tenth of a percent of the market might be organic gardeners. Second, Ford is also a truck company, and people who grow gardens tend to haul stuff they wouldn't want to shovel into the back seat of the family sedan. Thus, such a micromarket includes excellent prospects for pickup trucks.

Ford would first want to introduce these workers to each other, and suggest that they collaborate on building an organic gardening sub-site at ford.com—on company time of course. Imagine the enthusiasm that would result from being paid to do what you most love, instead of what you're told. Then Ford would find the best voices in this group—the most articulate, engaging and informed—

and sign them up as emissaries to the best *external* organic gardening website. Call it Organic Gardening World, OGW for short. These
ambassadors would then approach this best-of-breed site bearing
gifts: cash, server hardware, technical assistance, even reverse ad
banners to drive traffic from ford.com's homepage to this affiliate
micromarket aggregator. Say the OGW site has a regular audience of
5,000. Ford would want to increase this audience to 500,000 as
quickly as possible. It would also want an exclusive relationship with
respect to competitors. OGW could have other underwriters, just not
from the likes of GM, Daimler-Chrysler or Toyota.

Ford's money would enable the OGW site developers to quit
their day jobs in some corporate cube farm and devote full time to
doing what they love best. Notice that love is a powerful attractor
on both sides of the equation. And it is an equation—perhaps better, an *equator*. When organic gardeners click the banner on the
OGW homepage that says "Underwritten by Ford Motor Company,"
they would not be transported to ford.com, but instead to
ford.com/organic-gardening. And there they'd encounter Ford employees who understand and share their passion for mulch, for
good rich dirt, for corn-on-the-cob served five minutes from har-
vest. These two groups also share an active interest in pickup
trucks, automatic lift gates and power take-offs. Does this intersection of common interests hold more promise than conventional advertising? How much might it be worth to find out before competitors got the jump on the best voices emerging out there on the
web right now?

Imagine taking this one step further. Say Joe Smith is Ford's primary ambassador to the OGW site, and is highly visible in posting
there. It's part of his job. He doesn't write about Ford products, but
about his knowledge of organic gardening. He knows a lot, and he's
well respected for his advice. Now say Mary sends him private
email. "Joe, I know you work at Ford. I wonder if you can help me.
I bought an Explorer a while back, but the driver's side door is
sprung and my dealer is giving me the run-around." Joe promotes
this to the EVP Customer Service at Ford corporate, for which he has
hot-line priority, and 20 minutes later Mary gets the following note.
"Mary, Joe tells me you're having problems with your Explorer.
Sorry to hear it. Call Bill Smith at the number below and schedule

a time to have it fixed. I worked it out with Bill to take care of you at no charge." How many times would a company have to comp such service to gain word-of-mouth evangelists it couldn't buy with a $100 million ad campaign?

Welcome to gonzo marketing. As with the gonzo journalism from which it takes its name, this kind of engaged participation is the exact opposite of "objectivity" that pretends to have no perspective, no point of view. Every website worth its salt is an act of journalism, news of some passionate interest and engaged advocacy. By underwriting and participating in the life and growth of such sites, corporations can forge powerful relationships with emerging micromarkets. This is a win-win, not a zero sum, model. Everyone benefits: the corporation, its workers, external site producers, and their audiences.

Could there be problems of undue corporate influence on content? Sure. But these are no different from the problems faced today by traditional publishers, who set up "church and state" boundaries between advertising and editorial departments. A site with many underwriters will be safer from such influence—attempting which will be cause for terminating contracts. A company seeking unfair advantage would risk permanently ceding its relationship to a competitor. Not a real swift idea.

Why would a huge corporation get out of the way and enable mere workers to speak on its behalf? Workers are no longer valuable for their labor alone but also for their curiosity about the world *outside* the company—for their interests and passions and the uncontrived voices through which they express themselves. People want to talk to people, not flacks and lawyers and scripted marketing zombies with hidden and none-too-friendly subagendas.

Why would a company used to dictating to its markets via broadcast advertising suddenly switch gears and pay attention? Willie Sutton robbed banks, he said, because that's where the money was. Today, corporations must establish more intimate relationships with markets because that's where the knowledge is. Intellectual capital is no longer a strictly internal affair. Engaged conversations with relevant micromarkets will become a crucial source of insight and innovation, and the quality of this market intelligence will ultimately determine market share. Without such interactions, efforts to create competitive products and services risk taking place in a vacuum. At least one company understands this today, and many more will follow. "We need great ideas," says Nasser, "from people both inside and outside of Ford. We will listen to those ideas with respect and seriousness."

As products come to reflect genuine esteem for workers and customers instead of self-congratulatory ballyhoo and the adversarial targeting tactics that surround the concept of brand today, companies will be far better served, and so will their markets.

Gonzo marketing provides a model whereby companies can stop manipulating people as if they were abstract demographic data, and instead create genuine relationships with emergent online communities of interest: powerful new web micromarkets. The paradox is that companies can have everything they've always wanted. Greater market share. Customer loyalty. Brand equity. All those empty phrases that today make people blow coffee out their noses. But companies can actually achieve these goals. No, really. All they have to do is follow the advice my Junior High principal once shared with me. "Son," he said, shaking with anger, "you've got to get your thinking straight!"

Naturally, I didn't. Instead, I immediately began developing my notion of worst practices. Fortunately for you, the worst of the worst will not be covered here. Serious mistakes are critically necessary to the learning process. In my own case, since these mistakes have given me such a powerful competitive advantage, I'm afraid they must remain proprietary. Plus, there are certain statutes of limitation to consider. I've made more than my fair share of catastrophic errors. Make your own.

What the balance of this book does cover is a complex constellation of ideas capable of forging an entirely new kind of relationship between commercial organizations and post-colonial Internet cultural communities. Of course, they're *only* ideas. At present. But—as you may have already read somewhere—if they're any good, ideas propagate well over networks. And ideas create new markets.

The Value Proposition

*"**Value Proposition.** The reasons why a product is of
sufficient value to the customer to be well worth its price.
This term is often used in ad agencies as they
formulate their ultimate pitch. . .*

*Values. The deeply held beliefs and attitudes of
the members of a particular society."*

—THE PORTABLE MBA IN MARKETING [1]

*"The possession of wealth, which was at the outset
valued simply as an evidence of efficiency, becomes,
in popular apprehension, itself a meritorious act."*

—THORSTEIN VEBLEN [2]

"Money—it's a hit."

—PINK FLOYD [3]

THE SECOND CHAPTER OF *KOTLER ON MARKETING* IS TITLED "USING
Marketing to Understand, Create, Communicate, and Deliver
Value."[4] Maybe this will help me, I think. Maybe I'll get what I'm
missing if I read this bit. Yet out of 18 pages, there is no mention of
value until the 16th page, where all it says is: "The full positioning
of the brand is called the brand's value proposition. It is the answer
to the customer's question, 'Why should I buy your brand?'" Maybe
it's just me, but whether marketing was used or not, I have to say
that value—the core concept this chapter promises to unpack—was

not understood. Neither was it communicated or delivered. If it was created, it was created somewhere else. And that's my point. I'm not picking on Kotler, particularly. In fact, I like the guy. But this failure to communicate is not at all atypical. Business in general, and marketing in particular, seem to assume we know what they mean when they sling around terms like *value, brand* and *positioning*, and equate the resulting blur of vague ideas to something we might actually care about. This notion of value *was* created somewhere else—in some wish-fulfillment fantasy world where what is valuable to business maps seamlessly and unquestionably onto what is valuable to me. Value is value. It's obvious, isn't it? What if I said no?

It feels like spring, yet it's almost solstice, mid-winter coming in. Catching the light, a flock of pigeons turns through the sky over the highway and I remember. I couldn't have been more than 10 or 11, the age my daughter Selene is now. I raised pigeons, and every morning I would watch them fly out over the tilled adobe bean field, the huge fig tree at its center, the dairy where other, wild pigeons slept at night in the cow barn. We would go there with flashlights to try to catch them without waking the farmer, who was rumored to have a shotgun. This was California, the heart of Silicon Valley, though there wasn't any silicon there back then in the late 1950's. My heart would sing to see my flock tilt and wheel in the sun. I would feel something I couldn't describe, and still can't, to see them coming home at nightfall. I am driving and remembering and feeling how much is lost, how precious this life.

"I will survive" sang Jerry Garcia a year after nearly dying and eight years before he actually did.[5] Trying to explain The Grateful Dead is like trying to tell a stranger about rock and roll. No, it's like trying to tell the ungrateful, walking dead about life—that value has something to do with gratitude. Gratitude for the mystery of the world and the heart to feel into it. Diamonds in the dust. Value as treasure unrecognized. The story has it that Garcia found "grateful dead" in an old Funk & Wagnall's dictionary entry referring to a ballad in which a traveler takes pity and lays a wandering ghost to rest. Grateful, the dead man richly rewards the deed. Shades of "Finnegan's Wake," the traditional song on which James Joyce's sprawling novel of the same name was loosely (very loosely) based, in which Tim Finnegan's funeral gets entirely out of hand and his corpse comes back to life when some drunken reveler splashes whiskey on it. Or of the Egyptian Book of the Dead, which is purported to say: "in the land of the dark, the ship of the sun is drawn by the grateful dead." Or of Dylan Thomas, who sang in another key, "After the first death there is no other."[6] Or of *El Dia de los Muertos*, the day of the dead, when roses bloom in skeletal eye sockets and the people dance in the streets to a grim fandango celebrating life.

Among other things you may imagine at this juncture (and thanks for keeping them to yourself), this exercise smacks of what anthropologist Clifford Geertz calls "thick description."[7] Using a complicated tale about sheep and thieves and justice and the lack of it in colonial North Africa in 1912, he demonstrates that any time we attempt to describe "a particular event, ritual, custom, idea, or whatever," we end up spinning stories about other people's stories about yet other people's stories, and sorting it all out becomes next to impossible. It's a rich tapestry, and thick description, while it may seem confusing, often comes closer to what's actually going on than would "thin description"—the kind of succinct clear-cut abstraction that appears perfectly plausible, but totally distorts reality. Not that I'm claiming any methodological rigor in these musings, but the thickness I'm attempting to suggest is what music and painting and literature—what we roughly call The Arts—typically point to. And what the specialized languages of logic and science and business typically do not. It's a Zen sort of thing you could say. *I* could say; who's to stop me? Finger indicating moon-illuminated finger. The thickness of life as life is lived between the inexorable poles of birth and death. "Man is an animal suspended," says Geertz, "in webs of significance he himself has spun."[8]

Webs, yes. And although the Big Daddy web did not exist when that was written, that's why the choice of quote. That's where we're headed. It's where we already are. But wait. Though we have these words for our current situation—words like Internet and World Wide Web—it seems to me they obscure at least as much as they reveal. Because networks are inherently social realities, any attempt to definitively say what they are becomes immediately suspect. It depends on where you're standing when you look at them, and what sort of baggage you've brought along to the observation deck. "Meaning is use," said Ludwig Wittgenstein, meaning things mean what you make of them. But he also said, *"Die Welt ist Alles was der Fall ist"*— the world is everything that is the case. And really, how far does that get us? Except that "Case" is the main character in William Gibson's *Neuromancer*, which, when it was published in 1984, was the first entry in a then-hot new literary genre called cyberpunk. And in German, "neu Roman" means "new novel." The novelist then the new romancer. Sure, it's a stretch, but who knows what these creative types are capable of? Everything has at least two meanings.

Because it's expected, I guess, business tends to be way too serious. Tends to take language far too literally. "A thing *is* what it is called, and it could not be called anything else," writes Peter Berger in *The Social Construction of Reality*, explaining how children perceive the world. But the following shoe may fit much larger feet: "All institutions appear in the same way, as given, unalterable and self-evident."[9] His point being that they're anything but. As you may have already picked up from the book title, his point is that reality is socially constructed. And institutions are hardly exempt from such construction: the Church, the State, Fortune 500 corporations, the Internet, the World Wide Web. When you get online, as Gibson wrote, reality is a consensual hallucination. If you're lucky.[10]

Evidently, Friedrich Nietzsche liked to say "there are no facts, only interpretations."[11] Unlike myself, Geertz and Berger and Wittgenstein probably actually read the guy. He supposedly says this in *The Will to Power: Attempt at a Revaluation of all Values*, which sounds way too heavy for my head, and which, anyway, was patched together by his sister, who was married to a Nazi and took, shall we say, certain liberties with dearly departed Friedrich's notebooks, thus giving him a much worse rap than he might have had otherwise. Talk about your thick description. Admittedly, the rap was already pretty bad, because he's also the guy who lobbed the "God is dead" grenade into the middle of the Enlightenment garden party. To say the least, this did not ingratiate him with the God-fearing—though if they were really all that afraid, you'd think at least some of them might have taken this as good news of another sort. After all, a few hundred million Buddhists do. At any rate, what I think he meant, among other things I can imagine (which I am keeping to myself), is that divine authority was no longer what you might call a highly credible source in the working out of what certain things signified or what signified certain things. Like value, for instance, to loop back around to our theme, about which, at this point, *nothing* is certain. Well, good then. That means it's working.

As Nietzsche bought the farm in 1900, you can see that this sort of general shakiness about the meaning of things has been floating around for quite some time. Hell, you could go back to the classical philosophers. Say you're walking in Memphis, home of Elvis and the ancient Greeks.[12] Is what you think a thing to be what everyone else understands it as? Is the world as it appears to you, or does it look completely different to someone who *didn't* grow up in Darien, Connecticut, and get an MBA from Wharton? Of course, Plato and Aristotle and that lot wouldn't have been able to tell an MBA from a banana fish. And anyway, who cares? Who cares, especially, because such questions verge on dangerous ground, on terra incognita. Business prides itself on hard-nosed practicality and pragmatism, even if it gets all dewy-eyed wondering where its pragmatism came from. Philosophy, anthropology, sociology, linguistics? Leave that stuff to the longhairs. We got a business plan to write!

OK, so you write the plan. For a killer B2B e-commerce portal. And you structure the plan around the Holy of Holies, the infamous 4 Ps of marketing: product, promotion, place and price.[13] Of the four, only the last generates revenue; the others represent costs. Price is what you can charge based on some proposed value. If you're a consulting group, maybe you write a meta-plan, something for clients to chew on, if not perhaps entirely digest. If you're working at the Ernst & Young "Thought Center"—*From Thought to Finish*—you write this:

Moving From First Mover to First Prover:

The race for dominance in business-to-business (B2B) digital marketplaces is picking up steam....A winning business model is based on alignment of a company and its industry with how the company will achieve competitive advantage in each of four areas: the company's *unique value proposition; delivery chain management; functionality;* and *profit mechanisms.*[14]

Cool! And not only that, Ernst & Young also promises to "stress test" your business model. After they've created it, naturally (imagine something here about the fox guarding the henhouse). For this important work, the company has assembled a team with a "unique set of skills"—uniqueness having ultrahigh cachet at the moment—consisting of "investment bankers with top tier wall street experience, and academics and economists with diverse backgrounds including Harvard Business School."[15] Wow, huh? And probably cheap too. How could you go wrong? Except maybe by buying into the odd notion that a degree from Harvard ever qualified anyone for the diversity category.

Look, I have no particular animus toward Ernst & Young. I've spoken with some very smart people there over the years. But the fact is, you will find this sort of nonsensical no-nonsense cut-to-the-chase business rhetoric on thousands of corporate web pages today. Locating an example took me about two minutes on Alta Vista. Here's the search string; try it yourself:

+B2B +"e-commerce" +"value proposition"

More substantively, you could go wrong with any number of customers, prospects, partners or suppliers by creating a "value proposition" with zero idea of what value means to a couple-three billion people, each of whom is genuinely unique, and who, taken together, are a hell of lot more diverse—you can take this one to the bank—than a bunch of fucking academic economists. Assuming that its world is *the* world, choosing to be naïve about language to the point of volunteer autism, business ends up looking a lot less hard-nosed than soft-headed.

However, having thus blinded itself like Oedipus (what did it see that it couldn't bear to see?), business is reduced to common-sense dictionary definitions of value—though this "common sense," as we'll soon see, has nothing in common with the commons as construed to mean the people, the great seething mass of humanity that has been in these latter days transformed, as if by magic, into the miracle of global markets. That is to say, these definitions were largely created by business itself (more about the fox guarding the lexicon below). The *American Heritage Dictionary* includes the following definitions of "*value*":

1. An amount, as of goods, services, or money, considered to be a fair and suitable equivalent for something else. . .
2. Monetary or material worth. . .
3. Worth in usefulness or importance to the possessor; utility or merit. . . .
4. A principle, standard, or quality considered worthwhile or desirable. . . [16]

It seems reasonable to assume that considerations of what is worthwhile or desirable might have some bearing on price. You'd think, right? Business certainly thinks so. But the same dictionary defines "*price*" as follows:

1. The amount as of money or goods, asked for or given in exchange for something else.
2. The cost at which something is obtained. . . .
3. The cost of bribing someone. . .
4. A reward offered for the capture or killing of a person. . .
5. *Archaic.* Value or worth.

Though numbers three and four throw a bit of a curve—"every person has a price" and "a felon with a price on his head," the respective entries go on to explain—at least one and two are pretty much what you'd expect. The real zinger is the last item. Archaic? But wasn't value just explained in terms of cost? In fact it was: "an amount, as of goods, services, or money, considered to be a fair and suitable equivalent for something else . . ." And that, as the saying has it, is the price you pay.

Maybe it's some lexicographer's little joke, an Easter Egg like the ones Microsoft coders sneak into Office apps. Maybe the intent is to suggest that price *used to* reflect value, but that was then. Ha ha. Or maybe it means something far more ominous: that an older sense of value has been supplanted. For while Nietzsche never achieved his goal of revaluing all values, business has done precisely that. While nobody was looking.

In business, value determines price, or at least sometimes suggests it. Price is then a function of value—what something costs bears some relationship, we suppose, to what it's worth. But what about value in a larger framework than cost? What is the value of something to our lives? Without needing any fancy equations, we all know the value of oxygen even though it doesn't have an explicit price tag (yet). Aside from price, the larger value of products and services is connoted by a mystical constellation of values that are ideally supposed to be captured and represented by the concept of *brand*. The most successful branding campaign ever carried out was the branding of brand itself—getting human beings to accept the implicit assumption that all value is monetary, that everything has a price in dollars and cents (or currency of your choice). This largely unconscious theory of value is what defines and drives consumerism, in which identity is determined by what you have and can get instead of by who you discover you are or may become.

Because value is subjective and perceived differently by different cultures and communities, it cannot be reduced to fit neatly into a single systematic and comprehensive conceptual framework. However, this cultural relativity, this diversity of perspective and interpretation creates very large practical problems—especially for corporations committed to growth at any cost, especially for companies willing to let others bet, via the financial markets, on whether such growth is sustainable beyond, say, next Thursday. By revaluing all values in monetary terms and throwing out anything that didn't have an obvious rate of exchange, a sort of tacit universal metaphysics was born by default. God is dead, but business is alive and well. Long live McDonald's! Would you like fries with that? Long live Disney! It's a small world after all. Long live the Global Economy! Tagline pending.

In *Jihad vs. McWorld,* Benjamin Barber describes what he calls McWorld as a set of "onrushing economic, technological, and ecological forces that demand integration and uniformity and that mesmerize peoples everywhere with fast music, fast computers, and fast food. . . pressing nations into one homogenous global theme park, one McWorld tied together by communications, information, enter-

tainment, and commerce."[17] Later, contrasting Americans' choice of
multiple automobile brands with the non-choice of public vs. private transportation—a choice that was never explicitly offered—he
writes: "This politics of commodity offers a superficial expansion of
options within a determined frame in return for surrendering the
right to determine the frame. It offers the feel of freedom while diminishing the range of options and the power to affect the larger
world. Is this really liberty?"[18]

Freedom as nothing left to lose—Benjamin Barber, meet Bobby
McGee.[19] All values have been revalued. The frame has been hijacked. And as untold numbers of e-commerce pundits announce
with messianic fanfare and not a trace of irony: "Brand is everything!"[20]

It's Alive! It's Alive!

Love is not love
Which alters when it alteration finds. . .

—WILLIAM SHAKESPEARE[21]

Love is love and not fade away. . .

—CHARLES HARDIN AND NORMAN PETTY[22]

Entropy is the outward and visible sign of the second law of thermodynamics. In layman's terms, it means the house always wins,
but place your bets anyway ladies and gentlemen; there's one born
every minute. It means there's no free lunch and perpetual motion
devices make exceedingly bad investments. It means the transitori-
ness of the composite.[23] Because friction—there's the rub—is always
slowing things down, taxing energy transactions until there's nothing left to tax. And there's nothing left because, when things slow
down *enough*, they disappear. Ice Nine, if you've read Vonnegut, or
the fine print on those Dead albums: at absolute zero there's nothing doing. Entropy means that, once wound by the Big Bang, the
cosmic clock is always running. Running down.

The directional vector of this process is the gradient, the slippery
slope on which we build our hopes and dreams, technologies, em-

pires, civilizations. Steep grade ahead; test your brakes. Not much of a toehold really in the greater scheme of things. A fool's errand you might say. And yet, if all that's true, and things always move from a greater to a lesser degree of order and cohesion, then how is it that a point of no dimension whatsoever, one day before there were days to count, erupted with a violence so far beyond all measure that it's still red-shifting galaxies back to the beginning of what we lamely conceive of as time? Or that a handful of hydrogen comes to look around itself one day, at the world, the stars, the blackest, deepest night and says: "What a gas!"

That's the reversal.

We are dealing today with levels of complexity at which the immutable second law kicks in bigtime and begins to manifest as something tangible in our lives. The effect we feel is a kind of chaos in which things fall apart more readily than they come together. This downhill slide means more thankless work for everyone—desperately trying to manage the inherently unmanageable, with increasingly small returns on the investment. Despite the 1000-megawatt euphoria of ubiquitous technology cheerleaders, the answer is not faster chips and logic-gate flips, more FLOPS or more bandwidth. It isn't "enterprise-wide knowledge management" or whatever foolproof fad is circulating at the moment. The answer is that there is no answer.

We are drowning in complexity and the more we try to simplify things, the more complex we make things in the process. It's hopeless. There is no way out.

No *obvious* way, that is. And perhaps no permanent way. But there is one thing that seems to contradict the iron law of entropy. Life. Strangely opposite to the way we tend ourselves, the thermodynamic gradient is hell-bent for ultimate simplicity. And that simplicity is death. Simple atomic structures, perfectly equalized distribution, zero Kelvin. In contrast, life is complicated, as you may have noticed. Left to itself for billions of years, with no engineers in evidence and no management consultants, our planet suddenly became extremely complex as the result of contracting a virus. A billion years later, this viral anomaly developed into bipedal hominids with big brains and bigger plans. And we've been groping around ever since, blind, stumbling in the dark.

Sometimes a great wind comes out of space and shifts the points of the compass completely, revises longheld notions of what's valuable, what's worth spending life on. That's what happened to me in the course of writing this book. I fell in love. And how does something like that fit into the context of a business book? I ask you. I ask myself. Business books are boring. They're supposed to be boring. Dispassionate and objective, detached from personal concerns. The world of business is a world unto itself. Whatever insight business books may deliver, they must do so within a strictly circumscribed set of boundaries, within a framework that validates and reinforces their core subject. Which is of course: business. The tautology is so neat it's seamless. The business of business is business. Not even daylight can slip through the cracks.

But last time I checked, there was no world of business somehow separate from the world as a whole. There was no reality to the separation we speak so easily about between work life and private life—a.k.a. "real life." These are artificial distinctions, convenient fictions. But whose convenience do they serve? Yours, gentle reader? Mine? I don't think so. Something is desperately wrong here, I think. Then I think, well. . . maybe it's just me. Maybe I got bored with the power and majesty of commerce, with its challenges, obstacles, impact and opportunities. Got bored with its limits and limiting definitions of value. Got bored because I looked into my own heart and found something far more valuable there. I ask myself if I'm alone in this. And again, I don't think so. I think I've got company.

Hmmm, "company." Now there's a business word if there ever was one. But how does the company I've got in my boredom with business differ from the kind of company a business creates? Language is funny stuff, mixing us up at every turn. Or perhaps, since I love a good conspiracy theory as much as the next poor sod, being *used* to mix us up. *Webster's Third* provides help in the form of linguistic archeology. The word *"company,"* it tells us, comes from the word *"companion,"* which originally meant someone with whom you shared food—specifically, with whom you broke bread (*panis* in Latin).[24] That's strange. Gets sort of Biblical there, doesn't it? But maybe this is leading us further away from the inherent nature of value. Maybe I'm just tripping here, reaching for a rationalization for why I'm so bored with business. Me and all that company I suspect I've got.

But it gets even stranger. How does a company, a corporation, come into being? Not a trick question: it incorporates. But it is a trick answer. Back to the archeology, *corpus* in Latin means body. So to incorporate means to become embodied—to be made flesh. Is it just me, I ask myself, or are there linguistic clues here that business first sought legitimacy in the deepest mysteries of Christian theology? Maybe so. Legitimacy was certainly a problem for early business, dealing as it did with sublunary matters. There's a word you're not likely to find in your *Wall Street Journal.* And for good reason. The *Oxford English Dictionary* defines *"sublunary"* as:

> Existing or situated beneath the moon; lying between the orbit of the moon and the earth; hence, subject to the moon's influence. b. Inferior, subordinate (to). *Obsolete*
> Of or belonging to this world; earthly, terrestrial.
> Characteristic of this world and its affairs; mundane; material, gross; temporal, ephemeral.[25]

The sense comes through that the affairs of this world—perhaps business especially—were not terribly well thought of at one time. The Church, back when there was just one in Western Christendom, denigrated such involvement, to say the least. The whole idea of money was deeply suspect. We still speak of "filthy lucre," even if the modern use of the phrase is usually jocular. At one time, lending money at interest constituted the sin of usury. This explains why many more Jews than Christians went into banking—and also explains much of the resulting racial bias that has persisted to this day. Jews were not only the infidel, they became a sort of untouchable caste, performing necessary services for which they were, at the same time, deeply resented.

There was another community of practice whose concern with the sublunary sphere formed a counterbalance to the otherworldliness of the Church and its focus on the afterlife. To the alchemists, the material world was *prima materia*—the source of the earths and metals their art sought to transform. They were not just proto-chemists. They were philosophers working out a worldview that was heretical in the eyes of Rome. They immersed themselves in the material plane, the world of here and now—and out of this immersion came a powerfully legitimizing analogy for commerce.

In *The Business of Alchemy,* Pamela Smith writes that in the 17th century, commerce was considered an unproductive practice. Merchants were seen as taking without returning anything to the communities in which they lived. They did not produce anything themselves, but acted as parasites, feeding off the exchange between the people who made things and the people who bought them. "The unnatural offspring of this unnatural activity," writes Smith, "was money. Money was considered unnatural because it was a means of exchange that did not contain the seeds of its own regeneration."

Despite this strong prejudice, the paradox became obvious to many: money did seem to produce an increase in material well-being. It clearly created something valuable, but no one could quite figure out how. There was no model in nature—which, there being no venture capitalists at the time, is where you went to find business models in those days. This quandary had people scratching their heads and the merchant class hopping up and down on hot coals. Business desperately wanted to be accepted as legitimate, but in keeping with the perception of all things sublunary as inferior, subordinate, mundane, ephemeral and generally gross, the whole proposition smelled fishy.[26]

Enter the alchemist Johann Joachim Becher, who, as official physician and mathematician to the court of some now-long-since-deceased German dude (the precise historical details need not concern us here) supplied the missing link. Long story short:

Alchemy...became the vehicle by which Becher spoke to the court about production and material increase. The language of alchemy was particularly well suited to the discussion of commerce, for alchemical transmutation—the ennoblement of metals—provided an example of fabulous material increase and the production of surplus. This was especially true in Becher's theory of alchemical transmutation, which postulated that the multiplication of precious metals took place by means of consumption. Alchemy was thus a natural, virtuous activity within the compass of human art. . . [27]

It's hard to imagine today, when commerce has become the life blood—some would say the death knell—of the planet, that there was once a time when business had to stoop to higher authority. Clearly, it got what it wanted in the end, and it accomplished this largely the way it gets things done today: by influence peddling. Political lobbying not having yet been invented, the moneychangers went to the temple. Metaphorically speaking, of course. Max Weber's classic study *The Protestant Ethic and the Spirit of Capitalism* (1904) has been criticized as overly simplistic. Some argued that he put too much stock in the Calvinist notion of predestination and of wealth as an outward manifestation that the possessor was among the elect, i.e., those white, male Bürgermeisters lucky enough to be holding automatic get-out-of-jail cards and who were therefore and inevitably Bound for Glory, no thanks to Woody Guthrie. The book nonetheless brought much attention to the complex relationships that developed between ecclesiastical and earthly powers. This work was somewhat more successfully continued by Weber's student, R. H. Tawney, in *Religion and the Rise of Capitalism* (1926). Specifics of the Calvin-for-Capital controversy aside, it's clear that business went from cap in hand to calling the shots, and it did so through accommodation. Commerce went looking for, and found, strong support from religion.

So, could "*incorporation*" have been playing off the Christian mystery of transubstantiation—Word become flesh? Whatever the answer, the fact remains that this term we use every day, along with its shortened form, *corporation,* hides an anthropomorphic metaphor that has no basis in reality. No corporation has ever become embodied. But however mistaken, this metaphor has great power—more so because it is perceived subliminally. On the other hand, ad agencies apply a variation of it quite consciously in the process of product branding. Citing the Jolly Green Giant, the Michelin Man and the Pillsbury Doughboy, a book titled *Brand Spirit* states: "While there are many executional typologies in advertising, some of the most prevalent and successful are those which exploit brand anthropomorphy to the full."[28] The authors are associated with the advertising firm of Saatchi & Saatchi.

The embodied-corporation metaphor allows corporations to mimic human beings. To act as if. But the corporation has no heart.

The cries will go up at this one, I know. But the reaction is based on another misplaced metaphor. Forget how much your business gave to charity or how it's planting trees or teaching ghetto kids to use computers (so you can hire them later at minimum wage). I mean, the corporation lacks the physical organ we call the heart. That thing in your chest that goes thump-thump. Here, I'll make it easier for you: the corporation has no sex. Those who protest even at this obvious truth need to be reminded: it can only screw you *metaphorically*. But this is serious. This is important. Embodiment is a very big deal. Bodies don't come into being through mergers and acquisitions. They are born of woman, as King James put it. Bodies don't file for protection under Chapter 11. They die.

No corporation has ever fallen in love. Reflect on that a moment. Roll it around on your tongue, in the back of your mind. Does it seem a non sequitur, irrelevant? It's not.

Companies don't fall in love. But people do. And whether we speak about it publicly or not, as a species we tend to place great importance on this fact, this entry into a larger more connected world. Easy to ignore, forget, but this is vital. Love opens our hearts to each other, to people other than ourselves, and to the space we share as human beings cast into life without a manual, without a hardwired set of instructions. If, in our 100,000 years or so, we have made catastrophic mistakes, fought devastating wars, pillaged and raped and killed, we have also created complex cultures, built societies, created fabulous art out of nothing but imagination. Drawn on by the longing in our hearts, we have survived. Error but also Eros. Love has shaped and informed and colored our world as much as power. More. But we forget. We get embarrassed. Why? There is a reason, and that reason will unfold as we explore. This time of change is not any time. This world not any world. It is ours and we are here today, as never before, to chronicle and celebrate its wonders. To take it back.

When *The Cluetrain Manifesto* was published, a particular bit seems to have gotten left out. Perhaps someone got embarrassed. Because it's been on the website all along, it took me months to realize that what I'd written had mysteriously gone missing from the book. So, never having recanted anything, let me rectify the omission right now, in a place where it seems to me. . . ahem, appropriate. Whether or not it puts me in dire straits, let me step right up to the microphone. . . [29]

PEOPLE OF EARTH

The sky is open to the stars. Clouds roll over us night and day. Oceans rise and fall. Whatever you may have heard, this is our world, our place to be. Whatever you've been told, our flags fly free. Our heart goes on forever. People of Earth, remember.

Who are we? Look around you. Open your heart. Remember what you have forgotten.

"But what does this have to do with business?" business asks. The question itself reflects the problem. Blind to the central experience of our reality, business never thinks to wonder. Is never awed, inspired, never enthusiastic, curious, ecstatic. Business has *never* wondered—for the same reason that business has never fallen in love. Yet all these capabilities and qualities are intrinsic to the human character. They make us what we are. Corporations say, "We love our customers! You bet!" They say, "We love our workers! It's the people!" But these are lies. Corporations are incapable of love. This is not a moral condemnation, but a simple truth. They aren't equipped for it. Corporations have no heart. If you cut them, they do not bleed. If they die, no children mourn their passing. When they say "we love . . ." they are using words as counters in a game, as they count out money.

There is a conjurer's trick of language here, and at first it seems trivial, a mere convenience. Since companies are populated by people, the anthropomorphic projection sets off no alarms. As a result, we have gradually forgotten that "the company" is in many respects a reverse metonym—a figure of speech in which the whole takes on the qualities of its parts. It is not a reality. Companies produce goods, sell products, manage inventory. So far, so good; no problem. But later, closer to the present, companies begin to want our loyalty, our trust. They want us to be happy. Suddenly, big problem. The metaphor has gotten up off Dr. Frankenstein's table and is walking on its own. *It's alive! It's alive!*   .

But it's important to remember that it's not alive. The corporation pretends to subscribe to values it does not and cannot understand. Human values. Like love, like trust, like camaraderie and joy. These are things we genuinely value, but they have been devalued and denatured to advance the very different interests of the company. In the process, we are not only losing our language, we are losing our lives.

In the beginning was the Word, moving silent and unspoken upon the face of the deep.[30] But the word has been incorporated and co-opted into the service of another power, whose force is not grounded in the same spirit. We break bread in the company of strangers and it is as ashes in our mouths, giving no strength, no sustenance. Spirit, once sacred, has become an apparition, a ghost in the machine, and we are haunted by it. The historical journey from *Heilige Geist* to Zeitgeist moves from churchly dogma of the Holy Spirit to the secular and desacralized soul of a new machine.[31] And the word became dreck and the marketing communicators moved among us.

"Research on excellence and peak performance," writes Barry Heermann in *Building Team Spirit*, "confirms that high-performing teams and organizations consistently feel the spirit of the organization in their work, and that this feeling is an essential part of the meaning and value that members and observers place on their work."[32] And what precisely is this spirit? What *is* its meaning? What *is* its value? We cannot translate such terms into organizational "equivalents" without doing violence to what we once recognized as both most wholly other and most deeply human.

While religion staked out this territory long before business, neither has any rights of ownership. These feelings and meanings and values predate any institutional claim. "The spirit does but mean the breath," says Tennyson, and etymologically, he is correct. In the Vulgate Bible, the Latin *spiritus* was used to translate the Greek word for soul: *pneuma*, which means to breathe—the same word from which English gets *"pneumatic"*; the same concept from which we draw *"inspiration."* The first entry for *"spirit"* in *The Oxford English*

Dictionary reads: "The animating or vital principle in man (and animals); that which gives life to the physical organism, in contrast to its purely material elements; the breath of life."[33] Despite the preponderance of scriptural—and more recently, sports and business—uses, spirit does not depend on devotion to either eclesiastical or organizational objectives, and neither piety nor gung-ho are needed to understand the sentence: "The horse's spirit was broken."

Something animated and vital looks out from our children's eyes. Whatever it is, we recognize it and know it is precious. Yet except in rare cases today, that spirit is broken early and irreparably. The light goes out all too soon. We know, because at some inarticulate and dimly conscious level, we are those children. We feel the wind of spirit move us at odd moments, but put it down to nostalgia or temporary possession by some impractical flight of fancy. We shake it off and get back to work. Robbed of a voice to speak of these things, something animated and vital looks out from our own eyes, but only in rare, unguarded moments—and even then, wary, circumspect, suspicious. We let no one see what we fear no one will understand.

Where is the value in this, I wonder? What is the cost? Catching the light, a flock of pigeons turns through the sky over the highway. I am driving and remembering and feeling how much is lost, how precious this life.

There is an ever-present danger in such talk of authenticity and heart and wondrous awe—that it will come across like so much New Age trash. Naïve. Idealistic. Out of touch with economic realities and the challenges of global competition. Don't bet on it. The Internet has brought hundreds of millions of human beings together in an entirely new way, and we are using it to explore the things we truly value, genuinely care about. We are using the net to talk about the things that turn us on, about what and whom we love. It may not seem so from the outside, but we are sharing our hearts' desires in a way that could never have been imagined by business command and control or the stentorian voice of broadcast.

And as for Mr. and Mrs. America and all the ships at sea, I got your value proposition right here. Take a chance. Take a trip. Take a leap of faith. Incorporate for real. Take a walk on the wild side.[34]

The Red Queen Is Talking Backwards [35]

"Sing, O goddess, the anger of Achilles . . ."[36]

"Tell me, O muse, of that ingenious hero who traveled far and wide after he had sacked the famous town of Troy."[37]

Respectively, these two invocations launched the *Iliad* and the *Odyssey,* epic works that signal the dawn of Western civilization. But what does poetry have to do with business? In the era of the Internet, a lot. Paradoxically, the highest of high tech has created a doorway through which magic is re-entering the world.

The naive history books we read in school celebrated the triumph of science over ignorance and superstition. Experimentation based on empirical evidence gave us proven facts, not flights of fancy. Data won out over conjecture, and many times, knowledge over wisdom. Despite the miracles since wrought by science, the victim of this victory has often been imagination.

Today we want the cold, hard facts, the definitive word. We can't be bothered with perspective and opinion, hunches. We want to manage knowledge and make it "actionable." We want to "operationalize" intellectual capital. This is understandable given a view of the world as cold and hard, as a place where things can be known unequivocally, without a shadow of doubt. But this view born of scientific and technological tradition is just one way of seeing things. There are others.

"Content is King," the cliché tells us.[38] While the proposition has been widely debated, its obvious male bias has been ignored. Historically, science and technology have indeed been masculine pursuits. Both have shaped our world so long we can't remember anything that came before. And notice that both are about prediction and control. Cause and effect, action and reaction. Pull this lever, watch that plane incline. Provable. Repeatable. Powerful. Neat.[39]

But the world is not always neat. Most of it is extremely messy and, despite our erudition, still mysterious. The abstractions and reductions of rational logic try to explain the world, but they mainly explain what is already visible. Their built-in assumptions—for instance, that everything has a "scientific" explanation—blind this view to much of life. And literal, biological life is not a theory. We are inextricably embedded in it. Think about what really happens in a virgin forest. Think about what happens in the human heart.

These are deep waters with uncertain maps. Dark, hidden, flowing, oceanic, orgasmic, this is the realm of birth and death, of sex and passion, sleep and dream, of myth and intuition. Feeling not calculating. Yielding not controlling. This is the realm of the feminine.

Forget the sexual politics of gender. Yielding does not mean weak. Feminine doesn't even necessarily mean female. This is older knowledge. Much older. The ancient Chinese sages thought of Heaven as masculine, Earth feminine. Yin and Yang. Darkness and light. Complements, not polar opposites. Harmony comes from balance, not from victory of one over the other.

Yet in our culture today, science has won hands down, and its offspring, technology, has beaten all other views into submission. Technology begat big business and big business begat mass media. The intertwined histories of science, technology and commerce have left a legacy of domination and control—from the geographic colonialism of the so-called major powers to the more psychic forms of colonialism represented by media empires such as Yahoo and AOL, Disney and Rupert Murdoch's News Corporation.

In the marketplace, the mouthpiece of this colonialist impulse is broadcast. In the workplace, it is command-and-control management. Both are about imposing power top down. And both deliver the cold, hard facts in definitive, no-nonsense terms: work orders, database records, stock prices, sports scores, dispassionate and supposedly "objective" news reports.

This way of framing the world has collided head-on with the Internet. People have come to this medium by the tens of millions with other interests and concerns, high among them body-based emotions far from the mechanistic inclinations of the Business-Technology complex. The Internet has given everyone a voice. But *vox populi*—the voice of the people—is vastly more vital than the sterile pronouncements of corporations and media conglomerates.

The most fundamental quality of the feminine is mystery, not certain knowledge. Suggestion and connotation, not exhaustive description. Poetry and parable, not news analysis. As a culture, we are moving from cold hard facts to warm and fluid narratives. Warm as in body temperature, not chill robotics. Fluid as in organic forms, not rectilinear wire frames. And these human stories exert tremendous attraction. The god breathes into us and we are made alive. That is the etymology of "*enthusiasm.*" The goddess lends breath to voice and we are literally "*inspired.*"

Who is creating such stories today? Whose voices will draw new listeners the way Druids drew down the moon, the way Greeks drew a wooden horse to the gates of Troy? Tell me, O muse, of *those* ingenious heroes. Sing to me, goddess, of anger and estrangement. I'm a motherfucker, baby, your mind my sky, your eyes my fire. This world, this life so intricate, delicate, complex. Precious beyond measure. I'm slamming my head against the walls of empire, the habits of power, enraged. Blasting and burning for your love. Imagining the network finally connected. Imagining joy. A wall of horns and drums and dangerous magical noise. I'm bending over my Fender, working the circuits, incendiary, incandescent. Rocking in the free world, serving notice on Babylon. Ain't in for a dollar, ain't in for a dime. Ain't going down for no two-bit dream. Armed only with imagination, I'm back in your spiral arms tonight. Everything has at least two meanings. But one thing girl that I want to say, love is love and not fade away.

CHAPTER 3

Code Blue in the Marketing Ward

*"The propagandist's purpose is to make one set of people
forget that certain other sets of people are human."*

—ALDOUS HUXLEY[1]

*"The broad mass of a nation . . . will more easily
fall victim to a big lie than to a small one."*

—ADOLF HITLER[2]

"This little piggy went to market."

—ANONYMOUS

WHEN *ADVERTISING AGE* ANNOUNCED ITS 1999 MARKETING 100 AWARDS
ceremony—the magazine's eighth annual tribute to the people behind that year's hottest brands—some copywriter wrote: "The most
important element of a successful marketing plan is not the budget
or media selection, but the idea."[3] Roger Shiffman took home a top-
100 slot for marketing Furby, and Kenn Viselman won for promoting the Teletubbies. The event was sponsored by Comedy Central.
No lie. It may put things in perspective to realize that, among its Top
10 Jingles of the Century, *Ad Age* lists "I wish I was an Oscar Meyer
Wiener."[4] Remember: it's the *idea* that's important.

If you're not laughing, you're in deeper shit than you thought.
Chances are good that you *are* laughing, though. Or crying. Or saying, hot damn, that's right, or that's wrong, or that's utterly beside

the point. Whatever form they may take, the sum of such reactions, added to constant analysis and endless talk, constitute the global conversation I wrote about in *The Cluetrain Manifesto*. "Through the Internet, people are discovering and inventing new ways to share relevant knowledge with blinding speed. As a direct result, markets are getting smarter—and getting smarter faster than most companies." (Hang onto that thought for a minute and see if you don't pick up an echo.)

Now I can imagine some dyspeptic critic writing, "In what sense can it be said that these random views amount to '*relevant knowledge*'? Haven't we heard enough from these stridently opinionated web-heads like Locke and his ilk? Not one of these people has ever had to grapple with the daunting management challenges facing a Fortune 500 company or brought in a billion dollars in revenue. Who do they think they are to question the *genuinely* relevant knowledge hard-won from a century of hands-on marketing experience?" Something like that.

Or something like the assessment of *Cluetrain* that appeared in *The New York Times Book Review*. While granting that "the general thrust is on the mark," the reviewer accused the book of sloganeering. "What the Slogan Era's 'business revolution' is really about is not borrowed from politics; instead, it's a phenomenon that offers middle-aged managers a second chance to sound a barbaric yawp and imagine a new significance to their lives."[5] Not content to compare my deathless prose to Holden Caulfield's outpourings of teenage angst, *The Times* came back a few weeks later for a second round of recreational ass kicking. This article implied that certain aspects of the net are reminiscent of the '60s. One got the feeling this was not intended as a compliment. "The web, in Mr. Locke's view, brings the revolution against the sonorous all-knowing corporate voice to its inevitable climax and resolution in favor of the plebeians. 'The Internet enables people to talk directly to each other and to corporations,' he said. 'It is something businesses ignore at their own peril.'" The piece ends with a sneer: "Heavy, man, heavy."[6]

The point is not to complain of mediocre reviews—hey, if you piss on somebody's parade, you have to expect return fire—nor is it to out myself as a dope-smoking brimstone-hurling web-whacked anti-business middle-aged adolescent sloganeer. Rather, the point is to introduce someone who is none of those things—except possibly middle aged; it can happen to the best of us—but who has nonetheless been making some pretty radical pronouncements of late. "The bottom line is that *markets* are changing a lot faster than *marketing*," he writes in a book published 12 months after *Cluetrain*. And there's the echo you've been waiting for so patiently. "Today," he says, "most company marketing strategies are obsolete!" Emphasis and exclamation in original. And why is this so? Because, as he writes, "With the World Wide Web, we are moving into a new marketing era."[7]

Who is this masked man? And what gives *him* the right to yawp so barbarically? Let's just say he is to marketing what Werner Heisenberg was to quantum mechanics, or Jerry Lee Lewis to rockabilly. If marketing had a Godfather, a *capo di tutti capi*, Philip Kotler would be it. Since 1962, he has taught at Northwestern University's Kellogg Graduate School of Management, defined the field of marketing to generations of corporate vice presidents—his textbooks on the subject have long been required reading in MBA programs worldwide—and consulted to companies such as IBM, Apple, GE, Ford, AT&T, Motorola, Bank of America, Merck, Ciba Geigy, JP Morgan, Dupont, Westinghouse and Merrill Lynch. So when this guy says marketing is fucked, you best believe it. Though he didn't put it quite that way. Unlike myself, Kotler comes across as a gentleman.

I opened the last chapter by hacking on one of his books, but that came out in 1999, and a lot can happen in a couple years. Especially these days. We'll encounter him again below, and in another chapter for the seminal role he played in establishing the concept and practice of social marketing. For now, let's see what he's been saying about antisocial marketing. In the latest word on the profession, *Kellogg on Marketing*, he writes:

Industrial-Age marketing thinking is rooted in the metaphor of marketing as hunting. The marketplace is seen as a jungle. Marketers have to scope out the jungle (market research) and define the prey that they want to capture (target marketing). Marketers must study the prey's habits and habitats (consumer behavior). Marketers have to build a better mousetrap (product differentiation), lay traps and bait (advertising, direct mail, sales promotions), and secure the prey and prevent it from escaping (customer retention, relationship marketing).

The hunters/marketers assume that the prey is not as smart or well informed as they are. The prey acts on emotion (positioning), is easily seduced by trinkets (promotions), and wanders unwittingly into the danger zone (retail stores, salespeople). The hunter has extensive information about the whereabouts of the prey, and knows how to aim the rifle (value proposition) at the prey's soft spot.[8]

So let's cut the counterculture crap, OK? If people in general don't trust business, if they find it insulting and demeaning to be so cynically manipulated—and people do feel this way, in numbers far greater than corporate denial allows for[9]—it doesn't necessarily mean they're stoned. Or stupid. It might just mean they're not drinking the KOOL-AID® anymore.

"Discover the Kraft Family of Brands" the web page taunts me.[10] I am driven to kraftfoods.com in a masochistic fugue of documentary due diligence. As a responsible author, I must definitively determine who owns the KOOL-AID® trademark. But once there, I serendipitously discover this surreal exhortation: "Let the WIENERMOBILE™ take you to the OSCAR MAYER Virtual Lunchbox!" It's gotta be synchronicity. Even as I realize *Ad Age* got the spelling wrong, I start humming their Top 10 Jingle of the Century. "Oooooh I wish I was an Oscar Meyer Wiener . . ." And for some reason that will remain forever shrouded in the deep recesses of my tortured psyche, this causes me to suddenly recall the most frightening conspiracy theory ever circulated on the Internet. "What if," the message speculated darkly, "the Hokey-Pokey really *is* what it's all about?"

The Real Thing: Stories, Brands and Lies

"my heart is where it's always been. . . "

U2[11]

Richard Earle advised Johnson & Johnson during the Tylenol poisoning scare—an impressive credential indeed, as that company's public response was both fast and forthright. In *The Art of Cause*

Marketing, he explains why "art" figures in his book's title. Conventional advertising can be artful on occasion, he says, but seldom can it be called art. "True art is something that moves people in important emotional and personal ways," he writes, "something that stays with them and possibly affects their lives." Social marketing and cause marketing are themes we'll explore more deeply in a later chapter. For now, let's just say that the difference between traditional marketing and social marketing is critical. The first is focused on selling products; the second is aimed at raising awareness of issues that have high relevance to society as a whole. In the case of social marketing, Earle writes, "because the consequences are so far-reaching and because the objective is *always* to move people and affect their lives, it is very important that *every* piece of cause marketing be crafted as carefully as a serious work of art!"[12]

Though it was surely not the author's intent, this observation speaks volumes about conventional, non-cause marketing, correctly implying that most advertising does *not* move people in personal ways or intrinsically affect their lives, no matter how much companies try to convince us—and themselves—that their product pitches have such persuasive power.

Marketing has always been a black art—and it's getting blacker by the minute. In the sense of shrouded, invisible, unknown. In a fit of Amazon.com one-click-purchase possession, I recently bought 20 volumes of the *Harvard Business Review* Paperback Series. This collection covers more angles of business than you can shake a stick at (future stick-shaking was in fact my motivation for buying them): management, leadership, governance, performance measurement, information technology, you name it. However, in none of the book titles—nor in the titles of the 162 included *HBR* articles—does the word "*marketing*" appear. Not once. I find this curious.[13] It's there in the indices, of course. But the listings say things like: "Marketing strategy. See also brand building; mass media advertising; sales promotions; sponsorships." So if I do those things, then I'll be marketing, right? And to help me, the series does include a volume on *Brand Management*.

Almost en passant, Randall Rothenberg writes in *Advertising Age* that "it goes without saying branding has been exposed as a hoax." I like this guy—and not just because he sends email crammed with pointers to wonderfully germane books like Paul Lazarsfeld's *On Social Research and its Language* and James W. Carey's *Communication and Culture* (we got talking after he reviewed *Cluetrain*). I like him more because of the stuff he throws straight in the face of marketing's inner sanctum. "Brands are promises," he continues, "of service, quality, values and substance—made by a company to its own people, and thereon to its customers. To believe such a promise, which normally takes years to build, can be short-circuited by a multi-million-dollar network dump, in an economy where employees have the loyalty of rutting gerbils, strains credulity."[14]

Still, marketers invoke brand as if it were the Holy Grail. They speak of its power in hushed and reverential tones. The rest of us think they're barking mad. If marketing is only fully and completely understood by some elite priesthood of MBA-equipped professionals, then why should the market give a damn? If they haven't explained it to me—and they haven't—then something is very wrong here. There has been, to quote from *Cool Hand Luke*, a failure to communicate. The Big-M Marketing department behaves as if it isn't performing in front of a live audience. On the Internet, however, if there is no audience, neither is there a market.

But let's back up for a second to when we were all working without a net. I met Theodore Levitt in Pittsburgh in 1987. Cool guy. After his talk, I handed him a paper about the work I then did, called "Corporate Communications: Telling Stories That Transmit Vision." I was surprised to get a handwritten note a few days later saying he'd like to publish it in *Harvard Business Review*, of which he was then editor-in-chief. I'd just need to make a couple fairly simple changes, he said. Like a jerk, I never made them, and it never ran. Levitt had also written an important book called *The Marketing Imagination*—what a curious juxtaposition of words. Oxymoronic, you could almost say. Much earlier, in 1960, he had published a seminal article in *HBR* titled "Marketing Myopia," where he said: "Marketing is a stepchild. I do not mean that selling is ignored. Far from it. But selling . . . is not marketing. . . . selling concerns itself with the tricks and techniques of getting people to exchange their cash for your product. It is not concerned with the values that the exchange is all about."[15]

There's that maddeningly amorphous notion of value again. In 1975, *HBR* re-published this article along with Levitt's "Retrospective Commentary," in which he speculated as to why the piece had been so successful. At that date it had sold well over a quarter million reprints. And in this speculation he points to a dimension of value rarely if ever raised in marketing literature.

> Is it that concrete examples, joined to illustrate a simple idea and presented with some attention to literacy, communicate better than massive analytical reasoning that reads as though it were translated from the German? Is it that provocative assertions are more memorable and more persuasive than restrained and balanced explanations, no matter who the audience? Is it that the character of the message is as much the message as its content?[16]

Here, one of the greatest names in marketing returns the focus to the story and how it's told—and why it might *matter* how it's told. How provocative and persuasive are the stories marketing tells today? What is the character of the message?

In its first issue of 2000, *Fast Company* ran a piece of corporate puffery indistinguishable from advertising.[17] "Experience the Real Thing" the title beckoned. With no distracting hint of critical editorial distance, the text extolled in breathless prose "the Coca-Cola branding experience in Las Vegas, where nostalgia, storytelling, and technology create a magic formula." Storytelling seems to have achieved a certain cachet in corporate circles, though as an eviscerated, bankrupt concept. It's amazing to listen in on marketers trying to imagine what a story might be—almost like having a front row seat at a cargo cult ceremony. "We wanted to bring the brand to life, to tell the stories of Coca-Cola, and to express Coca-Cola's core values: fun, refreshment, and specialness in people's lives," says Deborah MacCarthy, manager of Coke's College Channel. Yeah, I can relate. I don't know about you readers out there, but for me, Specialness comes right after Truth, Justice and The American Way on *my* list of core values. Specialness? *Specialness?* What the hell are these people talking about? I'm getting spontaneous flashbacks of the Talking Heads movie *True Stories* intercut with *The Gods Must*

Be Crazy.[18] Ladies and gentlemen, please return your tray tables to the fully upright and locked position, suspend your disbelief and put on your tinfoil pyramid hats. We are now entering... [cue lights, cue music] the *Brand Dimension!*

> "Any presentation has to have a dramatic arc," [some brainless Coca-Cola flack] explains. "We wanted to create the sense of a journey, with a call to action at the end. If I give a presentation that's intended to sell, I tell a story whose call to action is 'Purchase my product.' In Las Vegas, our goal is to get people emotionally involved in the brand—so much so that they're ready to spend big bucks in the retail store downstairs."[19]

I can report that after reading this *Fast Company* article, I did get emotionally involved in the brand. I broke all the furniture in the office and swore a mighty oath to deconstruct such idiotic notions of "story" every chance I got. No time like the present, I figure.

Twice head marketing honcho at The Coca-Cola Company, Sergio Zyman, describes why, under his guidance, things went better with Coke: "We were successful because we never forgot that our goal was to get more people to buy more stuff more often so the company could make more money."[20] Stirring words, to be sure. But who cares? Really. While this is certainly what every company hopes to accomplish, do a company's atavistic wish-fulfillment fantasies constitute a story? Such empty and self-serving statements are not only insufficient today, they generate outright hostility. Once upon a time, such discussions took place in ultra-private mahogany-paneled board rooms, where it was safe to talk about how your marketing program pivoted on a devious remote-control trip to trick more demographic abstractions into buying more stuff. Today, such heretofore sensitive matters as "eyeball acquisition cost" are openly bandied about in the public Internet *agora*, where such talk has helped make it painfully obvious that companies seldom give a damn about what real people want or care about.

Even Zyman's own product—his book in this case—is now open to assessment in the networked marketplace, an assessment over which he as producer has no control. On Amazon.com, reader-reviewer Byron Menides, adjunct professor at Worcester Polytechnic

Institute's School of Industrial Management, writes: "I was disappointed after reading Sergio Zyman's book with the provocative title, *The End of Marketing as We Know It*. Old marketing based on mass merchandising with little attention to customer needs was dead years ago ... I am surprised that a book published in 1999 says so little about the impact and influence of the Internet in business to business and consumer marketing."[21]

But the fact that the Internet is missing from the discussion comes as no real surprise. This is marketing as it was canonized in the age of mass-market broadcast media, the dynamics of which differ deeply from those of the online world. The problem is not that marketing as Sergio Zyman knows it—manipulative, intrusive, gimmick-ridden and inherently dishonest—has come to an end. The problem is that this view of marketing remains unquestioned in most corporations and that its techniques are now being deployed in a new medium to which they have only negative relevance.

As Coca-Cola has been around for a long time, it may be tempting to think that its notions of marketing are typical of older, well-established companies, or of companies that offer commodity consumer products like fizzy brown sugar water. But much younger high-tech companies are prone to the same mentality and make the same mistakes. In an article titled "Legends in Their Own Minds," *Salon* looked at two business bestsellers: *High St@kes, No Prisoners* and *Renegades of the Empire*. Reviewer Thomas Scoville called them:

> ... particularly juicy specimens of the prevailing business rhetoric of the dot-com era. There is a kind of language—an amalgam of hyperbole, geek-speak, and pop-media code phrases, delivered in a perverse, super-desiccated and emotionally bankrupt tone—to be found in both of these books, and it is this contemporary mutation of language, rather than the stories themselves, that may ultimately communicate the Zeitgeist most effectively.[22]

To offer more than the facile business pitch, stories alone are not sufficient. What is critical is the intent with which they are told. The best stories arouse curiosity; they invite us to wonder. They may be captivating, but they aren't about capture and control. John Borthwick, a VP at AOL's Development Studio in New York, wrote to me after reading *The Cluetrain Manifesto*: "You talk about the importance of storytelling within organizations, and how stories humanize information. One reason I think this works is that telling stories encourages speaking from personal experience instead of talk based on corporate abstractions. Even when they're fictional, stories resonate because the back button is shared experience." While business rhetoric so often reflects the soulless quality of mass marketing, stories have a palpable heartbeat. Where the pitch seeks to isolate, reduce, to make us small and fearful, the story includes, expands, encourages. Imagination makes us larger.

At the end of the year 2000, *Context* magazine invited Sergio Zyman and Jerry Della Femina to interview each other about marketing online.[23] Della Femina has played an enormously influential role in the history of advertising, having first achieved notoriety in 1970 with his best-selling book, *From Those Wonderful Folks Who Gave You Pearl Harbor*. The title was a slogan he suggested to the Japanese electronics firm, Panasonic. It cost him his job, but the book hit the charts. Della Femina leads off by saying, "I don't know any advertising agency that has mastered the Internet yet. Being able to understand it and sell products on it through advertising seem almost impossible." He says that most online advertising creates resentment, working to shut down attention rather than elicit interest. And Zyman concurs: "I agree that banner ads are a joke."

It's refreshing to hear such overt skepticism about Internet advertising voiced by those wonderful folks who gave us so much vacuous handwaving in the first place. It's interesting, however, that adman Della Femina comes across more convincing than Zyman, the corporate marketeer. The latter, like so many of his brethren in The Craft (connotations of witchcraft fully intended), still invokes the concept of brand with all the crypto-mystical implications corporations insist on attaching to it. Zyman says: "The trick is to find ways of creating content that can actually communicate the benefits of a brand to consumers." And what "benefits" would those be? If there is any use at all in the litany of wondrous qualities a brand purportedly embodies, the advantage is to the company that creates such a mystique, not to the consumer. So Zyman is right. It is indeed a trick.

One turned far too often by corporations—and the reason emerging web markets are now turning the tables on the tricksters.

Zyman also provides unintended humor when he notes that "sometimes consumers can get manipulated." No! Do you think? And his comments on the opportunities for companies using the Internet "to grow bigger by building more powerful brands" are oddly anachronistic, if not just plain out to lunch. Leave it to a dyed-in-the-wool mass marketer to see economies of scale lurking in the wings just as one-size-fits-all "scaling"—going after larger and larger, but more mythical markets—is precisely the problem the Internet is best suited to solving.

In contrast, Della Femina doesn't use the word *brand* once, except in an almost opposite context. Where Zyman alludes to the mysterious *magic of brand*, Della Femina says: "We saw movies like *The Hucksters*, and we thought the ad executive did a particular *brand of magic*" [italics mine]. I couldn't help wondering if the subtly inverted trope was a conscious hack on the Big Guy from Coke. If so, score one for Jerry.

Della Femina says, "We're going to have to be clever and figure out different ways to reach people. But we're not going to reach them through advertising on the Internet." I think he's right, though I would shift the emphasis slightly. It's entirely possible to reach people through the Internet—just not through Internet *advertising*. This sort of neurotic attachment to labels is preventing business from realizing the genuine potential of the net. The typical syllogism runs like this. Marketing must be annoying, so if we're not annoying anyone, we must not be marketing, and therefore can't possibly make a profit. Ergo, the sky is falling.

At the end of the piece, Della Femina touches on an alternative to such turkey-in-the-rain stupidity, noting that companies are "trying to talk to people without the direct sell." Smart companies would do this, yes, though it seems that, on average, corporate IQs are still not breaking any records in this respect. I'd be a lot happier with this approach, if instead of leveraging what Della Femina rather loftily labels "truth-based communication," companies would just stop lying so damn much.

One form such lying takes is sucking up to particular demographic sectors that marketers drool over but don't even remotely begin to comprehend. A perennial favorite for these ministrations is the so-called youth market. On May 16, 2000, rock star Courtney Love ranted to the Digital Hollywood online entertainment conference in New York, among other things, about the time she entered into a sponsor relationship with a company that makes a popular brand of soda pop. She didn't mention whether it was Pepsi or that other one. And most likely, no one cared. What's the difference?

"It was really dumb," she said. "You had to buy the cola. You had to dial a number. You had to press a bunch of buttons. You had to do all this crap that nobody wanted to do." But that was just for starters. She also said she felt embarrassed to be shilling for a product she had no particular use for. And she didn't much like the marketers she was forced to deal with. "They treated me like I was an ungrateful little bitch who should be groveling for the experience to play for their damn soda. I ended up playing without my shirt on and ordering a six-pack of the rival cola onstage. Also, lots of unwholesome cursing and nudity occurred. This way I knew that no matter how tempting the cash was, they'd never do business with me again."[24]

Slice and Dice

A website accompanies Philip Kotler's textbook on *Marketing Management*, now in its tenth edition. In discussing chapter nine— "Identifying Market Segments and Selecting Target Markets"—the site says "To remain effective and profitable, marketers must strike the delicate balance between the ineffectiveness of trying to be 'all things to all people' through mass marketing products to everyone; and the cost prohibitive extreme of completely customizing a marketing mix to each individual."[25]

Like most marketing today, this logic admits—in principle—that mass marketing is a thing of the past. Mass markets, though once a huge source of profits, were in many respects a side effect of marketing inefficiency. As marketing adopted more sophisticated research tools, it became obvious that one size did not fit all. At first, divvying up mass markets into subcategories was a rough science, and the resulting segments were still very large. However, the process has become increasingly refined, to the point that, as the

Kotler site says, "segmentation becomes critical in the marketing process. Segmentation enables marketers to divide prospective customer groups into 'segments' that consist of people with similar demographic, psychographic or usage patterns."[26] Demographic slice-and-dice techniques are described in books such as *Divide and Conquer: Targeting Your Customers Through Market Segmentation*—the title as telling as the contents—and the far more technical and detailed exposition of *The Clustered World*.[27]

However, the admission-in-principle that mass marketing is no longer effective, or even particularly workable, hasn't changed the fundamental mindset that underlies it. The mass marketing mentality is well expressed by Zyman's "get more people to buy more stuff more often" mantra. Perhaps this is understandable coming from a marketer whose aim was to sell what is perhaps the archetype of commodity products. Despite trying to mind-meld it with phantasmagoric images of fun, refreshment, and let's not forget *specialness*, Coke is still just sugar-water in a can. In the grand taxonomy of product categories, cola is perhaps one evolutionary notch above coal and pork bellies.

Savvier marketers have grappled with the obstacles and opportunities attaching to segmentation in a more rigorous manner. Regis McKenna understood and articulated the value of niche markets and highly targeted marketing. In his 1986 book, *The Regis Touch*, he counseled a rifle-shot over a shotgun approach, saying that companies that tried to satisfy more than one niche were courting Chapter 11.[28] This advice was primarily aimed at startups such as Apple, with which he had worked from the earliest days. However, successful startups sometimes end up as Fortune 500 companies, as Apple did despite many missteps, and at that point the allure of mass marketing comes back with a vengeance. By 1991, McKenna was thinking out loud—in *Relationship Marketing*[29]—about a more generalized approach to market niches. This spawned an entire industry subcategory known as Customer Relationship Management or CRM (not to be confused with Cause Related Marketing, which we've touched on already and will encounter again soon enough).

At roughly the same time, Joe Pine was preaching a related new wrinkle in mass production and mass marketing in *Mass Cus-*

tomization: The New Frontier in Business Competition and a series of articles in *Harvard Business Review* that were eventually published in 2000 as *Markets of One: Creating Customer-Unique Value Through Mass Customization.*[30] The trajectory of these developments moved from focusing on undifferentiated mass markets to targeting highly selective niches, and culminating in "personalization" techniques such as the one-to-one marketing of Don Peppers and Martha Rogers.[31] Along this trajectory, these approaches increasingly acknowledge the importance of the Internet and electronic commerce. This new medium enabled marketers to reach individuals much more directly than, say, direct (snail) mail. However, the quotes around "personalization" are necessary because all these methods are still driven by database technologies. It is critical to remember the contribution of mass customization to this chain of development, because what "personalization" invariably boils down to is marketing to a mass of niches. In other words, and make no mistake, these purportedly "personalized" approaches to customers remain a form of mass marketing.[32]

An advanced personalization technique called *"collaborative filtering"*—which has been put to especially interesting use by Amazon.com—constitutes a potentially powerful exception. It's easy to forget that one of the primary uses of hypertext—the tangled web of stuff the web is based on—is to enable learning, which begins with establishing meaningful categories, connecting like to like. When I go to Amazon and see what other people found interesting enough to buy, I often gain valuable insight from a much larger social network than I could hope to connect with by any other means. Also, note that since Amazon's also-bought links are backed by nontrivial outlays of cold hard cash, they probably represent a more honest evaluation than the off-the-cuff opinions of friends and colleagues—or publishers' advertisements.[33] Collaborative filtering is the technology that enables the boundaries of such communities of interest to be determined. Malcolm Gladwell, author of *The Tipping Point*, wrote what is perhaps the best overview of this technology and its true significance—in *The New Yorker*, of all places. In "The Science of the Sleeper: How the Information Age could blow away the blockbuster," he says:

Collaborative filtering underscores a lesson that . . . humans have been stubbornly resistant to learning: if you want to understand what one person thinks or feels or likes or does it isn't enough to draw inferences from the general social or demographic category to which he belongs. You cannot tell, with any reasonable degree of certainty, whether someone will like "The Girl's Guide to Hunting and Fishing" by knowing that the person is a single twenty-eight-year-old woman who lives in Manhattan, any more than you can tell whether somebody will commit a crime knowing only that he's a twenty-eight-year-old African-American male who lives in the Bronx. . . . None of this means that standard demographic data is useless. . . . But the central claim of the collaborative-filtering movement is that, head to head, the old demographic and 'psychographic' data cannot compete with preference data. This is a potentially revolutionary argument.[34]

Meanwhile, back to the present point, which bears repeating in any case: *most* "personalization" is still a form of mass marketing. Historically, market segmentation has always been a top-down proposition, targeting groups of prospects according to the sales objectives of the company. But people are connecting with each other on the Internet bottom-up according to their own passions and interests, which seldom map directly to products. This bottom-up emergence of new markets is not an anomaly, but the continuation of a trend already well established before the net became a commercial force. It is hugely significant and will eventually become the primary source of corporate revenue. And here's the kicker: this entire phenomenon is invisible to current market research based on segmentation. Attached to their tried-and-true methods, corporations are literally running on empty, running blind.

Let's turn to Levitt again. In "Marketing Myopia," he said: "Industries that assume themselves to be riding some automatic growth escalator invariably descend into stagnation. The history of every dead and dying 'growth' industry shows a self-deceiving cycle of bountiful expansion and undetected decay." And even in 1960, he equated this blindness to a fixation on the economies of scale associated with mass production. "The tantalizing profit possibilities of low unit production costs may be the most seriously self-deceiving attitude that can afflict a company. . . . The usual result of this narrow pre-occupation. . . is that instead of growing, the industry declines. . . . The industry has its eyes so firmly on its own specific product that it does not see how it is being made obsolete."[35] He follows this with a brief synopsis of the buggy whip industry.

In his 1975 retrospective commentary on Marketing Myopia, Levitt blames the continuation of this trend on the sudden influx of "operating or financial executives" into industry. Today we would probably not be wrong to lump them into the general category of bean counters. "Executives with such backgrounds," he writes, "have an almost trained incapacity to see that getting 'volume' may require understanding and serving many discrete and sometimes small market segments rather than going after a perhaps mythical batch of big or homogeneous customers."[36] Levitt's use of "may re-quire" here should be read as high facetiousness. His point is that without *understanding and serving* no amount of *going after* is going to do much good.

Yet this is precisely what most data-based marketing technologies offer—deeper penetration and higher margins with only the *simu-lacrum* of understanding and the improved service capabilities such understanding might enable. But perhaps that's too abstract. Try this: do you feel all warm and fuzzy inside when you get email ad-dressed "Dear Bill" or "Dear Mary"? Assuming, of course, that one of those is actually your name. (Not taking anything for granted here. This is the remedial paragraph.) Do you feel that the company thus addressing you understands you and is therefore in a better po-sition to serve your deepest and most existential consumer whims? If so—and I'd really like to be more gentle about this, believe me, but—you are a fool.

The basic problem with this approach is that, in sharp contrast to television, the Internet has failed to produce sufficient fools. The de-pendable old mass-media trick—ramming canned commercial "mes-sages" down a one-way broadcast pipe—just doesn't get networked audiences to sit up and beg. It doesn't even get them to roll over. On TV, repeated pitches may create brand awareness. On the web, they create brand annoyance. This isn't the way we're communicat-ing with each other online. We argue, cajole, we joke, we talk. We tell each other stories. On television, a company has 30 seconds to be clever. But on the web, it has unlimited gigabytes to say what it's all about and why anyone should give a damn. This isn't a preview, like a TV ad. It's the main feature. If you advertise to us on your site once you've gotten us there, you've lost a prime opportunity to engage us, to converse with us, to tell us a story. You've blown it and we won't be back, no matter how big your banner budget.

The net has influenced the style of some broadcast advertising, but Internet audiences are hipper than many suspect. We see a knock-out ad on the tube and we're rolling on the floor laughing. At the same time, we know full well that we're unlikely to encounter the same mentality if we go to the website or call the customer service line. We'll get business as usual. When we appreciate certain ads, we're usually cheering for the agency creatives who conceived them. When I see a great spot for IBM, I immediately think "Man, somebody at Ogilvy is sure having fun!" I know from experience that no one is having fun logging trouble tickets at IBM's call center. It's a high-tech sweatshop.[37]

So what now? If a) the we-really-know-you-and-love-you-why-look-your-name-is-right-here-in-our-database gambit plays only with sub-morons on the net, and b) it turns out that the Internet is far less efficient than television in turning out sub-morons. . . then oh dear! What's a marketer to do? As we'll see next, some have gone off and thought about this problem deeply.

OverSimplicity®

Perhaps the real problem is that all that razzle-dazzle brand manipulation has consumers plumb tuckered out. Maybe the real problem is that it got too goshdarn *complicated*. In a nutshell, that is the underlying premise of *Simplicity Marketing: Relieving Customer Stress in the Digital Age*, by Steven M. Cristol and Peter Sealey.[38]

The fundamental axioms of business are precipitously red-shifting, receding at the speed of light from the power and relevance they once had with respect to pre-Internet commerce. "The Digital Age" is invoked in this book's subtitle for good reason: corporations are feeling—if not fully understanding—the enormity of this shift. It's good business these days to question core business assumptions.

One way of questioning the tried and true is to find a new lens through which to reassess long-established business practices. Deming's lens is a good example. By looking at the whole organization from the perspective of Quality, companies began to understand and accept the wrenching changes they would have to undertake to remain competitive in newly globalized markets.

Cristol and Sealey attempt to present Simplicity as an equally powerful explanatory and predictive lens for marketing. Markets are faced with a daunting array of product and service choices that have proliferated to the point of becoming counterproductive, driving customers away rather than attracting them. The authors emphasize stress as a major factor in contemporary consumer psychology, and stress reduction as a concomitant opportunity for business. They warn of the dangers of incrementally extending products and creating new brands. Instead they propose consolidating product and service functions via their "4 R's" approach to Simplicity Marketing—replace, repackage, reposition and replenish. All are aimed at alleviating customer anxiety.

But is Simplicity thus defined as powerful a lens as Quality proved to be? Paradoxically, the answer is yes only if we discount the real impact and ramifications of the digital age, and agree with the tacit but strongly implied message of *Simplicity Marketing*: that the Internet does not constitute a radical rite of passage into a truly new economy, and requires of business no dark night of soul searching.

The authors cite Seth Godin's book *Permission Marketing*, which holds out a similar promise to companies: that they can retain, or more accurately regain, some measure of control over their markets. However, the comfort this brings to marketers comes at the cost of self-delusion. Since the advent of the commercial Internet, markets are in control. And the First Step in any effective 12-step program of recovery has to be: get used to it. Business as usual is not alive and well. It's dying. The net has called code blue on the marketing department, and it's flatlining, monitors screaming that the patient's pulse is gone. When open heart surgery is the only recourse, suggesting a simplified lifestyle, or a please-and-thank-you rationale for the same old high-cholesterol spam, comes a day late and a couple trillion dollars short.

"As with the segmentation process, traditional approaches to pri-oritizing segments for targeting are not meant to be thrown out," *Simplicity Marketing* assures. "They are meant to be enhanced by considering customer stress as another important variable . . . "[39] But the dynamics the Internet brings to bear on market interactions raise fundamental questions about the viability of conventional segmen-tation and targeting. By freighting old concepts with new parame-ters, the authors seem to be suffering from their own denigrated in-crementalism.

While the authors acknowledge debate about whether the "4 P's" of conventional marketing remain valid in a digital economy, they choose not to engage the issue, instead positioning their own "4 R's" as complementary to existing practice. "Regardless of which side of the debate you're on, the 4 P's are still the foundation learned and used by most marketing managers for planning and execution."[40] And with that weak disclaimer—the familiar Everybody's-Doing-It defense—far more challenging and potentially enlightening ques-tions about how marketing fits into an altogether new kind of elec-tronically mediated commerce are neatly swept aside.

The same kind of slippery trope appears at the beginning of the book. "How," the authors rhetorically inquire, "did we get to a consumer world of 40,000 products in a supermarket, hundreds of long distance and cellular calling plans, 52 versions of Crest tooth-paste . . . ?"[41] But the crucial question of how we got into this mess is ignored. Historically, the explosion of consumer choice resulted from competition for unprotected niche market sectors, first from smaller domestic producers and later from large international compa-nies seeking to penetrate lucrative U.S. markets. These competitors were effective because the companies whose share they went after were often arrogant and complacent, believing they were impervious to attack. Think Honda Civic. Think Sony Walkman.

While the global economy and the economies of scope it spawned may be old news, most companies are still missing the fact that the Internet hugely accelerates this same trend. In the late '60s, auto executives dismissed the VW Bug. "Only students drive those," they said. Notice that 20 years later, business missed the significance of the early Internet for the same reason. "Networked Unix work-stations? But only students drive those . . . "

Today, competition is coming not from offshore, but from agile net upstarts catering to web-based micromarkets that don't yet raise a blip on the demographic oscilloscope. Even after decades of warning signals, most companies still believe they are in control of their markets, impervious to attack from below. But online, the market *is* the competition. Think Linux. Think Napster.

Through the reputation so many corporations have developed for self-serving consumer manipulation, marketers have lost credibility. Today the marketplace is connected, networked. Consumers are talking among themselves. And this changes everything. Cristol and Sealey argue that markets are stymied by too many options and must depend on vendors to make sense of their world again. For this they will be grateful, and gratitude will beget trust, trust will beget loyalty, loyalty will beget greater market share, and greater share will beget new profits. Thus runneth the prophecy. But the prophets are wrong and the profits are not forthcoming.

Markets are not stymied. They are not as confused as many companies nostalgically continue to wish they were. In the digital age, markets are rapidly becoming smarter than the companies that pretend to serve them. Faced with a broad array of choices, potential buyers are turning to the only source they trust: each other. Typical exchanges take place through email or online message boards, and they go a little like this . . .

QUESTION: I'm trying to get my head around the differences between products X, Y and Z. I'm getting a migraine from all the marketing double-talk. And the pricing schemes seem as if they were invented by Rube Goldberg. Can anyone help me sort this stuff out?

ANSWER (RECEIVED TEN MINUTES LATER): Forget any of the above. I've used them all and they all suck. Take a look at a little company a knowledgeable pal turned me on to. He thought highly of their product, and having used it for six months now, so do I. These folks got it right. Their site isn't fancy and they have no four-color brochures to send you, but there's an online demo that'll blow your mind. Also, because they haven't invested in the usual "brand" nonsense, you'll pay about 60% less than you would have for X, Y or Z—might as well pocket some of the difference in their banner ad budgets. This outfit deserves more recognition. If you're as impressed as I was, spread the word.

If X, Y or Z is your product, there goes your $10 million simplicity campaign. Because this word *will* spread. Like wildfire. This isn't "viral marketing" or "permission marketing" or "simplicity marketing." It's just real simple. Given the right vector—and the net has supplied it—people will talk about the products they hate and the ones they love. The latter will be well crafted, developed to address real needs, and backed up by friendly open straight-talking customer service. You got a problem? Well bummer, dude. And bam, it's fixed. That's simplicity.

"Entities should not be multiplied beyond necessity," said William of Ockham almost 700 years ago, a formulation that has come to be known as the law of parsimony or Ockham's razor. In non-philosophical terms it means: keep it simple, stupid. If marketing simplicity boils down to elegant, responsive product design, quality craftsmanship, a clear articulation of what the product does, and fast attentive customer service, then why inflate such a perfectly useful concept into a theory that invokes needless—and largely empty—neologisms such as *"overchoice," "brand soul," "brandscape"* and *"stressographics"?*

There's nothing simple about reducing people to databased demographic profiles, and nothing respectful about painting targets on their backs. If you really want simple, try telling the truth. But this prospect strikes abject terror into the hearts of those whose mission it is to package segments and deliver eyeballs.

A Hand Full of Gimme and a Mouth Full of Much Obliged

"Hey, baby, there ain't no easy way out. . . "

—TOM PETTY[42]

I first met Seth Godin in 1993, virtually speaking. He edited the *Information Please Business Almanac & Desk Reference* which included email addresses, something new at that time in a business publication. I contacted him. Later, I contributed to a book he put together called *E-Mail Addresses of the Rich & Famous*. When I found myself named in the acknowledgements, I emailed Seth, thanking him and expressing my surprise. "I should have dedicated the book to you," he replied. "You gave me more addresses than anyone else." We were never close pals, but we were friendly. By all accounts, he's a good guy with a working sense of humor. In *E-Mail Addresses,* he claims to have written "over 400 books, including *Valley of the Dolls, The Eiger Sanction, Catcher in the Rye, The Cat in the Hat,* and many others." All of which inclined me to like what he had to say. But I don't like what he's saying. I have trouble with his ideas for two reasons: 1) they've been enormously influential, and 2) they're fundamentally wrong. If not for 2, 1 would be cause for congratulation. Without 1, 2 wouldn't much matter. Together, it's a dangerous combination.

Godin is the most visible presence in online marketing today. I can't think of anyone else who comes close. And it isn't just because he was associated with Yahoo. His popularity is solely the result of his ideas. Despite the contributions of serious analysts like John Hagel (*Net Worth* and *Net Gain*), there was a perceived vacuum of solid ideas about e-commerce before Seth Godin came along. Or so anyone would have to conclude from the impact he's had. Marketers took up the banner of permission marketing with a vengeance.

"What do you consider your greatest professional achievement?" asks *The Industry Standard,* and Godin replies "I created the idea of permission marketing back when the web was all about Java, hits and push. Now, everyone from the press to key aggregators are rushing to embrace the idea that extracting attention and value from a relationship takes frequency and for that to happen online, you need Permission(TM)."[43] No kidding about the trademark. Looks like it's official then.

But the vacuum is still there. Godin does a good job on the ineffectiveness of broadcast advertising, on the annoyance of what he calls "interruption marketing," and on the way word-of-mouth works online. The problem is the service into which he presses these insights.

E-Mail Addresses of the Rich & Famous is out of print now, at which Godin breathes a sigh of relief.[44] Why? It raised quite a furor at the time about privacy and a neologism that had just come into the world: spam. Spam, as we all know today, is unsolicited commercial email. The offending item was a proposal the book tried to float.

A simple new convention will allow easy communication without overloading the system. . . . Just follow these two rules when mailing to someone you don't know: If you're sending unsolicited mail, precede your subject with a *?*. If you're sending a commercially related piece of mail, precede your subject with a *$*. This is a courtesy that will allow people to screen their mail and increases the chances that your mail will be read by someone who *wants* to read it. (italics in original) [45]

It didn't float. Nor did it just quietly sink. It caused a firestorm. Godin took a good deal of flameage for trying to rationalize a framework for sending ?$—which is to say, spam. He was obviously thinking early on about how marketers could use the Internet to reach prospects, and he's obviously been thinking about it ever since. He finally found his framework. In *Permission Marketing: Turning Strangers Into Friends and Friends Into Customers*, he calls permission marketing "the way to make advertising work again."

Permission Marketing. . . offers the consumer an opportunity to volunteer to be marketed to. By talking only to volunteers, Permission Marketing guarantees that consumers pay more attention to the marketing message. It allows marketers to tell their story calmly and succinctly, without fear of being interrupted by competitors or Interruption Marketers. It serves both consumers and marketers in a symbiotic exchange. [46]

I have to smile at the notion of calm, succinct, fearless marketers. The image that comes to mind is the used car sales division of the Power Rangers. But hold on just a second, I'm thinking. . . I turn the page. "I know what you're thinking," Godin says. "There's a catch." *Damn*, this guy is good! He's reading my mind.

If you have to personalize every customer message, that's prohibitive. If you're still thinking within the framework of traditional marketing, you're right. But in today's information age, targeting customers individually is not as difficult as it sounds. Permission Marketing takes the cost of interrupting the consumer and spreads it out, over not one message, but dozens of messages. And this leverage leads to substantial competitive advantages and profits.

Actually, I'm not thinking anywhere even close to traditional marketing—reader, back me up here—but I notice that the issue of personalization expense is raised, displayed to the congregation in the spirit of full disclosure—then neatly swept under the rug. These rhetoricians, I tell ya (it takes one to know one). In fact, the mention of personalization here is genuflection to an empty buzzword. The only "personal" element in the ensuing "symbiotic exchanges" is likely to be "Dear John." Some will argue that, no, customers are divvied up according to their expressed or demonstrated interest in certain product categories. But that's not *personal*. It's not something some person takes personally. It's good old traditional segmentation and targeting. For those who may have forgotten, a personal communication is more like this:

You have spaced out picking up the kids from day care for the last time. You're an irresponsible no-good drunk, Jim. Get help—from someone else. I'm leaving you forever.

—ALICE

Now let's ask ourselves: how much more information does Alice have about Jim than the typical permission marketer has about any given random pick from its base of five jillion target prospects? Alice may not *like* Jim a whole lot, but he knows right away on opening this mail that it's not a form letter.

Actually, there's not just one catch. There are two. The second gets talked about far less than the first (which doesn't get talked about much either, such is the raw corporate enthusiasm for this stuff), but it contains a bigger gotcha. Here it is now: and how do you *give* consumers the "opportunity to volunteer" to be marketed to? Well, er, ah, um, that is . . . The actual no-mumbling answer is simple: you spam them. The companies that have jumped on this bandwagon were already itching for a rationale to do just that—why let the MLM bottom-feeders have all the fun?—and Godin gave it to them on a silver platter. These companies aren't starting webzines and inviting a few dozen pals to sign up. They are sitting on databases that contain tens of millions of email addresses representing people they know no better than the Man in the Moon.

But perhaps you'd like a second opinion on this. Writing in *Harvard Business Review*, Peter Sealey says "Godin. . . concedes that permission marketers also rely on interruptions to introduce themselves to a broad base of customers. But the introductory ads can be quite simple because they don't need to sell the product. All they need to do is ask permission to say more. From that point on, all participation is voluntary." [47] Allow me to translate sans murky euphemisms: it's not voluntary *at first*. So what's for lunch, Mom? *Spam!!!*

Sealey goes on to say that "Permission marketing gives consumers *some say*, but the process is still *managed by the marketer*." In this case the italics are mine—to point out that the core program has not really changed at all. This is not about a new form of symbiotic exchange. It's about a very old form of command and control.

Godin has heard criticism like this before. To his credit, he hasn't blown it off as irrelevant, any more than he ignored the flames he fanned up with *E-Mail Addresses of the Rich & Famous*. He doesn't just listen, he takes it seriously, he thinks about it, mulls it over. Godin is trying to get it right. The question that motivated his latest book was clearly: How do you get people to give you permission to send them "exciting email offers" without having to first shotgun them with "invitations" that look like, smell like and—oh hell, why quibble—*are* in fact spam?

The opening page of *Unleashing the Ideavirus* frames the same problem in—you'll be unsurprised to learn—somewhat different language. "The #1 question people ask me after reading *Permission Marketing*: So, how do we get attention to ask for permission in the first place? This manifesto is the answer to that question." [48]

It's odd. Godin talks a lot about manifestos. Even though everyone knows those are the sorts of things that Godless communists produce. Introducing the basic concept in *Fast Company* before the book came out, Godin said: "an idea that moves, grows, and infects everyone it touches . . . that's an ideavirus. . . . It starts with an idea manifesto, a powerful, logical 'essay' that assembles a bunch of existing ideas and transforms them into a new, larger idea that's unified and compelling. . . As long as you can use your manifesto to change the way that people think, talk, and act, you create value. . . "[49] Right. As long as your "manifesto" doesn't spook companies like Procter & Gamble, Coke, Disney, Newscorp, IBM. What would companies of this towering stature make of a manifesto that said things like "Armed only with imagination, we're gonna rip the fucking lid off"?[50] Godin needed a more cleaned-up and presentable idea of what a manifesto should be. Maybe—why not?—it could be a sweepstakes or a lottery. A game. Something more *fun*. Who knows, maybe something that conveyed refreshment and specialness.

"So, is an ideavirus a form of marketing?" Godin asks. And he answers himself: "Absolutely! But today, what else is there?"[51] Well, gee, let's see . . . I can think of two things right off the top: 1) imagination and 2) ripping the fucking lid off—though I hope *Gonzo Marketing* as a whole will constitute a more rigorous and complete answer. The question itself implies everything this book deprecates, deplores and despises. To wit: that marketing has any future at all as a dressed-up tricked-out exercise in manipulating human beings, operating on the (entirely) base assumption that their only value is to consume commercial products for a price.

"But you're being unrealistic." I can hear the response already. Have heard it my whole damn life, as have we all. "That's impractical and irrelevant. Business is business and that's the way it's always been." Well guess what. That's not the way it is any more. Grow up. Get used to it. Power has shifted irreversibly while business continued to delude itself with laughable schemes, transparent lies and obsequious bullshit.

Yes, memic propagation *is* an important factor in how ideas move around online, but adding the commercial dimension is not just a minor wrinkle. It fundamentally changes the nature of the dynamic. Are marketers really naïve enough to believe that the same brain-numbing "key messages" their advertising and PR departments have been peddling all along are somehow going to magically "go viral" and capture hearts and minds?

"Contrary to what you may think," writes Godin in a moment of high levity, "the Macarena was not an organized, sinister plot; it just happened. But many other products, services, hit movies, or catch-phrases are the intentional acts of smart entrepreneurs and politicians who know that launching and nurturing an ideavirus can help them accomplish their goals."[52] This is marketing as information warfare—hardly a new concept. It's the same old spin and manipulation. Yeah, it's more sophisticated, but the main tactics are still target and attack. Using a slew of slick new-economy neologisms, Seth Godin has reinvented and repackaged a very old concept: propaganda.

Godin says that "the future belongs to marketers who establish a foundation and process where interested people can market to each other. Ignite consumer networks and then get out of the way and let them talk."[53] But what exactly is a "consumer network"? People tend to join into self-selecting communities online, but unless we're talking about buying clubs, they don't typically aggregate around products. Instead, they come together around common *interests*. They may "consume" products in the process, but this consumption is a side effect. They do not network as the "consumers" business has seen them as for a century, but as new tribes of hunter/gatherers. Often enough to constitute a trend, they are not only *not* hunting for products, they are hunting the businesses that make them— as radical bricoleurs, eyeing rusted-out corporations for spare parts. Too weird, you think? Too bizarre? Some companies have discovered large collections of MP3s cached deep within their firewalled IT fortresses. Who put them there? The company will never know. It was merely a temporary host. A convenient hard disk for a roving band of cultural nomads who have since moved on. A new species some speculate. It's 11 o'clock. Do you know where your children are?

In these subtle and often alien distinctions lie a world of difference—a chasm that business-as-usual can never cross.

But buck up, it's not *all* that grim. If you take the advice of the *Rocky Horror Picture Show*, liberation from these blues is just a jump to the left. And no, it's not a political thing. It's about getting your groove back, Jack. It's about joy, remember? But mostly, it's about *DOING THE TIME WARP AGAIN!* Cue the band. . .

In 1991, on a day that will forever live in infamy, MCI launched its "Friends & Family" marketing program. The basic idea was that, in exchange for lower rates calling them, you could drop a dime on intimate acquaintances, thus causing them to be mercilessly hounded by the company either a) forever, or b) until they had to be put on powerful prescription medications, whichever came first. This initiative was hugely successful up until the inevitable moment when participating MCI customers had lost all their friends and/or been disowned by their families.

A more sanguine and approving version of this story is recounted in a chapter on viral marketing in *The Anatomy of Buzz*, where it is explained that, while such campaigns are roughly as effective as feeding d-Con to rats, they tend to be prohibitively expensive. "If you're not a marketing executive at a telephone company," says author Emanuel Rosen, "you may think, 'Okay, but what can *I* do about this?'" On first reading, I thought to myself, "Yeah, how many tons of C-4 *would* it take to permanently remove MCI from the planet?" But more careful attention to the text alerted me that this was not the response the book was really calling for. I came to see that the author's rhetorical question was meant to imply that the typical marketing reader would be thinking, "Hey, how come *I* can't do this?" In the old days, it just wouldn't have been possible, we're told. But there's good news too. Now, "with the net," says Rosen, "this type of promotion is no longer limited to telephone companies."[54] Oh, aren't you *glad?*

Nonetheless, telephone companies seem to have a special bent for this sort of thing, having taken to the whole viral/permission idea as enthusiastically as the Black Death took to Europe in the 14th century. While writing this chapter, I woke up one morning to this crap from Sprint.

From: Sprint [r15901@discounts-direct.com]
Sent: Thursday, January 18, 2001 2:17 PM
To: clocke@panix.com
Subject: Dear Christopher, Sprint requests your permission

Dear Christopher,

Everyday more and more exciting and important information is being communicated via e-mail. In the future, Sprint would like to communicate with you via e-mail, and send you exciting and "Up to Date" information on new products and services that Internet users like yourself would have interest in. Sprint is presently seeking your permission for the privilege to serve you efficiently and electronically via e-Mail. Thank you!

Where in the world did a freaking Telco get the idea I might like to receive their "Up to Date" information "via e-Mail"? Who is responsible for this befuddled spew? Wait a second... I think I know—"seeking your permission" is a big clue—and I think a little payback is in order.

You may argue that a concept like "payback" has no more place in a serious business book than would that beastly trope so hated and shunned by people of good will everywhere: the *ad hominem* attack. But, while that is certainly true in the usual case, let us reason this out together. How many email addresses would you suppose are in Sprint's database of targets for this letter? Come on, pick a figure. OK, now memorize it and don't tell me. If you guessed any number smaller than the sum of all sentient beings in the known universe having both telephones and Internet access, you would be wrong. So now take this very large number and multiply it by the number of companies that want to establish a direct pipeline to your VISA card— approximately equal to the number of grains of sand in Hawaii—and you begin to get some idea of how many times you can count on being interrupted by some imaginative marketing oxymoron asking your permission to "serve you efficiently and electronically." Do you still think payback is out of line? Just as I thought. Thank you!

Gonzo Interlude in the Marketing Ward

"Your doctor has your written permission
to inject just about anything he wants into your IV bag."

—SETH GODIN, *PERMISSION MARKETING*

"You'll pay money just to see yourself
with Doctor Robert... "

—THE BEATLES, *REVOLVER*

I never should have taken the job. It was just after midnight in L.A. and I was sitting at the desk in my third-floor office drinking cheap whiskey from the bottle and watching a blood red moon rise over the City of Angels. A full moon. In Scorpio. The calendar had just ticked over to Friday the 13th. Could my luck get any worse? The phone rang.

Where do these studio execs get my unlisted number? PacBell says it values my privacy. Yeah right. It turns out to be Harvey Promoski over at Universal. What a loser. He's telling me the script writers walked out on his project today. No wonder. *Bottomliners* sounds like one of those films that should never be made. Not a lot there to distinguish it from every other POS these guys have cranked out in the last ten years, but hey, what do I know? Promoski's telling me there's big money behind the thing. Julia Roberts likes the storyboards, he says panting, all excited. Yeah? So who's she play? (Just asking. I'm not committing to anything here.) Martha Rogers, he says. He's impressed, I can tell. I can tell he wants company. And we're talking to Kiefer Sutherland and Kevin Bacon, he whispers (like it's a big secret if he's telling me), for Seth Godin and Sergio Zyman. Respectively, he says. Harvey reads the dictionary.

What are you telling me 'you never heard of them,' he yells into the line, like it's a personal affront. The actors, yeah, I say, but not the other ones. Was I supposed to? Maybe you better give me the plot. I listen. I tap my pencil on the blotter. I look at the clock. My luck has gotten worse.

Bottomliners. Whose godforsaken idea was this? I can't believe what I'm hearing. It seems a bunch of third-year grad students at the Kellogg School of Management figure out a way to experience Chapter 11 without really bellying up. They come back, he's telling me. Do you *get it?* They know what it's like to bore in, but they're still holding all their options! Wow, I say, not bothering to explain why. But get this, he says, they start having these, like, creeped-out visions, on accounta stuff they did. You know, customers they screwed, perpetrating boredom, lies. I can tell he's reading from the script. "Somehow we've brought our sins back physically. And they're pissed."

We even got the creatives working on it. *"Bottomliners*—Some lines should never be crossed." Whaddya think? Why do they call them "creatives," I'm wondering, but I know it's not worth asking. Yeah, I say, sounds hot. So what was it you wanted from me? He tells me again about the script guys taking a powder and the next thing I know I'm on a plane. They want to know what it's like to be at death's door. Background, he said, we need background. What can I say? I need the money.

I'm at the St. Vitus Dance Hospital for the Criminally Insane. I finally manage to find the staff lounge and here's my contact, Dr. Robert. Rising to shake my hand, he tells me everything's been set up. The marketing ward is right this way, he says, not wasting time, and I should follow him. He's got grand rounds, he explains, and they just got a wave of new admissions so it's pretty hectic. I can imagine, I say, looking around. I've never been in a marketing ward. How's your immune system, he asks, producing a paper mask from the pocket of his white coat. I dunno, I say, some days I get as many as 100 spams and I haven't crashed yet. That's nothing, he says. In the Level IV hot lab we've recorded over 100,000. No kidding, I say, bored already. I jot the figure in my notebook. Per minute, he says, glancing at me sideways. You don't want to go viral, believe me. I take the mask.

Good decision, he says, the place is crawling with MTDs. This is a new one on me, so I ask. Oh sorry, I forget, he says. Specialization, you know. Not fatal, usually, but they can be very nasty. Marketing Transmitted Delusions. I look at him. I don't say anything.

Dr. Robert takes the chart from the foot of the bed as he sweeps into the first room, all cheerful confidence. And how are we feeling today, Mr. Godin? I grab a look at the chart. Hey, isn't this the guy Harv mentioned? The doc looks over at me, annoyed that I'm interrupting. Form follows fiction, he says, winking, and jams a thermometer into Godin's mouth. Ooo didn ash my pamishon, he protests.[55]

The guy doesn't look good. Do they ever leave, I ask. Oh, they come and go, says the doctor, but the recidivism rate is high. Over 98 percent. This fellow's a regular, aren't you, Mr. Godin? He reads the thermometer. Frowns.

What about the ad agencies? says the guy in the bed. With so many talented people, why aren't they working to solve this problem?

There, there, the doc says, checking Godin's pupils for dilation. Don't you worry about the ad agencies. You're in good hands here.

Why's he talking about ad agencies? I ask, puzzled.

Oh, Seth here thinks a lot about advertising. It's his profession. When he's out there, that is. Got a thing about permission, though. It's odd. You should have seen it when we asked him to sign the permission forms. He smiled down at Godin as if he were a bad little boy. Took five orderlies to get this rascal into a straitjacket.

Early on at Yoyodyne, says Godin as if it just occurred to him, we discovered that we needed one full-time customer service person for every 10,000 people in the database.

And are we taking our meds like we talked about? asks Dr. Robert, ignoring him and surreptitiously rolling his eyes at the ceiling for my benefit.

Godin looks at him a minute, blank. Then says: Your doctor has your written permission to inject just about anything he wants into your IV bag.

That's correct, says Dr. Robert, approvingly. They've obviously been over this ground more than once. And are we cooperating with the staff? But Godin is counting on his fingers now, distracted. Suddenly he looks up at us as if coming to. One lucky customer could win a $100,000 shopping spree, he says.

I'll be back on Tuesday, assures the doctor. If there's anything you need, you just tell Nurse Ratshit. And he ushers me out. Yoyodyne? I ask when the door closes. What was that all about?

Dr. Robert looks concerned. He's been watching this *Buckaroo Banzai* video over and over and yelling 'Laugh-a while can, Monkey Boy!' Scares the crap out of the night desk. But look, we've got to keep moving.

Who's next, I ask as we walk down the long fluorescent hallway. The doctor checks his list. Hmmm, let's see. Today we've got Sergio Zyman, Don Peppers, Harry Beckwith, Steven Cristol, Peter Sealey, Geoffrey Moore, Al Ries, Jack Trout, Sam Hill, Glenn Rifkin ... quite a list. He flips the page on his clipboard. Oh, and Gary Hammel.

Are they all like him?, I ask, gesturing back to the room we've just left. Are they, all, like . . . you know.

I'm afraid so, the doctor replies, stopping to look at me full on. He takes his glasses off and rubs his eyes. Suddenly he looks weary. Beat. Been at it too long, I think. Must take a special kind of person. To keep it up. To keep the cheery smile in place while listening to such demented gibberish day after day. Personally, I don't see how he does it.

Broadcast: The Meme That Wouldn't Die

Although something clearly has to give, it is enormously difficult for any one individual, group or even company to drive the kind of change that's most required. The assumptions underpinning the business status quo are distributed across many organizations and corporate cultures interwoven in a complex ecological web involving companies, market research firms, advertising and PR agencies, and mass media. The complexity of these relationships, and the cross purposes these various factions are often pursuing, work against understanding, let alone creating, new and fundamentally different relationships to audiences and markets.

This tangled complex is the result of a viral pandemic so powerful that everyone's infected. But the nature of the contagion is such that hosts don't know they have it. The name of this disease is broadcast.

Business has become a dream world of nostalgia and denial, desperately trying to hang onto a memory that is fast slipping out of control. Too many companies today are on a collision course with a networked reality that doesn't recognize old notions of control and doesn't operate according to principles that once appeared to be timeless laws of nature. E-commerce planning founded on broadcast assumptions is guaranteed to fail. Catastrophically. When fantasy and reality clash, reality always wins.[56]

Broadcast is a genuine paradigm in the sense Thomas Kuhn defined the term in *The Structure of Scientific Revolutions*—an overarching theoretical framework that makes reasonably logical sense of the world, or some large part of it.[57] The part of the world that concerns us here is business—its aims, objectives, strategies and tactics. At the most fundamental level, the primary goal of any business is to create products or services it can sell for a profit. Strategies and tactics map to marketing and sales—how the business identifies potentially interested prospects and converts them to revenue-contributing customers.

For the past 100 years or so, the broadcast paradigm has colored, shaped and informed corporations' strategic market planning and the tactical implementation of those plans via specific sales initiatives. The broadcast paradigm made sense of a confusing array of data and helped to coordinate complex organizational efforts. It provided an effective basis for achieving goals and measuring progress. In short, it worked. And because it worked so well, the broadcast paradigm is now so deeply ingrained that its principles are taken for granted—universally accepted axioms that are transparent to the point of invisibility. Business is largely unconscious of these first principles. They remain unexamined. Ask a company why it behaves as it does with respect to markets and marketing and you're likely to get the answer a five-year-old might give: because. Businesses behave as they do because, well . . . because that's just the way things are.

Wrong.

And fatally wrong today. The Internet represents a genuine paradigm shift. The broadcast model never explained "the way things are" in some eternal and unchanging way. True, it explained the way things *were* for quite a long time. And that time was a time of great productivity and burgeoning wealth, both for companies and for society at large—First-World societies at any rate. For business, the first three-quarters of the 20th century constitute a sort of golden era, and the memory of this period still casts its Midas-touch aura over business thinking today. A critical factor in this auto-mesmerism, this attempt at self-hypnosis, is stonewall denial. That world was so good, it worked so well, so smoothly, and we understood how and why. Let's stick with that. Let's stick to our knitting, stay the course. Let's not admit that this fabled golden age is quickly fading.

But it is. The world is not fixed, immutable. It changes. Over the last several decades, two enormous forces have radically reshaped the world of business: the global economy and global networks. And these two powerful trends are linked in fundamental ways, though their linkage is still not obvious to most corporations. It is not obvious because business is blinded by nostalgia for the broadcast paradigm. Broadcast is the meme that wouldn't die.

To understand how "the way things are" has changed, it is necessary to grasp the way things were before, in those halcyon days of the broadcast era. Those days out of which the world is now passing forever. To understand and make effective use of the Internet, business must grasp how different it is from all that has gone before, and how much it has already undermined the broadcast model.

Broadcast is a media phenomenon. Specifically, it is a *mass* media phenomenon that arose in response to the needs of mass production and mass marketing. Media and business are often perceived as being separate, but this is largely a convenient fiction maintained at great cost to hide a powerful secret in plain sight: what we call "the media" today evolved and are only allowed to exist as the handmaidens of mass advertising. As soon as we call the Internet a "medium," we fall into the trap of assuming that it too must inevitably follow this pattern. If the net is a medium, then it must be an advertising medium. Right? From the perspective of business, that's what media are for—to serve its advertising needs. That's what media mediate. Otherwise, why would they exist?

To put it generously, this is a self-centered perspective. Less generously, it's a deluded perspective that explains why business has had so much trouble understanding how to work with the net. Why won't this damn thing behave itself? Why doesn't it do what it's *supposed* to do? The answer is that the "it" in this case is a different kind of it. Another animal altogether. While the Internet will eventually connect billions of people, it will never be a mass medium in the way television is a mass medium. The difference is crucial.

Mass media are "mass" because they have for so long served the core requirement of mass production: to move "excess" inventory. The more product such advertising could move, the more profit the company made, so obviously, the bigger the audience the better. Mass media are mass because they're huge. And the way such hugeness is achieved is by appealing to lowest-common-denominator tastes in terms of programming content. The program, the content, is merely bait to draw the audience. The real show, the real message, is the advertising. And advertisers want to lower the common denominator so that they can get everyone possible into the audience. The best medium is the most massive medium. The best place to place advertising is where the most eyeballs will be forced to eyeball it. This is why CNN loves Elián Gonzalez and Princess Di and OJ Simpson. This is why the cultural legacy we are creating and exporting to the rest of the world is a simpleminded sitcom with a dumbbell laugh track.

This is the broadcast model. Did somebody say MacDonald's?

People didn't come to the Internet for more of this featureless, characterless crap. They came for less. They came because they were bored silly by sterile vanilla one-size-fits-all commercial media. They came because they were hungry for something entirely else. And we found it: each other. The net enables people to speak, not just to listen. And to speak about things we're truly interested in. In 999 out of 1000 cases, we're not interested in talking or hearing about your product. This new empowerment of the audience is intrinsic to Internet technology. It's not something extra or something that can be taken away. It comes with the territory.

This is very bad news for mass producers. The good news is that there aren't many of those left. Look around. Since the advent of serious global competition, companies have not been able to rely on single products with long product cycles. Instead, they've been forced to create a wide array of options to compete with offshore producers and providers seeking to steal even tiny slices of their market share. As a result, markets that were once mass markets have exploded into a vast array of micromarkets.

Mass marketing to micromarkets is just plain stupid. And companies already know it. This insight has long been practiced in the form of demographic segmentation and target marketing. Companies that are already marketing to segments are clearly no longer marketing to the undifferentiated mass. In one sense, the web has merely put this powerful pre-Internet trend on a diet of steroids.

But there's another deeper sense in which networks are changing the fundamental nature of commerce. When companies use the techniques of demographic segmentation, they look at markets through the lens of product. "We have this thing. Who can we get to buy it?" In contrast, when online audiences look at this new medium, they look through the lens of interest. "I'm curious about this subject. Who can tell me more?"

People gravitate toward websites that feed their curiosity, that speak to their passions, their genuine interests. And in this process new micromarkets are just now emerging. Thousands of them. They are coalescing around voice: around people who are articulate, entertaining, knowledgeable and informative. These micromarkets are too small to show up on any demographic radar. To reach such micromarkets and form productive relationships with them, companies need to share the interests they represent. And to do so they must first stop speaking in the insistently demanding voice of command-and-control to which they became addicted in the days of broadcast. *Attention K-Mart shoppers!!!*

Instead of pitching products, corporate communications must seed conversations that become the basis for further community discourse. Effective communications will come not from traditional PR and marketing mouthpieces, but from employees spanning the corporation—real people with real passions, real enthusiasm. In contrast, one-way product pitches will fail to connect with genuine market interests. They will fall on deaf ears.

In the post-broadcast era, brand will become the sum of all a company has said and the *spirit* in which it has said those things— a powerful symbol of the state of the relationship between a company and *all* its stakeholders. In the best cases, brand will become a reputation for shared understanding and deep respect. Brands that do not convey these values will become embarrassing public flags signaling ignorance, arrogance and needlessly lost opportunity.

While broadcast is anything but subtle in its methods, understanding its full implications calls for a delicate touch. The dynamics of television and mass media have shaped and molded us, changed our minds in fundamental ways. But as we use those same minds to look at how media affects us, the effects can be extremely difficult to perceive. You're unlikely to see them by looking at yourself straight on. You'd probably want to change the channel after 30 seconds. You won't find them reflected in ratings statistics or in analysts' pie charts and spreadsheets. Occasionally, though, you may stumble across some odd exchange, a scrap of conversation that goes nowhere. Just words in passing. Ships in the night. It may look trivial on the surface. But look deeper. Wonder about it.

In March 1999, Brian Lamb interviewed NBC news anchor Tom Brokaw on C-SPAN's *Booknotes* program—Brokaw's book, *The Greatest Generation*, had just come out. And there's this nearly poignant moment where Lamb says, ". . . in television and radio, you almost become something other than what you are." Then he asks "Why has the business grown up that way where there's a lot of yelling and, 'We'll be right back after this!' You know, what's that come from? Because we don't talk to each other . . . "

For some reason that's not entirely clear—it's as if they're not talking to each other—Brokaw responds by reminiscing about the original broadcast announcers. "Edward R. Murrow was highly stylized," he says. "I mean, he's a reverential figure for all of us, but he couldn't get away with that now. You know, that cigarette smoke and the kind of the use of the language and how he did it and, 'the fault lies not in the stars but with us,' and that kind of thing . . . "

Lamb, evidently feeling that this response has not quite addressed the substance of his question, takes another shot. "Let me ask you again, though," he says, "why is it like in commercials, especially radio commercials, they're yelling at. . . what. . . what happened?" Brokaw digs way down deep this time. And comes up empty. "I. . . I don't know. I. . . there's this. . . it's probably the rock 'n' roll attitude about radio that it has to be louder."[58]

Sure, that's right. Blame it on rock and roll. But the fault lies not in the stars.

CHAPTER 4

Stories as Strange Attractors[1]

Control is the enemy of imagination. The two aren't just incompatible; they are inimical. One drives out the other. Deming, the Total Quality guy, said "drive out fear." Imagine.

DAVID WEINBERGER, GOOD FRIEND AND *CLUETRAIN* CO-AUTHOR, DEFINES the web as "many small pieces loosely joined." This chapter will be like that: an undone puzzle; a bit of sky here, a wisp of cloud, perhaps a shadowed face. This piece is also part of a larger piece. It's a story about stories that start conversations. A story about how conversations lay the groundwork for commerce—and how, sometimes, commerce grounds conversation.

But the story will not be linear. It will jump around. We expect this of fiction, but not of business writing, which should proceed in stately order, from one clear point to the next. However, since the arrival of the tangled higher-order logic of the web, business has become more dependent on narrative than on explication—and the narrative is no longer straightforward and predictable. It takes odd turns. It turns you on, then turns on you. It leaves you stranded. And then, just as you thought you'd reached a dead end, the road picks up again. The plot thickens. Stories are strange attractors.

Gonzo marketing isn't really about marketing at all. At least not the kind that mutters amnesiacally about the 4 Ps of Product, Place, Price and Promotion. Since the web came along, place no longer matters, the right price is often zero, and the first rule of promotion is to never talk about the product. Maybe instead, marketing should be about persuading people to listen, just as the goal of fiction is to get readers to willingly suspend disbelief. Hmmm, curious thought. But if that's the point, then "*marketing*" is probably the wrong word for the program. Which is why I call it gonzo marketing—a boring, not very friendly concept turned inside out and stuffed full of yarns and fables, myths and sagas, outright fictions: stories.

If I set out to tell you about my product, I'm already hosed, right out of the gate. You're not interested. Your eyes glaze over. And I can't *make* you listen these days—not with 30 bajillion web links beckoning every second. Certainly not the way I could make you listen with a 30-bajillion-dollar advertising budget and a populace hardwired to The Tube. Mass marketing is a special case of mass production in which the product is mass-produced commercial "messages." In the pre-net heyday of broadcast advertising, these messages had to appeal to the widest possible audience. Therefore they could offend no one. They could have no real personality. They had to be one-size-fits-all, bland, vanilla, preferably humorless. So pervasive was this jargon-ridden communicational "style" that even individuals deployed it in one-to-one business letters wherein they did such things as thank each other in advance for their earliest attention to those important matters impacting mutual concerns in re their earlier communication. Many businesses still think and talk this way.

With the advent of the Internet, markets have again become open, unconstrained conversations. Free talk. And the best conversations, the ones people gravitate toward, are based on stories. Stories, like conversations, don't have targets, fixed goals, Q2 objectives. They circumambulate their subjects. They explore. They don't have mission statements. If the pitch is the epitome of broadcast, the story embodies the essential character of the web.

Open-Source Marketing

It's Spring 1999 and I'm nearly broke. I'm getting worried. My phone rings. It's Steve Larsen, who was then senior VP marketing at Net Perceptions. I've known him since 1994, when he was at Prodigy and I was at Mecklermedia exploring a concept that would soon come to be called e-commerce. Now, he tells me, he's thinking about putting together a website focusing on personalization. I have to ask what that means. "Don't worry about it," Larsen says, "You'll pick it up real quick." Oh, so he's talking about a gig. Good timing. "Anyway, we were just kicking around who we could get to help us out with this, and at the same instant several people said 'Hey! This is a job for RageBoy!' So whaddya think? Are you interested?"

The result was that, for two years, I was editor-in-chief of personalization.com, and Net Perceptions was my client.[2] The project started with Steve and I experimenting with an idea suggested by something said by Eric Raymond, president of the Open Source Initiative. The web page at opensource.org explains the basic concept as it applies to software:

> The basic idea behind open source is very simple. When programmers can read, redistribute, and modify the source code for a piece of software, the software evolves. People improve it, people adapt it, people fix bugs. And this can happen at a speed that, if one is used to the slow pace of conventional software development, seems astonishing. We in the open source community have learned that this rapid evolutionary process produces better software than the traditional closed model, in which only a very few programmers can see the source and everybody else must blindly use an opaque block of bits.[3]

When he signed the manifesto at cluetrain.com, Raymond wrote: "The cluetrain is to marketing and communications what the open-source movement is to software development—anarchic, messy, rude, and vastly more powerful than the doomed bullshit that conventionally passes for wisdom."

What a terrific sound bite! But what if I took it seriously? Was it possible that there could be such a thing as "open-source marketing"? On its face, the idea seemed absurd. The canonical model for the open source movement is Linux, the development of which has been collaborative and widely distributed, percolating good ideas from the bottom up without explicit direction from any focal control point. How could marketing—competitive, centralized and highly managed via a top-down chain of command—bear any resemblance?

But the more Steve and I talked about it, the more we realized that an open-source marketing model fit with what we already believed. On the personalization.com site, we first banned any form of product promotion. We set up a forum for anyone who wanted to talk about the subject, pro or con, and we even published several articles that basically said personalization sucks. Then we decided to invite Net Perceptions' competitors to join in.

Steve had seen an early draft of *The Cluetrain Manifesto* and was interested in answering the question: If markets are conversations, how do you go about starting and sustaining that kind of conversation? We both felt that the success of the site should be measured on the quality of the content and the diversity of its sources—the number and variety of people participating—instead of by the sales leads it generated.

When the site launched, Steve wrote a column explaining what we were up to. He told the story about how we originally met (and how I got the name RageBoy from Esther Dyson). He followed with a telling comment: "I knew Chris would provide the separation from Net Perceptions necessary to the site being accepted as a legitimate source of high-quality information on an important topic and not just propaganda from some PR machine."

Separation as critical prerequisite for legitimacy? Isn't that kind of a weird concept for a marketing guy to be entertaining? No weirder, certainly, than putting his company's core market positioning into the hands of someone who calls himself RageBoy. But the response was fantastic. Many people wrote articles for the site (without pay, so it wasn't that). About 10,000 visitors—many from major corporations—subscribed to the newsletter I started putting out. The forum immediately started filling up with substantive discussion and lively debate. Links from other pages were plentiful and personalization.com got some great write-ups. Jesse Berst of ZDnet's *AnchorDesk* told his two-million-plus subscribers about the site: "Although it is sponsored by personalization vendors, it contains thoughtful commentary and information about the pros, cons and uses of personalization." And *USA Today* quoted me on the seed of an idea that eventually turned into the book you're now holding:

"In the days of broadcast media, pre-net, everything was outbound. You had these demographers slicing and dicing the market to see who the perfect target for their ads was," says Christopher Locke, editor of Personalization.com. "What's going on online now is the complete opposite of that; it's micromarkets which are emerging out of nowhere."[4]

But it wasn't all thoughtful commentary and penetrating insight. RageBoy, my psycho online alter ego, definitely put his oar in from time to time. Announcing the first Personalization Summit conference, held November '99 in San Francisco, he managed to break out of the leg irons, get control of my terminal and write to thousands of personalization newswire subscribers:

Hear!

[this followed by a list of well-known industry speakers]

Experience!

[followed by a litany of equally well-known companies]

- Steve Larsen, vice president of marketing, Net Perceptions, droning on interminably and telling really bad jokes.
- Christopher Locke, editor of personalization.com (securely restrained in a bamboo cage for your personal protection).

See!

1000 virgins sacrificed to the Great God Baal . . .

One CEO telephoned me within minutes of this crossing the net. "I've never seen a business newsletter quite like this," he said. He was clearly perplexed. I tried to be serious. "We only live to serve," I told him. But he registered anyway, as did hundreds of others. The conference sold out early. It was a standing-room-only success, exceeding everyone's expectations. And the newsletter was the only vector we used to flog the thing—if you don't count press releases, which are basically worthless. Did something strange happen to marketing while the world was busy making other plans? Yup. The web has turned the world upside down and inside out. When paradox becomes paradigm, worst practices work best.

Only Rock and Roll

In *The Cluetrain Manifesto* I talk about the ancient marketplace, the social hub around which civilization emerged. It was a confusing place, filled with noise, with talk, with song. Nearly 20 years ago, standing at a Tokyo news kiosk, I read an interview with Keith Richards in which he said he saw Mick Jagger and himself as being in direct line of descent from antique bards and medieval troubadours.[5] In place of "Let It Bleed" and "Sympathy For the Devil," I suddenly flashed on the lyric poet-musicians of the 12th century, on Beowulf, Homer, and even further back to bones and rattles and skin drums around some Neolithic campfire.

For me, this was a moment of radical reframing. Here was this roughneck rocker junkie talking about being connected to an authentic human lineage, which in turn connected him to both his own purpose as a man, and to his audience. Quite literally, to his market. Suddenly, Richards wasn't just a London punk grabbing for money and fame. He was reenacting and embodying a ritual that has united people at a primal, atavistic level for thousands of years—however dark, a powerful communion. Reading his almost throw-away comment revised my entire outlook on popular music. And on marketing.

Is the heritage of the ancient marketplace merely a legacy of barkers hawking their wares in some B-movie commercial carnival? Or was there ever poetry to it? Was there once upon a time some deeper story? Advertising shares certain qualities with the craft of storytelling. Unfortunately, the stories advertising tells are created to please clients, not the audience. That's upside down. Only a live and fully wide-awake audience—not a "focus group"—can truly judge a story's value. But instead of asking whether the story was effective, the ad agency today asks the client whether the story sold the product.

Because broadcast is intrusive, it's possible in that model for crappy stories—another way of saying ads—to sell mediocre products. However, the Internet is not broadcast. Broadcast assumptions—especially the high value advertising places on intrusion and manipulation—immediately fall apart on the Internet. If the story bombs online, that's the *end* of the story. If nobody listens, nobody buys.

I am inordinately fond of books. And I spend a lot of money acquiring them. It's a neurosis I've learned to live with. Who gets all this ill-gotten loot? Amazon. Certainly not because they're aiming spam and banner ads at me, but because of the stories and conversations there. "Huh?" you ask. "What stories? What conversations?" Perhaps you're too old, too set in your assumptions to see what's happening. Go to the Harry Potter pages. Slowly, haltingly, the children of the world are beginning to talk to one another. *They* understand. No one had to explain it to them. Barnes & Noble and Borders may have the same books, but they haven't yet embedded them in as rich and attractive a context. Not attractive as in pretty. Attractive as in magnetizing and awakening interest. Catalogs of bare product listings rarely have that effect, whereas interactions with other people often do.

New medium or not, companies are always going to try to sell us their stuff. It's what they do. It's what we expect them to do. But the point is no longer just to capture people's attention—though that remains critical. It's to encourage their goodwill. From this point forward, companies will never achieve substantial market share without first establishing an elusive quality called *"mindshare."* Do I want to obey my thirst and glug down a Sprite? Do I want to take the Pepsi Challenge? Do I care if you got milk? No, no, and no.

But I might care a lot if some company offered to hook me up with a bunch of interesting people who think sorta like I do, and have similar or complementary tastes and interests. People who could tell me stuff I wanted to know. Or even better, people good at telling stories, sharing experiences, insights, new perspectives. There are many places where that sort of exchange is happening on the net. But most of them are zines or e-mail lists or personal sites created by talented turned-on individuals.

Very few companies offer anything even remotely close. Sure there are huge chat conglomerates like ICQ and Yahoo and AOL, but they're just providing the tools or the pipe, not the juice. To them the stories are just message traffic and page hits. What about companies that sell other things, like cars or shoes or power tools? The sites that all these trillions of dollars of e-commerce are supposed to be coming from. Maybe I'm blind and I'm missing it. But I just don't see people hanging out at corporate websites. There's nothing to do there but buy more stuff so the company can make more money. Gosh, *that's* exciting! Thanks, Sergio.

To capture the interest of online markets, where we have gotten used to talking amongst ourselves in uncontrived, unpremeditated human voices, companies need to tell human stories. Not the smarmy, cloyingly sentimental "human interest" stories businesses are so fond of leveraging in support of some arcane brand mysticism, but rather, stories that come from having actually grappled with the class of problems the product or service purports to solve. In other words, companies need to tell stories based on genuine understanding, not purposeful misdirection. However, to tell such human stories, companies need human beings—a "product" with which they've never had much success. It's not that they lack the raw materials. They start with perfectly good stock. But they consistently turn out androids that sound like Tickle Me Elmo dolls.

Marketing Myopia Revisited

In the realm of technology, the unnatural spawn of Big Science and Big Business, it's all facts and figures. It's passionless objectivity all the way down. I woke up one day and said to myself: Yeah? Well, screw that. I was at an AI conference. Artificial intelligence not artificial insemination. And all these academic research types were arguing about natural language processing. They were arguing about it as if language was their personal property, something that they'd inherited along with their degrees and official membership in The Discipline. I remember getting angry. I remember thinking about the cave paintings at Lascaux and Altamira, about dictionaries as a form of lexical archeology, about Indo-European etymologies that went back the steppes of Asia, to people who rode into battle bareback and made up words for the sounds their swords and axes made, for the sounds of love, for the sounds of the night. And I thought, who do these hosers think they are, these long-winded doctors of philosophy with their anemic propositions and their feeble proofs? I walked away and never looked back.

I love language. And not just for what it can do. For what it is. But I'm also a working stiff. Somehow, I ended up in high-tech marketing. And for years I asked myself if there might be some way to combine my interest in language with my work in marketing. Could there be some hidden connection? This is one of those questions that is so profoundly stupid, you actually blush when you finally hear yourself asking it. "Hmmm, let's see . . . language, marketing . . . language, marketing . . ." And then the light bulb went off. Duh!

Could it be just remotely possible that the articulation of a company's history, direction and focus, what it cares about and spends its time doing, how it perceives its contribution to the world beyond itself . . . that all that could have some bearing on things like management, leadership, brand, positioning, value proposition and suchlike buzzwords? Double-duh! But companies mostly want to talk about just one thing: the product. And they mostly want to say just one thing about that: buy it! If markets are conversations, this makes for one hell of a dull conversation.

Why is corporate speech so unimaginative? In "Marketing Myopia," Theodore Levitt wrote:

> The reason [the railroads] defined their industry incorrectly was that they were railroad-oriented instead of transportation oriented. . . . What the railroads lack is not an opportunity but some of the managerial imaginativeness and audacity that made them great. . . . Even an amateur like Jacques Barzun can see what is lacking when he says: "I grieve to see the most advanced physical and social organization of the last century go down in shabby disgrace for lack of the same comprehensive imagination that built it up."[6]

Note here that Levitt turns to the amateur, and the amateur gets it right. Note also the references to imagination and audacity. Where professionals are cool and analytic, beginners and dilettantes often see things more clearly—and care more deeply about what they see.

The more people care, the more they are willing to risk. Concern, passion, shock, outrage: all tend to inspire engaged, audacious, imaginative speech. And such speech has true voice, the power to compel attention because—are you ready for this?—it is grounded in love.

In an era of networked markets, the love of the amateur and the delight of the dilettante represent a critical new dimension of economic reality, a powerful new market dynamic. The common online rabble—among which I definitely count myself—has no love for commerce and its convoluted, self-deluded marketing schemes.

Gonzo marketing is about reframing and recontexualization. Re-imagining. So imagine this: gonzo marketing is marketing from the *market's* perspective. It is not a set of tricks to be used against us. Instead, it's a set of tools to achieve what *we* want for a change. At the same time, it holds great promise for business, because . . . well, because we believed it all those years when business said it wanted to know what we really wanted. And for starters, what we want is for business to leave us the hell alone!

Fortunately for me, I'm schizophrenic—a definite plus when attempting to hold such views *and* make a living in the business world. So I actually do see the value of gonzo marketing to companies. I see it as a powerful form of market advocacy, which companies sorely need. They need it because, despite all the lip service, they are incapable of imagining what is going on in the minds of their own markets. Not so fortunately, the downside of this juggling act—where the "act" is telling the truth about things as I perceive them—is that I can only work for those rare companies that really want to know what their markets are thinking, as opposed to the many that merely pretend they want to know. But this market segmentation is OK by me. It prevents me from having assholes for clients.

You think this is Internet "attitude" talking? Ironic postmodern overstatement? Forty years ago, Ted Levitt speculated in some amazement about how the auto industry could have missed the public's clear preference for smaller, more fuel-efficient cars. "The answer," he wrote, "is that Detroit never really researched customers' wants. It only researched their preferences between the kinds of things which it had already decided to offer them."[7]

Narrative Goes Online

So-called personalization technologies purport to help companies understand their customers better. And in a way, they do. When Amazon tells you that "customers who bought this book also bought . . ." and gives you a list of titles, these *collaboratively filtered* results represent the collective knowledge of widely dispersed individuals. However, as used by most companies, personalization is an oxymoron. Without knowing anything about customers as people, it merely automates "cross-selling" and "up-selling" opportunities—a more sophisticated version of "Would you like fries with that?" Does this sell more fries? Yeah. But that's an extremely limited view.

Re-visioned from a higher vantage point, the view looks radically different. Collaborative filtering works bottom up by feeling out the edges of emergent micromarkets based on personal tastes and interests—in effect, defining potential online communities. This is a powerful capability, much better suited to a networked medium than the top-down demographic slicing and dicing typical of broadcast. Such techniques could enable companies to stop marketing altogether—at least in the sense of marketing *to* and marketing *at*. Instead, personalization could be used to get genuinely personal, connecting members of these emergent micromarkets *to each other*. Do that, and something different in kind results. People start talking, having conversations, telling stories.

Recall all those kids on Amazon vibing back and forth about Harry Potter. J. K. Rowling's first four *Harry Potter* books have so far elicited over 10,000 reader reviews—an incredible number. What's the commercial benefit? It's impossible to measure with scientific accuracy, but here's a clue. As I write this, the fifth volume in the series won't be published until next year—at least nine months away—yet today it's Amazon's #1 bestseller. Is that worth something in cold hard cash? You bet.

Amazon is facilitating this conversation and the resulting community of interest is far more likely to value the facilitator than if the company found a way to "message" at them more efficiently. Efficiency is not effectiveness. Talking about MyWidget—your wonderful product—is generally boring and tends to quickly turn into gush-ing, blatherous hype. But talking about the kinds of problems a product was created to solve, the opportunities and obstacles it was created to take advantage of or overcome—in other words, its larger market context—can often help people to decide why (and if) they should give a damn about it in the first place—a significant challenge for many companies these days.

Amazon.com's real innovation was to create a marketplace where customers, not advertisers and marketeers, could assess the value of products. For years, academic librarians built OPACs—online patron access catalogs—but to the best of my knowledge, none ever asked the reader, "so hey, did you *like* that book?" Back at the beginning of this chapter, I wrote: "sometimes, commerce grounds conversation." This is a good example. It took a commercial organization, not Yale or Stanford or the Library of Congress, to get ordinary people talking to each other about—of all things—books.

Do site visitors scanning reader reviews feel they are being advertised to? I don't think so. Especially when they encounter reviews warning off potential buyers: "This book sucks. It was a waste of money. Don't make the same mistake I did!" Is there slop in Amazon's system? Uh-huh. Are there design flaws? Definitely. Inequities? Possibly; I don't know for sure. But overall it's a great model. And it opens up rich possibilities, of which I suspect we've only seen the surface. The company is enriching its relational space—both hyperlinked knowledge and person-to-person relationships—in many ways: through its affiliates program, wish lists, member pages, reviews of reviewers, discussion boards, purchase circles, auctions, "Honor System PayPages," "Listmania" lists and so on.

The really interesting marketing action at Amazon is not how this information is being used to pitch products—"Would you like *War and Peace* with that?"—but in how it's being used to hook people up and get them talking with each other. "Hey, I just read *War and Peace*, and man, I gotta tell ya, this Tolstoy dood rulez!" So what's gonzo about that? Easy. It's anti-marketing. To be more precise, it's anti-marketing-as-usual—it's actually very *smart* marketing. Because people talking to each other don't sound like marketing droids.

Don't Examples

In 1996, Microsoft was running a thing called *Internet Magazine* on its site. The people responsible for putting it together got wind of my zine, EGR, and against all reasonable expectations, evidently liked what they saw. In fact, they said hey, write some of that gonzo stuff for us—none of this crap we get about how wonderful Microsoft's products are.

I was fascinated by the anything-but-our-product focus, so I tried to get to know the crew. One person sent me mail saying: "You wouldn't believe the background of this team: acupuncturist, MFA in poetry, mediaeval vocalist, '60s protestor for civil rights in the south, and many other secrets. Best of all, it's an ego-free-zone!" And then there was this, in response to my query about an odd quote in one of these Microsofters' sigs: "The Black Sabbath line comes from the convicted ex-journalist from S.F. He gets in every day at 7 a.m. and cranks up the volume and the writing. He also understands IE 4 better than most of the entire marketing team."

Remember: we're talking about the notorious Evil Empire here. The editor-in-chief was Emily Warn, a published poet. I bought one of her books, where I came across this: "But the haze in the hills is not fog or smoke from hermit fires. It is America breathing."[8] Wow, I thought, there is life in the trenches. Heart is still alive and beating inside the corporate monoliths. But a couple months later, Microsoft shut the project down.

Audioactive sells MP3 encoders and related sorts of things. I was impressed by the site when I first went there several years ago. It was funny and self-effacing. You could tell the crew was turned on, having fun. One page talked about the technology. This is pretty daunting stuff, it said. And it could be boring. Are you sure you want to wrap your head around the algorithms these wire-head scientists came up with?

The Audioactive site was good-looking and conveyed deep competence. I remember it a million sites later for only one reason: it had voice. I could feel there were real people on the other end. But when I went back to those pages to grab some examples, I couldn't find a single one. The site has been sterilized. The edge, the humor, the voice is gone. All the information is still there, and maybe the pages are a little slicker. But now the company sounds like every other e-bozo outfit on the web.

One day in June 1997, I hit the Microsoft website looking for some information now long forgotten. At the top of the main page was a headline about a recent deal: "Microsoft Invests $1 Billion in Comcast." Nothing very surprising there. What was memorable was the sub-slug: "We found some extra cash lying around in a sock drawer." Whoa! What was this? I ripped into the press release, hoping for more, but fell asleep at the terminal halfway through the obligatory Gates quote: "Today's announcement will enhance the integration of broadband pipes and content to expand the services offered to consumers." Zzzz . . .

I went back to the page for weeks afterwards, wondering if there'd be more inspired headlines, captions, further signs of life from whoever had produced the sock drawer line. No dice. Maybe one day I'll run into this person and hear the story of how she got demoted to Encarta shipping clerk for unauthorized cheek. Too bad. Too sad. Why do companies insist on being boring and character-free? Moreover, why do startups, those zany hackers with the wild ideas and boundless energy, insist on emulating big asleep-at-the-wheel companies as soon as they land their first-round financing? I imagine an exchange that goes something like this.

VENTURE CAPITALIST: "You fellows are bright as a pin and we like your spunk. Otherwise we wouldn't be handing you such a big wad of cash. But you have to realize this isn't a game anymore. No more goofing around. We expect to get a whopping return on this investment, and for that to happen, you're going to have to start acting and sounding like a real company."

DEVELOPER: "Gee. How does that work, exactly?"

VC: "Well, look at your Fortune 500 companies out there. You want to join them one day, right? We certainly want you to. You don't see them being funny do you? You don't see them making cracks about their products or management team. No, you don't. And you won't. Not ever. You have joined the ranks of serious business, and while you may find it a little plain, I can assure you this is how it's done."

In a medium well known for sites with names like "The Cathedral of the Hydrogenated Snack Cake," why would *any* company assume it needed to sound "businesslike"? Why would it ever write something like this unedited clip from a bona fide press release?

IBM is focused on delivering customized, flexible and scalable Internet solutions for companies of all sizes. Drawing on resources from across IBM and 90,000 IBM Business Partners, IBM's Global Net Generation Business helps Service Providers and other web-based companies (hosters, portals and born-on-the-web B2B and B2C companies) establish their businesses and become profitable in Internet time.[9]

Hey, in "Internet time" I'm snoring over here, guys. I'm cuttin' Z's again.

Rhetorical Questions

Steve Larsen periodically mails out an informal screed he calls Friends of Net Perceptions. It used to be Friends of Prodigy (which "had fewer friends" he notes), then Friends of CitySearch. He's been doing this for a long time now. In one of these he recapped the inside story of what it was *actually* like to go public. This was a hysterically irreverent look at what most company executives consider a sacred rite of passage into corporationhood. He ends thusly:

In the next bizarre iteration of this newsletter run amok, I'll clue you in on some other interesting stuff. If you are smart and value your sanity, you'll get off this list NOW! As always, getting off requires that you whirl a live chicken around your head three times on the night of a full moon while muttering lyrics from an obscure Doors tune . . .

He ripped off the chicken-whirling trope from EGR—though he tacked on the Doors bit, which I think adds a nice touch. Anyway, you get the idea. This isn't exactly your average business communiqué. It's solidly in the gonzo camp. Yet he sends it out to clients, journalists, industry analysts, even to investors. Steve doesn't hesitate to tell these readers to subscribe to my EGR ravings, where—trust me on this one—they are liable to encounter all manner of unseemly and highly unbusinesslike content. I ask him whether this isn't . . . uh, just a little risky. "Marketing is about real relationships," Larsen replies. "I tell my friends about stuff I like, no matter how off-the-wall. They don't always share my tastes, but they end up knowing me better."

Only in a world gone crazy would that be gonzo. But the business world today is not just crazy. It's headed for the rubber room. In "Fear and Loathing on the web" (gonzo ported from Las Vegas to AltaVista), I quoted David Weinberger, who said: "The dogs have it right. Customers want to take a good long whiff. But companies so lobotomized that they can't speak in a recognizably human voice build sites that smell like death." That was one thread, one shared stream of consciousness that led to the cluetrain manifesto, where later I would write:

> To speak with a human voice, companies must share the concerns of their communities. But first, they must belong to a community. Companies must ask themselves where their corporate cultures end. If their cultures end before the community begins, they will have no market. Human communities are based on discourse—on human speech about human concerns. The community of discourse is the market. Companies that do not belong to a community of discourse will die.[10]

I'm cautiously edging toward a theory of rhetoric here. The word *rhetoric* often causes eyebrows to be raised, and is sometimes even met with alarm. This reaction involves the conflict between two contradictory sets of semantics:

rhetoric, noun

1. persuasive speech or writing: speech or writing that communicates its point persuasively
2. pretentious words: complex or elaborate language that only succeeds in sounding pretentious

From ancient times to the present, the study of rhetoric has always focused on effective, persuasive communication. However, lacking a theory of rhetoric—an informing overall set of communicational principles and a sense of what they are to be used for—institutional speech has largely been reduced to the second definition.

Stories often employ figures of speech: similes, metaphors. They use these rhetorical devices to ground abstractions in the familiar—like the face of a friend emerging from an anonymous crowd. Slacking off and surfing around one day (my usual routine), I came across an article titled "Ashby's Law Revisited."

> Where before, companies could get away with making the right noises about flexibility but really remain as rigid as they want to while instead trying to pull political and other strings to control the environment, they can't any more—trying to do this in the current environment will be akin to bolting the stable door after the horse has fled and is already out there in the wild mounting many mares and making many foals.[11]

The writer's name is Olu Oni. When he wrote this, he was just some guy, one of millions of people posting pages to the web. However, when the weekend is over and he puts on his shoes and tie and business suit, he is Assistant Vice President for Global Markets Technology at Chase Manhattan Bank. When he writes like this, he isn't speaking on behalf of his company. He is very careful to say so. But when he leaves for work, does he leave the poetry at home? I doubt it. Consider the metaphor of the horse. Notice that it is drawn from the world of the living. Notice that the horse is wild, that it has broken free. Notice that its first thought is to replicate itself.

Some metaphors are so powerful they speak directly in the language of the collective unconscious. In an e-mail conversation we got into about cluetrain and his paper on Ashby's Law, Olu wrote: "Markets have strong supernatural and spiritual bearings in Yoruba culture and indeed the reason for the adage 'do not buy from strangers' is because of the belief that spirits also came to the market to transact in souls . . . Buy from a stranger and the transaction may cost you more than you bargained for."

The best stories can become myths that draw people together, create entire cultures. The people within the culture so created are not strangers to each other precisely because they know the old stories. They share and reflect on them. They remember together. This creates powerful cohesion, even identity. And sometimes the stories are warnings. They persist because they continue to protect the people, often from great harm. Is the notion of a market traffic in souls merely superstition? If it's just a metaphor, what is it a metaphor *for?* Is it possible that the engine of commerce decoupled and estranged from the concerns of any human society could actually steal people's souls? In some real sense, destroy their life force? Perhaps it's not a metaphor at all.

If you think deeply about this story, it becomes an allegory—richer, deeper, entangled with other meanings. You turn it over in your mind. You talk about it and retell it. This is how stories travel through time, as word of mouth from ancient days. This is how stories replicate themselves.

For a long time, all our lives in fact, the engine of commerce roared on, insatiably devouring the 20th century. The deafening sound it made was not only the noise of industrial factories, but also of the mass communication machines that pumped out an endless stream of mesmeric anti-myth—the empty stories that were advertising. Then along came the web and the Thorazine wore off, the hypnotic spell began to break. As networking replaces broadcasting, communication must become richer and more interesting—not just louder and more insistent. It must have character, invite participation. Must differentiate itself from the plethora of uncommunicative corporate blather, which by its sheer volume—in both senses—threatens to drown out all memory of life-before-the-brand.

For purposes of such differentiation, it's a good idea to explore styles and concepts that corporate communications are apparently incapable of even conceiving. Such radical approaches include, but are not limited to:

- being funny
- being playful
- being angry
- using big words
- using bad words
- using parody and satire
- dropping arcane literary allusions
- admitting to heavy use of illegal pharmaceuticals

And, for extra credit, most outrageous of all:

- telling the truth

The challenge today is to engage with people in something larger than yourself. Something you have in common. Something murky and ill-defined that's hovering on the edges, waiting to be discovered. Whatever that something is, it's out there on the web. Lurking. The world has changed. Fundamentally and irrevocably. The comforting certainty of the database, the fixed field, the form, is gone forever. Good. The fill-in-the-blanks approach to information and knowledge, to life, is what T.S. Kuhn—The Paradigm Guy®—called puzzle solving: the slavish, formulaic rule-following that comes between revolutions, scientific or otherwise. It's stupid, stultifying, boring. And on the Internet at least, it's over, finito, dead, kaput. Hail Eris!

Marketing has an agenda, an objective. It wants us to do something, buy something. Now! Stories aren't like that. They suggest, they explore, they imagine. They say, hey take your time. Become larger. The web is storyspace. It's its own strange attractor.

But wait. Doesn't all this reduce to some vague form of muddle-headed web mysticism? Gonzo or not, shouldn't "marketing" have something to do with making money? Absolutely. The real question is whether websites emulating the lowest-common-denominator style of mass media will be effective at bringing in new business. Today, it may seem so. But tomorrow, attempting to please everyone is likely to please no one.

Brand Id

I first heard from Brian Millar soon after the cluetrain manifesto appeared on the web. At the time, he was working at RMG International, a subsidiary of The WPP Group. WPP is arguably the world's largest advertising and public relations conglomerate—we're talking motels on Boardwalk. Brian sent me e-mail that became an article, "Modern Life is Rubbish," which I published on personalization.com. "We now benefit from economies of scale at the cost of any modicum of humanity creeping into our dealings with brands," he wrote. "But I think that it's a temporary problem, because many of these Industrial Age monoliths are pretty doomed."[12]

He has since left RMG and WPP and started a company of his own, called myrtle. The site says:

> myrtle is a new company which helps brands communicate in an accelerated culture. Yes: people are more contradictory, more aware of choice, more demanding and less ready to be talked down to or imposed upon than ever. No: they can't be bribed, they don't think your ads are entertaining any more and they resent being sneaked up on. Yes: our work starts with consumers. We find patterns in the chaos of their lives.

By the way, myrtle is also his dog's name. "In a market that's accelerating in incomprehensible ways," Millar explains in e-mail, "doing nothing is the greatest risk of all. And in a market that's a conversation, the winners are going to be the people with something to say. Our website represents our brand's id. All the sneaky little things we've always wanted to do and say are out there for everybody to see."

Sneaky little things like what, precisely? Well . . . myrtle imagines "ultranarrow ultramodern microchannels" offering endless loops of sampled video—people swearing for hours on end, for instance, or interminably strung-together car chase scenes. "It's a meaner, more lizardly attitude to our treasured media archives," Millar admits, tongue firmly in cheek. "But then, nothing's sacred." Brian tells me that myrtle is also offering "Turin Shroud duvet covers. The extraordinary deposition image, only shown in public once per generation, preserved on your comforter forever. A gift to treasure. Yes. What have Turin Shroud duvet covers got to do with running an ad agency? Frankly, nothing as far as I can work out. But I bet they'd look nifty."

And then there are a number of items such as . . .

Human Crisps: If it's okay for vegetarians to eat, say, bacon-flavour snacks because it's just "pretend" or "bacon-effect" and contains no actual animal products, then we want to eat human-flavoured crisps. It's only fair that carnivores get a share of the new fiction-food market too. So while you're thinking, hmm . . . who do I want to eat the most, please understand we don't want just any person-flavour. We crave celebrities, novelists, philosophers, stars of stage and screen, athletes, musicians and (where available) leading figures from history. In snack form. Let's be clear—there's no actual human in them, so it isn't cannibalism, just hugely similar, and about as close as we'll ever get in today's world. Yum.

The message isn't "here's how we'll help you sell." Instead, it's "here's how we think." There's an exuberance to the site that's tangible, infectious. We won't even try to describe the blipvert for "Transparent Bone-less Lions"—except to repeat the tagline claim: "They're educational!" One gets the feeling that myrtle represents a significant departure from the kind of advertising and branding Brian Millar previously did for companies like Compaq, IBM, Mercedes-Benz and British Airways. Call it a wild hunch.

So is gonzo marketing just whacked out, undisciplined indulgence run amok? Partly, yes. But that's not necessarily the point. Nor is there any point at all without some deeper substance—the dimension of character, of voice. The myrtle site, for instance, is pure voice. Uncut, undiluted. If you become their client, what you see is very likely what you're going to get. This has manifold ramifications.

For one thing, it signals: this is who we are. In the same breath, it gives fair warning: who we are is non-negotiable. If you can't dig it, just go away.

Gonzo marketing has attitude to spare, but it's not the attitude of the poseur. Gonzo is not a style that can be faked. Sophistry is not an option. We're not talking about some generic class of "free-age" nouveau-consultants here, or camouflaged faux-hip cyber-alley suits with a fast rap. Instead, what is emerging from the huge new mind-space the Internet has opened up is a new breed of professionals-turned-dilettantes—who work for delight more than dollars and value the work itself above company or client. These creative Ronin first ply their marketing skills by representing the things they passionately care about. Their websites are their resumes, attracting precisely the sorts of people they want to—and are willing to—work with. A company doesn't hire such people, it woos them. It doesn't control them—it finds the best possible fit, then takes the trip.

But why would a company brook such unconscionable independence? Why would it ever agree to such risk? The answer is simple: because the risks of continuing in status-quo mode are infinitely greater. Authentic, engaged voice is precisely what companies desperately need today. Lacking that, they're sunk. Networked markets are smart markets. To these new audiences, the broadcast pitch is a carrier wave for unadulterated boredom. The faintest hint of hucksterism triggers an inattention so profound it constitutes a form of commercial catatonia. The billions being spent on e-commerce marketing of this sort might just as well be flushed down an enormous toilet. If somebody put up a webcam and streamed the video, it might even draw as big a crowd as the one that thronged the Dancing Hamsters page. Good show. A million laughs. But what can you do for an encore?

Most companies needn't look far to find genuine voices within their ranks. All they have to do then is get out of the way. They don't need "empowerment" programs. Such paternalism is just as stifling as the control it tries to mask. What they need are nonintervention treaties. A model already exists for this in the publishing world. Without a voice, a newspaper is nothing. So newspaper companies search out voices they respect and make them editors. Then the company stays out of the editor's face. The publisher—that is, the business side of the house—doesn't tell the editorial side what to write, or how to write it. There are plenty of instances in which this arrangement is honored in the breach, but it exists and it mostly works. It's referred to metaphorically as Church and State. Given such a setup, it shouldn't come as a great surprise that gonzo first emerged in the world of journalism. But nothing inherently limits it to that world. Gonzo marketing simply represents business getting the clue about 30 years late.

Nine Maxims

OK, time to regroup, mop up and get out. Time to try to reassemble what these many small loosely joined pieces have been intimating, insinuating, hinting at, suggesting.

Marketing has become irrelevant. As practiced today, most marketing is dependent on assumptions that may still hold true with respect to broadcast media, but have little relevance to the Internet.

Best practices usually aren't. Techniques that have worked in the past tend to be misleading and even dangerous when change is extremely rapid.

Frustration is inspiration. People who work for companies *want to believe.* They want to engage with each other and with the market, but they're hobbled by functional categories and bureaucratic management that militate toward group stupidity.

Gonzo is a terminal response. Adopting worst practices is an extreme response to frustration with existing practice. People finally engage because they care. Better engaged than enraged—though gonzo marketing is often both.

Permission is the critical hurdle. Frustration is not enough. There has to come a moment in which people give themselves permission to speak—just as gonzo journalism offered new freedom of speech to a whole generation of writers. Inspiration must pass through rationalization and fear. Only then can voice emerge and true words go forth. Such words pass the same permission on to others. Things ignite.

Storytelling is the path. True voice is the articulation of craft, and craft cares about quality. That's what defines it as craft, as art—"good enough" is not good enough. Storytelling is the path and primary tool of gonzo marketing. It's pragmatic, it's opportunistic, it's about what works. Even if what works breaks all the rules. And it will.

Gonzo marketing is market advocacy. The goal of gonzo marketing is not to better "penetrate" markets, but to better represent the market's interests—in every possible sense.

Companies aren't real enough to speak. Gonzo speech is what companies need right now, but they can't produce it. By nature, they have no personality, no character, no subjective take, idiosyncratically engaged or otherwise. Plus, they can't relinquish control, can't loosen up, let go. They are bound by the paranoia they have created.

Only individuals can be gonzo. Only people can convey enthusiasm through their stories. The marketing department doesn't have a story. Neither does the company. The discovery of worst practices is imagination replacing control. Worst practices tend to be radically anti-corporate, anti-marketing—but only because they are unconditionally human.

I opened this chapter by quoting W. Edwards Deming's dictum: "drive out fear." Deming also said if you want quality, shut down the Quality Control department. Make quality everybody's job. Companies that need marketing that actually works could take a tip from Deming. Shut down the marketing department. Then get out of the way. We'll take it from there. Hell, we'll take it anyway. What's happening in this medium is crucial, epochal. But what is unique and most consequential about the net is not what most companies are pursuing. At best, their bread-and-circus sideshows are temporary holding actions. Temporary insanity.

Today we need anthems more than analysis. We need to tell new and deeper, larger stories. Stories about ourselves—the kind of creatures who invent them, and why their creation is so important. Stories about why we can't afford to lose such a precious human legacy in a din of charlatanism and slobbering artless venality. The promise of the net is the promise of humanity coming together, seeing itself for the first time, as we saw ourselves from the moon more than three decades ago, saw the breathtaking blue planet spinning out there. Out *here*. This time it's much more intimate. Maybe we can't see the faces yet, but we can read the words and begin to sense the lives behind them.

CHAPTER 5

Social Marketing and
Public Journalism

> *"Social capital is about networks,*
> *and the Net is the network to end all networks."*
>
> —ROBERT D. PUTNAM IN *BOWLING ALONE* [1]

ON THE SURFACE, SOCIAL MARKETING AND PUBLIC JOURNALISM MAY seem only vaguely related to gonzo marketing. But they're highly germane to where we're headed. For two reasons. First, both represent significant attempts to get closer to audiences, to become more relevant and credible to smaller, more focused niches. The Internet is a more intimate medium than broadcast or mass publishing ever was. Whether with respect to markets or readerships, both social marketing and public journalism are attempts to establish more intimate relationships. Second, both developed before the Internet became a big deal, and therefore do not depend on hyperactive tub-thumping about the wonderful new world of e-commerce. Too much thinking about business today relies on a highly questionable form of pretzel logic that did not exist before 1995. The Internet can make companies a lot of money. Money is good. Therefore the Internet is good. Or . . . the Internet cannot make companies a lot of money. Therefore it is bad. Either way, *quod erat demonstrandum.* Such fatuous syllogisms aside, I wanted to find evidence of trends that were already underway when the net and business began to intersect, and thus had at least an outside chance of being based on something more substantive than the promise of instant e-riches—or the pall of e-poverty.

I am not proposing social marketing and public journalism as models in the usual sense—as templates on which to build further. Instead, I find social marketing and public journalism interesting for what they say about the limitations of broadcast marketing. Both are direct responses to those limitations—detached, impersonal, bland and humorless one-size-fits-all mass communications. These movements make an appearance here because they deal with fundamental issues—both problems and potential—that have a large bearing on the alternatives this book does propose.

Neither social marketing or public journalism is likely to continue very long in its present form. Though they will continue for a time, the dynamics of the net will ultimately cause a definitive interruption of these courses, just as they will for mass marketing and broadcast. They will not survive because both seek to salvage the conventional institutions in which they are embedded—in one case broadcast advertising, in the other mass-media journalism. This point is crucial, but involves a longer story—one that I hope will make better sense when we return to it at the end of the chapter. For now, let's just say that both rely on business as usual continuing essentially unchanged. Does the expression "fat chance" mean anything to you?

Despite these caveats and disclaimers, social marketing and public journalism constitute instructive precursors—call them foreshadowings, intimations—of what I'm calling, for better or worse, the gonzo model.

Social Marketing

Everyone has experienced social marketing in some form—media campaigns to raise awareness about the dangers of cigarettes, illegal drugs, sexually transmitted diseases and various other health and environmental hazards. Social marketing was first defined in 1971 by Philip Kotler and Gerald Zaltman.[2] Eighteen years later, in 1989, Kotler and Eduardo Roberto wrote *Social Marketing: Strategies for Changing Public Behavior*, the subtitle underscoring the cultural dimension. They describe the scope of the discipline as follows: "Social marketing is a strategy for changing behavior. It combines the best elements of the traditional approaches to social change in an integrated planning and action framework and utilizes advances in communication technology and marketing skills."[3]

The goal of social marketing is to change minds—values, beliefs and behavior—not to promote products with price tags attached. If a campaign is successful, the only "product" is the effect produced: revised attitudes about some issue thought to be of high relevance to society as a whole.

But thought to be relevant by whom? Because it does not attempt to get people to buy products, social marketing is often perceived as more credible than commercial advertising. However, it also risks creating resentment. "Who are 'they' to tell me to quit smoking?" While many public service campaigns are created by major advertising agencies and delivered through conventional mass media channels, bottom-up local programs are usually more effective. When members of a particular group use marketing tools in their own behalf, the message is less likely to be perceived as coming from some paternalistic outsider whose intentions may be suspect.

Fostering Sustainable Behavior: An Introduction to Community-Based Social Marketing makes the point that attempting to change people's behavior works best when you talk to people directly. "The emergence of community-based social marketing," the authors write, "can be traced to a growing understanding that conventional social marketing, which often relies heavily on media advertising, can be effective in creating public awareness and understanding of issues . . . but is limited in its ability to foster behavior change."[4] It's limited because people tend to blow it off. The distance that broadcast inevitably creates is, well . . . distancing. The message seems to be aimed at someone else. It isn't immediate, doesn't apply to my life here and now.

At first, some big issue (say cancer awareness) is socially marketed by a big non-profit org (say the American Cancer Society) using the resources of a big advertising agency (say Ogilvy & Mather). But then, smaller organizations, even neighborhoods, realize they can do something similar—set up a block watch program, for instance. In such cases, word of mouth works much better than mass marketing. And note that, on the Internet, "community-based" need not imply geographic proximity. Online communities can be globally distributed, yet still act as communities with respect to shared interests, values and objectives.

Social marketing has been extensively deployed in the third world, especially in public health programs. *Social Mobilization & Social Marketing in Developing Communities* notes that "little success has been achieved in developing countries using a strictly mass media model." AIDs education is a case in point. Author Neill McKee writes that "mass media is seldom sufficient to bring about behavior change. Networks and peer counseling are needed, involving those most at risk."[5] While community involvement is crucial to the effectiveness of such initiatives, it is not easily accomplished, nor is this an area in which traditional marketing has much experience—or much interest. Traditional marketing is designed and delivered from the top down. It does not usually elicit input and involvement from its targeted markets.

This criticism of mass marketing echoes the feelings of many in the general online population. Because Internet audiences self-organize around common interests, and therefore tend to form natural communities, people are generally much more interested in each other than in intrusive marketing messages. In this respect, the net world begins to look a lot like the Third World.

Participatory Development Communication: A West African Agenda recaps the history of many "modernization" programs in which wealthy Western countries attempted to help less fortunate global neighbors. "Such modernization was planned in the national capitals under the guidance and direction of experts brought in from developed countries," writes Chin Saik Yoon. "Often, the people in the villages who are the 'objects' of these plans would first learn that 'development' was on the way when strangers from the city turned-up, frequently unannounced, to survey land or look at project sites."[6]

Programs like this are modeled on the top-down methods of mainstream marketing and mass media. A central organization determines what is in the best interests of their "backward" beneficiaries, then goes about implementing its "altruistic" plans without bothering to consult with the targets of their largesse. Such paternalism smacks of Rudyard Kipling's infamous "White Man's Burden," a phrase that Microsoft defines via its *Encarta World English Dictionary* as "the supposed responsibility of Europeans and their descendants to impose their allegedly advanced civilization on the non-Caucasian original inhabitants of the territories they colonized," adding that the phrase is often considered offensive.[7] No shit, Sherlock.

> *Take up the White Man's burden—*
> *Send forth the best ye breed—*
> *Go, bind your sons to exile*
> *To serve your captives' need;*
> *To wait, in heavy harness,*
> *On fluttered folk and wild—*
> *Your new-caught sullen peoples,*
> *Half devil and half child.*[8]

The white man's burden trope was an important ideological component of a much larger agenda called colonialism. This agenda is hardly an artifact of yesteryear. The attitude of large corporations coming onto the Internet has all the same earmarks. Call it e-colonialism. Here we were, all these wild and sullen half-devil children fooling around with the net, engaging in bizarre rituals and idolizing false gods. Then along came the Fortune 500 to civilize our heathen asses and get us all to worship at the Church of the One True Disney.[9] Wow, thanks.

Practitioners of participatory communication take an altogether different approach, not just teaching, but also learning from the people with whom they work. The impetus for the participatory approach grew out of anthropological field work, in which it became obvious that researchers often brought their own biased cultural assumptions to their description of non-Western societies. Recall here anthropologist Clifford Geertz's notion of thick description, which was an important step in the attempt to cure this sort of transcultural arrogance. But ultimately, there is no cure, for the simple reason that there is no ultimate authority to appeal to on questions of whose culture is better, more advanced, more civilized. These are inherently judgments of value, which cannot be decided by scientific method, no matter how rigorously applied. In response to these issues, Elaine Lawless developed the concept of reciprocal ethnography, in which the people she is observing are invited to observe her in the same manner, and to question her own assumptions, biases and beliefs. "My work is 'reciprocal,'" she writes, "in that we [herself and the people she is studying] . . . have established a working dialogue about the material, a reciprocal give and take."[10]

It is precisely this kind of give-and-take that is noticeably absent from traditional marketing. Most conventional marketers don't even seem to notice its absence, having apparently forgotten that it was ever important to speak with real customers—except perhaps in the context of focus groups. In heterogeneous societies, however— whether we're talking about the vastly varied nations of Africa or the global Internet—focus groups can be extremely misleading, as outside marketers are thrust into an unfamiliar constellation of cultural beliefs. Social marketers in developing countries focus on participation, both because they are highly sensitive to the colonialist impulse, and because they have a different set of objectives from those of commercial marketing. These differences are reflected in the following passage from *Participatory Development Communication*:

> Commercial stations which are caught-up in "rating-wars" and competition for the advertising dollar probably do more elegant audience research than participatory media managers. But there is a very fundamental ideological difference . . . Commercial stations aim to capture "market segments" which they can then sell to advertisers for a profit. Their loyalty in business is to the advertiser. Participatory media's loyalty is to the people.[11]

Among the techniques used to foster participatory communication, the author includes listening, negotiation, sensitivity to local language, appreciation of traditional customs and folklore, facilitating the sharing of knowledge, understanding acceptable methods of entering the community, knowing when and how to leave it, and keeping in touch afterwards. To say the least, these are not matters that conventional marketing pays much attention to. But ignoring them can result in ugly charges of cultural manipulation. And here—let me say it again—the net world begins to look a lot like the Third World.

Of course, conventional marketing has refined manipulation to an art form. And on that note, complicating the issue of credibility even further, we come to the closely allied notion of *"cause-related marketing,"* or often simply *"cause marketing."* But hold that thought. We'll come back to it in just a second. This is pretty dense stuff, so let's take a little break.

Intermission

Got your popcorn right here. There you go. What's that? You want a Coke? Sorry, no Coke. Pepsi.

In *The Blues Brothers* movie, Dan Aykroyd, in his character as Elwood Blues, repeatedly repeats: "We're on a mission from God." He is dead serious, which is why it's funny. The mission is to put the band back together and save the orphanage. You get the picture. Consider how many people who build personal websites feel they're on a mission from God. Some might even use the expression to denote a kind of ironic self-awareness of their own obsessive focus on something that's so tiny and trivially insignificant compared to all the Big Deal doings of E-Commerce, from Amazon to Yahoo. Now consider that a mission is a kind of *cause*. It may not be Cancer Prevention or World Peace. It could be anything that generates the same kind of hell-bent mania with which the Blues Brothers brought Chicago to a screeching halt. It could be day trading or javascript programming, home schooling, quantum physics or amateur pornography. It could be chinchilla ranching. Whatever it is, it could also be hugely effective in bringing people together who share that particular passion. Finally, consider that—without any commercial product being involved—Napster was on such a mission and had such a cause. Working bottom-up, using a community-based approach, it fostered social behavior change on a global scale. It got millions of kids to stop buying music from large multinational entertainment cartels. I'm not saying this is good or bad, mind you. It's just so. As Elwood says: "It's 106 miles to Chicago, we've got a full tank of gas, half a pack of cigarettes, it's dark and we're wearing sunglasses." And without missing a beat, Jake replies, "Hit it!"[12]

Don't ask. It's just so. The net is just like that. But we're getting ahead of ourselves.

Cause for Concern

Back to the difference between social and cause marketing. A few examples of the latter include Ben & Jerry's promoting peace with popsicles and American Express sharing its spare change with the homeless. It was in fact AmEx that first coined the *cause-related marketing* usage in 1983, when it agreed to donate a penny to the Statue of Liberty restoration project every time anyone used their card, and a buck for each new account. What they meant by the term was "the marketing of a product or service by using commercial exchanges to trigger donations, thereby raising money and visibility for a cause."[13] *Cause Related Marketing: Who Cares Wins* defines cause marketing in pretty much the same terms: "a commercial activity by which a business with a product, service or image to market builds a relationship with a cause or a number or causes for mutual benefit."[14]

In February 2001, *New York* magazine began running an ad for Absolut vodka that was created by the advertising firm TBWA/Chiat/Day. As in all the entries in this long-running campaign, it features the distinctive Absolut bottle, this time representing the logo of GLADD, the Gay and Lesbian Alliance Against Defamation. In his *New York Times* advertising column, Stuart Elliott writes that the ad "is indicative of two trends that are helping to reshape how advertisers appeal to consumers." The first is cause-related marketing, "which seeks potential customers by supporting causes they themselves support." The second is niche marketing, "which seeks potential customers among narrow demographic segments rather than the general population." The article notes that these interrelated approaches have also been adopted by much larger companies such as American Express, General Motors and Procter & Gamble.[15]

There is fast-growing interest in cause marketing, and no lack of enthusiastic proponents on both sides of the corporate/cause equation. Among the most eloquent is Bill Shore, founder and executive director of Share Our Strength. SOS describes itself as "one of the nation's leading anti-hunger and anti-poverty organizations." It has raised over $65 million for such causes since 1984. Among the many partners SOS has attracted are America Online, American Express, Barnes & Noble, Bloomingdale's, Coors Brewing, KitchenAid, Kraft Foods, Macy's, The Home Shopping Network, Williams-Sonoma, and Yahoo. SOS speaks in uncharacteristically entrepreneurial language for a non-profit. "Share Our Strength understands the return on investment these relationships provide for our partners and our work to end hunger."[16] Shore argues that people have a deep-seated desire to contribute to society, and that organizations like SOS provide an opportunity to do so. In *The Cathedral Within: Transforming Your Life by Giving Something Back*, he writes about doing something that counts:

> All of us have strengths we need to share. . . It's not just about volunteering or trying to be a better person. It's not about making your community a better place. It's not about service being good for your soul. It is more fundamental, almost primal. It is what the species instinctively wants to do: to perpetuate itself by leaving something behind; to make a mark that lasts; to make ourselves count.[17]

The corporate world finds strong appeal in such ideas. Businesses are tired of being perceived as heartless. There's only one catch: they *are* heartless. No incorporation for the corporation. No body, no heart. Remember? Or did you skip that chapter? While it's true that many *individuals* involved in business enterprises might love to feel they were giving something back—or perhaps just leaving a legacy to a monumentally engorged ego—they can only do so within the corporate framework if they can prove the ROI on such gifts.

There is no doubt cause marketing can do real good. But no matter how good the concept sounds, we're still talking about companies aligning themselves with sympathetic social causes primarily so they can move more product. The terms *"social marketing"* and *"cause-related marketing"* are often used interchangeably, which is seriously misleading. An otherwise excellent book on the subject, *The Art of Cause Marketing*, unfortunately perpetuates this confusion. "Cause marketing informs about and creates action on behalf of a cause," writes author Richard Earle. So far so good. But he then says, "Advertising which does that is also widely classified as 'social marketing.'"[18]

This conflation of labels glosses over a critical distinction. Kotler and Andreason define cause-related marketing as "any effort by a corporation to increase its own sales by contributing to the objectives of one or more non-profit organizations."[19] They also define social marketing: "Social marketing seeks to influence *social behaviors* not to benefit the marketer but *to benefit the target audience and the general society*."[20] The italics are in the original, indicating that the authors thought it was important whether a product was being sold or not. And they say this multiple times in various different wordings. For instance, the goal of social marketing "is not to market a product or service *per se* but to influence a social behavior . . . Its sponsors simply wish to make the society a better place, not merely benefit themselves or their organization."

Why all this emphasis? Why is it so important to distinguish social marketing from cause marketing, which often adopts the same terminology? "There is . . . a legitimate concern," write Kotler and Andreason—and remember, these are dyed-in-the-wool mainstream marketing guys, not flaming Marxists—"that, without careful training and monitoring, those adopting social marketing will employ some of the more unsavory persuasive strategies that have helped create economic successes of a number of socially dubious products and services." And then they go even further: ". . . in stating that social marketing involves customer behavior that the marketer thinks is socially desirable, we make no judgments about whether in any given circumstances they are right. Sound marketing approaches and techniques can be used as easily by a Hitler or a Charles Manson as by a Mother Theresa or a Pope John Paul."[21]

Contrast these powerfully cautionary notes with the following statement which appears in the foreword to *Brand Spirit*, a book on cause marketing by two writers associated with the advertising firm of Saatchi & Saatchi. Here, Edward de Bono both acknowledges serious flak and in the same breath discounts it.

> Some might think that Cause Related Marketing is simply a cynical exploitation of public sympathy for the sake of profits. There will always be people who take it upon themselves to make these sorts of judgments on behalf of others. However, consumers always have the power of the final choice and if most of them felt it was cynical, then CRM would cease to exist.[22]

To be generous, this is an extremely weak argument. It is not only legitimate, but a thoroughly excellent idea to question the implications and effects of corporate sponsorship—on *anything*, cause-related or otherwise. The disparity in knowledge resulting from huge differences in power and financial resources between corporations and de Bono's trusting "consumers" makes the asking and answering of questions about exploitation far more than a rhetorical parlor game. The operative concern is a little item called corporate influence. If consumers didn't like nuclear power plants so much, we wouldn't be spending billions of dollars to clean up the poisonous shit they dumped into our world, right? Point being, powerful corporate interests sold consumers on the wonders of having a plutonium breeder in their very own back yard. Speaking of poisonous shit, has the intellectual caliber of television *really* been degraded by commercial sponsors? We all pretty much know the answer to that one without having to launch another study. And while we're at it, are kids adversely affected by companies sponsoring school events? Many reasonable parents find the implications seriously upsetting. This doesn't make them cynics.

By whatever name they call it—social or cause marketing—corporations are allying themselves with social issues as a way to better position their products. And what they're up to isn't always crystal clear from a quick scan. For instance, Novartis has mounted several extensive "social marketing" campaigns targeting diseases such as leprosy and epilepsy in third-world countries. While such programs may deliver solid, dependable information, their overall credibility cannot help but be colored by the fact that Novartis is a

Global 500 pharmaceutical firm that makes drugs specifically indicated for these illnesses.

In *"A Short Course in Social Marketing,"* Novartis blurs the distinction between social and cause marketing when it says that in social marketing "demand has to be created for the idea or product concept, such as family planning, as well as for the tools or *product itself,* such as condoms."[23] (My italics.) The Ciba-Geigy Leprosy Fund described in the report hinges on drugs that are manufactured by Novartis. Is the company profiting from leprosy? Not a nice thought. As it turns out, Novartis has suspended commercial sale of these products, and has committed to donate them to the World Health Organization in sufficient quantities to cure everyone suffering from the disease. This obviously makes a huge difference in assessing the company's motivation. Because the tangible products are not for sale, it is legitimate to call this program social marketing. On the other hand, Novartis does sell its anti-epileptic product, which, as the company explains in "Social Marketing for Epilepsy," has been on the market for many years. "The commercial objectives are to expand the anti-epileptics market by closing the treatment gap and to maintain or increase the market share of Tegretol® in a growing market."[24]

Such ambiguities of intent have generated skepticism and even overt hostility. The December/January 2001 issue of *Ms.* magazine featured an article about cause-related marketing, noting that between 1990 and 1998 corporate investment in such programs leaped from $125 million to $545 million—an increase of over 400 percent. Unlike many glowing words written on the subject by participating companies and marketing consultants, this spike in cause marketing was not reported as cause for joy. "Doubts about the motives behind these campaigns are being raised by consumers, charities, and cause-related marketers themselves," the article says, sharply criticizing campaigns by Philip Morris, American Express, the Internet-based Hunger Site, and Benetton.[25]

The United Weirdness of Benetton

Ah, Benetton, certainly the most controversial practitioner of cause marketing. For a $2+ billion company selling clothing, fashion accessories and sporting goods, the company sure has some strange ideas—and an attitude that never quits. Of all the cause-related sources I looked at, only Kotler and Andreason mention the company at all, and then only to say that "Benetton produces shocking ads designed to energize consumers to care about AIDs."[26] Kotler also puts founder Luciano Benetton on his list of 30 "marketing visionaries."[27] However, most cause-marketing aficionados seem to want to distance themselves from Benetton's bad example. Personally, I find myself drawn to the company's approach—precisely because it's so outré. It looks a lot more authentic from where I'm sitting than the squeaky-clean go-team boosterism that characterizes so much of this kind of marketing.

Benetton's $15 million "We on Death Row" ad campaign ran full-page photographs of condemned U.S. felons along with the company logo. This brought howls of protest and several lawsuits. But the company held its ground. "When we talk about death row or AIDS or war or peace, it's not a contrived topic," said Mark Major, director of communications for Benetton USA. "It's definitely something that people at Benetton feel very strongly about. We don't apologize for the fact that dual purposes can be achieved. We can raise brand awareness that we are a company that cares about capital punishment and we can get people engaged in the topic."[28] The *Ms.* article charges that Benetton made no financial contribution to the fight against capital punishment, but fails to acknowledge how much this kind of publicity would normally cost. On the other hand, many felt it was negative publicity. Much to its credit, in my opinion, Benetton doesn't seem to give a damn. If brand meant what the *people* in a company actually believe in—beyond the sheer wonderfulness of the company's products—I might take the concept of branding more seriously. Typically, brand has nothing to do with what anyone believes, unless a belief means something you trick someone else into.

"Benetton likes to shock," writes *The Economist* in a burst of reserved British understatement. "The company has a history of running provocative advertising campaigns that seem quite unrelated to the buying of T-shirts and jeans."[29] These have included images of neon condoms, a war cemetery, horses copulating in a field, a very raw-looking newborn infant with umbilicus still attached, and dying AIDS patients. They are the work of Oliviero Toscani, acclaimed photographer and advertising *enfant terrible*. Both Toscani and

Benetton have been accused of ruthlessly exploiting social issues to enhance the company's appeal to the "youth market." But while their advertising has generated enormous outcry, I think these guys are not so easy to dismiss as blatant hucksters.

"We're more interested in discovering people than in selling them dreams," said company founder Luciano Benetton, who once posed nude to raise money for the homeless. "Here is the discovery of beauty without stereotypes; here is diversity highlighted by uniqueness."[30] Are such sentiments genuine, or do they simply represent a higher order of cynical market manipulation? To my own ear, Toscani comes across as pretty credible. In an interview on the *Salon* website, he says, "I hate to make advertising by saying that it goes to charity." And he brutally mocks companies that publicly pat themselves on the back for giving to the poor. "Oh, we're doing an eight-course charity dinner," he mimics in scathing parody of such self-congratulation. Then, "Fuck you!" he explodes. "I hope your eight-course dinner is poisoned!"[31]

This may be as close to genuine gonzo as an advertiser has ever come. If it's a staged posture intended to improve his company's positioning, the subterfuge sets a whole new standard in rhetorical sophistication. But it doesn't appear to be fake. "Media is just a bunch of bullshit," says Toscani. "Media is the real advertising. And they belong to big companies. There are some newspapers and TV companies that can't talk about certain things because they belong to General Electric or some big gas company."[32] This isn't the kind of talk you're real likely to overhear in a hallway at, oh say, American Express or AOL.

But is such an outspoken, against-the-grain approach to marketing viable? Can it last? *Business Week* reported that this style of advertising was over. "Now, though, Luciano [Benetton] says 'shock' images are a thing of the past."[33] That was obviously wrong, however. The article was written in 1995, and since then, Toscani's work for Benetton became even more outrageous.

In April 2000, Benetton and Toscani finally did part ways. Was the company displeased with the controversy he had created? It's impossible to know for certain, but the company explicitly thanked Toscani for his "fundamental contribution to a new advertising concept" that supported the company's "brand communication requirements." Toscani appeared to be undaunted. "Fortunately, nothing lasts forever," he said.[34] He is now creative director at *Talk* magazine, working with equally controversial editor Tina Brown, formerly of *The New Yorker*.[35] We'll see how long that lasts. The venture is backed by Miramax Films and Hearst.[36]

Meanwhile, even with Toscani gone, the madness continues at Benetton. Drawing on ten years of images that appeared in its magazine, *Colors*, the company has created an exhibition in the Leopolda train station in Florence. The press release called Colors Extra/Ordinary Objects "an anthropological report on our world." There's also a website, but of course. The first item there reads: "Fatherly love—More than 850 million Roman Catholics worldwide regard the Pope as the 'earthly representative of Jesus Christ.' They also believe that he's infallible when speaking on moral matters." Pictured alongside this entry is the Official Pope John Paul all-day lollipop. There is also a Pope John Paul II bottle opener. The text reads in part: "'Does the Pope use this opener?' we asked the Vatican Press Office. 'That is a ridiculous question,' they snapped and promptly hung up." Rounding out the Western religious paraphernalia category is this: "Nun bra—Nuns of the convent of St. Rita . . . shop for their underwear at religious underwear suppliers in Rome. St. Rita's nuns prefer the Cross Your Heart model from Playtex in beige. It's unlikely St. Rita herself was so well supported during her lifetime—she's the saint of desperate causes."

But it's not just all anti-clerical fun. Also included in the collection is a land mine, which the site calls "a favorite toy of generations of Afghan children. . . Children just love the bright green color and wings of the 'butterfly,' as it's nicknamed." The introduction to the show was written by rocker Peter Gabriel. Book by—who else?— Oliviero Toscani.[37]

This form of marketing begs many questions, and many are radically unsure of Benetton's motives—at least among those who haven't already decided they despise the company. To me, Benetton's brand of drive-by semiotics has more credibility than the safe, please-all-the-people-all-the-time approach of most cause marketing. Benetton positions itself by actually taking positions, even though its stance is liable to alienate as many customers as it attracts. Somehow, I don't get the impression of marketing committees behind these acts. Rather, I sense something quite rare and wonderful in the commercial world: intelligent, quirky human beings possessed of genuine character and a thoroughly gonzo sense of humor.

Segue: Social Capital and
The Common Good

Let's pull back a bit from the close-up view of how any one company connects with any particular social issue. If we look at the phenomenon in broader perspective, it becomes clear that cause marketing is part of a larger, deeper trend. "A big new idea is emerging in America," writes Harvard Business School's Rosabeth Moss Kanter. "Everywhere I look, businesses are discovering social values, and social purpose organizations are discovering business principles. And both are finding that they can create new benefits for their stakeholders by reaching out to the other."[38] Sounds terrific. In fact, we're exploring these matters in such depth because gonzo marketing sees similar potential in the intersection of community and commercial interests. For our purposes, these communities are indeed "social purpose organizations"—passionate, highly voiced websites and the new audiences coming together around them.

The Kanter quote is from a book titled *Common Interest, Common Good: Creating Value Through Business and Social Sector Partnerships,* which includes a chapter on cause-related marketing. However, common interests aside, business has often been perceived not as the friend, but as the enemy of the common good. While business obviously doesn't like this perception, it has become a lot harder to dodge as communications have become faster, more efficient and more global. It is no longer possible for companies to quietly clearcut ancient forests or to pollute a thousand miles of pristine coastline with impunity. People care, and people are talking—across previous cultural and geographic boundaries, across obsolete demographic sectors. Across the Internet. It is no longer possible to run a sweetly profitable sweatshop operation in Southeast Asia without having dozens of websites spring up including photos and firsthand interviews with exploited women and children workers.[39]

Companies that are charged with such offenses usually question the interpretation of the events on which they are supposedly based. Do such allegations, they ask, reflect objective reality? And then we're thrown back into the ontological soup and the endless morass of philosophy. Because the real question is, whose reality trumps whose? We'll soon return to the vexing issue of objectivity. For now let's agree that many corporations want to align themselves with the common good. It's just none too clear to whom this "common good" is common.

Related is the notion of the *commons*, "a tract of land, usually in a centrally located spot, belonging to or used by a community as a whole," says *The American Heritage Dictionary*. This has become extended to mean any place where people gather to converse about issues that affect their collective well-being. In 1968, an influential paper on this subject appeared: "The Tragedy of the Commons."[40] The central metaphor involves a common grazing area, large enough that each farmer can raise a single sheep on this communal tract. However, without enforcement of who does what, various farmers—thinking what the hell, more for me—begin to add two sheep, then three, and soon the commons becomes overgrazed and worthless to all. Bummer. Perhaps the modern commons is our collective attention. Every media outlet, advertiser and politician wants to put another sheep on our cognitive pasture. The attention we need to pay to public matters is thereby rapidly depleted. Whatever the cause, something has certainly made people—Americans anyway—pull back from public involvement.

Robert Putnam is one of the prime purveyors of the concept of social capital. In *Bowling Alone: The Collapse and Revival of American Community*, he argues that sociability has taken a steep downturn in American society. The title refers to significant attrition in previously popular social involvements, such as league bowling. He voluminously documents many other examples. The cost of this downturn in community engagement is a critical measure of the social cohesion necessary to maintain a healthy democracy. What is being lost is social capital. "The core idea of social capital theory," writes Putnam, "is that social networks have value . . . social contacts affect the productivity of individuals and groups." He defines social capital as "connections among individuals—social networks and the norms of reciprocity and trustworthiness that arise from them."[41] While individuals gain from these networks, so does the larger community in which they are embedded—the public sphere. "Social capital can thus be simultaneously a 'private good' and a 'public good,'" Putnam says. "Some of the benefit from an investment in social capital goes to bystanders, while some of the benefit redounds to the immediate interest of the person making the investment."

But what precisely is this benefit? What accrues to the public good? Simple. "A society characterized by generalized reciprocity is more efficient than a distrustful society," says Putnam. "Trustworthiness lubricates social life."

Business Week criticized what it took to be the pessimism of *Bowling Alone*. "The Internet is creating new networks and communities," wrote By Farrell. "Putnam ends up documenting the decline of a particular type of social capital tied to an industrial economy—even as more heterogeneous, eclectic forms of social capital emerge in the Information Age."[42] However, Putnam makes much the same point:

> Community, communion, and communication are intimately as well as etymologically related. Communication is a fundamental prerequisite for social and emotional connections. Telecommunications in general and the Internet in particular substantially enhance our ability to communicate; thus it seems reasonable to assume that their net effect will be to enhance communication, perhaps even dramatically. Social capital is about networks, and the net is the network to end all networks.[43]

The Internet is the most powerful means we have today for building social cohesion, yet it is being used by business without regard for the larger interests of society. Gonzo marketing involves a more integrated approach, whereby corporations and markets can genuinely collaborate in the creation of social capital.

In *Knowledge and Social Capital*, Eric Lesser extends the concept of social capital into the workings of business organizations.[44] While many companies are beginning to see the advantages, they generally want to leverage, own and manage these benefits for themselves. This could be a showstopper with something called *social* capital, unless you believe that the organization constitutes a society unto itself. It's true that social networks exist within companies, and that understanding how they operate is valuable to the organization. But companies exist within a social context larger than themselves, and while they may greatly influence and shape this context, they do not control it. Lesser's book has much to say about reciprocity as it affects organizational dynamics, but includes little discussion of reciprocity between the organization and the wider community—a.k.a. the market. It is mysterious behavior, yet entirely typical of business-as-usual, to exclude the market as an integral part of the organization's social network, context and reason for existing. This should come as no real surprise, however, as Lesser is (and I quote) "an Executive Consultant with the IBM Institute for Knowledge Management and a member of IBM's Global Knowledge Management and Solutions Practice." But maybe that's just me. When I hear the word *"solutions,"* I reach for my revolver.

Having thus savaged the guy, let me praise his other book, *Knowledge and Communities.*[45] This collection reprints the brilliant paper by John Seely Brown and Paul Duguid on "Organizational Learning and Communities of Practice."[46] This was the foundation for the authors' critically acclaimed 2000 book *The Social Life of Information.*[47] There's that word again: *social.* It sure is getting popular in business circles these days. Had you noticed? If not, notice.

But business tends to talk about communities of practice the same way it talks about social capital: in terms of the internal workings of the organization, and not so much in terms of interaction with the marketplace. This is odd, since customers often have more collective knowledge about a company's products or services than the company itself. Networked communities of practice—and of plain old garden-variety *interest*—are certainly crucial. But to be genuinely useful to a corporation, they must extend beyond the corporate borders and include a much larger external audience—present and potential markets.

Gonzo marketing is a way for companies to create genuine relationships with external web-based markets. One important difference from traditional marketing—and a crucial prerequisite for success—is that the company will not *own* or *manage* the knowledge developed in these communities. It will be outside the corporate sphere of influence—at least where influence is construed to mean control.

Such border jumping has an interesting precedent. *"Benchmarking"*—the search for best practices—not only cuts across internal functional boundaries, it also gets people talking across companies, or even across entirely different industries. But there's always a trade-off in such exchanges, especially where direct competitors are involved. How much do you share relative to the knowledge advantage you expect to receive in return? If you keep the kimono closed, you get nothing. If you open it too far, you could lose it all. In fact, the whole tit-for-tat best practices gambit is based on paranoia symptomatic of closed systems knowing that they must become open systems or die, but kicking and screaming a lot in the process. Under such trying conditions—i.e., constant kimono checking—best practices become dysfunctional. It takes so long to reach consensus about anything important, that the results are either trivial or patently wrong.

Nonetheless, given the internetworking of markets, opening up closed systems has become more critical than ever—getting outside the box, outside the beltway, outside the insular frame of mind that has kept the audience "safely" removed from business decisions about strategy and tactics. The same pressures apply to the media business, though—being a very different sort of business—they apply in a different way.

The Case and Cause of
Public Journalism

The aims of social marketing are in many ways congruent with those of public journalism, a ten-year-old movement started by journalists who feel that reporting is too top-down, too much shaped by national polls, veiled political agendas and corporate press releases. They have sought to become more engaged in local civic concerns and tend to take positions on issues rather than pretend to a remote and questionable "objectivity." Recall here Hunter Thompson's definition of gonzo as engagement. We'll soon be hearing more from him and others on how such engagement—and the engagement called for by public journalism—is impossible under traditional media standards of objectivity.

Public journalism could be seen as a form of cause marketing, where the cause is democracy and the associated product is the local paper. Trying to resurrect democracy within the context of a media business's profit mandate is a tricky proposition. Trickier still, the ills that public journalism seeks to cure are not merely tactical mistakes, but inherent qualities of mass media. It does little good to ameliorate symptoms without acknowledging the disease that causes them. However, the goals of public journalism are laudable, even if they seem Quixotic in the context of conventional media. Jay Rosen chronicles the ups and downs of the movement in *What Are Journalists For?* On Amazon, he posted an overview, from which the following is excerpted.

> Countering spin, hype and entertainment with real news of public import is tougher than ever, especially when the company that owns your operation pushes it onto a more commercial grid. . . . What happens in the public arena still matters to people, even if a game show does better in the ratings. . . . journalists need democracy if their work is to make a difference. But were they doing enough to make democracy work? And what could they do differently? We can reduce some of our engrained [sic] cynicism, they answered, because it distorts our outlook, and the audience can sense it. We can try to provide a better forum for discussion, and connect the talk there to problems in real life. We can lend our reporting talent not only to problems, but to possible solutions where they might exist. Going further, we can attempt to engage people in civic life, and give them more help when they take that step. At times, we can be a convener or catalyst in local communities just as we are, at times, a watchdog and critic. And we can do all this without abandoning our role as truthteller and information source.[48]

The New York Times review charges that public journalism's "most ardent supporters have taken on the trappings of evangelists." Note that evangelists is used here as a code word. The implications are not good, as Real Journalists are supposed to be "unbiased," which means they would never dream of evangelizing. Too engaged. Too *involved.* "Its detractors have denounced it as a fad, a gimmick, a commercial ploy or an idea that was not new at all," the review continues. Then interestingly, the paper invokes its own views. How much more unbiased can you get? "Influential journalists from *The New York Times* have been more scathing. In a signed Editorial Notebook article, Howell Raines, *The Times*'s editorial page editor, said James Fallows's much-discussed 1996 book, *Breaking the News*, posed an 'insidious danger, and that is that reporters and editors become public policy missionaries with a puritanical contempt for horse-race politics.'"[49]

Much of this debate centers on the slippery concept of "objectivity." What Fallows actually said, among many other juicy provocations, was this: "One of public journalism's basic claims is that journalists should stop kidding themselves about their ability to remain detached from and objective about public life. . . . They inescapably change the reality of whatever they are observing by whether and how they chose to write about it."[50] He's surely going to hell for that one. Imagine the nerve. Disrupting the profound majesty of those scintillating horse races.

From the perspective of the Internet, which—in case you've somehow missed it—is my perspective in this book, this debate is absurd. We don't need press credentials to have a point of view, and in expressing such views we don't pretend to be omniscient or impartial. For better or worse, we call em like we see em. But the debate is extremely serious from the perspective of conventional media, which either a) have not grasped the true significance of the net, or b) having grasped it just fine, are terrified by the implications. All of which could be ignored as insignificant inside-the-metaphorical-media-beltway navel-gazing except for one critical fact: old media is where business gets its news about new media. The irony here is that, in defending its high standards of objectivity, traditional media have betrayed a bias that is tantamount to a news blackout. The real Internet—the net as it is, as it actually operates—doesn't fit traditional models of media *or* business. Ergo, that Internet doesn't exist. The media has created an image of the net that appeals to business and what business already knows—which is television. But this view is a complete fiction. When the net fails to "live up" to this projection, it is judged anarchic, wild, untamable—or simply a failure. Things were simpler in the old days. All you had to do was shoot all the buffalo and the Indians.

Nearly all the controversy surrounding public journalism has come from the establishment press, which has lobbed charges of "advocacy journalism." For traditionalists, expressing a point of view breaks the first commandment of reporting: thou shalt remain impartial. These complaints would have greater moral weight if many of the mass media publications from which they come were not themselves open to charges of corporate and government influence. The principle of "Church and State," which is supposed to insulate news reporting and editorial opinion from the potential sway of advertising dollars, is often honored more in the breach than the observance. Because such bias is hidden and benefits the highest bidder, it is far more pernicious than journalists actively engaging in civic debates whose outcome they honestly care about.

The most biased and unbalanced claim the mainstream press ever made is that it is objective. Is there anyone stupid enough to believe that what is presented is "the facts and nothing but the facts," or even "all the news that's fit to print"? The press itself certainly doesn't have any illusions about the illusions it projects. Yet it wants us to take them as an undistorted reflection of "reality." This represents either towering arrogance or a degree of uncritical ignorance that should disqualify the media from reporting on anything more complex than Johnny's birthday party.

Writing about the role of the press as defender of the republic, Rosen writes

> the litany of government lying during Vietnam, the showdown with the White House over the Pentagon Papers, and the triumph of the *Washington Post* during Watergate convinced a generation of journalists that official authority was not to be trusted. From there it was a short step to concluding that their own authority rested on rituals of mistrust. Any criticism of those rituals could be seen as a demand to "soften" the news, a deadly epithet, for to go soft was to lose your commitment to truth and thus all your credentials.[51]

And, Rosen adds, "This was not an irrational fear." The pressure on journalists to keep things crisp and snappy and not too intellectually challenging came from many quarters, notably, strong competition from *USA Today* and concurrent demands from the business side to staunch the bleeding that newspapers were experiencing as a result of dwindling subscriptions. In an interview discussing his book, *Deadlines & Datelines: Essays at the Turn of the Century*, Dan Rather says this. Can you see him making the air-quotation-marks? Sort of like air-guitar, but with just two fingers.

> I think the audience says, "Well, listen, the evening news has sort of gone into," quote, "News Lite," as some evening news broadcasts have. I consider it part of my job to keep the *CBS Evening News* hard news, as hard as we possibly can, but I wouldn't kid anybody that there are great pressures to make it more entertainment, quote, "soften it up" because the belief runs strong if you do that, you attract a larger audience.[52]

A larger audience equals a mass market—and the "editorial content" is only advertising bait. Howard Kurtz, press critic for the *Washington Post*, is considerably more forthcoming. In *Media Circus: The Trouble with America's Newspapers*, he tells this delightful little story.

> "Look at the front page," Mike Barnicle says. "More often than not it's full of what I call made-up stories, ideas they cook up at these cluster-fuck meetings: 'Go out and do left-handed teenagers who are thinking of becoming gay.' They do trends, they don't do news. There's a burnt fuse, a lack of connection between people in the business and a large number of people who read newspapers."
>
> Our efforts to repair this burnt fuse are rather awkward. We hire teenagers to review movies for other teens and pretend that we've plugged into the youth culture. We assign reporters to cover shopping malls. We ballyhoo the local football team on the front page. We serve up modest portions of News Lite, congratulating ourselves for not overtaxing the poor reader.[53]

Media critic Jon Katz, discussing his book *Virtuous Reality* on *Booknotes*, says that if Thomas Paine were alive today, he'd be writing on the Internet. "He couldn't get a job at any newspaper in America," observes Katz. "He certainly did not believe in objectivity and he was far too outspoken and independent-minded to work in a news-room. And he would not have liked corporate media in the least." He speculates that if Paine had followed the dictates of objective jour-nalism, *Common Sense* would have begun "A spokesperson for the British says the colonies should remain attached, and a spokesperson for the colonists says it shouldn't." And the American Revolution would still be the subject of the world's longest filibuster.[54]

In *Custodians of Conscience: Investigative Journalism and Private Virtue* the authors open a chapter called "The Paradox of the Dis-engaged Conscience," as follows:

> If investigative reporting is American journalism at its most rigorous, it is also American journalism at its most paradoxical. The essential energy of investigative reporting is still best characterized as "right-eous indignation," a term coined by Ida Tarbell a century ago as the anthem of the muckrakers. . . But this unmistakable tone of moral engagement stands in apparent opposition to the presumed objec-tivity of news. How can journalists function as the custodians of conscience and at the same time claim to be mere observers of fact? That is, how can they expose wrongdoing without making moral judgments?[55]

The reprehensible advocacy public journalism is accused of, in fact, takes its place in a long tradition of investigative reporting. If engagement and advocacy are perceived as impediments to the media, then something is inherently wrong with the media, not with the basic human inclination to engage and advocate. Trying to sup-press these inclinations artificially for the sake of some elusive no-tion of balance is not only futile but psychologically dysfunctional. People care. They are not simply cameras passively recording ran-dom events with no emotional valence. The pretense of such "ob-jectivity" not only damages the pretender, but also deeply unravels the social fabric (or capital, if you prefer) of the society that depends on observant, informed, articulate and *engaged* reporters to better understand and appreciate itself.

But the truth is that "objectivity" is a McGuffin here, a diversion-ary tactic. The real objective is to gather the largest possible audience for advertisers. The pretense of detachment is merely camou-flage for media whose prime directive is to serve the mass market-ing requirements of business.[56]

Tom Wolfe's 1973 book, *The New Journalism*,[57] took the impulse to engage a step further than social muckraking. Journalists are re-ally frustrated novelists, said Wolfe, and what they really want to do is what novelists do: make stuff up. One branch of this genre turns into literary journalism, which claims such practitioners as Tracy Kidder *(Soul of a New Machine, House)*, Joan Didion *(The White Album, Miami)*, John McPhee *(The Curve of Binding Energy, Annals of the Former World)* and Wolfe himself *(The Electric Kool-Aid Acid Test, Bonfire of the Vanities)*.[58] These authors brought to the report-ing of fact an attention to detail and a style of writing more gener-ally associated with fiction. Another, smaller and much stranger branch turns into gonzo journalism and claims one king-hell king-pin, Hunter S. Thompson *(Fear and Loathing in Las Vegas, Gener-ation of Swine)*.

"The 'new journalism' attracted attention," writes Jack Fuller in *News Values*, "especially when it ran in newspapers or was written by people whose names were identified with newspapers, by its fundamental violation of the old traditions of the craft, beginning with the tradition of colorlessness of expression."[59] Thompson is colorful all right. In this mode of writing, it would be unusual to read about the Justice Department deciding to break up Microsoft. Instead, you might get a detailed description of how giant vampire bats ate Bill Gates' brain. And what it tasted like. Thompson not only used novelistic techniques, he made real events seem stranger than fiction. Which, as we all know, they often are. And he's still doing it. In a recent screed on *ESPN*, he wrote about the night of the 2000 U.S. national election. On hearing that CNN had awarded Florida to Gore, he says "My own immediate reaction was baffle-ment and surprise. . . I was troubled by waves of Queasiness & shudders of Gnawing Doubt. I felt nervous & vaguely confused, as if I had just heard a dog speak perfect English . . . That will get your attention, for sure."[60] Thompson gets people's attention. For sure. And ESPN knows it. In another column there he writes about the Oakland Raiders football team, bemoaning their currently kinder, gentler ways. "The Raiders of yore had no mercy on anything they could get their hands on," he says. "They strangled cops and ate their own babies." It must be true. I read it on the web. Yeah, it's a little weird, but that's OK by me—and a few million others. It sure beats reading marginally rewritten press releases and the Sunday *Parade* supplement.

David Mindich opens *Just the Facts: How "Objectivity" Came to Define American Journalism* by stating that "if American journalism were a religion. . . it's supreme deity would be 'objectivity.'" No other book explores this article of faith in such historical depth. Calling the phenomenon naïve empiricism, Mindich writes: "It is no less than remarkable that years after consciousness was complicated by Freud, observation was problematized by Einstein, perspective was challenged by Picasso, writing was deconstructed by Derrida, and 'objectivity' was abandoned by practically everyone outside newsrooms, 'objectivity' is still the style of journalism that our newspaper articles and broadcast reports are written in, or against." Most relevant to our purpose here, the book—which mostly focuses on the 19th century—concludes by talking about the Internet. ". . . [A]n explosion in new media has again threatened the elite, 'objective' journalists. With so many storytellers (each of the thousands of homepages, for example, is a separate news source), and with so many departing from the 'information model' of 'objective' news, journalists are called on once again to define themselves."[61] It is no surprise, Mindich says, that the issue of objectivity should arise at this critical juncture. What is a surprise are the very real alternatives the web presents to getting past the current denial about the function of journalism. Telling stories that make sense of the world is something human beings have always done, and will continue to—not within the confines of a conflicted media industry, but within the context of a diverse and vibrant global culture.

Shallow Babble and the Shock of Recognition

In a review of Rosen's *What Are Journalists For?*, *The American Prospect* notes that public journalism continues a much earlier debate between the journalist Walter Lippmann and the philosopher

John Dewey. "Lippmann had questioned the ability of ordinary citizens to be objective enough to exercise their democratic responsibilities," writes the reviewer, while "Dewey had more faith in their collective judgment and insisted that democracy can't be left to the elites."[62] Uh-huh. And in support of public journalism's position, Rosen also quotes from *The Structural Transformation of the Public Sphere* by Jürgen Habermas. It is no accident that Habermas would later go on to write *The Legitimation Crisis*, attempting to read which book made my head hurt.[63] However, from an intensive five-minute scan, I can summarize its findings as follows: "Says who?" This basic uncertainty at the heart of our culture was explored in depth by continental thinkers such as Jacques Derrida and Michel Foucault and the fundamental query was expanded into a larger challenge to the entire Western intellectual tradition: "You and what army?"

Steve Martin liked to say that he studied just enough philosophy in college to fuck him up for the rest of his life. We can all sympathize, I'm sure. But look, it's really simpler than all that. Leaving out certain American politicians, most of us have gotten past the notion of the divine right of kings. That was once the font from which legitimacy issued. We got past it with the alternative—if admittedly radical—notion of democracy. But there are holdouts and throwbacks hidden in plain sight today. One of them is "objectivity," of which some purport to have more than others. If this means being fair and balanced and trying to understand complex debates by taking both sides fully into account, then cool. But it often means something that's at the same time a lot larger and a lot less explicit—that some group has privileged access to The Truth, and you're not part of it. Hey, don't you know anything? Read your newspaper!

The Internet and the web have quietly but inexorably undermined our willingness to cop to this implied elitism. Why write a letter to the editor when you can start your own web site? If it's good, you could get more traffic than the paper has subscribers. Love him or hate him, Matt Drudge did exactly that. But is news on the web dependable? Is it true, is it *trustworthy?* Is it legitimate, the way the "legitimate press" is supposed to be legitimate?

Jay T. Harris is chairman and publisher of the *San Jose Mercury News*. In April 2000, he delivered the keynote address to the 36th annual Scripps dinner at the Reynolds School of Journalism and Center for Advanced Media Studies. That certainly has an insider ring to it, eh? But just wait. In his talk, "New Media in the New Millennium," Harris warned that since the Internet enables almost anyone to publish whatever they please, readers will have a hard time telling the difference between the output of bona fide journalists and the ravings of "plain old crackpots." Personally, I think the latter will be pretty easy to spot, as they're generally a lot funnier. Brilliantly clarifying the distinction between net-based communications and journalism—they "are not the same thing," he said. "More often than not, they are different."—Harris further explained that journalism is "a profession committed to informing the public about public issues and significant events," which mission is to be carefully distinguished from the "the shallow babble of the masses."[64] After all, without the special secret decoder rings issued to Official and Authorized members of the Legitimate Press, how could shallow babblers like ourselves possibly determine the deep significance of historic public figures such as O.J. Simpson, Princess Di, and "Little Elián Gonzalez"?

Journalism is a noble profession and my intent is not to vilify its practitioners. Why, some of my best friends are journalists! (And of course, book reviewers are not included in this critique.) However, the notion that journalism brings to the reporting of events a magical "objectivity" that is somehow sacrosanct or received from a higher authority is clearly crap. Nonetheless, the net has come in for plenty of abuse from such defenders of the purportedly privileged relationship the press has with its various audiences. More various than it cares to admit. *The San Jose Merc*'s Jay T. Harris is hardly an isolated example; there are plenty like him. First, such guardians of the public good ignored the Internet. Then they got seriously spooked by the attrition of their readerships to online alternatives. Then they pandered to "the New Media," and pontificated about its impact as if they'd actually spent time on the web, which most clearly had not. Much of the mainstream media reaction to net journalism has been either violently negative or pedantically patronizing.

The news media have been on the defensive for a lot longer than the net has been around, and it has often made of the net a convenient whipping boy for what public journalism's Jay Rosen calls "the troubles in the press." Cataloguing its problems in detail would be an exhaustive undertaking, which, fortunately for us, has already been undertaken by others. A brief scan of the titles of a handful of books on the subject tells a tale that can't credibly be pinned on the Internet: *Uncertain Guardians: The News Media as a Political Institution*; *Unreliable Sources: A Guide to Detecting Bias in News Media*; *Rich Media, Poor Democracy: Communication Politics in Dubious Times*; *Republic of Denial: Press, Politics and Public Life*; *When MBAs Rule the Newsroom*; *The Control Room: How Television Calls the Shots in Presidential Elections*; *Media Circus: The Trouble with America's Newspapers*; and a book by James Fallows that *really* pissed off a lot of publishers, *Breaking the News: How the Media Undermine American Democracy*.[65] The list could go on. And does. But we should trust established media and distrust voices from the net. Maybe I need to have this explained to me again. I don't get it.

In many respects, the press has itself to thank for the outpouring of public discourse on the Internet. People came to the net in droves (a drove representing roughly ten million souls) and responded with enormous enthusiasm to anything *different* from the bland and boring fare they'd been force fed for so long by broadcast journalism. Who created this audience? In many ways, mainstream media did. As Frank Zappa once remarked (at rather high volume), "Do you love it? Do you hate it? There it is the way you made it." This was on the album *Absolutely Free*. And freedom is the issue here. Not as in the problem, but as in the result. We may not be able to say with much certainty what the ultimate "objective" truth about the world is, but on the Internet we've given ourselves and each other an increasing measure of liberty to say what it feels like to be living in whatever version of this world we can manage— the freedom, in fact, to say whatever comes into our heads. Inevitably, this horrifies the self-appointed arbiters of taste and the elite interpreters of what is good and real. So what? Freedom is *not* just another word for nothing left to lose. Freedom is wild in the litany of senses Gary Snyder enumerated, one of which was "far out," if you recall.[66] The web is not a definitive history or a map of the stable reality so many seem to long for. The web is a non-stop planet-spanning celebration. And we ain't goin' back in the box.

The box being "objectivity," of course, which implies accepting the idea that someone else, someone "well placed," some "credible informant," some unnamed and faceless source close to the president (whether of the country or the corporation), will speak to us, channeled through some official interpreter, and tell us how it is. Hey, don't you know anything? Turn on your radio and listen to the rap that Tipper Gore and her ilk have taken such pains to label offensive—and that will get more offensive the more it's so labeled. Turn on your web browser and your email client and your MP3 player. Listen. *There's* the news that didn't fit. *That's* the way it is, Walter. And it ain't goin' back in the box. Baby.

Democracy would be a lot easier to buy if it weren't for the free speech addendum. And democracy is still a highly tentative experiment. There are plenty who feel we'd be better off if we had just the true stuff. The real stuff. The official version. Then everyone would know what was going on. Only problem is, this is called fascism. If not for the Internet, we might already be there. But even before the net—yes, kids, it's true, this stuff goes way back—there were people who didn't give a flying fuck about the official version. Artists, they're sometimes called.

Seen in historical context, gonzo journalism continues a long tradition of highly unofficial chroniclers, writers whose take on the world offended popes and kings and even commoners, their tastes attenuated to a hot-house frailty that suited the refined and elevated sensibilities of their betters. Take another look at literature. At the nasty bits of Ovid, Chaucer and Boccaccio, Rabelais. At Cervantes, Voltaire and Jonathan Swift, Lewis Carroll, Charles Dickens. At Thomas Paine and Thomas Jefferson. At Upton Sinclair and Sinclair Lewis. At Pasternak, Solzhenitsyn, Nelson Mandela. At John Steinbeck, Henry Miller, Kurt Vonnegut, Salman Rushdie. All these authors were censored or suppressed at one time. And that's the short list. While *The Canterbury Tales* were first published at the end of the 14th century, none of this is ancient history. Chaucer was challenged in a 1988 court case in Florida, the initial complaint citing sexual references, vulgarity and "the promotion of women's lib."

More specifically, the plaintiff objected to the use of the words *"ass"* and "fart" in The Miller's Tale.[67] Today, one suspects this individual has probably not availed his family of the rich resources the Internet provides. The Alta Vista search engine returns 76,095 hits for the query term "fart." Google returns 173,000. See, for instance—offered in the spirit of social commentary on such censorship—the interactive audio permutations on this theme at www.createafart.com.

While gonzo journalism is in good company with respect to its disrespect for normative social strictures, it cares deeply about the "objectivity" debate. In his acid-tongued (and -headed) obituary for Richard Nixon, Hunter Thompson says Nixon's casket should have been "launched into one of those open-sewage canals that empty into the ocean just south of Los Angeles" and that "his body should have been burned in a trash bin." It seems fair to say that Thompson was not terribly fond of this particular president, calling him many vile and terrible names.

> Some people will say that words like *scum* and *rotten* are wrong for Objective Journalism—which is true, but they miss the point. It was the built-in blind spots of the Objective rules and dogma that allowed Nixon to slither into the White House in the first place. He looked so good on paper that you could almost vote for him sight unseen. He seemed so all-American, so much like Horatio Alger, that he was able to slip through the cracks of Objective Journalism. You had to get Subjective to see Nixon clearly, and the shock of recognition was often painful.[68]

Politics aside, the gonzo turn was a crucially important response to the notion that, to be "legitimate," journalism had to be distanced from personal perspective, that it had to be cool, impartial and detached. That it had to be everything, in other words, that the net is not.

Getting Subjective

While worlds apart in many respects, social marketing and public journalism share a desire to get closer to audiences than was possible with mass media broadcast techniques. They also raise deep issues of motivation and credibility. Who is seeking to engage our attention, and why? Who can we believe? Both also deal with relevance and interest as determined by audiences themselves, bottom-up, rather than being predetermined top-down by publishers and media conglomerates. Public journalists ask their readerships what issues are important to *them*, irrespective of Gallup and CNN polls. Social marketers speak of participatory communication in which the values and beliefs of the audience are considered from the outset.

The corporate appetite for cause marketing runs headlong into the law of diminishing returns. Companies use a mass marketing metric in determining the appeal of such causes. AIDS is good, for instance. Lots of upscale youth market pull. Arthritis, on the other hand, is far less sexy. Though many more people may feel its effects, a) it is not fatal—critical to establishing deep empathy—and b) it does not target the bloated belly-of-the-bell-curve demographic that broadcast aims to reach. As more companies graze their products on the pastures of our civic concern, that concern is proportionally diminished. The tragedy of the commons is inevitably repeated when our attention to the public sphere is attenuated by too many profit-driven appeals to the common good.

The gonzo approach of a Thompson or a Toscani strikes me as much more intrinsically interesting than the earnest exhortations of the public journalists, even though their intent can easily be made to look more thoughtful and serious. I mean, who's going to dis democracy? But the paradox is that by taking on the role of guardian of democracy, public journalism risks a higher-order public paternalism. And in this it looks not a lot different from the attitudes of mainstream media. The charge of "advocacy" has never carried more weight than it does in the following gonzo critique by America's foremost sociologist and culture critic. I'm referring of course to Dave Barry. In his first work of fiction, *Big Trouble*—called out on the cover as "an actual novel by Dave Barry"—he describes the frustration of a journalist whose newspaper management wants him to write articles that, he believes in his heart, nobody wants to read:

> They preferred issues stories, which were dense wads of facts, written by committees, running in five or six parts under some title

that usually had the word "crisis" in it, like "Families in Crisis," "Crisis in Our Schools," "The Coming Water Crisis," et cetera. These series, which were heavily promoted and often won journalism contests, were commonly referred to in the newsroom as "megaturds." But the honchos loved them. Advocacy journalism, it was called. It was the hot trend in the newspaper business. Making a difference! Connecting with the readers![69]

Barry's character resolves this plot conflict by putting his foot through his managing editor's computer screen. The author comments laconically: "He'd burned a bridge there." Perhaps relevant to our current cogitations, the guy ends up doing advertising and PR.

Noam Chomsky is a very different sort of thinker. Unlike Dave Barry, very few have ever accused him of being funny. But while humor is a powerful weapon, there are more serious charges to be laid at the door of the press than its inability to entertain. In *Manufacturing Consent: The Political Economy of the Mass Media*, authors Herman and Chomsky write:

> . . . the democratic postulate is that the media are independent and committed to discovering and reporting the truth, and that they do not merely reflect the world as powerful groups wish it to be perceived. Leaders of the media claim that their news choices rest on unbiased professional and objective criteria. . . . If, however, the powerful are able to fix the premises of discourse, to decide what the general populace is allowed to see, hear, and think about, and to "manage" public opinion by regular propaganda campaigns, the standard view of how the system works is at serious odds with reality.[70]

This is also a reality that public journalism sidesteps no less than the traditional press. Public journalism is nothing more than a naïvely optimistic band-aid if it assumes that its audience-driven agenda will not run into headlong conflict with the powerful corporate interests that own or control an overwhelming share of conventional (i.e., non-Internet) media. And this is not an oh-by-the-way observation. It represents a crucial and defining factor in the options that will be available—or not—to any form of future journalism. We should care about this, as one of those options involves the continuance or termination of a free and open society.

The challenges faced by social marketing and public journalism stem largely from the institutional dimension of both: the institution of corporate advertising, the institution of the press as it is currently constituted. If the attempt to hew to these old models is removed from the equation, many "problems" of credibility and objectivity disappear. Much hand wringing about these matters represents a last-ditch effort to preserve Big-A Advertising or Big-J Journalism at all costs.

But Internet audiences don't care about saving these institutions. They may care a lot about preserving "a free press." But that concern doesn't map to GE, Viacom, Disney, Bertelsmann, Time Warner/AOL or News Corp—the six companies that basically own global media today.[71] Net audiences want information that's relevant, credible and engaging. If those criteria are met—contrary to the esoteric brand cabalism of mass media empires—they don't much care where it comes from. Given that many web sites are overt acts of passionate advocacy journalism, companies need to find a way to underwrite the best of breed without expecting to own them, control them or otherwise influence their independent editorial perspective. And there is a way—surprisingly simple and sane—for companies to do just that. We'll soon be exploring this alternative: the gonzo model.

This is not to say I don't care about the quality of journalism or the press as it exists today. I value the press. I hope it gets better. And it will—to compete with thousands of new voices percolating up from the nether regions of the net. If it can't compete, whether for economic or journalistic reasons, I don't think any amount of civic concern will bail it out. I'd join in thinking such an eventuality was tragic if I didn't believe that at least some of the new voices coming from the bottom up won't be as good as anything we've seen from journalism so far. And they won't need "the media" as it exists today in order to survive.

At the end of his book, *Deciding What's News: A Case Study of CBS Evening News, NBC Nightly News, Newsweek and Time*, sociologist Herbert Gans proposed something he called "multiperspectival news."[72] It would be bottom-up, he said, not top-down like traditional broadcast media. "For example," he wrote, news about Federal (and corporate) policies would "be accompanied by reactions not just from high officials, but from citizens in various walks of life who would be affected by these policies." This sounds very much like the agenda of public journalism, though Gans was writing in 1979, at least a decade before that initiative began. Multiperspectival news would also include what Gans calls "subcultural programming," content created to satisfy a broad and heterogeneous array of "taste cultures"—audiences having distinct shared aesthetic values and standards. Unfortunately, this increased coverage would also require many more delivery channels than existed at the beginning of the '80s, so it seemed wildly impractical.[73]

Who knew then that the web was on the way?

CHAPTER 6

From Micromedia to Micromarkets

*"The prevalence of mass marketing has obscured the fact that for
centuries consumers were served as individuals."*

—ARMSTRONG AND KOTLER, *MARKETING: AN INTRODUCTION*[1]

OVER THE LAST SEVERAL DECADES, NEWS, INFORMATION AND ENTERTAINMENT
have come to be controlled by a rapidly conglomerating collection
of corporate media empires. When Ben Bagdikian wrote *The Media
Monopoly* in 1983, 50 firms dominated U.S. media. By the second
edition, the number had shrunk to 29; by the third, 23; by the
fourth, 14; by the fifth, 10. The sixth edition, published in 2000, lists
only six companies that together control the vast majority of journalism that Americans see and hear—news and information that
also colors and shapes, if not defines, what the rest of the world believes about itself. The Big Six are General Electric, Viacom, Disney,
Bertelsmann, Time Warner/AOL and Rupert Murdoch's News Corporation.[2]

At the end of January 2001, the Walt Disney Company announced
it was deep-sixing its Internet portal site, Go.com. Where were *you*
when the news came? I'm sure we all shed a silent tear. *The New
York Times* quoted Disney CEO Michael Eisner as saying the company would "refocus its efforts on the web sites related to its broad-

cast and entertainment brands." Disney decided on the move because "the advertising community has lost faith in the Internet and
specifically in portals," according to Eisner, who reported that the
future of the Internet is—now here's a surprise—"interactive television and pay-per-view."[3]

This story is a classic. We got brands, we got broadcast, we got
tee-vee. Who was it said, "What else *is* there?" We even got lost faith
and redemption. You gotta love the way these guys talk. But listen,
can we, like, refocus our efforts on reality for just a second? Complaining that the Internet fails as a mass medium for broadcast advertising is like being disappointed that a BMW makes a lousy trac-
tor. "That's right, Farmer Bill, the damn thing keeps getting stuck
between the furrows. Hell, Ol' Bessie never useta get stuck!"

Motley Fool noted a number of factors working against Go.com,
not least of which was "the questionable idea of creating an umbrella site for an in-house family of brands, no matter how individually strong those brands may be." The article mentions that, rely-
ing on essentially the same strategy, "Time Warner's Pathfinder, a
pioneering online newsstand for Time Inc. magazines, had already
been through several failed incarnations by the time plans for
Go.com were being hatched."[4] Being kinder than I, the author does
not emphasize the obvious: that *it's not like those failures were exactly a big secret at the time.* Why is it that we all remember the bit
about the pain in the dinosaur's tail taking so long to get to the dinosaur's brain? It must be one of them Jungian archetype things.

The truth is, the net takes to advertising the way fish take to bi-
cycles. Search engines—a de-buzzed synonym for *"portals"*—are a
great idea, sure. People use them all the time, which is why they always rank highest in the Whopper Site Sweepstakes, the mine-is-
bigger-than-yours measurements of who's going where most. In
every respect that counts—and there's really only one: where deep-
pocket advertisers will plunk down their media-buy megabucks—
these metrics are indistinguishable from Nielsen ratings as applied
to TV sitcoms. While considerably less amusing, the portals are a lot
more efficient in delivering audience stats. And who doesn't love a
pie chart?

"According to Media Metrix (December 2000), Walt Disney Internet Group's combined web sites collectively represent the eighth

largest web property, attracting more than 20 million unique visitors representing 25% of the web universe per month."[5]

That's massive. But not massive enough for true King-of-the-Hill mass media players. Michael Wolff, duly infamous author of *Burn Rate*, writes about Eisner in *New York Magazine*, saying there are really two Eisners, one good, one bad. "The good Michael is the no-Hollywood-jive, drooping-sock Michael, the faithful-to-his-wife Michael, the decent, goofy, puppy-dog Michael. The Michael played by Tom Hanks." That doesn't sound so good to me, actually, but then Wolff has never been much noted for sucking up. It gets worse, of course. "And then there's the bad Michael: controlling, vindictive, dissembling Michael. The avaricious Disney-is-too-small-and-no-company-is-too-big-for-Michael-Eisner Michael."[6]

This is not just a passing observation. The operative concern here is scale, as in "economies of." We are observing a game of monster-media hubris that would make Caligula blush, played out by titanic egos risking everything—going for broke as if the world were coming to an end. And it is. Their world anyway. Accompanying its story on Disney's no-Go, *The Financial Times* ran a timeline showing that in June 2000, General Electric's NBC Internet dumped several web offerings and a month later Viacom changed its mind about launching its online MTVi music network. By January 2001, AltaVista had announced layoffs for the third time, NBC Internet and CNN had made deep staff cuts, and News Corp had decided to can its Fox internet division. All for the same reasons: audiences declining and advertisers taking a hike as a direct result.[7]

But Internet audiences are not really declining. There are more people online than ever. They've just found better ways to spend their time. People do go to portal sites, in droves. But they go there to search for somewhere *else* to go. Could be why Disney named it GO.com, eh? They don't go to click on banner ads. They don't go to "interact"—at least not in the sense Eisner means when he talks about interactive TV. As I was writing this chapter, an item arrived from *Wired News*, titled "Placing Product Before Art."

Game shows and advertisers have been quick to embrace interactive programming . . . But independent filmmakers at the Digital Independence conference said the real money to be made doesn't come from creating interactive programming for sitcoms and hour-long dramas; it's in product placements similar to those seen in *The Truman Show*. . . . the founder of the first 24-hour television-shopping network . . . encouraged directors to build that product inter-activity directly into films and television . . . "Interactive television gives . . . viewers the opportunity to drill down and find out more about the products they might want."[8]

Right. In the big love scene, what we really want to do is mouse on the lipstick and get some hot makeup tips. We want to click on the tires in the hair-raising car chase. "Honey, wouldn't those look great on the SUV?" And she says, "You touch that remote, Frank, it's over. I mean it."

Since the mid-'90s, the topic of "interactive media" has been the focus of innumerable articles in the popular press. But most of these have looked at the phenomenon through a mass-media lens, with "interactivity" reduced to advertising links and "Buy It" buttons. At base, however, the Internet is a *publishing* medium, allowing indi-viduals to express views, opinions and perspectives in a way that was never possible before its arrival. "Freedom of the press," wrote A. J. Liebling in 1960, "is guaranteed only to those who own one."[9] His witticism has taken on a double irony today, as the Internet and World Wide Web have in fact reduced the cost of owning one by orders of magnitude.

The barriers to entry are lower in this medium than in any that preceded it. The net has given writers, artists, musicians, hackers and other creative defectors from the homogenized wasteland of mass media a place to express themselves. These expressions are not uniformly compelling, to be sure—many are godawful by con-ventional standards. But their worth is not determined by conven-tional standards. That is to say, it is not determined by the expecta-tions of media conglomerates bent on appealing to the lowest common denominator and therefore, by the inexorable and inflexi-ble logic of broadcast, to the largest possible collection of passive ad receivers. In contrast, these network-mediated communications are valuable to whatever degree they can draw an audience, be it two or two million. They are valued by whomever comes back.

The Internet is still young. Very young. But people have already learned to use the search engines and all the nifty little bookmarking doo-dads. They've learned to use email. They've learned what they like, and they've told their pals. No wonder traffic passing through ad-infested portal sites is down. What they like is not advertising. It's voice. Websites that have genuine voice are where people are beginning to congregate online, where they *do* hang out. Not in the huge aggregations demanded by traditional media-cum-marketing expectations, but in pockets, in ecological niches too small to attract the notice of the Eisners and the Murdochs. However, the size of these audiences is directly proportional to the perceived quality of the voice that attracts them and the cogency of what it has to say, whether the delivery vector is a word processor, an overdriven guitar amp, or a can of spray paint. An entirely new class of micromarkets—small, but growing fast—are forming around such micromedia sites today.

Micromedia

Because entry costs require high returns on investment, broadcast media rarely offer emergent voices a hearing. The Internet reverses this trend, providing many low-cost vectors for small-scale publishing—micromedia, as opposed to mass media. Low-budget bottom-feeder webzines don't worry much about size of readership. With little investment at risk, the primary motive is personal gratification, seldom profit, and the style of such publishing is therefore often quirky and experimental. If there's an audience that clicks with the material, *that's* the market—and it shows up via word of mouth. The process works bottom-up, by attraction, not top-down by intrusive demographic targeting.

A handful of webzines such as *Salon* and *Feed* are professionally produced, including the work of many journalists. They emulate the "controlled circulation" model of offline publications wherein subscription is free, with costs and profits covered by advertising. These sites have had a hard go of it, as this model requires a relatively large audience. But *Salon* and *Feed* are exceptions. Most zines and other forms of micromedia—email lists, web conferencing sites, chat boards, Usenet newsgroups—typically do not have business plans, advertisers or investors. Instead, they are independent efforts by individuals or small groups with nothing much to lose, and a possible audience to gain

One of the latest and most interesting additions to the suite of micromedia tools are weblogs—simply *"blogs"* to the faithful. There are a lot of faithful. Blogging exploded across the non-commercial regions of the Internet like a global pandemic—the real thing, not a drummed-up marketer's dream of manifesto destiny.

A weblog is a little like an online diary. Date-stamped entries are usually in the form of short observations or opinions of the moment, often including hyperlinks to news items and other web pages of interest to the author. Several startups now offer free weblog services to make such postings a piece of cake. At first glance, weblogs don't seem like anything new. Given a little effort, anyone with a text editor, an FTP client and a web page could put one together. But how much effort is too much? The requirement to write HTML would probably exclude most people right off the bat. Remember when URLs that came in email had to be cut and pasted into a web browser? Once it was possible to click directly on emailed links, the web took a huge leap forward. As Malcolm Gladwell demonstrates in *The Tipping Point*, little things can have disproportionately large consequences.[10] Weblogging appears to be one such wrinkle in the web today. And one thing you can count on: there will be more. Such tools will keep getting better, connecting more people entirely outside the big-media sphere of influence.

Dave Winer created weblogs.com to advance the phenomenon. "A weblog is kind of a continual tour," he says, "with a human guide you get to know. Each guide develops an audience, and there's camaraderie and politics between the them. They point to each other in all kinds of structures, graphs, loops, etc. They also point to the sites they read."[11] If you look at a few random weblogs, you might come away thinking that they're simply another form of random link lists. In a way, they are. But they're also much more. Something profound is going on here. The incestuous linking and camaraderie Winer talks about constitutes a powerful form of bottom-up news filtration and consensus building. The best voices emerging via weblogs and other micromedia are forming the kernels around which new networked communities of interest will coalesce—micromarkets *in potentia*. The Internet has always demanded that business read between the lines. Weblogs raise the bar. Now the challenge is to read between the sites.

And the micromedia phenomenon is growing—in the number of tools available to create and support them, in the number of sites coming onstream, in number of links among them, in number of loyal fans they are attracting. How many times have you gotten email—"Trust me, you really *need* to check this out!"—accompanied by some exceedingly strange URL like www.goatsatemywashingmachine.com or www.sweetfancymoses.com. It might be the worst garbage you've ever seen. Or it might have you laughing so hard inside of ten seconds that you marvel once again at the inventiveness of the human species. And instantly you know your friend was right: you *did* need that.

Fortunately, *Goats Ate My Washing Machine* is not a real site. Not so fortunately, *Sweet Fancy Moses* is. Be forewarned, you could end up wasting a lot of time on this utterly bent "online journal of wit." And you're too busy for that, I know. But trust me, you really *need* to check this out! To illustrate the point, I asked Brian Crowley if I could quote a clip from his "Pretty Damn Good Dream Analysis." He agreed to this, writing back via his editor: "And feel free to tell Mr. Locke that the author toils each day in the marketing world, so he writes from experience." See? These are not just a bunch of kids fooling around. These are dedicated professionals.

Dream: "I am in my childhood home standing in front of the door to my bedroom, which is closed. I reach out to pull the door open, but someone inside the bedroom is holding it shut. I pull harder and harder, but the person is too strong, almost inhumanly so. After struggling with the door for many moments, I slump to the floor and catch my breath. 'Why won't you let me in?' I whisper into the door. A voice from inside the room answers, 'Because you are not ready.' I immediately recognize the other voice as my own."

Analysis: The dreamer is most likely troubled by pressures at work—an upcoming financial report for stockholders, perhaps. The dreamer's inability to open the door signifies his real-life failure to make third-quarter earnings reflect a significant growth to stockholder market shares. His ass is really on the line this time.[12]

What's more interesting about this piece than its high hilarity (though I think it's pretty funny) is the level of audience sophistication it depends on. The site says of itself: "Our obsession is to build a collective work where intellect, humor, and voice come together in orgiastic triple climax." And this expectation has not gone unmet. Traffic to *Sweet Fancy Moses* has done a hockey-stick ramp in the few months since a handful of writers got together and decided to launch it on the web. This is not stuff you'd be likely to encounter in the Sunday supplement of your local paper, or even in online publications with a broadcast-oriented business charter. Nonetheless, unsuspected and unpredicted by market segmentation analysis, there is a smart and avid audience emerging here. And new audiences hold the potential to become gateways to new micromarkets. This potential, however, will not be fulfilled through the usual traps and snares of traditional advertising.

In a moment of advanced procrastination—of which I experienced several thousand in the course of writing this book—I decided that I should explain this core principle of gonzo marketing in exhaustive detail on *Sweet Fancy Moses* itself, thus using the site as both example and delivery vehicle. Sparing you the full scope of my self-indulgence (masochists see endnote), here's part of what I wrote there:

In general, vice presidents of marketing working in large corporations think we are morons. Takes one to know one, I guess they figure. For decades, they have been sponsoring "content" that fits their bell-curve-driven dreams of mass market penetration. Bend over, here comes another sitcom. They will tell you they only sponsor this sort of thing for the mindless, shuffling Thorazine-Drooler category, which however, comprises 98.74% of all Americans. Because when they ask them "Who wants to be a millionaire?" every hand in the house goes up. Of course, they'd get the same reaction if they said, "Who wants to go to Arts and Crafts now?" or "Who needs to use the bathroom?" But the marketeers will tell you they've conducted extensive, expensive research. They'll tell you this is what the people *want*.

Yeah, but look who they asked! Forming a focus group is like jury selection at the OJ trial. "Not that one. He sneered. Swear to God, I saw his lip curl! And not the one laughing into her laptop, either." They never ask the smart people. They never ask us. And you know why? Because they know what we'd tell them. To stick it up their Nielsen ratings. Sure they do these multiple choice questionnaires. "Do you like *Friends* better than *Cheers?*" And maybe for the octogenarians: "Did you like *Cheers* better than *Mork and Mindy?*" But they never give you any *real* options, like: "If given half a chance, would you strangle Robin Williams with a length of rusted barbed wire dipped in botulism toxin?"[13]

While it's a perennial favorite, black corporate humor is obviously not the only focus of such micromedia attractors. It might be artistic, a real-time performance piece in which the Zapatistas take over Mexico—like www.ezln.org. Or political—like www.artcrimes.com. Slashdot is a community of Linux users that hacked together a web conferencing platform that has served to connect people who share that particular interest (maniacal obsession perhaps comes closer). The Slashdot platform is open-source software, which means it can be modified by other groups with different interests. The latest site to adopt the Slash code is *Plastic,*[14] masterminded by Joey Anuff, one of the original founders of *Suck.com*[15]—spawned out of *HotWired*— and Steven Johnson, co-founder and editor of *Feed.*[16] *Suck, Feed* and *Plastic* have recently shut down. But their problems have little to do with content quality, and much to do with the advertising model on which they depend. The audience size of any single micromedium is minuscule compared to broadcast media. But taken together, micromedia could easily eclipse television. And soon.

Whether hotshot media management types in New York and L.A. choose to believe it or not, these net-based publications are overt acts of journalism. In 1998, Jamie Heller, then executive editor of *TheStreet.com*, wrote a piece in *The New York Times* titled "Online Journalism Coming Into Its Own." It ends: "whatever the conventional media elite may think, online journalists might have decided that they're already arrived—and are happy to stay right where they are." Sounds good. Change comes to MediaLand. However, what has lent the Internet validity—for Heller, as he says in the article, and many others who originally came from the print side—is the immigration of known and respected members in good standing of the *legitimate* press.[17] This is a rather colonial perspective. A view from the Raj. Gin and tonics with the natives. A spot of hunting. "Indjya, old man, nothing like it! Great fun. Take the missus."

This is not to denigrate professional journalists—if their expertise is in researching issues and events and articulating their findings in—as the *Miami Herald's* Carl Hiaasen suggested—a kick-ass delivery modality.[18] As in when you go, "Wow, that piece whomped serious butt!" But if—how should I put this?—the *specialness* of having worked in conventional media is based on the mystique of the secret "objectivity" handshake. . . well, we've been over this already, haven't we? Don't get me started. Don't make me have to come over there! In fact, by jettisoning (or more likely, never having thought of) such primitive beliefs about "objective" and emotionally disengaged reporting, many *un*known, *un*credentialed *non*-pro web journalists are already doing—effortlessly, unselfconsciously, without a second thought—what public journalism has had so much trouble attempting to accomplish within the institutional framework of commercial broadcast, online or off. That is, these new web journalists are engaging people's real-live vital concerns and exploring issues percolating from the bottom up, not imposed top-down by polls and pundits. This is bona fide journalism, even if nobody official gives it official sanction. Badges? We don't need no steenkin badges![19] In *The World Wide Web and Contemporary Cultural Theory*, Steven Jones writes:

> Journalism on the web is not journalism as we have known it thus far. It creates a different order of content. . . It asks us less to attend to "the latest" and more to attend to what we find interesting; less to synthesize and understand a "who, what, when, where, how, and why" and more to attend to "what's next?"; less about a "them" and more about an "us". . . The range of possibilities has widened: we are no longer certain of what is reported in the news, and we are much more likely to allow alternative explanations. . . It

is not so much that we do not believe what we read, see, and hear in the news as it is that we are inclined to believe that there is more . . . As Marshall McLuhan put it, "'content' . . . is always another medium. The content of the press is literary statement, as the content of the book is speech, and the content of the movie is the novel." It is now more clear than ever that the content of the web is news, though not necessarily journalism.[20]

In an article called "The Dotcom Brain Drain," *The American Journalism Review* reported that a surprising number of reporters are abandoning print publications to write on the web. "Web sites are basically about conveying information in engaging ways," says veteran journalist Nick Denton, adding: "That's what journalists do."[21] And that's what Denton did. For eight years, he wrote for *The Economist* and *The Financial Times*. Then in 1998 he founded Moreover.com, which delivers news stories from thousands of sources to websites across the planet. "Traditional Internet technology leaves a significant blind spot around dynamic content," says Moreover.com. "Information that changes quickly is either omitted or delivered too late to be useful."[22]

The New York Times writes about the company in "Mining the 'Deep web' With Sharper Shovels," noting that only a tiny fraction of the estimated 500 billion "pieces of content" on the net are visible to conventional search engines.[23] The cliché has it that 99% of this stuff is junk. But the cliché reflects the primary bias of broadcast media. It's "junk" only because the people who want to find it don't aggregate into large enough segments to constitute sufficiently lucrative advertising targets. It's "worthless" only because media moguls like Michael Eisner and Rupert Murdoch can't figure out how to make a buck off it. Randall Rothenberg frames the problem neatly in *Advertising Age*:

. . . while the Internet destroys many existing economic models, it doesn't necessarily replace them with something equally viable. I've written about the radio's problem: with universal broadband penetration, the individual listener has access to thousands of stations, serving every niche interest imaginable. With any 17-year-old with a handful of MP3s and some time on his hands able to have his own global network, the value of brick-and-mortar stations, which has skyrocketed in recent years as conglomerates tried to assemble national networks, erodes. How do you rebuild—or sell advertising within—an industry composed of a kazillion stations, each with a handful of listeners? [24]

And he answers his own question: "Damned if I know." At least he's honest. But the real problem lies in automatic assumptions of how to parse "equally viable"—usually construed to mean something you can sell advertising in, around, about, over, under, sideways, down. But many "insignificant" niches can add up to a lot of people. *The Times* "Deep Web" story reports that in December 2000, some 340,000 people hit the Moreover site, adding "and that is without any consumer marketing from the company."[25] Advertising isn't the only way to make a buck. Moreover is both giving away its service to smaller independent web sites, which spread awareness of the company and its tools, while licensing its core engine to major corporations, where it's being used to assemble and annotate distributed topical knowledge bases on the fly.

So far, most of the news stories served by moreover.com come from traditional publishers: newspapers, the financial press, big-media web sites. But that's changing fast. The company has partnered with Blogger, an explosively expanding online startup that produces software for creating and maintaining personal weblogs.[26] The result is newsblogger.com, which not only lets small sites publish links to late-breaking news stories, but lets editors at those sites add their own commentary.[27] This constitutes something completely new in the world, a form of populist metajournalism. The commentary is often sophisticated media criticism—noticing how the publication plays up certain aspects of a story and plays down others. For an example of such media criticism, you really *need* to go check out *Online Journalism Review*.[28] It's not a weblog, it's a website, but here the point is not the mechanism, but how these tools are being used to comment and expand on mainstream news, to which people previously had no way to respond outside of token letters to the editor. In a similar (though non-populist) vein, *Slate*'s excellent Daily Papers feature is worth looking at. This email-cum-web column is teaching many thousands how to read and deconstruct the deep rhetoric of newspaper layout decisions, such as the significance of how an article is placed on or absent from Page One at publications like *The Wall Street Journal*, *The Washington Post* and *The New York Times*.[29] Such unprecedented and fast-growing popular sophistication with respect to media is a direct result of the net.

But back to blogs. Because moreover.com also indexes an increasing number of small indie weblogs, things are starting to get recursively tangled beyond all recognition out there. It's getting hard to tell who's "in the business" and who's doing it for love. "ALL THE NEWS THAT'S FIT TO BLOG" reads the motto on the newsblogger site. "What could be more intuitive than a list of chronological, commented links?" asks a piece in *digitalMASS* about Moreover's offbeat alliance. "It's only natural that a company like Blogger would be helping publish blogs with names like Deadman and Brainsluice alongside corporate news services."[30]

On Tom Peters' web site, Tom or someone near and dear to him explains weblogs and their significance. "A lot of people keep online 'blogs'—or 'weblogs'—as personal journals, or just as a running series of observations about anything under the sun. We've created a series of blogs in order to make a running commentary of neat, weird, or odd ideas that have to do with corporate culture, work, online commerce, or a variety of other topics."[31] Thus a phenomenon that grew bottom-up out of the deep, invisible web wins endorsement from the world's numero uno business consultant. Hands have been laid on. Yeah, it's dangerous, out of control. Yeah, it trashes all sorts of sacred-cow boundaries. But it's cool to like this stuff. Tom Peters turns serious webhead. I love it.

The stars of this new medium are just now emerging. Don't think Matt Drudge, think Walter Cronkite. Individually, their audiences will be much smaller than those of today's mass-market broadcast channels, but taken together, the total audience will be much larger. Within a few years, many thousands of quality news, entertainment and information sources will spring up on the Internet to serve highly specific communities of interest. These micromedia sites will constitute an increasingly important vector for electronic commerce, serving as possible points of entry into a huge collection of web micromarkets.

Micromarkets

Microsoft's *Slate* represents an interesting modification of the strictly advertising-based webzine model: corporate underwriting. The company owns the site and pays the considerable costs of producing it. But this begs the age-old journalistic question of influence—the separation of powers (or lack thereof) between editorial and business interests. How credible is *Slate* in reporting on the Microsoft antitrust case? Ownership isn't everything. In cases like this, it can be an impediment. What if, instead of launching *Slate* itself, Microsoft had bankrolled an indie zine with proven editorial appeal, then adopted an ironclad hands-off policy with respect to content? If corporations underwrote externally produced webzines and were careful to preserve site independence, the resulting sites could be far more credible attractors than are most current corporate web pages. This sort of enlightened patronage first appeared in the Renaissance when the Medici banking family supported artists like Botticelli, Michelangelo and Leonardo da Vinci. Strangely perhaps, it could work again today, financially rewarding quality site producers and enabling companies to better connect with nascent web micromarkets.

But these are hints of things soon to come—both in the next chapter and the near future. At present, micromarkets don't yet exist. Micromedia do exist, and are growing rapidly. Audiences are coming together around these new bottom-up sources of news and views. But these audiences will not become markets until business finds a viable way to interact with them. Markets exist only in the eye of the beholder—this is the view from the world of commerce. If business doesn't learn how to behold online markets—doesn't come to perceive them for what they really are—these markets will *never* come into being as such. Like any market, micromarkets are relational affairs. They do not exist independent of their observers in quite the same way as shoes and ships and sealing wax. This may seem an abstruse philosophical point, but it has critical ramifications for business, so pay close attention here. People in the microaudiences coalescing around micromedia do not think of themselves as micromarkets. *They think of themselves as people.*

This is perhaps the greatest shift in the balance of power between companies and what they have viewed until now as "consumers"—people whose only function was to buy products. The net has helped human beings to rediscover other, and often more interesting, uses for their humanity. Because of this shift in perspective—which has caused online markets to radically realign priorities and allegiances—business needs to be especially wary of using old broadcast terminology as if it still applied in familiar ways. "It looks like a medium, so it must be like television." Or "I see a lot of eyeballs out there, so it must be a branding opportunity." Just because some of the words sound the same doesn't mean they describe the same realities. In *Principles of Marketing*, Philip Kotler and Gary Armstrong talk about *micromarketing* in the following terms:

> Segment and niche marketers tailor their offers and marketing programs to meet the needs of various market segments. At the same time, however, they do not customize their offers to each individual customer. Thus, segment marketing and niche marketing fall between the extremes of mass marketing and micromarketing. Micromarketing is the practice of tailoring products and marketing programs to suit the tastes of specific individuals and locations. Micromarketing includes local marketing and individual marketing.[32]

What they mean by *local marketing* is street-level GPS coordinated with point-of-sale data. Real sophisticated. Real complex. Real spooky. I don't mean that. What they mean by *individual marketing* is mass customization, one-to-one stuff, "personalization." I don't mean that either. In fact, I don't talk about "micromarketing" at all. Or marketing *to* anybody, for that matter. That's still the whole targeting trip. Ready, aim, *sell!* Instead, I talk about *gonzo* marketing *for* and *with* micromarkets. As used in this book, "*micromarkets*" are not hash-browned or refried databases. Neither are they individuals, so-called "markets of one." Instead, they're genuinely *social* social groupings. Little ones perhaps, at first, but they're collections of people, communities joined by shared interests. And (this part is probably important too) they're groups you actually *belong* to, that you *interact* with—not by punching buttons and entering your zip code, but by exposing something real about who you are.

This kind of interaction—unlike Michael Eisner's variety—applies to *everyone* who wishes to be part of the community. Even businesses. Companies that want to relate to these communities as markets, must first become active participants. No more remote-control media buys. No more painting bull's-eyes on the backs of abstract demographic segments. So maybe this is a good time to let you in on a little wrinkle in the unified revised standard theory—gonzo marketing isn't really marketing at all. It's market advocacy.

On the net, advertising works against itself. Because it relies on scattergun tactics guaranteed to repel more attention than it attracts, it needs as large an audience as possible. If only 2 percent of the audience will even register an ad, much less act on it, the advertising model needs sites 50 times larger than sites in which everyone is paying attention. However, sites that much larger cost that much more. Therefore they must be even bigger to cover costs and bring in more eyeballs to satisfy more advertisers so more people will buy their products more often. It's a rat race. Critically, this never ending upward spiral directly degrades the quality of content. To attract a larger audience, content must be less challenging, more popular— less focused on specific interests, more broadly appealing. In other words, more generic. And because every other site with mass media pretensions is offering the same kind of generic information, it becomes a commodity, readily available in so many places that no one site can attract a critical mass in terms of audience share. This may have been OK for early TV, where the audience was captive and all the broadcast networks offered essentially the same fare. And by God, anyone who didn't like it could move to Russia! But on the web, it's not so OK. We don't have to move anything but our index fingers. Click. We weren't looking for commodity information anyway. We were looking for voice.

Meeting market expectations is a way for a business to be predictable, yes, granted. It's also a way to be *boring as hell*. Some will be tempted to argue here that at least it's safe. Don't. It's not safe. Boring is dangerous. Boring communicates that you have no guts, no heart, no soul. Conventional market research offers black-and-white certainty—or at least insinuates that it can provide powerful predictors of future market directions. Let's take a look at how this works. Say Nirvana hits big in Seattle, and OK so your big-assed record company missed it, but you pick up on the trend right away—and sign a thousand mediocre grunge bands. If Apple makes a sort of blue computer housing and it catches on because every other computer ever made was that puky off-ivory, then hey, you make yours sort of chartreuse. If everyone suddenly wants to be a millionaire, you launch a game show where the contestants get a wheelbarrow, a truss, and 10-minute pass to Fort Knox. Your time-slot competitor hits you with brilliantly creative programming about people stranded on a desert island with no sex? No problem. You strike back with strongly competitive programming about people stranded on a desert island with lots of sex and rabid half-starved monitor lizards. See? Difference is minimized. Expectations preserved.

Only by then, your market's gone. Your audience has long since split.

The Internet is entirely different. It's not an opportunity for viral marketing. We *are* a virus and we want to multiply. We *are* the audience. We *are* the market. We are in it and of it. This is not just our "positioning," it's our position. And we won't recant or renege or back down. Where would we go? What else *is* there? This is market advocacy. This is gonzo marketing. You don't have to be nuts, but it helps to have been there. Because when you get personal with so many people, you begin to get stretched, to blur at the edges. You don't define your product—you discover who you are. Prepare for deep existential terror at times. And, if you really connect, for the rush of your life.

Let's turn to Kotler and Andreason one last time. These guys are all right if you overlook their proclivity to prepend "target" to "audience."

Marketers who constantly keep attuned to their target audience are confronted again and again by the market's diversity. As a consequence, they assume markets almost always must be segmented with strategies fine-tuned to the needs and wants of each subpopulation. Closeness to consumers also leads to recognition that *traditional demographic approaches are seldom adequate* to capture the rich diversity in target audience's needs, wants, life-styles, perceptions, and preferences.[33]

Within a few years, thousands of quality news, entertainment and information sources will spring up on the Internet, each serving a highly specific community of interest. Around many of these micro-media, a web of intercommunicating micromarkets will emerge in a band of spectrum invisible to conventional marketing. The stars of this new medium are just now emerging. Don't think Dan Rather, think Chaucer, Cervantes. Think Dante. Don't think Jerry Springer, think Rabelais and Shakespeare. Don't think George W., think Winston C. Don't think Oprah, think the Oracle at Delphi. Human beings have always discovered magic and magnificence within themselves. It wasn't created by media marketeers—they just saw an opportunity to make a killing. The magic was there all along. It still is.

CHAPTER 7

The Gonzo Model

"As the chief and only true gonzo, Thompson, in his famous 'Fear and Loathing' reportage for Rolling Stone *magazine, wasn't just a passive observer but played his own freaked-out part as unofficial Tom O'Bedlam to the events he covered."*

—THE OXFORD ENGLISH DICTIONARY QUOTING *NEWSWEEK*[1]

"Orr was crazy and could be grounded. All he had to do was ask; and as soon as he did, he would no longer be crazy and would have to fly more missions."

—JOSEPH HELLER, *CATCH-22*

THOUGH MANY READERS MAY SKIP TO THIS CHAPTER FIRST, ITS LOGIC will probably be perplexing without the circuitous route that leads to the gonzo model being proposed here. That route is not defined by the previous chapters in this book, but by the history of business in the 20th century. Let's briefly recap the essential elements. Mass production and its attendant economies of scale typified business for most of the past 100 years. Because this mode of production was so enormously successful, it has continued to shape and color the conduct of business even long past the ascendancy of the industrial model out of which it grew. Perhaps the major reason for this long and painful hangover is the persistence of mass media, which were spawned in response to the needs of business as critical vectors to mass markets. Like the management of large industrial corporations with many thousands of workers and millions of customers, broadcast advertising partakes of the same top-down style of command

and control. Both employees and customers were told what to do—whether to work hard or shop hard—but not asked in any substantive way for their input or opinions.

This basic mass marketing–mass media scenario was already changing in fundamental ways long before the advent of the Internet. Because of the vastly expanded range of products and services that became available through global competition once mass markets began to fragment into many segments and niches. The same competition brought enormous pressure to bear on companies, forcing them to turn to their entire workforce in search of process improvements and new product ideas. Though loudly proclaimed by many companies, the "empowerment" of workers to contribute such insights—as though this were a "privilege" granted thanks to corporate largesse—has done little to change the inherently authoritarian nature of management. Command and control remains the order of the day. And the same is true with respect to markets. Through there is much talk these days about the empowerment of the customer, companies still communicate their demands by broadcasting them to demographically determined abstractions about which they know very little, and with which they have little in the way of genuine relationships.

The coming of the Internet has greatly accelerated these trends. While the net did not cause these long-term shifts, it has catalyzed a much faster evolution of business than would have been possible without global networks. This change in the speed of business has also produced a change in the *kind* of business that will be viable from this point forward. With the reality of interconnected audiences and markets, something fundamental has changed in the world, and the world continues to change as a result. The catalyst has triggered an irreversible chain reaction.

However, both mainstream media and corporate marketing are blind to these changes inasmuch as they continue to rely on deep-seated yet tacit assumptions attaching to the pre-Internet broadcast model. The strategy of the ostrich notwithstanding, blindness never offers protection, only higher—since unacknowledged—risk. Four decades ago, one of best minds in marketing, Theodore Levitt, wrote about the catastrophic impact of a similar blindness on an earlier business era.

Even after the advent of automobiles, trucks and airplanes, the rail-road tycoons remained imperturbably self-confident. If you had told them 60 years before that in 30 years they would be flat on their backs, broke, and pleading for government subsidies, they would have thought you totally demented. Such a future was simply not considered possible. It was not even a discussable subject, or an askable question, or a matter which any sane person would consider worth speculating about.[2]

Using only slightly different language, anyone daring to challenge the "obvious" and unshakable supremacy of the railroad barons would have been considered gonzo. Whacko. A nutcase. Today, anyone failing to genuflect to the similarly "obvious" and unassail-able hegemony of AOL/Time Warner, Disney, News Corp and other such media empires is also thought to be demented, deranged—or perhaps just hopelessly ignorant and naïve. But these Masters of the Mediaverse betray a confidence just as blind as that of the railroad companies a century ago. And they don't have 60 years, or 30, to figure it out. They don't even have three.

So what happens if the great "iron horses" of broadcast are about to encounter the media equivalent of the automobile and the air-plane? What if their millions of miles of inflexible track, laid at such great cost, are about to be made superfluous by alternate routes ap-pearing out of a dimension invisible to the imperturbably self-confident chieftains of these great conglomerates? But "what if" has nothing to do with it. These eventualities are not forthcoming; they've already materialized. A quick change of transportation metaphors is now called for, from railroads to shipping, because however cleverly Michael Eisner, Rupert Murdoch, Steve Case and the rest of these broadband tycoons rearrange the deck chairs on their respective *Titanics*, an even more titanic iceberg with their names carved into it has already calved off some remote Arctic ice shelf and is inexorably drifting their way. That iceberg, of course, is the Internet. If a just God grants my fervent prayer that I may be the James Cameron of their fateful rendezvous, my heart will go on and on. Film crews are standing by on seven continents. The revolution will be streamed in MPEG.

And what will happen to business then? What will happen if companies are left with no way to advertise? But this is the wrong question entirely. Companies don't give a damn about advertising—any more than they did about railroads. What they cared about 100 years ago was getting goods to market by whatever means was most effective. What they care about today is connecting with potential customers by whatever means is most effective. In the pre-Internet days, when broadcast was the only way to accomplish that—the transcontinental railway of marketing—advertising was a foregone conclusion. But advertising is not only exorbitantly expensive, it's a ridiculously inefficient means of attempting to reach and form productive relationships with an increasingly fragmented array of networked markets. Many of these markets are just now emerging bottom-up from the web, and are completely invisible to the traditional analytic tools of market research.

These micromarkets are forming around micromedia, myriad small online publications that are beginning to attract millions beneath the notice (and contempt) of convention marketing radar, and which *could*—given a framework radically different from broadcast advertising—serve to mediate between companies and potential customers. This framework is what the gonzo model aims to provide.

Implementing the Program

The balance of this chapter describes how, by adopting this model, companies can open up to new markets in ways that are smarter, friendlier and far more effective than outmoded legacy marketing methods—the unnecessary baggage business has so far brought to the Internet. If you skipped over Chapter 1, pretend *this is a hypertext link*. Before you read on, go back and scan the section about what Ford Motor Company is up to—"Ripping Out the Wall"—and the speculative "Preview of the Gonzo Model." We're about to delve into the nuts and bolts. Without the contextual connections those previous bits provide—the conceptual bolts—the following may strike you as merely nuts.

Motivation and Resources

Paradoxically perhaps, there are several reasons why Global 1000 corporations may have the best advantage in the early stages of the transition from traditional marketing to more intimate micromarket relationships. This does not mean that smaller companies are excluded from adopting this model, or that they would reap less benefit. It's just to suggest that very large companies may well be first in to the pool (last one's a rotten investment).

First, these companies are most dependent on broadcast advertising, and therefore most at risk from its failure to port from conventional media to the Internet. While most are unaware of the reasons for this failure, many are exploring other avenues to reach networked markets. Given the near-religious fervor with which some of these companies have responded to approaches like permission marketing, this exploration often telegraphs to markets a counterproductive aura of desperation. These companies are ready for something different, but they're not quite sure what it is. The old broadcast model does not offer much help in assessing why one method is more likely to work, or fail, than another. Or worse, it leads to false predictions. This has caused much costly thrashing— companies going overboard for flavor-of-the-moment nostrums such as "push," "personalization" and "permission," which turn out to have the half-life of late-August fireflies.

Second, these companies are currently spending prodigious sums on adverting—in both offline media and on the more broadcast-oriented forms of web marketing. The funding for initial gonzo-model testbeds will come out of such supersized media budgets. And testbeds will be crucial. No company is going to shift a major portion of its marketing resources into this mode without testing the waters first. Micromarkets are not mass markets, or even the type of large market niches business has typically pursued. While this may seem obvious, it's important to understand the implications. Each micromarket will represent a much smaller percentage of revenue potential than the markets currently targeted through conventional segmentation. Therefore, companies will need to establish a much broader array of micromarket partnerships. Using a fairly random example, if each external micromarket partner represented 1/10 of 1% of overall revenues, the company would eventually need to establish 1,000 such relationships to replace earnings generated by its current marketing methods.

Third, these large global companies have very sizable and diverse workforces. This is critical, as what underpins the gonzo model are personal interests and passionate engagement around those interests. The first tactical step for companies is to determine what these interests are. Today, most corporations have little idea.

Intellectual Capital Audit

Intellectual capital has been the subject of much discussion in business journals, conferences, and high-level corporate think tanks. And lately, nascent ideas about social capital have been folded into the mix. However, most of this discussion has focused on knowledge about products and production processes, or social relationships within the organization. This self-reflexive and insular examination leaves the lion's share of existing intellectual and social capital lying on the table. It's there in plain sight, but the legacy of command and control prevents most companies from seeing it. They are blind to enormously valuable assets they're already holding.

In the first half of the twentieth century, nearly all industrial companies had a "check your brain at the door" policy. While not explicitly written into official employee handbooks, workers knew it was there, and behaved accordingly—keeping perfectly viable process improvement ideas to themselves. When Total Quality Management began to reverse this trend, and self-directed teams were given unprecedented authority to design their own work environments, management was often surprised to learn how much these workers knew. "How come you never told us any of this?" the bosses inquired. "How come you never asked?" the workers replied.

But here we're talking about a different sort of intellectual capital that has been undervalued to the point of invisibility. What are employees interested in *outside* the framework of "the job"? Human Resources never asks, except perhaps to fill in those trivial "other" fields in the resumé database—hobbies, club memberships, neighborhood action groups, whatever. The company yawns. The company doesn't really care. But it should. What drives the self-selection process whereby communities of interest come together on the Internet is not products—Seth Godin's notion of "consumer networks" is little more than a convenient fiction. Instead, what unites these communities of interest is—duh!—their common *interests*.

Sometimes these shared interests have a political dimension, as with "interest groups" that make common cause to advance some desired change. More often, though, these are common, garden-variety interests, as in rock music or opera, historical biographies or mystery fiction, home schooling or scuba diving, or any of thousands of other interests workers pursue outside of their paid involvement with the company. While most of these are understandably avocational, many are related to the individual's professional work, whether it be accounting practice, computer programming or some aspect of business management. Whatever form they take, all are potential points of intersection with external communities of interest currently emerging on the net. As such, these interests are like diamonds in the dust in a networked economy.

Companies need to understand the worth of these interests, then identify their specific focus. This will require more than vague statements about valuable employees. It will require the establishment of serious programs to encourage and showcase such interests, and to develop and nurture communities of interest within the company.

Long ago, AOL created a content incubator, a "greenhouse" in which to let various creative talents show what they could produce. AOL promoted those it thought best into its commercial offering. Companies can follow a similar model. It's not rocket science. All that's required is a large and unconstrained web space behind the corporate firewall—and a top-management-blessed invitation for people to build sites around subjects they really care about. Given the "check-your-brain" hangover, most employees will contribute nothing. Incentives should be carefully considered, such as time off regular work to produce these sites. However, incentives that are too enticing across the board could remove an important quality filter. Those who are naturally inclined to contribute will be driven by an extra degree of enthusiasm to communicate their passions—and this is the most valuable stuff a company can elicit. Such passion and enthusiasm forms a good fit with the Zeitgeist of the web.

Once the program gets underway, the developers of these internal sites will begin to realize that they share interests with other workers they've never met. In a company with 100,000+ employees, this is no big surprise. The company should encourage collaboration between such individuals and groups. The goal is a single site on each topic of interest, incorporating whatever talents and expertise members of the community can bring to the party. In themselves, such initiatives are likely to surprise the companies that seriously encourage them, if only through the *Hawthorne effect*—the phenomenon whereby the productivity of workers increases any time management pays attention to them, that being such a rare event. A less academic way of describing this is to recall the question, "How come you never asked?"

Identifying best of breed

However, the point is not productivity. The point is marketing. There is a trajectory to such work, and it's vector is through and beyond the corporate firewall. The point is to connect with external micromarkets. To accomplish this, the company needs to assess the sites it has nurtured through such a greenhouse program, and select the best results for further development. There are two critical measures of what "the best" means here. The first could be a serious challenge for many corporations. It entails understanding what "voice" is. A good metric to use in this regard—a worst practice, if you're keeping track—would be to select sites as distant as it's humanly possible to get from the vacuous rhetoric of the typical corporate home page. Elements to look for include personal style, differences of opinion, humor, deep knowledge of the territory—and an ability to articulate it—plus, if you're lucky, that indefinable quality of gonzo. Companies that promote the bland, the vanilla—in other words, the kind of crap they're used to delivering through their current "marketing communications"—might just as well not embark on this route. They'd be wasting their time.

The other measure of what constitutes best of breed entails fit with the company's markets. This is tricky ground. In the earlier Ford example, there is a distinct (if non-obvious) connection between organic gardening and the company's products—specifically, no one is going to haul manure in the family four-door. But such an explicit tie-in need not exist. If enough people outside the company are interested in cooking, say, such a focus could be attractive to certain web micromarkets even if the company offers no products that are directly related. If the markets it wants to attract are fairly general, it makes little difference. As long as its products or services *could* be useful to such an audience, such topical interests should not be excluded out of hand. However, if the company makes molybdenum gears for bulldozers, cooking might be a bit far afield. In making decisions about which areas to focus on, companies will use whatever insight they've garnered from previous demographic segmentation efforts. They'll also use gut feel. And they'll make mistakes. The latter is unavoidable, but since this is not a mass market strategy, and dozens or hundreds of sites will be offered to the web at large, no one bad call will be fatal. On the other hand, the near certainty of error makes it critical to establish out front a way to reset from such missteps such that none is catastrophic or ends up generating bad will either inside or outside the organization.

Identifying external partners

The challenge here is to locate independent external websites that form a natural fit with the internal employee interests identified in the previous step. Matching the interests of people in the company to those of people in the marketplace offers the potential for engendering conversations on matters of actual interest to emergent web micromarkets. No matter how hard companies wish for it, these micromarkets are unlikely to give their permission to talk about the wonders of your company's product. However, they may well grant permission for individuals who happen to work for you to join in discussions already underway—the nature of which discussions being what brought the micromarkets into existence in the first place.

Actually, these are not markets at all until the company is able to sell to them, and—critical paradox alert!—they will never *become* markets as long as the company's main purpose is to do so. It is crucial to understand that the primary objective of such internal/external intersections is to establish relationships of genuine trust among people sharing specific focal interests. Any attempt to undermine or short-circuit this process using intrusive marketing techniques will have devastating instant-karma consequences.

In looking for external web partners, the knowledge of employees already engaged in these programs will be critical. The most knowledgeable and articulate voices on the company side will also tend to be intimately familiar with relevant external web resources. They will know which sites are best, which worst, which marginal, and this information will be essential to making good micromedia partnership decisions. Usually, such expertise will be closely related to an individual's specific interests. However, some employees may have more general web sleuthing skills and a good nose for promising sites, whether or not they are well versed in the particular subject area. Companies should consider turning these generalists into dedicated web scouts, analogous to the A&R (artist and repertoire) scouts that major music recording labels employ to search out new talent. Identifying newly emerging web micromarkets will be an ongoing involvement, and such A&R scouting will soon form an important aspect of corporate marketing—as it should have from the beginning of corporate entry onto the web.

The best external candidates for partnership will not necessarily be the best established. The slicker the site and the greater the size of its existing audience, the more expensive the relationship is likely to be. This is where "radar for voice" can pay enormous dividends. A nascent site that is interesting, engaging, compelling, creative, independent, and again, if you're lucky, a little gonzo, is the ideal candidate. Such a site will have great potential to draw an audience. It is less likely to be encumbered by restrictions stemming from previous marketing or venture capital relationships. And critically, it will need resources of the sort that corporate underwriting can provide.

Underwriting

What exactly does *underwriting* mean? In essence, underwriting is a form of patronage, in the sense the term was used in the Renaissance. In fact, the practice it describes largely kicked off the Renaissance. In the 14th century, the Medici banking family served as a powerful patron to artists such as Botticelli, da Vinci and Michelangelo, whose work we might never have heard of without such corporate support. True, the word *"patronizing"* has come to have extremely negative connotations—as in, "don't patronize me!" We'll deal with these in the section below on the problem of influence.

Isn't *underwriting* just a fancy word for sponsorship? As the term is being used here, the answer is a resounding and definitive no. In the corporate marketing mindset, sponsorship is indissolubly linked to advertising, and underwriting does not involve advertising. In fact, it is a more effective alternative to advertising's inherently distanced and impersonal methods. The aim of underwriting external sites is to establish strong *personal* relationships between a company and emerging web micromarkets in which the company has a perceived future stake, and in whose subject matter company employees have a preexisting *personal* interest.

There is one important sense in which underwriting and advertising are linked. As the former will increasing replace the latter, the financial resources required to support these micromarket initiatives will come out of current media budgets. For this reason, the marketing department has to fully buy in. Achieving consensus on this point will constitute a substantial challenge for many corporations— an insurmountable hurdle in some cases. As this book has shown, marketing is set in its ways, and many of those ways are grounded in realities that ceased to apply decades before the Internet became a major avenue to markets. On the positive side, the decreasing effectiveness of current methods should act as a strong incentive, encouraging marketing to look beyond "best practices" that have long since become liabilities in a networked world.

So, what sorts of resources do these external sites need? The usual: time and money. Micromedia sites tend to be labors of love. Their developers are typically working to make ends meet while keeping their sites afloat on nights and weekends. The first contribution of corporate underwriting is to enable these creative principals to quit their day jobs in some cube farm, thus freeing them to devote full time to their primary passion. Companies can simply underwrite external partners by giving them money with which they can purchase needed resources. However, other forms of support tend to forge closer relationships—and as that's the whole idea, this should be considered. Companies can lend or donate computer equipment, disk space, bandwidth, and render various forms of technical, design and artistic assistance. They can also develop or license content relevant to the specific interests of these communities and make it freely available to them. Such content would be more welcome, and therefore more effective in creating recognition and goodwill, than the majority of current expensive-but-empty "branding" ploys.

Companies can also direct traffic to these partner sites from their web pages—a sort of reverse advertising. The objective is to grow these sites in which the company is investing. Just because they're micromarkets today doesn't mean they have to remain so. It is in the mutual interest of underwriters and external partners to announce the existence of partner sites and encourage customers and prospects to visit them. The set of micromarket partnerships a company engages in becomes an important component in its brand. Think of Benetton here. Its employees care—so the company tells us—about issues like AIDs and racial equality and capital punishment. The company further assumes that its market shares similar concerns. So it welds its brand to those issues. If it loses some customers in the process, it figures it will attract others more sympathetic to its positions. Benetton's radical experimentation along these lines is understandably terrifying to most companies.

However, the issues that interest people need not be "issues" at all; these interests extend far beyond the realm of heated political or cultural debate. A company may underwrite micromedia sites focusing on subjects as commonplace and uncontroversial as baseball, wine collecting, javascript programming, film noir, telecommuting, or notable bassoon performances. Though the last is a little unlikely (unless, of course, the company manufactures bassoons), a company will identify itself with emergent markets by the underwriting positions it takes, and the collection of these positions will say a lot about the character of the company as a whole. Companies should neither embrace nor sidestep controversy based on ulterior marketing considerations, but should take positions their employees truly support and consciously choose to align themselves with. This is a roundabout way of stating the obvious: that companies should tell the truth about who they are instead of representing themselves as airbrushed fictions.

Bottom line: *the fundamental message of marketing must change from "we want your money" to "we share your interests." In this respect, corporate underwriting is a way—perhaps the only viable way at present—for companies to put their own money where their mouth is.*

Structuring the relationship

If money is changing hands, you can bet that lawyers will be involved. They will. These won't be casual handshake deals but formal contractual relationships. Both parties will want to maximize the value of what they give and what they get for it. Both parties will want to minimize their risk. One tradeoff involving both value and risk will be the term of such contracts. As noted already, a company might find a smaller, newer micromedia partner attractive because the relationship will be relatively cheap. The site has little but sweat equity and voice to show; the rest is potential. The company is investing in this voice in the reasonable expectation that the audience it is able to attract will become more valuable over time. Plus, the company is agreeing to provide certain other valuable resources (as described in the last section) to assist in the success of the site. The company will want to extend its relationship for as long as possible at the same level of financial support, and not be penalized—through a ramping schedule of payments—for a success it has helped to secure. But too long a term might not be in the company's best interests either. There is no rule of thumb at this point on the optimal length of these relationships, and there may never be—many factors will have to be taken into account, and these will differ from company to company and site to site. The two parties will have to work out a compromise amenable to both. Exit protection for both sides therefore becomes especially important—one form of which might be yearly or biannual renewal options with plenty of notice given if one party intends to bail, or feels that renegotiation is warranted.

One protection the company will (and should) require is *exclusivity with respect to the domain*. While a site may have many underwriters—the more the merrier, for reasons we'll see below—it should be precluded from having more than one in any single competitive market arena (hereinafter, as those lawyers might say, the *domain*). In simpler terms, if a site enters into an underwriting relationship with Ford, it will not be able to ink a similar deal with General Motors. In the case of a coveted potential web partner, this will engender competitive bidding, which is good for the site. However, the site should take many other factors besides money into account. Prime among these is cultural fit. Do the parties "speak the same language"? Do they see eye to eye on expected results? Are both being honest and above board? If these questions are not explored, nasty surprises could result. If the answers are not in the affirmative, one party or both is going to be unhappy with the marriage.

But back to competitive bidding for a moment. If a company identifies a candidate site early enough, and offers it fair underwriting terms, price inflation due to bidding may be avoided. There are tradeoffs here on both sides. Should the site wait to get other companies interested, or are immediate funds more valuable than a potentially greater sum later? This is simply the old bird-in-the-hand question—though exclusivity considerations make it crucial to chose well here. As to the company, should it invest in the relationship now, at a lower price, or wait to find a possibly better candidate? The company is not explicitly bound by exclusivity—it would be too difficult to define, for one thing—but a) will not usually wish to underwrite competing sites, and b) resources are, after all, finite. So the company will obviously need to choose well too.

Despite these tradeoffs and admittedly gnarly considerations, companies will clearly attempt to sign quality partners before competitors can scoop them up. Without pretending to cover all the details here—as we say on the net, IANAL: I Am Not A Lawyer—contracts will have to spell out who gets what, for how long, and how the relationship will be continued beyond the contract term—or dissolved with the least damage to either party. More important than the letter of the law, however and as usual, is a sense of goodwill and a spirit of enthusiastic collaboration. These hookups should be joyous affairs. If they're not, they'll be disappointing. Or nightmares. There's not a lot of middle ground. Sure, problems will arise and need to be ironed out. Sure unforeseen factors will come to light and need to be dealt with. But this will only work if both sides basically respect each other.

Influence: Church and State

Mutual respect already has a deep tradition in conventional media. And this is one convention worth preserving. The separation of "Church and State" refers to the longstanding rule that editorial content must not be swayed by advertising dollars. The number of ad pages Microsoft buys in a magazine, for instance, should have no bearing on the review of Windows 2010. While this principle is often honored in the breach, it remains an excellent idea—for both the publication *and* the sponsor. If corporations are too often successful in influencing content decisions, readers begin to notice that the publication has sold out, and they soon go elsewhere for opinions they can trust. Ultimately, this is a pyrrhic victory for the advertiser, as it thereby loses a critical path of communication with the market. Understanding how this works is hardly a new thing in mainstream media. The general outlines of the principle were articulated by Adolph Ochs, publisher of *The New York Times*, as far back as 1916:

> It is an axiom in newspaper publishing—'more readers, more independence of the influence of advertisers; fewer readers and more dependence on the advertiser.' It may seem like a contradiction (yet it is true) to assert: the greater number of advertisers, the less influence they are individually able to exercise with the publisher.[3]

Within the framework under discussion, an important difference lies in the "more readers" argument, which itself reflects old broadcast and advertising axioms. Micromedia sites are not playing quite the same numbers game. A site far too small to attract broadcast advertisers can be highly sought after by multiple underwriters. But aside from considerations of audience size, Ochs's dictum still applies, albeit in somewhat restated form: the more *underwriters,* the more independence of voice is assured. Agreeing not to bring undue influence to bear on editorial content will be an important item in contracts. An underwriter attempting to do so will automatically be in breach and risk losing its long-term exclusive position. If competitors are avidly waiting in the wings for this to happen, it very likely won't. A company would have to be crazy to hand such advantage to a rival.

This is a delicate aspect of the relationship between companies and their micromedia partners. The diciest situations will be where the content of the external site has a direct bearing on the company's products—for example, if Toyota were to underwrite a site equivalent to *Car & Driver* magazine. This might be a dynamite idea. It's certainly not one to be avoided. But in cases like this, the company will need to sit on its hands and count to ten when the site reports that its latest product bites. Of course, it can argue and debate the opinion—it just can't threaten to penalize the site. If it does so, it paradoxically opens the door to Mitsubishi taking over its slot. This would obviously constitute a Very Bad Move. As a result of this dynamic, micromedia underwriting partners will be *better* protected from corporate manipulation than are their mass media counterparts in the broadcast world.

However, the influence problem probably won't be a very big deal overall. If Ford underwrites an organic gardening site, for instance, the company is highly unlikely to use its financial clout to sway readers' views on the best way to mulch carrots. So everyone can just relax. An excellent tactic in any case.

Why do it?

So far, this book has mostly looked at the negative motivations for gonzo marketing. Radical alternatives tend to appear when nothing else really works. The main agenda up to this chapter has been to show that marketing as currently practiced is badly mismatched to the culture and dynamics of the Internet. But the gonzo model goes beyond critique. Following the steps outlined above, companies can encourage authentic voice and genuine conversation within their walls, then break down the walls and connect those conversations to related exchanges already underway in the networked marketplace. Let's take a brief walkthrough of how this could work.

Say you're currently interested in K–12 education. You've got two kids and you're worried they're getting shortchanged in the public schools they go to. You want to know why and you want to explore your options. There's a lot of debate on this topic and sorting it out isn't easy. The conclusions that seem most obvious turn out to be questionable. The "definitive sources" you once might have trusted seem like mouthpieces for the status quo, or seem as if they've got hidden vested interests. But you've got little time to research all this. You care, but you also have to go buy a computer. Otherwise the kids won't be able to keep up with their schoolwork.

You go to the Dell site—let's say; this is entirely hypothetical—to start trying to figure out what system you need and how much it's going to set you back. To your amazement, right there on the homepage, you see a banner saying something like "Visit Our Home Schooling Community." As you watch, the banner changes. Next it says, "Visit Our Personal Investing Community," then "Visit Our Gonzo Tasmanian Chinchilla Ranching Community," but you're not interested in those (you're not even sure what that last one means). When the home schooling banner rolls back around, you click, and—hey, look at that!—there's a well produced web magazine addressing all your questions. The first thing you notice is a graphic saying "Underwritten by Dell." This is strange. And now you're curious. You click on this graphic assuming it will take you back to the Dell home page you've just come from. But another surprise: it doesn't. Instead, you end up on another sections of the Dell site where employees of the company are writing and talking about the very issues that have been bugging you. Intrigued but skeptical, you click around and scan a bunch of articles. The site is substantial and there's more to explore than you possibly could in one sitting. You bookmark the main entry point and pop over into email to send the URL to the half dozen friends you've lately been talking to about these school issues. "Look what I just found," you write. "I know, it's weird to find this on a computer company site, but what's even weirder is that there isn't any advertising."

Of course, there are links to Dell's regular site—this is a company page, so the frames are the same, with buttons for products and support and such. There are also links to many more of these "communities" Dell seems to be "underwriting." You explore the school pages some more and discover contributions by Dell people who think home schooling is the greatest, and Dell people who tried it and thought it sucked. They talk that way too—as if no one is controlling what they say. And they all have email addresses listed with invitations to comment on their views. You decide this must be bogus, some kind of advertising gimmick after all. But you email one person whose perspective you particularly agree with. To your astonishment, you get a reply 20 minutes later answering the question you asked, then adding "You know, it's a highly individual decision. Ask around, but go with your gut." Aside from a signature block that identifies this person as a Dell employee and a URL back to the Dell home schooling site, the message contains no pitch to buy anything. You forward it to the same six friends. "I can't believe these people have time to respond to stuff like this. Their company must be supporting this in a big way. I don't know why." But your skepticism is melting. You're impressed. You write back to the person who mailed you from Dell. "Wow, that was fast. Thanks. By the way, what do you do there?" The reply comes back even quicker this time. "I'm in customer service. Let me know if you ever have questions on that side of things. Doesn't matter if you have a Dell or something else. I know how they all work. ;-)"

As you browse around—you've come back several times now—you do find an article or two about Dell products. Aha, you think, this is where they get the payoff. But both sound like good advice on buying systems best suited to kids. "Forget the more expensive lines" one says. "Those are either for road-warrior business types or they're servers. Unless your kid is making a full-length movie (mine is, actually), you don't need that much power." Accompanying the piece is a chart laying out an optimal configuration for homework, gaming and Internet browsing. For less than you thought you'd have to pay. You click again. You buy it. While the price was a nice surprise, it wasn't the reason you bought the computer—and you didn't shop around as you were planning to. You bought it because you were impressed by what this company was doing. The next week, in the school parking lot, another parent mentions she's been thinking about a new computer for Billy. "Have you looked at the Dell site?" you ask. "I know you're interested in K–12 education. . . Here, let me write down this URL. It's really quite amazing."

Notice that there's nothing particularly gonzo about this little scenario—except that its approach to marketing breaks every accepted "rule" and notion of best practice. Also note that it focuses mainly on the company side of the micromarket partnership. In fact, the boundary between the two would be pretty permeable. There would be lots of links back and forth between the company site and its external underwriting partner, to content and resources existing on both sides. The partner would provide many pointers to Dell, and Dell would send as many people as it could to the partner site. They would be complementary, building in-depth understanding of the related issues, familiarity with regular contributors, and confidence in the company's intentions. They would also build customers. Loyal customers. But more than that, this combination would create more credible *evangelists* than any company could ever hope to generate, no matter how big its advertising budget.

There are other reasons why this model would be a major win for companies. Like attracting and holding onto the best and brightest talent—environments like this would be highly seductive to creative individuals. Like giving stockholders a better view of employee morale and the corporate culture's overall health than can be conveyed in a quarterly spreadsheet and a glad-handing annual report. Like giving journalists a thousand reasons for writing about the company. Like giving the net-at-large a million reasons to link to your web pages. Like the fact that what the gonzo model actually creates is a gigantic wide-area knowledge-acquisition filter attached to thousands of intelligent agents—a.k.a. knowledgeable human beings— and that this speaks directly to the capacity for innovation and the ability to remain competitive. There are many reasons for adopting the gonzo model, but the best will only be discovered in the course of exploration and experiment.

Why do it? Wrong question. The real question is, why not?

The Coming Internet Land Rush

I've always wanted to write The Coming Something-or-Other in a business book. It sounds so, you know, business-bookish. Don't worry, though, this is no convoluted consulting jive, compadres. You may think the net has been a big deal up to now, but you ain't seen nothing yet. Frankly, reviewing most of the corporate Internet gambits we've seen to date is not essentially dissimilar from watching a monkey trying to. . . (down, RageBoy, down!) fondle a football. In contrast, though mistakes will certainly be made, the model we've been circumambulating here will spur greater and faster development than everything that's happened on the net so far.

All it will take to torch it off is a few major corporations establishing the first micromarket partnerships. As soon as word leaks out that this is happening, their competitors will freak—with good reason. A company moving quickly to lock in relationships with the best voices in its areas of interest will reap substantial first-mover advantage. The next company to go looking will be looking at candidates of lesser quality. Competitors who wait a year or more to get started will find themselves picking over factory seconds. It's so simple. Deadly simple.

The result will be an Internet land rush of nearly unimaginable proportions. Imagine corporate buckboards lined up along the Internet border. Imagine B-movie thunder and lightning, sturm und drang. Imagine a light. . . over at the Frankenstein place. . . Imagine joyful anarchy and wild-eyed chaos as the empires of business-as-usual finally come crashing down of their own top-heavy weight. It's just a jump to the left. And it's about bloody time.[4]

So, if you run a website worth its salt, be prepared to see company A&R agents come calling, and soon. If it's not worth its salt, get busy. Gonzo marketing is market advocacy, remember? Despite the very real advantages to corporations, this one's for us. Be prepared to work with companies who get what you're up to and want to help circle the wagons around real—not bogus "consumer"—communities. As for the rest, the arrogant bastards had it coming all along. Enjoy the last laugh. Take no prisoners.

CHAPTER 8

Champions of the World

"Devil or angel, I can't make up my mind. . . "

THE PLATTERS [1]

"You don't know where you belong. . . "

CYNDI LAUPER, *SISTERS OF AVALON* [2]

SOMETIME BACK AROUND THE 3ʀᴅ CENTURY A.D., IF YOU CAN REMEMBER back that far, a certain meme got loose in an area roughly corresponding to what we now call the Middle East. Historically, quite a few whacked out ideas have originated in this region, most of them involving, in one way or another, the sacrifice of goats. Dave Barry can laugh at Santería all he wants, and we can all wonder what was up with those Aztecs, but this ancient proclivity to off the living in the pursuit of supernatural favor must reflect some deep, bloodthirsty need in the human soul. Or maybe—not to be insensitive to multicultural considerations, you understand—it was just an atavistic form of influence peddling. "Hello, God? Got a nice goat here for you. Uh-huh, hope you like it. Now about that Babylonian land development deal I was telling you about . . ." In all likelihood, we'll never know for sure.

Anyway, this meme came to be called *Manichaeism*—or if you happened to be in any way attached to a pope back in those days, the Manichean heresy. The core idea here was that nature and spirit are opposed and at war. Now, you can see right away how this would cause papal heartburn, as this was clearly encroaching on the monopoly turf of the whole Judeo-Christian setup. Gnostics and Buddhists horning in on the act clearly wouldn't do. To get the general flavor of this, think Microsoft and Netscape without Janet Reno. As if that weren't bad enough, Manichaeism also ticked off the Zoroastrians, from whose tradition it had borrowed certain critical elements, to the point that they finally did a drive-by on the rapper who was laying this stuff down—the dude's street name was Mani—and that was basically that. Or so everybody thought.

But these ideas continued to spread. They held a powerful attraction. God all-knowing and powerful, man stupid and weak. Spirit pure, flesh evil. Heaven good, earth bad. (You can see how the top-down thing got going.) This perspective simplified things a lot. And it had a straightforward agenda: the end of life and the destruction of the world. Talk about your perfect elevator pitch. What's to not understand? Much as I disapprove the fire-in-the-belly CEO-like qualities of Torquemada—who, granted, didn't get the Spanish Inquisition into high gear until much later—I think I might have been among the inquisitors on this particular Manichean issue. Fundamentalist dualism fundamentally sucks. Let's not quibble: any kind of dualism sucks. It's dumb. But it's understandable, I guess.

Historically, human beings have attempted to reduce the world to fit some overarching paradigm, some all-inclusive explanatory framework. Without such a worldview, the thinking goes, we would be left with only confusion and chaos. But the complexity of the world is such that every attempt to reduce it to fit such conceptual models impoverishes not only the world, but ourselves. Nonetheless, we can't seem to resist asking questions of the form: *which side are you on?* In the case of the Manichean debate: are you for the world or against it? But this attempt to simplify matters is naïve in the extreme, simplifying—and signifying—nothing. Instead, such black-and-white categorical distinctions mask what is truly interesting about the diverse ways in which people have come to perceive and value experience.

However, extreme naïveté never having posed much of a hurdle to human judgment, it should come as no surprise that the ancient Manichean war between matter and spirit has continued unabated to this day. Benjamin Barber writes of *Jihad vs. McWorld* and the binary, zero-sum implications seem unavoidable. This is a war between fundamentalist spirituality and fundamentalist materialism. Which side are you on? Are you for the world or against it? Come on, join up, take sides! But let's back up a minute. I want to make two points about materialism, the first personal and contemporary, the second cultural and historical, revisiting the dawn of business.

I have not been easy on business in this book. I have kicked asses and taken names. Applying the which-side-are-you-on filter, many may therefore conclude that I'm down on "materialism"— which translates into being rabidly anti-business. In fact, that stance is increasingly popular these days. You know the catechism. Business is evil, money is theft, corporations are rapacious juggernauts out of control, which left unchecked will destroy the quality of life on earth and the earth itself.

Paradoxically, the old Manichean agenda to put an end to the world, once based on spiritual opposition to the material plane, is now within the reach of the worldly powers. And this is no joke. Think global warming. Think industrial pollution, acid rain, break-neck deforestation. Business often seems to be at war with "the *environment*"—our more sophisticated way of referring to what the ancients simply called the world. It would be a serious mistake for business to take such anti-business sentiment lightly or to think that opposition to the bright and shiny vision of McWorld is safely localized in Islamic nations with unreasonably resistant notions about modernization and the wonders of a global economy. Next time you get a chance, drop by a demonstration against the World Trade Organization. Those are your children getting their heads busted open in the street.

So yeah, I share these concerns. But does this make me an "anti-materialist"? The quotation marks here and above, around "materialism," are necessary because these are essentially silly conceptual categories, setting up a bogus straw-man opposition between options that are not really optional. Abstruse philosophizing aside, the material world is not a concept. Whatever I may think about it, I remain in it and of it. If I question the attitudes and actions of business, does this mean I must "renounce the world" in favor of penitential sackcloth and ashes? If I think that business assumptions that applied in an earlier epoch have become dysfunctional in a networked society, does it mean I must go to the desert, wear funky sandals and eat locusts? It better not. Such either-or thinking constitutes a conceptual booby trap. Although the "logic" is usually transparent and invisible, when we think this way we are invoking extremely old binary opposites. Spirit good, world bad. World good, spirit bad. But such zero-sum, heads-I-win-tails-you-lose alternatives are suffocating and insufferable. I don't want to take sides. I don't want to be lumped into such confining categories. I want an olive tree *and* a Lexus. I want a Big Mac *and* a jihad.[3]

Let me try to explain this a different way. In the course of writing this book, in which I have admittedly given business a bad time, I have also given business quite a lot of . . . well, business. As you might expect, I pretty much have no life. I'm plugged into this monitor every damn day, online more than off. It's pathetic, I know. I'm a slave to the web. But I also eat and drink like mere mortals. I drive a car. I even wear clothes on occasion. The point is, I buy stuff. It's just that, being lazy, I buy it, whenever I can, on the net. Just while I was laboring over the last couple paragraphs, two delivery trucks arrived. The first brought ink cartridges for my printer; the second some really cool cooking software (I eat therefore I cook) and two boxes of *Harry Potter* audio CDs (they're not for my kid, they're for me). In the past several months I've ordered lots of stuff off the web: a Maxtor 80 gigabyte hard drive, a super-nifty Iomega Predator CD burner, an HP OfficeJet all-in-one printer/scanner/copier/fax combination, Iris OCR software and handheld text scanner, a Microsoft Encarta DVD encyclopedia upgrade, a Sony handheld digital voice recorder, a Sony digital camera, a CD Walkman, music CDs, DVD and VHS videos, a stereo with an integrated DVD player, (yet another) desktop computer, an online subscription to the *Grove Dictionary of Art*, an offline subscription to *Harvard Business Review*, and, of course, endless and innumerable books.

"Sure," you say, "you're an information junkie. That kind of stuff is all you net-heads ever buy." But *au contraire, mon frere*. I also purchased—again, from the web—all manner of clothing, toothpaste, vitamins, deodorant (very necessary in my line of work), several items of furniture and luggage, a pasta maker, a waffle iron, a crepe maker, a bread machine, a food processor, a microwave oven, a cast-iron barbecue grill, and—against all my better judgment, of which I haven't much to begin with—a Roland guitar synthesizer whose technology is sufficiently advanced as to be indistinguishable from magic.[4] OK, so maybe this doesn't qualify me as the world's greatest online shopper, but neither does it exactly brand me as a sworn enemy of e-commerce. While I strongly resist the idea that my identity is defined and bounded by my role as consumer, all in all, I think I've more than earned the sanguine salutation so typical of spammers: Valued Customer. Aside from a certain gender disparity, I'm right there with Madonna when she says, "I am a material girl."

But am I therefore a material-*ist?* I don't think so. And perhaps the information-junkie dimension constitutes some sort of skeleton key here, not just to my own behavior, but to that of the hundred-million-plus who have come online since I started writing about the Internet a decade ago. My personal buying habits aren't very interesting in themselves, unless you're my accountant (be glad you're not). They aren't interesting at all unless they represent some larger trend. But I think they do. I think they represent an enormous shift, not just in market attitudes and expectations, but in—for lack of a better phrase—collective consciousness. A deep and profound shift.

Among many attempts to explain the rising importance of computer-generated data was what Nicholas Negroponte saw as a critical differentiation between informational bits and "atomic" matter, upon which he expounded in *Being Digital*.[5] However, I've never been able to get very excited about this distinction. It seems to me yet another binary opposition. Bits good, atoms bad. Or—in the amphetamine-jazzed rhetoric of *Wired* magazine, where Negroponte flogged this simplistic concept to within centimeters of the grave—bits wired, atoms tired. While I know it's true that you can jam a webzine down a net connection a lot easier than, say, a pair of Nikes or a Ford Mustang, this doesn't do much to reduce my need for shoes and transportation. At the end of the day, after finally getting my head around the crucial difference between an HDTV signal and a chunk of Wisconsin cheddar, I'm not entirely sure what conclusion I am meant to draw from the bits-v-atoms argument—except maybe, the blur between content and advertising being what it is today, that I need to renew my subscription to *Wired*. Get some more hot tips on technofetishism.

But here's a tip of an altogether different stripe. Information is halfway between matter and spirit. I want to be very careful here. I don't mean that information is somehow sacred or spiritual in itself. I'm not trying to launch a new religion. Neither do I mean that information is superior to hula hoops but inferior to the angelic choirs. Instead, what I mean is that information mediates the spirit in which we perceive and value the material world. This mediation, which is neither inherently "spiritual" nor "materialistic," has a bearing on what we mean today by "*media*," and how our cultural perception of that concept has changed over time.

Take the neologism "*multimedia*," for example. This term partakes of a sort of meta-ambiguity, referring as it does to two distinct meanings of media without being very clear about either. In the first case, the multiplicity of multimedia refers to various *media of expression*, such as words, pictures, and sound. In the second case, the term refers to various *communication media*—such as newspapers, radio, television, and the Internet—through which such hybrid assemblages can be delivered. This latter sense has all but eclipsed the former, and in doing so has turned yet another of those sleight-of-tongue pop-philological tricks that serve to make meaning opaque, and eventually meaningless. As when someone protests— one of my personal all-time favorites—"Come on, that's just semantics. You know what I *mean*."

No, I don't know what you mean. Yet it's never been more important for all of us to understand what we mean by "*media*" and what it is that media mediate. Business understands this mediation as providing a vector for advertising—a channel through which to connect the dots from product to consumer. But let's go back to the older sense of *media*. A writer's medium is inscribed language; a painter's, color and form; a sculptor's, stone or metal; a musician's, sound and time. The medium is the means of conveyance, but what is conveyed is (usually) more than the material employed. Art communicates a *sense* of the world, not in literal terms, but by attempting to reproduce in another soul some deep, intangible and otherwise inexpressible quality of how the artist *experiences* the world—how the world *feels*. Art mediates spirit.

It is in this spirit that human beings, unbidden and uninstructed, have begun to use the Internet. Just as we used colored earths and

stone tools to create mimetic images of bison and horses in Neolithic caves. Just as we constructed monumental architectures hon-
oring gods now long forgotten. Just as we invented symbols and
emblems that pointed beyond themselves, hieroglyphics, pic-
tograms, alphabets, stories, epics, novels, histories. Just as we invented ecstatic dance and ritual music. Yeah, and so what? What
does it all *mean*, Mr. Natural? While nobody can say with any certainty, it is certain that whatever human beings have been attempting to express all these millennia continues to hold huge fascination
for human beings today. And this isn't some academic exercise in
art history. We practice what we preach. It's in our bones. It's in our
blood. It's in the beat of some larger heart. Perhaps the Stones said
it best. "I know, it's only rock and roll, but I like it."[6]

Billions of people will soon be connected to the Internet. They're
not all here yet, but they're coming. Writing in *The New York Times*,
Thomas L. Friedman reports that "Chinese will be the most popular
language on the web by 2007."[7] They're coming, and what they're
coming for is what the net mediates: the beat of that larger heart.
The net is not intrinsically a medium for advertising. They're not
coming for product brochures or lower prices. They're not coming
for some ersatz Disney World "experience." Instead, the net is an
artistic medium. It mediates spirit. Whatever spirit we bring to it, we
are coming for that. We are coming to discover who we are.

But let's not set up another Manichean spirit/matter dichotomy
here. Rock and roll good, e-commerce bad. The problem with materialism is not that it loves the world too much, but that it does not
love the world *enough*. If the dictates of business are causing the
exhaustion of planetary resources, something is clearly wrong with
its system of valuing matter. Not all value reduces to dollars and
cents. Most people I know detest being addressed as "Valued Customer" because they understand precisely what they're being valued
for: the chance that they'll fork over the purchase price. Any other
dimension of our existence is outside business's concern, beneath
its interest, immaterial. And, that's exactly right. This dimension *is*
immaterial. What does a company care that your dog can speak
Urdu? That your daughter is dying of leukemia? That you almost
broke under the pressure once, but somehow you survived. That
tonight the air feels the way it did the first time you fell in love?

These are matters that matter to people who appreciate and value your spirit. They are not material to a materialism that views human beings only through monetary criteria of value.

In adopting such a one-dimensional perspective, business has devalued the world it once represented. This stance is not an intrinsic aspect of business. It's not a given, not irreversible. Historically, the only-money-is-material attitude is fairly recent. I'm always amazed to hear people singing the Queen lyric—"we are the champions of the world"—after their team wins a football game.[8] I suspect the inspiration for this song had about as much to do with sports as the Star Spangled Banner had to do with web advertising. It's not about taking home the trophy. It's about *championing the world*. Four definitions are listed for *"champion"* in *The American Heritage Dictionary*. The first two involve contending and winning prizes. But the second two entail speaking on behalf of, or defending the honor of, some other entity. "3. An ardent defender or supporter of a cause or another person: a champion of the homeless. 4. One who fights; a warrior." Business was once a champion of the world in this larger sense.

Do you remember the sublunary sphere we talked about back toward the beginning of all this? Skipped that bit, did you? It figures. Well, for you slackers then, the sublunary sphere was the material world and *all* its material girls—the world, literally, under the orbit of the moon. In the eyes of the early Christian Church, the "things of this world" were mundane—that is, *"worldly"* in a highly pejorative sense. The other world (as in *"otherworldly"*) was the only world worth having any truck with: the destination of the just: heaven. What happened down here below on earth was of no interest or importance except as it related to getting *out* of this world, escaping this vale of toil and tears for a purely spiritual realm, "a better place." This was echoed in the Manichean dualism with which we opened this final chapter: world bad, spirit good. Simply put, matter didn't matter.

To say the least, this is a dim view of life on earth. What changed it was largely business. Business championed the world as no other segment of society had dared. It concerned itself with people and their needs, their hopes and dreams. It trafficked in desire and traded in "filthy lucre." It made the world its home base and permanent headquarters. It also made the world a better place. Less toilful for many. Less tearful for most. It did not eradicate pain and injustice. It did not create heaven on earth. But that was never its aim. Always in favor of the pragmatic business plan, its aim was earth on earth. And no apologies.

Historically and culturally, this was a huge accomplishment, and in many respects, a great leap for civilization. Significantly, business did not accomplish this by opposing matter to spirit and winning in a head-to-head contest, but rather by accommodating itself to the world of spirit and showing that the two were not incompatible. Commercial and ecumenical values were shown to be non-exclusive. But over time, business came to recast *all* values that were once commonly held by the inhabitants of this worldly sphere in terms that were conducive only to its own interest in maximizing profit. In an ironic reversal, business has become the new Church, with an equally inflexible, if secular, binary dogma. Now money is everything, and personal wealth the Promised Land. The produce-market-consume cycle is all that matters, and anything falling outside it simply noise. Simply a challenge that can be steam-rollered with a better jingle, a shinier brand, a bigger advertising budget. If something comes along that business doesn't quite understand, something that doesn't fit its value proposition, hey, no problem: invoke the ancient catechism. But first, give it to the boys in marketing to give it a bit of a hook and a better spin. Disney World good, Internet bad.

And so the thrashing continues, from pole to pole, until we're exhausted and ready to scream. Black vs. white. White vs. black. It's been going on for centuries. But quick, choose camps. Which side are you on?

It doesn't have to be this way.

We are people of earth. Feet firmly on the ground, we dream, but we also buy shoes. We explore each other's heads and hearts, but we also rent the occasional video, buy the occasional car or house or—whoops, there goes the neighborhood, honey—Eminem CD. Explicit lyrics and all. We value the spirit of the world that holds our lives in the balance so tentatively, but we also buy computers and carpets and zucchinis and vacuum cleaners and a million other things we need or want or decide—though we know it's not true—

that we just can't live without. And it's OK. All of it. It's OK that business makes stuff and tries to get us interested in buying it. It's OK that we're often interested in more than what business has to offer. We *might* be interested if only business came across a little less lame, a little less blind to what we're all about. We are not the devils of McWorld. We are not the angels of Jihad. We are both and neither. We are people of earth.

While dogma tends to limit and shut down the realm of the possible, contradiction and uncertainty enrich it. We have a name for people who deal with confusion without trying to reduce and simplify it, who enter into an open conversation with the world. We call them artists. Without artists, the world would be one big billboard. Without artists, the human dream would be over. Fortunately, it's not. Around populist artists—though most wouldn't call themselves that—new communities are emerging bottom-up on the net. An artist who connects with such a community is a shaman, a healer. And the disease that's gone truly viral, the malady that most needs a cure today is Either-Or Syndrome. Paradoxically, given where this emergence is taking place, being an artist is about being *non*-digital, *non*-binary. Not this versus that. Not that versus this. We are both and neither. We are more than is dreamed in your marketing plan, Horatio.

But isn't all this talk about artists (*artists* for God's sake!) really just more harebrained, impractical net-head bullshit? One last time, here's Philip Kotler, perhaps the world's most highly credentialed marketing authority, writing in *Harvard Business Review* five years ago—just as the Internet was getting off the ground and the notion of community as local and geographically bounded was being redefined as borderless and globally connected.

> By supporting the arts, businesses demonstrate good citizenship, add polish to their corporate image, enhance their community's quality of life, and promote goodwill among customers, clients, and employees. Moreover, a thriving cultural community helps businesses recruit and retain highly educated and talented people. The collective power of these benefits allows businesses to attribute many of the cash expenses of collaborative ventures to marketing rather than philanthropic budgets.[9]

The most critical factor in creating collaborative alliances between business and the arts, says Kotler, is trust. Internet artists and corporate underwriters must come to understand each other's view of the world. There is nothing written in stone that says the two must forever remain incompatible. But trust, says Kotler, "cannot be built in the abstract by thinking, planning, and talking about it. The best way to build trust is to get to work."[10]

Commerce and culture don't need to be at war. They need to be reintegrated. The bellicose imagery of business—waging campaigns, penetrating markets, beating the competition with killer-apps— won't be changed by adopting a new net-correct vocabulary or more worshipful protestations about Valued Customers. Fears about a global economy replacing indigenous customs with cheap made-in-America media trash, and enslaving the populations of poor countries as indentured sweatshop workers, won't be ameliorated by breaking windows at anti-WTO rallies. Maybe there's no hope for such an integration. Maybe business and society are bound for head-on collision or head-on collusion and there's no other way out. In which case, we are all well and truly fucked. Either way, the end of life and the destruction of the world are guaranteed. The Manicheans get the last laugh. And we can all go to heaven happy.

On the other hand, the challenge may not be so daunting after all. That's what I'm betting. That's what this book has been about. The dot-com meltdown of 2000 didn't prove that commerce is unworkable online. It only proved that get-a-bigger-hammer tactics based on antiquated notions about mass markets and broadcast media are unworkable online. Even for high-latency MTFTTB (Mean Time From Tail To Brain) dinosaurs, the message is slowly sinking in. Business is tired of playing the clueless bad guy. People are tired of working for and buying from clueless bad-guy businesses. The gonzo model is a way that companies and Internet communities can begin to work together in genuine partnership. The net has heightened our consciousness of ourselves as a species. This is a profound shift, the implications of which we can barely glimpse, still only guess at. There is more to the world that's coming than electronic commerce. For one thing, there's a potential Renaissance waiting in the wings, an explosion of art and culture greater than that touched off 500 years—not incidentally, by a form of corporate underwriting. Florentine bankers wanted to be remembered for their patronage of the arts. We remember them today because it worked. But the rifts between workers and companies, between companies and their markets, are profound and the negative effects of these rents in the social fabric touch nearly everyone on the planet today. The healing has to begin somewhere. Commerce is an excellent starting point.

The ideas in this book will be only ideas at first, bloodless and abstract. But as people in corporations and Internet communities begin to get to know each other *as* people—as acquaintances, friends and even sparring partners—begin to expect the unexpected. You know the cartoon that shows a scientist working out the formula for the Big Bang, and right in the middle it says "then a miracle occurs"? Expect that. Gonzo marketing is market advocacy. It's not zero-sum, not us-against-them. It's about lighting up the human network, creating a more humane global society—and achieving undreamed-of market efficiencies in the process. While the reasons the gonzo model is necessary and inevitable may be complex, the method is simple. Hook up, connect, co-create, procreate. Redeploy. Foment joy. Brothers in arms, sisters of Avalon, champions of the world get to work.[11]

notes

Introduction

1. *Encarta Book of Quotations,* developed for Microsoft Corporation by Bloomsbury Publishing, 1999.

2. Look for the January 2001 Forrester Report "The Snooze Factor: Sleepy Time in the Management Aisle." You won't be able to find it, however, because it doesn't exist. If you believed it did, seek immediate help from a professional gullibility counselor. Harley Manning, on the other hand, is a real research director at Forrester who reads Entropy Gradient Reversals and does, in fact, believe that most business books are better than Valium for getting to sleep at night. Much to the credit of both Manning and his company, this gratuitous chain yanking is published with knowledge aforethought and prior consent. Whatever those mean.

3. Johan Huizinga, *Homo Ludens: A Study of the Play Element in Culture,* Beacon Press, 1955. First published in Dutch, 1938. Quotes from the original foreword.

4. *Encarta Book of Quotations,* op. cit.

5. Claude Levi-Strauss, *The Savage Mind,* University of Chicago Press, 1966. Originally published in French as *La Pensee Sauvage,* 1962.

6. David Gates, "Will We Ever Get Over Irony?," *Newsweek,* January I, 2000, p. 90.

7. Nitin Nohria and James D Berkley, "Whatever Happened to the Take-Charge Manager?" *Harvard Business Review,* January, 1994, p. 128.

8. No, we're not really putting down the fine indigenous cultures of Borneo and New Guinea. See irony, supra. Even better, see a headshrinker.

9. Huizinga, op. cit.

10. http://www.ibm.com/lous-grooves.html Unfortunately, this page now reports "Our apologies. . . 404 multifail."

11. Daniel J. Boorstin, *Hidden History,* Vintage Books, 1989.

12. Shunryu Suzuki, *Zen Mind, Beginner's Mind,* Weatherhill, 1972.

13. Hunter S. Thompson, "The Kentucky Derby is Decadent and Depraved," included in Tom Wolfe, *The New Journalism,* Harper & Row, 1973. p. 179.

14. Hunter S. Thompson, *Fear and Loathing in Las Vegas: A Savage Journey to the Heart of the American Dream,* Vintage Books, 1971.

15. Motley Fool, http://www.fool.com

16. Gary Snyder, *The Practice of the Wild,* North Point Press, 1990.

17. *The I Ching or Book of Changes*, translated by C. F. Baynes and R. Wilhelm, Princeton University Press, 1967.

18. Hunter S. Thompson, op. cit.

Chapter 1

1. Taken from an obscure and badly translated Japanese arcade game, this meme burned up the net for a time. If you have to ask what it means, it's already too late. http://www.scene.org/redhound/AYB.swf. See also Jon Carroll, "All your base are belong to us," *The San Francisco Chronicle*, February 20, 2001. "The Net revealed how slow the media were, maybe how slow they had always been. By the time something hit the mass media, it was over." http://tribalwar.com/forums/showthread.php?threadid=24539

2. William Gibson, *Neuromancer*. New York: Ace Science Fiction Books, 1984.

3. Part of this section appeared on *Feed*.http://www.feedmag.com

4. Courtney Love, speaking to the Digital Hollywood online entertainment conference in New York on May 16 2000, as reproduced on *Salon* –http://www.salon.com/tech/feature/2000/06/14/love/index.html

5. This section originally ran on Byte's web site on February 21, 2000.

6. Entropy Gradient Reversals lives at http://www.rageboy.com

7. *The Economist*, "Lost in cyberspace," December 16, 1999.

8. For a sampling of the companies from which EGR draws subscribers, see http://www.rageboy.com/domains.html

9. As transcribed from the RealAudio file on Ford's website.

10. *The New York Times*, May 13, 2000; "Ford's Admission Perplexes the Neighbors in Henry's Hometown."The full Ford "1999 Corporate Citizenship Report" is at: http://www.ford.com/default.asp?pageid=399&storyid=387. The Ford "Sport Utility Vehicle Case Study" is online at: http://www.ford.com/default.asp?pageid=399&storyid=742

11. Jac Nasser, "Letter to Ford Stakeholders" at http://www.ford.com/default.asp?pageid=399&storyid=733

Chapter 2

1. Charles D. Schewe and Alexander Hiam, *The Portable MBA in Marketing*, John Wiley & Sons, 1998. Quotes taken from the glossary section, p. 473.

2. Thorsten Veblen, *The Theory of the Leisure Class*, 1899.

3. Pink Floyd, "Money," on *Dark Side of the Moon*, 1973. Lyrics by Roger Waters.

4. Philip Kotler, *Kotler on Marketing*, Free Press, 1999, pp. 17–34.

5. The Grateful Dead, "Touch of Grey," on *In the Dark*, 1987. Lyrics by Robert Hunter.

6. Dylan Thomas, "A Refusal to Mourn the Death, by Fire, of a Child in London," from *The Poems of Dylan Thomas*, New Directions, 1971.

7. Clifford Geertz, "Thick Description: Toward an Interpretative Theory of Culture," in *The Interpretation of Cultures*, Basic Books, 1973, p. 6.

8. Ibid. p. 5.

9. Peter L. Berger and Thomas Luckmann, *The Social Construction of Reality: A Treatise on the Sociology of Knowledge*, Anchor Books, 1966, pp. 59.

10. William Gibson, *Neuromancer*. New York: Ace Science Fiction Books, 1984.

11. Friedrich Nietzsche, *The Will to Power*, Random House, 1987. See also http://plato.stanford.edu/entries/nietzsche/

12. Marc Cohn, "Walking in Memphis," on *Marc Cohn*, 1991. Also performed by Cher on several albums and probably at least once in Las Vegas, home of the pyramids. The Talking Heads, "Cities," on *Fear of Music*, 1979. While it's not clear how many Greeks were in Memphis at any one time, David Byrne seems to have believed they were there in force. On the other hand, he's on the money about The King. Perhaps he believed, as I do, that Elvis said it best: "we can't go on together with suspicious minds."

13. Philip Kotler, *Marketing Management: The Millennium Edition*, Prentice Hall, 2000, p. 15.

14. http://www.ey.com/global/gcr.nsf/US/First_Mover_to_First_Prover_-_Thought_Center_-_Ernst_&_Young_LLP (emphasis in original)

15. http://www.ey.com/global/gcr.nsf/US/Marketplaces~Business_Model_eBusiness_-_Ernst_&_Young_LLP

16. *The American Heritage Dictionary of the English Language, Fourth Edition*, Houghton Mifflin, 2000.

17. Benjamin R. Barber, *Jihad vs. McWorld: How Globalism and Tribalism Are Reshaping the World*, Ballantine Books, 1995, p. 4

18. Ibid, p. 220.

19. Kris Kristofferson, "Me & Bobby McGee." Also performed by Roger Miller (1969), Janis Joplin, and Jerry Lee Lewis (1972). "Freedom's just another word for nothing left to lose."

20. For instance: Duane E. Knapp, *The Brand Mindset: Five Essential Strategies for Building Brand Advantage Throughout Your Company*, McGraw-Hill Professional Publishing, 1999. See also the related site where the quote appears http://www.brandstrategy.com/m_ebrand.htm. Also: "Our brand is everything to us," says Valerie Oberle, Vice President of Business Development at the Disney Institute – http://www.qualitydigest.com/jan97/disney.html Also: "The brand is everything," says Bloomingdale's CEO Michael Gould – http://www.columbia.edu/cu/business/botline/marketing.html

21. William Shakespeare, Sonnet 116.

22. Charles Hardin and Norman Petty, "Not Fade Away." Originally performed by Buddy Holly in 1957. Recorded by the Rolling Stones on their first album in 1964 and again in 1972 on *Exile On Main St.*

23. Gampopa, *The Jewel Ornament of Liberation*, translated by Herbert Guenther, Shambala, 1959.

24. *Webster's Third New International Dictionary: Unabridged*, electronic edition, Merriam Webster, 2000.

25. *The Oxford English Dictionary*, second edition, Oxford University Press, 1989.

26. *The Business of Alchemy: Science, Culture and the Holy Roman Empire*, Pamela H. Smith, Princeton University Press, 1994. pp. 7–8.

27. Ibid. p. 9.

28. Hamish Pringle and Marjorie Thompson, *Brand Spirit: How Cause Related Marketing Builds Brands*, John Wiley & Sons, 1999, p. 57.

29. Dire Straits, "Sultans of Swing," on *Dire Straits*, 1978. Thank you, goodnight, now it's time to go home.

30. Recast from *The Old Testament*, Genesis 1:2, King James version.

31. Tracy Kidder, *The Soul of a New Machine*, Little Brown and Company, 1981. See also, Laurie Windham, *The Soul of the New Consumer: The Attitudes, Behavior, and Preferences of E-Customers*, Allworth Press, 2000.

32. Barry Heermann, *Building Team Spirit: Activities for Inspiring and Energizing Teams*, McGraw-Hill, 1997. From the introduction, online at http://www.coax.net/spirit_at_work/intro.htm. See also, John W. Newstrom and Edward Scannell, *The Big Book of Team Building Games: Trust-Building Activities, Team Spirit Exercises, and Other Fun Things to Do*, McGraw-Hill, 1998.

33. *The Oxford English Dictionary*, second edition, Oxford University Press, 1989.

34. Lou Reed, "Take a Walk On the Wild Side," on *Transformer*, 1972.

35. Jefferson Airplane, "White Rabbit," on *Surrealistic Pillow*, 1967.

36. Homer, *The Iliad,* translated by Samuel Butler.

37. Homer, *The Odyssey,* translated by Samuel Butler.

38. See "Content is King," a talk delivered by Bill Gates, Chairman of Microsoft Corporation, January 3, 1996. http://www.microsoft.com/billgates/columns/1996essay/essay960103.asp

39. David Noble, *A World Without Women: The Christian Clerical Culture of Western Science*, Knopf, 1992.

Chapter 3

1. Aldous Huxley, *The Olive Tree And Other Essays*, 1936.

2. Adolf Hitler, *Mein Kampf*, 1933.

3. http://adage.com/news_and_features/special_reports/mktg100–1999/index.html

4. http://adage.com/century/jingles.html

5. Rob Walker, "Biz.Com: Four e-business journalists offer a guide to the new capitalism in the Internet age," a review of *The Cluetrain Manifesto* in *The New York Times Book Review*, March 26, 2000.

6. Leslie Kaufman, "Tuning In the New Way: The Internet Scene May Just Have a Lot in Common with the 1960's," *The New York Times*, April 10, 2000.

7. Philip Kotler, "Reflections on Marketing," the preface to The Kellogg Marketing Faculty, Northwestern University, *Kellogg on Marketing*, Dawn Iacobucci (editor), John Wiley & Sons, 2001.

8. Philip Kotler, "Marketing in the Age of Information Democracy," in The Kellogg Marketing Faculty, Northwestern University, *Kellogg on Marketing*, Dawn Iacobucci (editor), John Wiley & Sons, 2001, p. 387.

9. Christopher Locke, "Take My Word for It," *Journal of the Wild-Assed Guess*, September, 1995.

10. http://www.kraftfoods.com/html/brands/brands.html

11. U2, "Even Better Than the Real Thing," *Achtung Baby*, Island Records Ltd., 1991.

12. Richard Earle, *The Art of Cause Marketing: How to Use Advertising to Change Personal Behavior and Public Policy*, NTC Business Books, 2000. Italics in original.

13. After writing this, I discovered that the *Harvard Business Review* Paperback Series does include two volumes with "marketing" in their titles, though both are much older. *Sharpening the Marketing Edge* was published over 10 years ago, and *Consumer Marketing Strategies* is out of print.

14. Randall Rothenberg, "What Makes Sense, and Doesn't, or How to Resist Internet's Song," *Advertising Age*, August 5, 2000. http://adage.com/news_and_features/rr_viewpoint/archives/rr20000508.html

15. Theodore Levitt, "Marketing Myopia," *Harvard Business Review*, July-August 1960.

16. Theodore Levitt, "Marketing Myopia," *Harvard Business Review*, reprinted September-October 1975. The quote is from Levitt's "Retrospective Commentary" on his original 1960 article.

17. Jill Rosenfeld, "Experience the Real Thing," *Fast Company*, January/February 2000.

18. David Byrne (director), *True Stories*, 1986. A highly satirical look at a small Texas town during its "celebration of specialness." Jamie Uys (director), *The Gods Must Be Crazy*, 1980. A Coke bottle falls from the sky in the Kalahari desert causing severe cultural disruption to a tribe of Bushmen.

19. Jill Rosenfeld, "Experience the Real Thing," *Fast Company*, January/February 2000.

20. Sergio Zyman, *The End of Marketing As We Know It*, HarperCollins, 2000.

21. Quoted with the permission of the poster.

22. Thomas Scoville, "Legends in Their Own Minds," *Salon*, December 16, 1999. http://www.salon.com/tech/books/1999/12/16/renegades/index.html

23. Jerry Della Femina and Sergio Zyman, "It's a Mad, Mad, Mad Ad World," *Context*, December 2000/January 2001. http://www.contextmag.com/setFrameRedirect.asp?src=/archives/200012/thelastword.asp

24. Courtney Love, speech at the Digital Hollywood online Entertainment Conference, New York, May 16, 2000. Published on *Salon* as "Courtney Love Does the Math" http://www.salon.com/tech/feature/2000/06/14/love/index.html

25. Susan Sesolak, "Discovering Sources for Segmentation Data." from the companion website to Philip Kotler, *Marketing Management: The Millennium Edition*, Prentice Hall, 2000. The quote is from an "Internet exercise" dealing with chapter 9: Identifying Market Segments and Selecting Target Markets. http://cw. prenhall.com/bookbind/pubbooks/kotler5/chapter9/deluxe.html

26. Ibid. Susan Sesolak, "Discovering Sources For Segmentation Data."

27. Harry Webber, *Divide and Conquer: Targeting Your Customers Through Market Segmentation*, John Wiley & Sons, 1998. Michael J. Weiss, *The Clustered World: How We Live, What We Buy, and What It All Means About Who We Are*, Little, Brown and Company, 2000.

28. Regis McKenna, *The Regis Touch: New Marketing Strategies For Uncertain Times*, Addison-Wesley, 1986.

29. Regis McKenna, *Relationship Marketing: Successful Strategies for the Age of the Customer*, Addison-Wesley, 1991.

30. B. Joseph Pine II, *Mass Customization: The New Frontier in Business Competition*, Harvard Business School Press, 1993. See also: James H. Gilmore and B. Joseph Pine II, *Markets of One: Creating Customer-Unique Value Through Mass Customization*, A Harvard Business Review Book, 2000.

31. See for instance, Don Peppers and Martha Rogers, *Enterprise One to One: Tools for Competing in the Interactive Age*, Doubleday/Currency, 1997.

32. In 1999, I created personalization.com for Net Perceptions. At the beginning of 2001, I handed off my position as editor in chief to Eric Norlin. In June 2001, Net Perceptions decided to close down the site. http://www.personalization.com

33. See a somewhat more detailed discussion in Christopher Locke, "Beyond Purchase Circles," *personalization.com*, November, 1999. http://www.personalization.com/soapbox/columns/clocke-column–3.asp

34. Malcolm Gladwell, "The Science of the Sleeper: How the Information Age Could Blow Away the Blockbuster," *The New Yorker*, October 4, 1999. http://www.gladwell.com/1999_10_04_a_sleeper.htm

35. Theodore Levitt, "Marketing Myopia," *Harvard Business Review*, July-August, 1960, pp. 45–65.

36. Theodore Levitt, "Marketing Myopia," *Harvard Business Review*, reprinted September-October 1975. The quote is from Levitt's "Retrospective Commentary" on his original 1960 article.

37. Some of the material in this section is from an interview I did for the journal of the American Association of Advertising Agencies: "The Fortune Tellers," *Agency* (Vol. 10, No. 1), Winter 2000.

38. Steven M. Cristol and Peter Sealey, *Simplicity Marketing: Relieving Customer Stress in the Digital Age*, Free Press, 2000. Much of the material in this section is from my article "Smart Customers, Dumb Companies," *Harvard Business Review*, November-December, 2000.

39. Ibid. Cristol and Sealey, p. 201.

40. Ibid. Cristol and Sealey, p. 190.

41. Ibid. Cristol and Sealey, p. 7.

42. Tom Petty, "I Won't Back Down," on *Full Moon Fever*, MCA Records, 1989.

43. http://www.thestandard.com/people/display/0,1157,1043,00.html

44. Personal communication.

45. Seth Godin, *E-Mail Addresses of the Rich & Famous*, Addison-Wesley, 1994. p. viii.

46. Seth Godin, *Permission Marketing: Turning Strangers Into Friends and Friends Into Customers*, Simon & Schuster, 1999.

47. Peter Sealey, "How E-Commerce Will Trump Brand Management," *Harvard Business Review*, July-August 1999.

48. Seth Godin, "Unleash Your Ideavirus," *Fast Company*, August 2000, p. 115. http://www.fastcompany.com/online/37/ideavirus.html

49. Seth Godin, "Unleash Your Ideavirus," *Fast Company*, August 2000, p. 115. http://www.fastcompany.com/online/37/ideavirus.html

50. Christopher Locke, "Internet Apocalypso," *The Cluetrain Manifesto*, Perseus, 2000.

51. Seth Godin, "Unleash Your Ideavirus," *Fast Company*, August 2000, p. 115. http://www.fastcompany.com/online/37/ideavirus.html

52. Seth Godin, "Unleash Your Ideavirus," *Fast Company*, August 2000, p. 115. http://www.fastcompany.com/online/37/ideavirus.html

53. Seth Godin, *Unleashing the Ideavirus*, electronic edition, Do You Zoom, Inc., 2000. http://www.ideavirus.com

54. Emanuel Rosen, *the anatomy of buzz: how to create word of mouth marketing*, Doubleday/Currency, 2000. p. 195.

55. With the exception of this statement, all Seth Godin's remarks in this section are direct quotes from his book, *Permission Marketing: Turning Strangers into Friends and Friends into Customers*, Simon & Schuster, 1999.

56. Parts of this section previously appeared in different form as "The Halcyon Days of Broadcast Ad Model Fade," *Digitrends*, October 2000. Also online at http://www.digitrends.net/marketing/11542_12584.html

57. Thomas S. Kuhn. *The Structure of Scientific Revolutions*, third edition, University of Chicago Press, 1996. Originally published in 1962.

58. From an interview on C-SPAN's Booknotes, March 7, 1999. http://www.booknotes.org/transcripts/50506.htm

Chapter 4

1. A different version of this chapter ran in Esther Dyson's *Release 1.0* in February, 2000.

2. http://www.personalization.com. After creating the site and getting the core community together, I passed the project on to Eric Norlin, who is now editor in chief.

3. http://www.opensource.org

4. Elizabeth Weise, "Future Will Be Up Close And Personal," *USA Today*, November 23, 1999.

5. I forget the publication this interview appeared in. Email me if you know.

6. Theodore Levitt, "Marketing Myopia," *Harvard Business Review*, July-August 1960.

7. Theodore Levitt, "Marketing Myopia," *Harvard Business Review*, July-August 1960.

8. Emily Warn, *The Novice Insomniac*, Copper Canyon Press, 1996.

9. IBM press release, "Web Integrators, Hosters and Incubators Now to Provide IBM Offering for Internet Start-Ups," Partnerworld, Atlanta, GA, February 26, 2001.

10. http://www.cluetrain.com

11. Olu Oni, "Ashby's Law Revisited," http://members.home.net/onis/articles/feature1.htm

12. Brian Millar, "Modern Life is Rubbish," *personalization.com*, www.personalization.com/soapbox/contributions/millar.asp

Chapter 5

1. Robert D. Putnam, *Bowling Alone: The Collapse and Revival of American Community*, Simon & Schuster, 2000, p. 171.

2. Philip Kotler and Gerald Zaltman, "Social Marketing: An Approach to Planned Social Change," *Journal of Marketing*, July 1971, pp. 3–12.

3. Philip Kotler and Eduardo L. Roberto, *Social Marketing: Strategies for Changing Public Behavior*, Free Press, 1989, p. 24.

4. Doug McKenzie-Mohr and William Smith, *Fostering Sustainable Behavior: An Introduction to Community-Based Social Marketing*, New Society Publishers, 1999.

5. Neill McKee, *Social Mobilization & Social Marketing in Developing Communities: Lessons for Communicators*, Southbound, 1993.

6. *Chin Saik Yoon*, "Participatory Communication for Development," in Guy Bessette and C.V. Rajasunderam (editors), *Participatory Development Communication: A West African Agenda,* Stylus Publications, 1996.

7. *Encarta World English Dictionary*, 1999. Developed for Microsoft by Bloomsbury Publishing Plc.

8. Rudyard Kipling, "The White Man's Burden," *McClure's Magazine*, February, 1899. http://www.boondocksnet.com/kipling/kipling.html in Jim Zwick, (editor) *Anti-Imperialism in the United States, 1898–1935* http://www.boondocksnet.com/ail98–35.html (January 8, 2001).

9. Ariel Dorfman and Armand Mattelart, *How to Read Donald Duck: Imperialist Ideology in the Disney Comic*, International General, 1984. While it pre-dates the net by a bit, this seems relevant to the general theme.

10. Elaine Lawless, *Holy Women, Wholly Women: Sharing Ministries Through Life Stories and Reciprocal Ethnography*, University of Pennsylvania Press, 1993. Special thanks to my sister, Elizabeth Locke, who pointed out the potential relevance of reciprocal ethnography to gonzo marketing.

11. *Chin Saik Yoon*, op. cit.

12. *The Blues Brothers*, Universal Pictures, 1980.

13. Shirley Sagawa and Eli Segal, *Common Interest, Common Good: Creating Value Through Business and Social Sector Partnerships*, Harvard Business School Press, 1999, p. 117.

14. Sue Adkins, *Cause Related Marketing: Who Cares Wins*, Butterworth-Heinemann, 2000, p. 11.

15. Stuart Elliott, "Advertising: Absolut to Salute GLAAD," *The New York Times*, February 22, 2001.

16. Share Our Strength is online at http://www.strength.org

17. Bill Shore, *The Cathedral Within: Transforming Your Life by Giving Something Back*, Random House, 1999.

18. Richard Earle, *The Art of Cause Marketing: How to Use Advertising to Change Personal Behavior and Public Policy*, NTC Business Books, 2000, p. 3.

19. Philip Kotler and Alan R. Andreason, *Strategic Marketing for Nonprofit Organizations*, fifth edition, Prentice Hall, 1996, p. 304.

20. Philip Kotler and Alan R. Andreason, *Strategic Marketing for Nonprofit Organizations*, fifth edition, Prentice Hall, 1996, p. 389.

21. Philip Kotler and Alan R. Andreason, *Strategic Marketing for Nonprofit Organizations*, fifth edition, Prentice Hall, 1996, p. 388.

22. Hamish Pringle and Marjorie Thompson, *Brand Spirit: How Cause Related Marketing Builds Brands*, John Wiley & Sons, 1999, p. xix. Edward de Bono has written many books, perhaps the best known of which is *Lateral Thinking*.

23. "A Short Course in Social Marketing," Novartis Foundation for Sustainable Development, 2001. http://www.foundation.novartis.com/social_marketing.htm

24. "Social Marketing for Epilepsy," *Novartis Foundation for Sustainable Development, 2001*. http://www.foundation.novartis.com/social_marketing_epilepsy.htm

25. Dan Bischoff, "Consuming Passions," *Ms.* magazine, December 2000/January 2001, pp. 61–65.

26. Philip Kotler and Alan R. Andreason, *Strategic Marketing for Nonprofit Organizations*, fifth edition, Prentice Hall, 1996, p. 306.

27. Philip Kotler, *Kotler on Marketing*, Free Press, 1999, p. 14.

28. Evantheia Schibsted, "Shock It to You," *Business 2.0*, May 1, 2000.

29. "Advertising and death," *The Economist*, February 17, 2000.

30. Luciano Benetton, March 1998, http://www.benetton.com/wws/aboutyou/peopleplaces/file2063.html

31. Debra Ollivier, "The Colorful Dissenter of Benetton," *Salon*, April 17, 2000. http://www.salon.com/people/feature/2000/04/17/toscani_int/index.html. Some quotes are from the associated interview, "Toscani in His Own Words," which begins at http://www.salon.com/people/feature/2000/04/17/toscani_int/index1.html

32. Ibid.

33. John Rossant, "The Faded Colors of Benetton," *Business Week*, April 10, 1995.

34. Benetton corporate press release, "Benetton Advertising: Toscani Passes The Baton," Ponzano, Italy, April 29, 2000. http://www.benetton.com/press/sito/press_releases/press2000/communication/oting.html

35. *Talk* magazine, "the Players" (editorial team), http://www.talkmagazine .com/players/index.html

36. Reviewing *Talk* magazine, Alex Kuczynski writes: "Of 22 articles in the first four issues written by people in the film industry or about people or characters in the film industry, 11 featured people recently or currently affiliated with Miramax or Disney Projects." As reported in "The Critics: Mainstream Media," *Columbia Journalism Review*, March/April 2000. On the other hand, Michael Wolff reports on an interview with Tina Brown about *Talk*. "We want it to have the feeling of the voices of the Web." Wolff notes that she adds "Of course we want it to be accurate." Michael Wolff, "All Talk," *New York Magazine*, January 25, 1999.

37. Oliviero Toscani, *1000 Extra/Ordinary Objects*, Taschen America, 2000. http://www.benetton.com/wws/aboutmake/colors/index.html

38. Rosabeth Moss Kanter in the preface to Shirley Sagawa and Eli Segal, *Common Interest, Common Good: Creating Value Through Business and Social Sector Partnerships*, Harvard Business School Press, 1999.

39. See for instance: NikeWatch at http://www.caa.org.au/campaigns/nike/index.html; Corporate Watch at http://www.corpwatch.org/trac/nike/announce/nikes.html; and the Boycott Nike site at http://www.saigon.com/nike/. These are just near-random examples of the kind of public corporate oversight the web has enabled.

40. Garrett Hardin, "The Tragedy of the Commons," *Science*, 162, 1968, pp. 1243–1248.

41. Robert D. Putnam, *Bowling Alone: The Collapse and Revival of American Community*, Simon & Schuster, 2000, p. 19.

42. By Farrell, "Bring Back the Quilting Bee," a review of *Bowling Alone* in *Business Week*, June 26, 2000.

43. Robert D. Putnam, *Bowling Alone: The Collapse and Revival of American Community*, Simon & Schuster, 2000, p. 171.

44. Eric L. Lesser, *Knowledge and Social Capital: Foundations and Applications*, Butterworth-Heinemann, 2000.

45. Eric L. Lesser, *Knowledge and Communities*, Butterworth-Heinemann, 2000.

46. John Seely Brown and Paul Duguid, "Organizational Learning and Communities of Practice: Toward a Unified View of Working, Learning, and Innovation," originally published in *Organization Science*, February, 1991. The George W. Bush quote is purportedly from a talk he gave in Arlington Heights, Ill., on Oct. 24, 2000. "It's important for us to explain to our nation that life is important. It's not only life of babies, but it's life of children living in, you know, the dark dungeons of the Internet."

47. John Seely Brown and Paul Duguid, *The Social Life of Information*, Harvard Business School Press, 2000.

48. Jay Rosen, posted to Amazon.com November 22, 1999. http://www.amazon.com/exec/obidos/tg/stores/detail/-/books/0300078234/reviews/

49. Tom Goldstein, "Good Question" (review of *What Are Journalists For?*), *The New York Times*, November 14, 1999.

50. James Fallows, *Breaking the News: How the Media Undermine American Democracy*, Vintage Books, 1997, p. 260.

51. Rosen, *What Are Journalists For?*, Yale University Press, 1999, p. 34.

52. From an interview on C-SPAN's Booknotes, July 25, 1999. http://www.booknotes.org/transcripts/50525.htm

53. Howard Kurtz, *Media Circus: The Trouble with America's Newspapers*, Times Books/Random House, 1993, p. 341.

54. Jon Katz discussing his book – *Virtuous Reality: How America Surrendered Discussion of Moral Values to Opportunists, Nitwits & Blockheads Like William Bennett* on *Booknotes*, Air Date: March 23, 1997. http://www.booknotes.org/transcripts/50404.htm

55. James S. Ettema and Theodore L. Glasser, *Custodians of Conscience: Investigative Journalism and Private Virtue*, Columbia University Press, 1998, p. 61.

56. For an interesting note on McGuffins, see http://nextdch.mty.itesm.mx/~plopezg/Kaplan/Mcguffin.html

57. Tom Wolfe, *The New Journalism*, Harper & Row, 1973.

58. Kevin Kerrane and Ben Yagoda (editors), *The Art of Fact: A Historical Anthology of Literary Journalism*, Touchstone Books, 1998. Also: Norman Sims (editor), *The Literary Journalists*, Ballantine Books, 1984. Also: Norman Sims (editor), *Literary Journalism: A New Collection of the Best American Nonfiction*, Ballantine Books, 1995.

59. Jack Fuller, *News Values: Ideas for an Information Age*, University of Chicago Press, 1997, p. 136.

60. Hunter S. Thompson, "The fix is in," *ESPN, Page 2,* http://espn.go.com/page2/s/thompson/001127.html

61. David T.Z. Mindich, *Just the Facts: How "Objectivity" Came to Define American Journalism*, New York University Press, 1998.

62. Mary Linsky, "The Public Interest in Journalism," *The American Prospect*, January 17, 2000. See also, Walter Lippmann, *Public Opinion*, Free Press Paperbacks (Simon & Schuster), 1997. Originally published by Macmillan in 1922.

63. Jurgen Habermas, *Legitimation Crisis*, Beacon Press, 1975. German edition originally published in 1973. Jürgen Habermas, *The Structural Transformation of the Public Sphere: An Inquiry into a Category of Bourgeois Society*, MIT Press, 1991. German original published 1962.

64. Scott Sonner, "Publisher Sees Newspapers Flourishing in Internet Era," Associated Press, dateline: Reno, Nevada, April 1, 2000, available at http://www.sfgate.com/cgi-bin/article.cgi?file=/news/archive/2000/04/01/state0401EST0107.DTL.

65. Bartholomew H. Sparrow, *Uncertain Guardians: The News Media as a Political Institution*, Johns Hopkins University Press, 1999; Martin A. Lee and Norman Solomon, *Unreliable Sources: A Guide to Detecting Bias in News Media*, Lyle Stuart,

1990; Robert W. McChesney, *Rich Media, Poor Democracy: Communication Politics in Dubious Times*, University of Illinois Press, 1999; *Republic of Denial: Press, Politics and Public Life*, Yale University Press, 1999; Doug Underwood, *When MBAs Rule the Newsroom*, Columbia University Press, 1993; Martin Plissner, *The Control Room: How Television Calls the Shots in Presidential Elections*, Free Press, 1999; Howard Kurtz, *Media Circus: The Trouble with America's Newspapers*, Times Books, 1993; James Fallows, *Breaking the News: How the Media Undermine American Democracy*, Vintage, 1997.

66. Gary Snyder, *The Practice of the Wild*, North Point Press, 1990.

67. Dawn B. Sova, *Banned Books*, Facts on File, 1998. The series includes four volumes: *Literature Suppressed on Political Grounds, Literature Suppressed on Sexual Grounds, Literature Suppressed on Religious Grounds,* and *Literature Suppressed on Social Grounds*—the Florida (Chaucer) case appears in the last, pp. 64–65. All the authors listed in this paragraph are included in the series.

68. *Better Than Sex: Confessions of a Political Junkie—The Gonzo Papers, Volume 4*, Hunter S. Thompson, Ballantine Books, 1994. p. 243. Italics in original.

69. Dave Barry, *Big Trouble*, Berkeley Books, 2001, pp. 14–15.

70. Edward S. Herman and Noam Chomsky, *Manufacturing Dissent: The Political Economy of the Mass Media*, Pantheon Books, 1988, p. xi.

71. Ben H. Bagdikian, *The Media Monopoly*, Fifth edition, Beacon Press, 2000.

72. Herbert J. Gans, *Deciding What's News: A Study of CBS Evening News, NBC Nightly News, Newsweek, and Time*, Vintage Books, 1989, p. 313.

73. Herbert Gans, *Popular Culture and High Culture: An Analysis and Evaluation of Taste*, Basic Books, 1999, p. 175. Originally published in 1974.

Chapter 6

1. Gary Armstrong and Philip Kotler, *Marketing: An Introduction*, fifth edition, Prentice Hall, 1999, p. 183.

2. Ben H. Bagdikian, *The Media Monopoly*, Fifth edition, Beacon Press, 2000. pp. x–xxi.

3. Saul Hansell, "Disney to Abandon Portal Site," *New York Times,* January 30, 2001.

4. Nico Detourn, "Was Disney's Go.com a Goofy Idea?," *Motley Fool,* January 30, 2001. http://www.fool.com/news/2001/dis010130.htm

5. Walt Disney Internet Group investor relations page, http://disney.go.com/investors/wdig/invest.html

6. Michael Wolff, "Eisner Un-Moused?" New York Magazine, July12, 1999, http://www.newyorkmag.com/page.cfm?page_id=143.

7. Source is a timeline accompanying Christopher Parkes, "Disney ends Go.com portal," *The Financial Times,* January 29, 2001.

8. Brad King, "Placing Product Before Art," *Wired News*, February 1, 2001.

9. Abbot Joseph Liebling, "Do You Belong in Journalism?," *The New Yorker*, May 14, 1960.

10. Malcolm Gladwell, *The Tipping Point: How Little Things Can Make a Big Difference*, Little Brown, 2000.

11. Personal communication

12. http://www.sweetfancymoses.com/crowley_dream

13. Christopher Locke, "Writer's Bloc," *Sweet Fancy Moses*, http://www.sweetfancymoses.com/locke_bloc.htm

14. http://www.plastic.com

15. http://www.suck.com

16. http://www.feedmag.com

17. Jamie Heller, "Online Journalism Coming Into Its Own.," *The New York Times*, August 3, 1998.

18. Carl Hiaasen, *Kick Ass*, University Press of Florida, 1999.

19. "Badges? We ain't got no badges. We don't need no badges. I don't have to show you any stinking badges!" Dialogue from *The Treasure of the Sierra Madre*, 1948.

20. Steven Jones, "The Bias of the Web," in Andrew Herman and Thomas Swiss (editors), *The World Wide Web and Contemporary Cultural Theory*, p. 177. The embedded quote is from Marshall McLuhan, *Understanding Media, The Extensions of Man*, Penguin, 1964, p. 266.

21. Paul Farhi, "The Dotcom Brain Drain: Print Journalists Are Heeding the Siren Song of the Internet," *American Journalism Review*, March, 2000.

22. http://w.moreover.com/site/about/team/index.html#nickdenton

23. Lisa Guernsey, "Mining the 'Deep Web' with Sharper Shovels," *The New York Times*, January 25, 2001.

24. Randall Rothenberg, "What Makes Sense, and Doesn't, or How to Resist Internet's Song," *Advertising Age*, August 5, 2000. http://adage.com/news_and_features/rr_viewpoint/archives/rr20000508.html

25. Lisa Guernsey, "Mining the 'Deep Web' With Sharper Shovels," *The New York Times*, January 25, 2001.

26. http://www.blogger.com

27. http://www.newsblogger.com

28. http://www.onlinejournalism.com

29. Scott Shuger and others, "Today's Papers" (ongoing column), *Slate*, http://slate.msn.com/code/TodaysPapers/TodaysPapers.asp

30. Julia Lipman, "Weblogs Crawl Out from Underground," *digitalMASS*, December 13, 2000. http://digitalmass.boston.com/columns/internet/1213.html

31. http://www.tompeters.com/content/weblogs/index.html

32. Philip Kotler and Gary Armstrong, *Principles of Marketing*, 9th edition, Prentice Hall, 2001, pp. 247–248.

33. Philip Kotler and Alan R. Andreason, *Strategic Marketing for Nonprofit Organizations*, fifth edition, Prentice Hall, 1996, p. 397. Italics added.

Chapter 7

1. *Newsweek*, May 12, 1980, as quoted in *The Oxford English Dictionary*, second edition, Oxford University Press.

2. Theodore Levitt, "Marketing Myopia," *Harvard Business Review*, July-August 1960.

3. Adolph S. Ochs, in an address to the Philadelphia convention of the Associated Advertising Clubs of the World, June 26, 1916. Cited in Elmer Davis, *History of the New York Times, 1851–1921*, which is in turn cited in Walter Lippmann, *Public Opinion*, Free Press Paperbacks (Simon & Schuster), 1997. Originally published by Macmillan in 1922.

4. Thanks and a tip o' the hat to *Rocky Horror*. If you're not familiar with this film, go rent it, Frederick. Give yourself over to absolute pleasure. Find out what bottom-up is all about. Oh, Frankie!

Chapter 8

1. Blanche Carter, "Devil or Angel." Performed by The Clovers in 1956; also by Bobby Vee in 1960.

2. Cyndi Lauper and Jan Pulsford "You Don't Know," *Sisters of Avalon*, Epic (Sony), 1997.

3. Benjamin R. Barber, *Jihad vs. McWorld: How Globalism and Tribalism Are Reshaping The World*, Ballantine Books, 1995. Thomas L. Friedman, *The Lexus and Olive Tree*, Farrar Straus & Giroux, 2000.

4. "Any sufficiently advanced technology is indistinguishable from magic." The line appears in Arthur C. Clarke, *Profiles of the Future: An Inquiry into the Limits of the Possible*, 1962.

5. Nicholas Negroponte, *Being Digital*, Knopf, 1995.

6. Mick Jagger and Keith Richards, "It's Only Rock & Roll," performed by The Rolling Stones on *It's only Rock & Roll*, 1974.

7. Thomas L. Friedman, "Hype and Anti-Hype," *The New York Times*, February 23, 2001.

8. Freddy Mercury, "We Are the Champions," performed by Queen on *News of the World*, 1977.

9. Joanne Scheff and Philip Kotler, "How the Arts Can Prosper Through Strategic Collaborations," *Harvard Business Review*, January 1996, p. 52.

10. Joanne Scheff and Philip Kotler, op. cit.

11. Mark Knopfler, "Bothers in Arms," performed by Dire Straits on *Bothers in Arms*, 1985.

index

1–to–1 marketing, 12, 78
4 Ps of marketing, 47, 103

ABC, 173
Accenture (Andersen
    Consulting), 5
Advertising Age, 65, 68, 69–70,
    175
advocacy journalism, 151, 153,
    161, 163
Africa, 45
AIDS, 132, 141, 161, 194
aircraft design, 9–10
alchemy, 54–56
Altamira, 27, 110
AltaVista, 23, 48, 159, 167
amateur spirit, 4–5
Amazon.com, 13, 72–73, 78,
    109, 113–114, 135, 149
American Airlines, 36
American Express, 136, 137,
    140, 142
American Journalism Review,
    175
American Revolution, 153
Anatomy of Buzz, The (Rosen),
    92

AnchorDesk, 106
Andersen Consulting
    (Accenture), 5
Andreason, Alan R., 138, 141,
    191–192
anthropology, 45, 47, 133–134
anthropomorphism, 56, 58
antisocial marketing, 67–68
Anuff, Joey, 173
AOL (America Online), 12,
    23–26, 62, 74, 109, 142, 189
    and Share Our Strength, 137
    /Time Warner merger, 24–26,
    163–166, 185
Apple Computer, 67, 77
Aristotle, 47
Armstrong, Gary, 165, 179
Art of Cause Marketing, The
    (Earle), 68–69, 138
Ashby's Law, 119–120
AT&T (American Telephone &
    Telegraph), 67
Audioactive, 115–116
automobile industry, 34–41,
    186, 196
Aykroyd, Dan, 135

B2B (business-to-business)
  commerce, 47–48
Bagdikian, Ben, 165
bandwidth, 25, 52, 194
Bank of America, 67
Barber, Benjamin, 50–51, 204
Barne's & Noble, 109, 137
Barry, Dave, 161–162, 203
Beatles, 93
Becher, Johann Joachim, 55
Beerbohm, Max, 1
"beginner's mind," notion of, 5
Being Digital (Negroponte),
  207
Bell Atlantic, 25
Ben & Jerry's, 136
benchmarking, 148
Benetton (company), 140–144
Benetton, Luciano, 141, 142,
  143–144
Berger, Peter, 46
Berlin Wall, 34
Berst, Jesse, 106
Bertelsmann, 36, 163, 165
best of breed, identifying,
  190–191
Big Trouble (Barry), 161–162
Bloomingdale's, 137
Blues Brothers (film), 135
Boorstin, Daniel J., 4–5
Borthwick, John, 73–74
Bottomliners, 94–95
*Bowling Alone: The Collapse
  and Revival of American
  Community* (Putnam),
  145–146
BP Amoco, 34

brand(s)
  equity, 41
  magic of, 75
  use of the term, 50
  value proposition of, 43–63
Brand Spirit, 56, 138–139
Breaking the News, 150
bricolage, 2, 3
British Airways, 123
broadcast paradigm, 97–102
Brokaw, Tom, 102
Brown, Tina, 143
Browne, Jackson, 7–8
Buddhism, 5, 45, 46–47
Building Team Spirit
  (Heermann), 59
Bush, George W., 24
Business of Alchemy, The
  (Smith), 55
Business Week, 142, 146

Calvinism, 56
Camerson, James, 185
"Car Talk" (radio show), 12
Carey, James W., 70
Case, Steve, 185
Catch–22 (Heller), 183
*Cathedral Within:
  Transforming Your Life by
  Giving Something Back*
  (Shore), 137
cause marketing, 68–69,
  135–140
Cause Related Marketing
  (CRM), 139
*Cause Related Marketing: Who
  Cares Wins*, 136

CBS (Columbia Broadcasting System), 152, 163, 173
censorship, 160
Chase Manhattan Bank, 119
Chaucer, 159
children, perception of the world by, 46
Chomsky, Noam, 162
Christianity, 54, 59–60, 143, 204, 210
Church, and State, 40, 46, 151, 197–201
Ciba Geigy, 67, 140
Citicorp, 34
Click and Clack, 12
Cluetrain Manifesto: The End of Business As Usual (Levine, Locke, Searls, and Weinberger), 28, 33–34, 57–58, 66–67, 74, 108
CNN (Cable News Network), 20, 100, 154, 161, 167
Coca-Cola, 71–72, 73, 77, 90
collaborative filtering, 78–79, 113
colonialism, 62, 133, 153
Colors magazine, 143
Comedy Central, 65
common good, 144–148
common sense, 48, 153
Common Interest, Common Good: Creating Value Through Business and Social Sector Partnerships, 144
Communication and Culture (Carey), 70

communities of interest, 13, 41, 177
Compaq, 123
complexity, 52, 81
computers, provision of, to employees, 34–38
Conde Nast, 34
Conoco, 34
Context (magazine), 74
contractual relationships, 195–197. *See also* partnerships
convergence, use of the term, 25
Coors Brewing, 137
Cristol, Steven M., 81–82
CRM (Cause Related Marketing), 139
CRM (Customer Relationship Management), 77
cross-selling, 113
Crowley, Brian, 171
C-SPAN, 102
Custodians of Conscience: Investigative Journalism and Private Virtue, 153
Customer Relationship Management (CRM), 77
cyberspace, coining of the word, 21

Daimler-Chrysler, 39
Deadlines & Datelines: Essays at the Turn of the Century (Rather), 152
De Bono, Edward, 139
Della Femina, Jerry, 74, 75
Dell Computer, 199–201

Delta Airlines, 36
Deming, W. Edwards, 36, 126
democracy, 4, 20, 145, 149,
    155–156, 159
  and cause marketing,
    136–137
  and micromarkets, 181
  and social marketing, 161
demographic(s), 41, 72, 113,
    191
  and micromarkets, 181
  profiles, 14
  segmentation, 101
  slice-and-dice techniques, 77
  and youth markets, 76
Denton, Nick, 175
Derrida, Jacques, 155, 156
Dewey, John, 155–156
Didion, Joan, 154
Digital Hollywood
    entertainment conference,
    22, 76
Direct Marketing Association, 5
Disney, 62, 90, 163, 165–167,
    185, 209, 211
Druids, 63
Dupont, 67

Earle, Richard, 68–69, 138
Easter Eggs, in software, 49
economies of scale, 75, 79–80,
    167, 183
Economist, The, 31–32, 141,
    175
ecosystems, 7
EGR (Entropy Gradient
    Reversals), 28–33, 115, 118

Egyptian Book of the Dead, 45
Eisner, Michael, 165–167, 169,
    175, 180, 185
Eli Lilly, 20
Elliott, Stuart, 136
Ellison, Larry, 17
E-Mail Addresses of the Rich &
    Famous (Godin), 86–87, 89
Encarta (Microsoft), 116, 133
End of Marketing as We Know
    It, The (Zyman), 73
Entropy Gradient Reversals
    (EGR), 28–33, 115, 118
entropy, law of, 52
Ernst & Young, 47–48
ESPN, 154
ethnography, reciprocal, 134
Excite, 23
external partners, identifying,
    191–192

Fallows, James, 150, 158
Fast Company, 28, 71–72,
    89–90
Fear and Loathing in Las Vegas
    (Thompson), 10, 15
Feed, 169, 173
financial markets, 23
Financial Times, The, 167, 175
Finnegan's Wake (Joyce),
    44–45
First Union Bank, 5
Floyd, Pink, 34, 43
focus groups, 28–38, 108
Ford Motor Company, 34–41,
    186, 196
Forrester Research, 1

Fortune 500 corporations, 46, 77, 133

Fostering Sustainable Behavior: An Introduction to Community-Based Social Marketing, 131

Foucault, Michel, 156

From Those Wonderful Folks Who Gave You Pearl Harbor (Della Femina), 74

FTP (File Transfer Protocol), 170

Fuller, Jack, 154

Gans, Herbert, 163–164

Garcia, Jerry, 44

Gartner Group, 5

Gates, Bill, 116

Gates, David, 2–3

Geertz, Clifford, 45, 46, 133

gender, 62

General Electric, 36–37, 67, 163, 165, 167

General Motors, 37, 39, 136

Gerstner, Lou, 4, 28, 31

Gibson, William, 21, 46

GLADD (Gay and Lesbian Alliance Against Defamation), 136

Gladwell, Malcolm, 78, 170

Go.com, 23, 166–167

Godin, Seth, 85–91, 93, 95–96, 189

Google.com, 159–160

Gore, Al, 24, 154

Gore, Tipper, 159

Grateful Dead, 44

gratitude, 44

Greatest Generation, The (Brokaw), 102

Gutbrodt, Fritz, 6

Guthrie, Woody, 56

Habermas, Jürgen, 156

Hagel, John, 86–87

Hardin, Charles, 51

Harris, Jay T., 156–157

Harry Potter books, 109, 113, 206

Harvard Business Review, 3, 48, 69–71, 78, 89, 144, 206, 212

"Hawthorne effect," 190

Heermann, Barry, 59

Heilige Geist, 59

Heller, Jamie, 173

Heller, Joseph, 183

Hiaasen, Carl, 174

Hitler, Adolf, 65

Homer, 61

Home Shopping Network, 137

Homo Ludens: A Study of the Play Element in Culture (Huizinga), 1–2

HotWired, 173

HTML (HyperText Markup Language), 170

Huizinga, Johan, 1–4

Hunted, The (Leonard), 15

Huxley, Aldous, 65

IBM (International Business Machines), 4, 28, 31, 37, 67, 81, 90, 117, 123, 147

ICQ, 109
Iliad (Homer), 61
imagination, 63, 111–112
individual marketing, 179
Industry Standard, The, 28, 86
*Information Please Business
    Almanac & Desk Reference*,
    85
Intel, 36, 37
intellectual capital, 188–190
Internet Magazine, 115
interruption marketing, 86–87
IPOs (initial public offerings),
    23
ISPs (Internet Service
    Providers), 23

Jagger, Mick, 108
Japan, 74
Jews, 54
Jihad vs. McWorld (Barber),
    50–51, 204Johnson, Steve,
    173
Johnson & Johnson, 68–69
Jones, Steven, 174–175
journalism
    advocacy, 151, 153, 161, 163
    gonzo, 10–11, 40, 154, 160
    literary, 154
    meta-, 176
    and micromedia, 169,
        173–175
    and objectivity, 148–150,
        152–159
    and social marketing,
        129–164
    and subjectivity, 160–164

Joyce, James, 44–45
JP Morgan, 67
*Just the Facts: How "Objectivity"
    Came to Define American
    Journalism*, 155
J. Walter Thompson, 34

Kanter, Rosabeth Moss, 144
Karsax Online, 7
Kellogg Graduate School of
    Management, 67, 94
Kellogg on Marketing, 67–68
Kesey, Ken, 9
Kidder, Tracy, 154
Kipling, Rudyard, 132
K-Mart, 101
Knowledge
    acquisition, 37
    relevant, 66
Knowledge and Social Capital
    (Lesser), 146–147
Kotler, Philip, 44, 67, 76, 130,
    138, 141, 165, 179,
    191–192, 212–213
Kraft Foods, 137
Kuhn, Thomas, 97–98, 121
Kurtz, Howard, 152

Lamb, Brian, 102
Larsen, Steve, 104–105, 107,
    117–118
Lascaux, 27, 110
Latin, 59
Lauper, Cyndi, 203
Lawless, Elaine, 134
Lazarsfeld, Paul, 70
legitimacy, 54, 106, 156–157

Leonard, Elmore, 15
Lesser, Eric, 146–147
Levi-Strauss, Claude, 2
Levine, Rick, 28
Levitt, Theodore, 70–71, 79–80, 111–112, 184
Lewis, Jerry Lee, 67
Liebling, A. J., 168
Linux, 37, 84, 105, 173
Lippman, Walter, 155
local marketing, 179
Locke, Selene, 44
love, 51, 57, 58–59, 193
Love, Courtney, 22, 76
loyalty, 41, 58
Lycos, 23

MacCarthy, Deborah, 71
MacDonald's, 100
McKee, Neill, 132
McKenna, Regis, 77
McPhee, John, 154
Macy's, 137
Magliozzi, Ray, 12
Magliozzi, Tom, 12
Major, Mark, 141
Manicheanism, 203–205, 210
manifestos, 89–90
Manning, Harley, 1
Manufacturing Dissent: The Political Economy of Mass Media (Chomsky and Herman), 162
marketing. See also micromarkets
  antisocial, 67–68
  cause, 68–69, 135–140

"4 Ps" of, 47, 83, 103
  individual, 179
  interruption, 86–87
  local, 179
  myopia, 79–80, 110–112
  niche, 12, 77, 83, 129, 136–137, 176
  one-to-one, 12, 78
  opensource, 37, 104–108
  permission, 37, 83, 85, 88–89, 93
  simplicity, 81–85
  social, 67, 69, 129–164
Marketing: An Introduction (Armstrong and Kotler), 165
Marketing Imagination, The (Levitt), 70–71
Marketing Management (Kotler), 76
Marketing Myopia (Levitt), 79–80, 111
Markets of One: Creating Customer-Unique Value Through Mass Customization (Pine), 78
Martin, Steve, 156
Marxism, 138
Mass Customization: The New Frontier in Business Competition (Pine), 78
materialism, 205, 210
MCI, 25, 92
Mecklermedia, 104
Media Circus: The Trouble with America's Newspapers (Kurtz), 152

Media Metrix, 166
Media Monopoly, The
   (Bagdikian), 165
Medici banking family, 193
Menides, Byron, 72–73
Mercedes-Benz, 123
Merck, 67
Merrill Lynch, 67
Miami Herald, 174
micromarketing, Kotler and
   Armstrong definition of, 179
micromarkets, 12–14, 84,
   100–101, 165–182,
   186–188
   basic description of, 12
   creating relationships with,
      40–41
   and identifying best of breed,
      190–191
   and identifying external
      partners, 191–192
   partnerships, 195–197, 202
   replacement of mass markets
      by, 38
micromedia, 13, 165–182,
   186–188, 193–194
Microsoft, 23, 37, 49, 133
   antitrust case against, 154,
      178, 204
   Encarta, 116, 133
   Internet Magazine, 115
   Office, 49
   Slate, 176, 178
   Windows, 197
Millar, Brian, 122–123
Mindich, David, 155
Miramax Films, 143
Mitsubishi, 198

modernization programs, 132
motivation, 187–188
Motley Fool, 12, 166
Motorola, 67
MP3, 3, 21, 91, 115, 159, 175.
   See also music industry
Ms. magazine, 140–141
MTVi music network, 167
muckraking, 154
multimedia, use of the term,
   208
Murdoch, Rupert, 25, 62, 165,
   169, 175, 185
Murrow, Edward R., 102
music industry, 22, 44–45, 102,
   108–110

Napster, 21–22, 37, 84
NASDAQ, 36
Nasser, Jac, 35, 37, 41
National Public Radio, 12
NBC (National Broadcasting
   Corporation), 102, 163, 167,
   173
Negroponte, Nicholas, 36, 207
Net Perceptions, 104, 106–107,
   117
Netscape, 204
Neuromancer (Gibson), 21, 46
New Journalism, The (Wolfe),
   9, 154
newsblogger.com, 176–177
News Corporation, 25, 62, 90,
   163, 165, 167, 185
News Values (Fuller), 154
Newsweek, 2, 163, 183
New Yorker, The, 78, 143
New York magazine, 136, 167

New York Times, The, 28, 35,
66, 136, 149–150, 165, 173,
175, 177, 197, 209
niche marketing, 12, 77, 83,
129, 136–137, 176
Nietzche, Friedrich, 46–47,
49–50
Nixon, Richard M., 10–11, 160
Nordstrom, 34
Novartis, 139–140
NYSE (New York Stock
Exchange), 36

objectivity, 40, 110, 145
and journalism, 148–150,
152–159
Ochs, Adolph, 197
Ockham's razor, 85
Odyssey (Homer), 61
Oedipus, 48
Office (Microsoft), 49
Ogilvy & Mather, 34, 81
*On Social Research and its
Language* (Lazarsfeld), 70
one-to-one marketing, 12, 78
Oni, Olu, 119
Online Journalism Review, 176
OPACs (online patron access
catalogs), 114
Open source marketing, 37,
104–108. *See also* Open
Source Movement
Open Source Movement, 105,
173. *See also* open source
marketing

Paine, Thomas, 152–153
Panasonic, 74
Paradigm Guy, 121

*Participatory Development
Communication: A West
African Agenda* (Yoon),
132, 134
partnerships, 195–197, 202
paternalism, 132–133, 161
PeopleSoft, 5
Peppers, Don, 78
permission marketing, 37, 83,
85, 88–89, 93
*Permission Marketing: Turning
Strangers Into Friends and
Friends Into Customers*
(Godin), 87–89, 93
personal computers, provision
of, to employees, 34–38
personalization, 12, 78, 79,
106–107, 113
Personalization Summit
conference, 107
Petty, Norman, 51
Petty, Tom, 85
Philip Morris, 140
Pine, Joe, 77–78
piracy, 22
place, as one of the 4 Ps of
marketing, 47, 103
Plato, 47
play, importance of, 1–2
pneuma, 59
*Portable MBA in Marketing,
The*, 43
Practice of the Wild, The
(Synder), 14
pragmatism, 3, 47, 126
price
determination of, by value,
50

as one of the 4 Ps of
marketing, 47, 103
use of the term, 49
Principles of Marketing, 179
Procter & Gamble, 90, 136
Prodigy, 104, 117
product
as one of the 4 Ps of
marketing, 47, 103
placement, 28
professionalism, 4–5
promotion, as one of the 4 Ps
of marketing, 47, 103
*Protestant Ethic and the Spirit
of Capitalism, The* (Weber),
56
Putnam, Robert D., 129,
145–146

racism, 54
RageBoy, 30–32, 105, 107
rain forests, 7
Raines, Howell, 150
Rangaswami, J. P., 6
Rather, Dan, 152, 182
Raymond, Eric, 105
Reeves, Keanu, 26
reframing, 112
Regis Touch, The (McKenna), 77
Relationship Marketing
(McKenna), 77
Renaissance, 193
Reno, Janet, 204
return on investment (ROI), 137
Reuters, 34
rhetoric, 118–119
Richards, Keith, 108

Right Stuff, The (film), 7, 9
Right Stuff, The (Wolfe), 9
RMG International, 122
Roberto, Eduardo, 130
rock and roll, 44–45, 102,
108–110
Rogers, Martha, 78
ROI (return on investment), 137
Rosen, Emanuel, 92
Rosen, Jay, 149, 151, 155–158
Rothenberg, Randall, 69–70,
175
Rowling, J. K., 113
Rüschlikon conference facility,
5–6

Saatchi & Saatchi, 56, 139
Salon, 73, 142, 169
San Jose Mercury News,
156–157
Savage Mind, The (Levi-
Strauss), 2
Scoville, Thomas, 73
Seal, 7
Sealey, Peter, 81–82, 89
search engines, 23–24, 160,
167, 175
Searls, Doc, 28
Shakespeare, William, 51
Share Our Strength (SOS), 137
Shiffman, Roger, 65
Shore, Bill, 137
*Short Course in Social
Marketing*, A, 140
simplicity marketing, 81–85
*Simplicity Marketing: Relieving
Customer Stress in the*

Digital Age (Cristol and Sealey), 81–83
Slate (Microsoft), 176, 178
Smith, Pamela, 55
"Snooze Factor: Sleepy Time in the Management Aisle" (Manning), 1
Snyder, Gary, 14, 158
social capital, 144–148
Social Construction of Reality, The (Berger), 46
Social Life of Information (Lesser), 147
social marketing, 67, 69, 129–164
  definition of, 130–131
  in the third world, 132–134, 139
Social Marketing: Strategies for Changing Public Behavior (Kotler and Roberto), 130
Social Mobilization & Social Marketing in Developing Communities (McKee), 132
spam, 20, 27, 30, 82, 87, 88, 89, 95, 109, 207
spirit, 59–60, 92–93, 101
startups, 77, 116
storytelling, 12, 74, 108, 126–127, 154
Structural Transformation of the Public Sphere, The (Habermas), 156
Structure of Scientific Revolutions, The (Kuhn), 97–98
subjectivity, 160–164

Suck.com, 173
Sun Microsystems, 5
Suzuki, Shunryu, 5
Swiss Re, 5

Talking Heads, 71
Talk magazine, 143
Tawney, R. H., 56
TBWA/Chiat/Day, 136
TCI, 25
team spirit, 59–60
thermodynamics, 52
TheStreet.com, 173
thick description, use of the term, 45, 46
Thomas, Dylan, 45
Thompson, Hunter S., 9–11, 15–17, 148, 154, 160–161
Time Warner, 24–26, 163, 165–166, 185
Tipping Point, The (Gladwell), 78, 170
Toscani, Oliviero, 141–143, 161
Toyota, 39, 198
trademarks, 68
transubstantiation, 56
trust, 58–59, 146, 156
truth, 75, 121, 156
Tylenol poisoning scare, 68–69

U2 (rock band), 68
underwriting, 193–195, 213–214
up-selling, 113
USA Today, 106, 151–152

value
  proposition, 43–63
  and social marketing, 131
  use of the term, 44, 49
Veblen, Thorsten, 43
Viacom, 163, 165, 167
Virtuous Reality (Katz), 152–153
Viselman, Kenn, 65
voice, 12, 126

Wall, The, 34
Wall Street Journal, The, 28, 54, 177
Warn, Emily, 115
Washington Post, The, 35, 151, 152, 177
Weber, Max, 56
weblogs, 170–171, 177
Weinberger, David, 17, 28, 103, 118
Welch, Jack, 36–37
Westinghouse, 67
What Are Journalists For? (Rosen), 149, 155
Whitman, Walt, 22
Will to Power: Attempt at a Revaluation of all Values (Nietzche), 46
"Will We Ever Get Over Irony?" (Gates), 2–3
William of Ockham, 85
Williams-Sonoma, 137
win-win model, 40
Windows (Microsoft), 197

Winer, Dave, 170
Wired, 207
Wired News, 167–168
Wittgenstein, Ludwig, 46
Wolfe, Tom, 9, 154
Wolff, Michael, 167
Worcester Polytechnic Institute, 72–73
World Health Organization, 140
World Trade Organization, 205
World Wide Web and Contemporary Cultural Theory, The (Jones), 174–175
WPP Group, 122

Yahoo!, 23, 62, 86, 109, 135, 137
Yeager, Chuck, 9
Yoon, Chin Saik, 132
Young & Rubicam, 34
youth markets, 76

Zaltman, Gerald, 130
Zappa, Frank, 158
ZDnet, 106
Zeitgeist, 59, 190
Zemke, Debbie, 36
Zen Buddhism, 5, 45. *See also* Buddhism
Zero Wing, 19
zero sum models, 40
Zyman, Sergio, 72, 74–75, 77

Christopher Locke
clocke@panix.com

Named in a 2001 Financial Times Group survey as one of the "top 50 business thinkers in the world," Locke is author of *Gonzo Marketing: Winning Through Worst Practices*, co-author of *The Cluetrain Manifesto*, president of Entropy Web Consulting, and editor/publisher of the widely acclaimed and justly infamous webzine *Entropy Gradient Reversals*. Now based in Boulder, Colorado, has worked for Fujitsu, Ricoh, the Japanese government's "Fifth Generation" artificial intelligence project, Carnegie Mellon University's Robotics Institute, CMP Publications, Mecklermedia, MCI, and IBM. He has written extensively for publications such as *Forbes, Release 1.0, Information Week, Publish, The Industry Standard,* and *Harvard Business Review*, and his professional work has been covered by *Fast Company, Wired, Advertising Age, Business Week, The Economist, Fortune, The New York Times, The Wall Street Journal* and many others.

He has never recanted anything.

CITY OF LIKES

CITY OF LIKES

A NOVEL

Jenny Mollen

Nacelle Books

For Sid and Lazlo

CHAPTER ONE

I shot up in bed, convinced that I'd just felt a cockroach tiptoe across my forehead. Repulsed, I raked my fingers over my scalp and ran my tongue along the inside of my mouth. "Oh my god!" I screamed. "I think I might have eaten one!"

"You didn't eat one!" My husband called out from behind the bathroom door.

I switched on the light and scanned my bedside table, expecting to see a chorus line of roaches staring back at me. There was a flicker of movement behind the pile of childhood development books I'd spent the last six months forcing myself to read. It was as if the pests were taking a short break to change costumes before remounting their attack. "Iliya, this is insane! We can't stay here."

"It's here or my mother's place," he calmly reminded me.

"How are those our only two options?"

According to the alarm clock, it was almost seven in the morning, but from where I sat, in our windowless tomb of a bedroom, it could just as easily have been the middle of the night. I raised my water bottle and slammed it hard onto my nightstand, determined to draw blood.

"You're not gonna get them," Iliya said. "They're too fast."

"I don't want to get them! I want to call an exterminator!"

"You can't call anyone. We're not on the lease. We're not even supposed to be here."

"How are you so mellow about this? We are living in a roach-infested apartment with two children! This isn't something we can just wait on." I got up and stomped toward the bathroom door and flung it open.

Iliya was leaning into the mirror, flossing his teeth in his neurotic way, until his gums bled. "Cockroaches don't hurt children," he slurred, then spat into the sink before turning toward me. With his angular cheekbones and piercing blue eyes, he looked like one of those male models from a high-end cologne commercial. The kind of guy who says nothing until the last moment, when he locks eyes with the camera and whispers something nonsensical like, "Set your heart on fire with ice."

I folded my arms and glared. "I'm calling Ken."

"You've already called him five times," he said. "You look psycho."

"I *am* psycho!" I exclaimed.

"Besides, Ken's on location."

"In Toronto! That's like five minutes from here." I turned around and headed back into the bedroom, closing the bathroom door on his annoyingly Photoshopped body.

"By what, rocket ship?" Iliya laughed as he caught up with me. "He's busy shooting. You know actors. Give the guy a minute."

"So now he's all Daniel Day-Lewis and too deep in his craft to deal with a roach infestation at his apartment? Is that *really* going to be your defense?"

"Ken is a great guy and he's letting us stay here for free," Iliya said for the millionth time. "You don't even want to know what the roaches look like in Coney Island."

Iliya was right. I didn't want to know what the roaches looked like in Coney Island, nor did I want to know what his mother looked like without clothing. I watched him help himself to two identical black T-shirts in a basketful of clean laundry on the floor.

When Chelsea House offered Iliya the promotion, they expected him to jump without thinking twice. And he did. We all did. Head of global membership was a coveted position, one that he'd been gunning for since his early days with the club. It was, according to Iliya, "an opportunity too good to refuse," even if the bump in pay wasn't that substantial. The company provided us with a small relocation fee, enough to cover the money we lost breaking our lease in LA and throwing our furniture into storage. But there were still hundreds of things to figure out. Iliya was tasked with finding us a temporary place to stay while I focused my attention on getting our tuition back from our son's preschool and enrolling him in another one, selling our car on Facebook, and setting up goodbye playdates and drinks with every friend, co-worker and dog groomer we'd known for the past decade.

I sunk back onto the edge of the bed. "I should have known this was too good to be true. Wait a minute," I said, redirecting my anger. "*You* should have known this was too good to be true." I watched Iliya study the two T-shirts and pretend not to hear me. "A spacious loft in Tribeca for just as long as we needed it? Of course, that's not a real thing! If Los Angeles taught us anything it's to never believe the empty promises of actors." I flopped backwards on the bed, then remembered the roaches. I sprung back up and gave myself a thorough TSA patdown. "Why would Ken do this to us?" I wailed.

"Hey. Ken is a good friend who's worked his ass off for the current success he's having, so I'm not going shit-talk him. His show is doing better than any other show on the History Channel." Iliya was proud of his former AA sponsor. Ken was the only person I'd ever seen Iliya have a phone call with that lasted longer than five minutes.

"Not to be a total buzzkill, but it's about the Oregon Trail." I couldn't resist. "Eventually everybody loses an axel or dies of dysentery." Iliya didn't respond, most likely because he had no idea what I was talking about. His education was cut short at age fifteen, when he escaped the antisemitism of Ukraine and moved to Brooklyn with his mother and little sister. He never ended up re-enrolling in school. In order to help support the family, he went to work right away, promoting clubs and restaurants around Manhattan. And now, all these years later, he was back where he'd started.

Iliya's plan was always to save up enough money so that he could open his own restaurant. It was going to be high-end and Russian, a spruced-up version of Veselka, his favorite East Village joint. He'd been nurturing this dream ever since we met at Geiko, a Japanese steakhouse in Hollywood where all of the waitresses were forced to dress like horny geishas and where we both worked.

I let off a sigh. "Tell me why I agreed to do this again?"

"You didn't like Los Angeles either," Iliya reminded me. "You hated the traffic." He was speaking as if we were two octogenarians reflecting on a life we'd lived centuries ago instead of one we'd abandoned just three weeks prior.

"Everyone hates the traffic, Iliya!"

He winced. "And the endless sun."

"That's just you. I have nothing against the sun. In fact, I like sunshine, and palm trees, and nice people who say 'excuse me' when they bump into you on the street."

"There's a difference between nice and fake. And how many of those 'nice' California people ever offered you a job? The kind of job you deserve?" He tilted his head. "You have to believe me. This city is going to change your life."

It was true, my life in LA hadn't been perfect. I felt trapped in my air-conditioned apartment in the valley. My friends were either singles who suggested we meet for dinner at 9:30 p.m. or new moms who lived all the way out in Brentwood and refused to cross the

405 for playdates. Which meant I was alone ninety percent of the time. And while I wanted to get back to work, I couldn't get hired to save my life. I'd only recently started trying to find a job, after Roman had turned four, but it felt as though the entire industry had changed in the few years I'd been sitting on the bench. New platforms were popping up quicker than I could download them, let alone figure out how to optimize them.

New York was the biggest marketing hub in the world. The city was bursting with energy and opportunity. And not just professional ones. Whenever we visited, it felt like a giant cruise ship where I could be a parent upstairs but also disappear downstairs to a life that was entirely my own. In theory, it was everything I'd been looking for. But the reality was already proving to be different from the postcards.

"Which of these shirts do you like better?" Iliya asked, switching gears.

I stared at him blankly. "Is this a trick question?"

"No. Why?" Iliya looked at me with that foreign-guy cluelessness that he'd perfected.

I shook my head. "They're the exact same shirt."

"No they aren't."

"Umm. Yeah." I showed him the matching Gap tags.

"One is more washed. It's a different vibe."

"Feels like the same vibe to me," I muttered. "I guess go with whichever makes you feel richer and skinnier?"

"I'm already skinny." Sometimes my humor was wasted on him.

While Iliya pulled one of the shirts over his head, I marveled at the body of the man I happened to marry. Towering over me at six feet three inches, Iliya was more masculine than any guy I'd ever been into. Which wasn't saying a lot, as the guys I dated before him turned out to be gay. Iliya gave me a warm smile. "It's going to be okay, Meg. This isn't our new home. It's just until we can afford our own place." He kneeled down to kiss me. "I gotta hurry," he said. "Saro is flying in from London." Saro was the CEO and founder of Chelsea House, someone Iliya emulated and feared in equal parts. "I'm still taking Roman today, right?" Iliya was waiting to see if I would offer to take our son to school.

"It's your turn," I said, trying to stand my ground. I'd taken the kid to the last ten drop-offs. "Speaking of Saro, I saw that Chelsea House is hiring someone to run their website. Did you know about that?"

"I didn't," he said, averting his eyes. "Have you seen my wallet?" I grabbed a pair of jeans sitting on top of the dresser and fished out a dilapidated Velcro billfold. Iliya had used the same wallet since he'd turned twenty-one and refused to replace it. He claimed it kept him humble. It also served as a reminder that he hadn't yet reached his financial goal. Over the years, people would give him new ones, which he would graciously accept then cast off into one of his junk drawers.

"Well, they are," I said, my voice slightly quavering. "And I'd kill that position."

Iliya held up his hand and shook his head. "You don't want to run somebody's website. And you know how I feel about us working together."

"But we met working together."

"And you hated me."

It wasn't until after Iliya fired me that we ended up getting together. And it wasn't until after our first child that I forgave him for firing me. "But we're stronger now, and we need the money, and I am good. Really good."

"You're better than good," he said. "Running a website isn't what you were born to do. You're a writer."

"A copywriter," I corrected him. "There's a difference."

"And Chelsea House is cheap. You need to find a job that pays real money. Otherwise, what is the point of you going back to work?"

I balled my hands into fists. "The point is that we can't afford to live in New York if both of us aren't working. And if I keep hearing the *Paw Patrol* theme song all day every day, I'm going to have a psychotic breakdown."

"Summer is over," he said. "Roman is back in school."

"Well Felix isn't," I reminded him. "And you're missing the point!"

"Look, I want you to be happy too," he said. "I just don't like the optics. I barely know this New York team. Imagine me going in today telling them that they needed to hire my wife, who hasn't had a job in nearly five years."

"Wow." My voice cracked. "That was really low."

"I'm sorry, that's not what I meant. It's not that I don't think you're qualified. I just think it comes off as nepotism."

"Said the guy who works for a glorified fraternity," I shot back. I found it absurd that Iliya, a dude who could not have been less moved by popularity, was the gatekeeper to one of most sought-after membership clubs in the country. He didn't disagree, not deep down anyway.

But he was a hard worker. And if he didn't want to lose his job, it was best not to think too hard about Chelsea House and all that it stood for. I hated the late nights, the drunken douchebags, the posers who spent all day scrolling their own websites on their laptops, the married women who were always slipping Iliya their room keys. I even hated the maddeningly hot waitstaff who waited twenty minutes before asking if you wanted a glass of water.

But running the club's membership gave Iliya a cachet that no previous job ever had. People kowtowed to him. The club's younger members invited him to their weddings and the older ones to their children's bar mitzvahs. It was silly, but it felt good. And hopefully it would prove beneficial when he finally decided to do something on his own.

"You're going to get a job you love," Iliya said. "You had an interview yesterday, you have more today. You're doing everything right. You don't need me to hook you up with nonsense."

"Thanks," I said, wishing he could see how lost and obsolete I felt.

"You are going to be more than fine." Iliya kissed me on my forehead like I was a child. I hated when he did that.

CHAPTER TWO

I stopped working when I had Roman because we couldn't afford help. I didn't have an extended family that I could lean on, and my mom was only capable of intimacy with cats. My goal was to be the mother that I'd always wished someone had been for me.

Turned out my happiness wasn't to be found at the bottom of a heap of burp cloths and breast pumps. I found myself falling deeper and deeper into a depression. In high school, I worked as a stock girl at Blockbuster video. It was a two-year stint during which I'd watched and internalized the message of every rom-com I was supposed to be rewinding. According to Hollywood, I could have it all! I could have a baby, then take off for the woods of Vermont to make homemade applesauce, only to reemerge as the CEO of my own company with a sensitive-yet-stable veterinarian husband, a cherubic and potty-trained toddler, and a closetful of matching flannel pajamas.

Instead, I found myself isolated and unfulfilled. The highlight of my week was taking Roman to the grocery store and letting him feast on all the free samples so I could get out of making dinner. Being a mom wasn't enough for me. And New York was my chance to finally get it right. I was going to go back to what I knew before kids. I was going to find a job —something fulfilling that would make me not just a more joyful person but a better parent. I was going to beat my depression, finally get my head screwed on straight. I was going to be me again. My reverie in the shower was broken by the sound of my four-year-old son shrieking.

"He better not have seen a fucking roach," I shot to Iliya as I rushed out of the room.

Roman stood naked at the front door shaking like a nervous

Chihuahua. "RiRi is here," he said excitedly.

I heard the raspy mutterings of what sounded like an angry Russian prostitute on the other side of the door.

"Is that you, Marina?" I asked, double-checking that it was indeed my sister-in-law and not some belligerent neighbor.

"Of course, it's me! Who else would it be?" Marina exclaimed, bursting through the door the moment I unlocked it. In her platform suede boots, skintight jeans and bright orange Hermes belt, she looked like one of those high-priced call girls who sit in the lobby at the Beverly Hills Hotel staring at their phones and eating Chex mix.

I tried not to judge her babysitting attire as I made my way to the other side of the room, toweling off my hair and scanning the area for roaches with each step. Normal rent for a one-bedroom in Tribeca was ten to twelve grand, at the minimum. But Ken's apartment, along with two others that had better views of the bumper-to-bumper traffic on Canal Street, wasn't technically in Tribeca. Instead, it was situated in a sort of no-man's-land once referred to as West Soho and most recently deemed Hudson Square. Developers had tried to buy the building just after Hurricane Sandy, thinking that with all the water damage, they could score it for a deal. But as Ken had explained to us, the owner was unmoved by the offer. The shady cash-only bodega downstairs generated more than enough money that selling low wasn't worth it. Unfortunately for us, keeping the bodega running was all that mattered to him. Any issue upstairs — whether it was plumbing, electric, or even pest-related — went ignored.

Marina sidestepped around her nephew, making a beeline to the kitchen sink with a half-spilled latte in her hands. "What happened to your clothes, Roman?"

"They were too tight."

Marina threw me a look.

"What was too tight?" Iliya walked out of the bedroom busily answering morning emails on his phone.

"My pants. They were a little tight but also very loose," Roman supplied.

"Roman, they're cotton and tagless," I told him. "You picked these sweat suits out and you promised that you would wear them. We have seven of them now and I'm not giving them away." Roman's pre-K in LA had thrown around the term "sensory" when it came to his strange predilections and more than occasional tantrums. I was still hoping that this phase would be something he'd outgrow. The older he got, the easier he was to negotiate with. Read: Bribe. Unfortunately, the whole thing was like a game of whack-a-mole. The minute I helped him move on from one issue, a new one would pop up. Currently, it was all — and only — about clothes.

"I'm pretty sure Marina brought something for you," I said. "And if you can get dressed, I bet she'll give it to you."

Roman lit up and began to bounce up and down for Marina like a fan girl sitting front row at a Taylor Swift concert. I envied the power she had over him. She was the fun aunt. She was also the only aunt. Which only made her more fun. I was jealous not just that my son adored her but that she only got the best of him. They'd laugh, they'd play, and then she'd get her things and go. She didn't have to deal with the chaos of getting him dressed, the irrational scenes over the food he didn't want to eat or the three-hour adventure that was bedtime. As far as Marina was concerned, kids were easy. It was moms that were hard.

"Okay, look everybody," I said, glancing at my watch. "We've got to get a move on things. Roman's school starts at nine. It's Iliya's morning to take him and —"

"NOOOOO!" Roman cried, digging his heels into the hardwood floor. "I want Mommy to take me!"

I glanced at Iliya, who was in the room physically but may as well have been at his office. He was terrifically engrossed in his emails. "Mommy has an interview today," I reminded the entire room.

"I thought you did that yesterday." Roman blinked at me, confused.

"This is a different job. It's a new day. New day, new job." I tried to sound positive. I wanted Roman to see me as a winner even if I couldn't see myself as one. "And it's *two* interviews. I'm meeting with two different companies, so that's even more of a chance for success, right?"

Roman stared at me blankly, then farted. Defeated, I made my way over to Ken's mini kitchen. While I measured out three cups of formula for Felix, I gave Marina the rundown. "We don't have a microwave, so you need to heat the bottle in a pot. Felix can sleep for another half hour but then you need to wake him, or he'll be off his schedule for the rest of the day. Oh, and we already fed Red, but he still needs to go out and pee," I instructed, lining the cups of formula along Ken's hotplate.

"Aren't you wondering why I spilled my latte?" Marina looked at me, clearly offended that I hadn't yet given her my undivided attention. Before I could come up with an excuse, she launched into her rant, half talking to me, half checking out her manicure.

"So, this dickhead started screaming at me when I pulled up because I wouldn't unlock my car doors and let him in."

"Language!" Iliya hissed to his sister. He drained his coffee and deposited the empty cup by the sink.

"Quiet, both of you," I said gently. "The baby is still asleep. We want him to go for another half hour."

Marina ignored me, focusing on scowling at her brother and then continuing her rant. "It's like, not every Mercedes SUV is an Uber, dude." Marina scoffed as she rummaged through the cabinets for a morning snack.

"But I thought you *were* an Uber driver," I said, taking my time washing Iliya's cup to be sure he saw me doing it.

"A Wing Woman, Meg. That means female passengers only. My car, my choice. Eww! You guys have roaches!" she shrieked, dropping a box of cheddar bunnies to the floor and watching them fly everywhere.

"*Zatknis!*" Iliya cried, shaming his sister in Russian. "The baby!" It was my job to drop to my knees and scoop up the bunnies.

"I'm not gonna lie, guys," Marina said. "This already feels like a hostile work environment."

"Nobody is being hostile," Iliya and I said in unison, terrified that she might pick up her knock-off Chanel purse and its fifteen-pound makeup bag and storm out of our apartment. Marina looked at me, about to say something, when Roman interjected. "Can I have my present now?"

"When your clothes are on," Marina instructed firmly, pointing to the sweatshirt portion of the tracksuit on the floor. And like a miracle, Roman promptly complied.

Looking as proud of herself as if she'd just taught our dog to speak, Marina sauntered over to her bag and pulled out a Super Mario figurine. "It's from when your daddy and I were children. I got him off eBay. Originally he was a prize in a cereal box." Marina could make anything sound exciting, even dry old cereal.

"They used to put toys in cereal?" Roman looked like his mind was about to explode.

"Believe it or not, they still do. If your mommy buys the fun kind." Marina shot me a vengeful smile.

"Roman, we gotta go!" Iliya said, sounding jumpy.

"But I want Mommy to take me!" Roman flung himself between my legs as I made my way toward him with his backpack.

Iliya looked at me, then again at his phone. God, he was so pathetic. "Fine," I said. "Just go. You can do tomorrow's drop-off." Before Iliya and I could kiss goodbye, Felix started screaming from behind a sheet of drywall that Ken had put in place to give the illusion of a second bedroom. His high-pitched cries reminded me of those techno sirens that go off whenever somebody orders a Sex on the Beach shot in Tijuana. I threw up my hands, defeated. "*Annnd* the baby's up!"

"Don't look at me!" Marina said.

"*Pizdets!*" Iliya cursed in his native tongue and turned to me, sheepish as he grabbed his keys. "Please don't hate me."

I watched my gorgeous husband slip out the door, wishing I could hate him.

"How long do you need me today?" Marina asked when her brother was out of earshot. "I made it to the focus group round of my Lastrelle study."

"Your what?" I asked, hurrying to rescue Felix before he combusted. Unbothered, Marina slicked down her vixenish high ponytail and walked to the full-length mirror to admire her outfit and then start to pick apart a face full of makeup. She was beautiful like her brother but hid it under half a dozen layers of foundation that she insisted was "just a little powder and bronzer."

"Lastrelle," she called out. "It's a new technology that takes off four or seven layers of skin and makes you glow. But first you look like a lizard person for a week."

I reappeared holding Felix. At just five months old, he was a clone of his big brother, with Iliya's dark hair and my curled upper lip. "Did you already have this procedure?" I inquired, concerned she was about to peel her entire face off in front of me.

"Not yet," she said. "Later today."

"Mommy! I'm waiting!" Roman was keenly attuned to any and all gravitational shifts in my attention. The desperation on his face said that he'd just been abandoned in a hot car.

"Okay. Yes. We're going." I hunched down on the floor, balancing Felix in one arm as I attempted to wedge Roman's little feet into his tiny shoes. "You wanna grab Felix?" I asked Marina. But she was in a trance, squeezing a nonexistent zit on her chin.

If I were interviewing nannies to help me out with the kids, Marina would have been my last choice. She was messy, unreliable, and always looked like she was dressed in a slutty Halloween costume. But she wasn't a child molester, didn't wear my shoe size, and my kids adored her. Also, she was cheap.

"So what time do you need to leave?" I asked, trying not to let my frustration show. This was so typical of Marina. She would always pretend to want to help but when the time came, she'd find a way to weasel out.

"Like three-fifteen. Latest." She shrugged, finally taking Felix into her arms and beaming like she was Mother Teresa.

"Ok. That's the soonest I can get here," I said. "Roman's school isn't out until three." I looked at Roman, who was starting to pull on his shirt. If I didn't get him out of the house, he was going to be naked and sobbing within the next two minutes. "Right," I said. "Okay. Fine."

"Oh, did I tell you about the dentist?" Marina asked just as I was about to grab my bag.

I tried to be polite while still gathering up my things, laser-focused on Roman like he was a Jenga tower that might fall at any moment. "I have a date with a dentist who offered to make me a free night guard," Marina continued. "God, this place really is a shithole…" She touched the wall. A sliver of old paint broke off and fell to the floor. "Are you sure it's safe to live here?"

Roman perked up. "What's a shithole?"

"Nothing, honey." I shook my head. "Take your backpack. Don't forget to take Red out!" I reminded Marina as I kissed Felix one last time.

"Da, Da, Da!" she nodded. "Oh, and don't forget to text me your Wi-Fi password, your Netflix info, and your Seamless account!"

"You got it," I called back, slowly realizing that I'd just gone from having two children to three.

CHAPTER THREE

The city was ridiculously hot for September. Way hotter than Woody Allen movies had led me to believe, with their depictions of autumn in New York as a season that called for oversized blazers and tweed slacks. I didn't have access to any oversized blazers that weren't Iliya's, and I didn't have any slacks that weren't maternity wear. The last time I shopped for myself was before I had Roman. Once he was on the scene, he was the priority and every bit of extra cash I'd squirreled away went toward buying onesies and then the next size up in whatever leisure suit he was currently obsessed with. My go-to outfit was black jeans with some kind of band tee that made me look like I was a prepubescent boy permanently stuck in the bleachers at a Death Cab for Cutie concert.

But I had an interview today, so I tried to class things up with a ruffled button-down blouse and mules that I could half-walk in. "Let's take a picture to remember this moment!" I said, pulling out my phone and snapping a shot in a mirrored wall of what I hoped would be my last day of unemployment. I uploaded the picture to Instagram. My account was set to private and not even my husband followed it. It was half diary, half vision board, a way to catalog my life. I used it to look back and see what my body had looked like six months ago or to approximate how happy I'd been the year prior. I also posted pictures of experiences I longed to have, the Italian grottos and Tibetan temples I hoped to visit. I never had the money to do one of those study-abroad programs in Europe, and the only place I'd ever traveled for work was Nashville, to supervise a biscuit mix commercial.

Sweat dripped down the back of my neck as I stuffed my phone back into my purse and rushed across Canal Street, heading south.

Reaching into a sandwich baggie filled with what had now been coined by Marina "boring" cereal, Roman pulled out a handful of whole grain oats and sprinkled them on to the sidewalk, leaving himself a trail back to Marina in the event that we got lost.

Sunlight seeped through the cracks of the few prewar spice warehouses still waiting to be converted into ten-million-dollar lofts. Men pulling breakfast carts lined with donuts and everything bagels ambled across the vacant cobblestone streets, expertly avoiding potholes and sidewalk scaffolding. Iliya had explained to me that Tribeca was always under construction, always reinventing itself. The neighborhood was like a cat who'd lived nine lives, or Madonna before she started adopting all those Malawi children. What had started out as farmland had morphed into a hub of wealthy white people crammed into brightly lit buildings, as if afraid of the dark.

I'd never been wealthy by any stretch of the word. I grew up poor with an English teacher mom who had three kids by three different men. My dad owned his own plumbing company and did okay but got remarried and moved to Palm Springs with his new family when I was still in middle school. He always sent me a card on my birthday but sometimes got my age wrong in his inscription.

With Iliya's new bump in income, we were better off than we had been in a while. We'd saved a tiny bit and probably could have afforded a down payment on something modest in my hometown of Salem, Oregon. But New York was a whole different stratosphere. It would have taken a lucky lottery ticket or some elderly gentleman making Iliya an indecent proposal for us to even dream of living like the people who seemed to levitate around us. When I took Red out for his late-night walk, I liked to stand on the street corner while I waited for him to pee, looking up at my neighbors and trying to guess what they had ordered for dinner or what they were watching on TV. It was fun to admire them though, pacing back and forth in their all-glass habitats in the sky like wild animals on display.

From Beach Street to Barclay, blondes pushing sticky-fingered children in geared-out strollers barreled down the sidewalks like drag racers, brushing past each other without so much as a glance or nod of acknowledgment. Everybody was frantic and frazzled, even when there was no reason to be. People didn't meander in New York. Even when you tried to stand still, you almost had to fight against some unseen current constantly propelling you forward.

Roman had been in his new preschool for just over two weeks, and I had yet to remember to pack his lunch. There was just so much going on. By the time I got both kids to bed, I could barely remember to brush my teeth and charge my cell phone before burrowing under the sheets and passing out. Lunch was always one step beyond me.

Roman didn't seem to mind my forgetfulness, as it gave us a few extra minutes of time together before drop-off. We popped into a sweltering deli to pick up a sandwich and an apple, and then completed the walk to his modestly air-conditioned school.

"I love you, Mommy," Roman said when we reached the top of the school steps. He held my face, kissing me more intensely than any man ever had. No goodbye with Roman was ever easy. It was always hard to tell who was feeding off of whose anxiety.

He still clung to me as he ran through his ritualized list of questions. "Where are you going to be?" "Will you pick me up?" "If I want to call you, will the teacher let me?" I nodded over and over, offering whatever reassurance I could.

"I don't want to go," he whimpered softly into my sleeve. Kids and parents were streaming past, and I didn't dare look up. I didn't want to see their pity and judgment.

"Roman, you can do this," I said, prying myself free and steering him toward his classroom. Before Roman could lunge for me, I raced back downstairs, where a mother gave me a rueful smile. She was wearing a fashionable peasant dress and carrying a bucket bag with fabric samples spilling out of the top. A bright yellow bike helmet jauntily dangled from her elbow.

"It's hard, but trust me, by next year they will turn into different kids," she said.

"You promise?" I followed behind her and watched her unlock her bike.

"That's what everybody says, anyway." She shrugged. "Where are you guys thinking of for kindergarten?" Her tone was a mixture of curious and competitive.

"Still figuring it out," I said noncommittally. Ken's place was only temporary, and I couldn't enroll Roman anywhere until we had a permanent address.

The mom gave a flat smile. "If you're thinking of going private, you'd better get it figured out soon."

I held back a groan. My friend Bethany had warned me that New Yorkers were obsessed with private school. Getting your kid into the right school was a ferociously competitive sport that made the Hunger Games look like ping-pong. At the time, I'd tuned her out. We could never afford the hefty price tag of private school. But the more people talked about it, the harder it became to ignore.

New Yorkers had this weird way of both lauding and shaming you. If you opted for public, you were gritty and cool. But if you didn't try for private, you were a greedy monster who clearly cared more about yourself than setting your kid up for success.

"Well, before you make any decisions, you may want to do a neuropsych eval on him," the mom suggested.

"A what?" I looked at her in confusion.

"Just an assessment of what you're dealing with. It's like a blueprint for your child's brain. He seems wonderful, but he clearly has... needs." She gave me a slapped-on smile.

"What needs?" I felt queasy. "*Special* needs?"

"I'm not an expert," she said airily. "But everyone has needs. My daughter has her own cornucopia of shit going on. It's just the world we live in now. Imagine if our parents had actually taken the time to figure us out."

Roman had never been easy. I was the first to admit that. But he was smart and always seemed to be on the right track developmentally. I had struggled with dyslexia as a kid, but I was fairly certain that that wasn't his problem. There were other things that concerned me though, and other people were starting to see them too.

The mom watched me as her words sank in. "You just want to be sure that he's going to a school that can support him not just academically but emotionally," she added gently. "I'm Sari, by the way."

With her curly strawberry blond hair and the tiniest smattering of freckles across her nose, she looked like the middle-aged version of my childhood Cabbage Patch doll — only richer.

"I'm Meg," I said with a smile that I hoped would conceal the intimidation inspired by her supersized diamond engagement ring.

"Is he your first?" Sari asked as she walked her bike toward the street corner.

"Yeah. He has a baby brother at home," I said, following along.

"Eldest kids are always the most difficult." Sari sighed knowingly. "He's probably a genius. My daughter is either going to be a CEO or a serial killer. She's smart as hell but when it comes to empathy or normal social cues, she doesn't have them. That's why we're doing private. I can't let her get lost in the system."

I could feel the corners of my mouth quivering. Was that what I was doing to Roman, setting him up to get lost?

"It's expensive," she went on, "but I just want her to have all the tools she needs. You only get one shot, you know?" I could feel my armpits dampening. "Yeah," I trailed off.

"I hate to sound like a snob because I'm really not a snob." Sari was talking faster now. "I'm super down to earth. I live in *Brooklyn*, for god's sake, but public schools in the city are a shit show. And if you have any issues at all, you slip through the cracks. It's sad. So sad."

"What cracks exactly?" I asked.

"In public school, the ratio of students to teachers is like 30 to one. Also, lice," she added in an ominous tone.

"So which school is your daughter going to go to?" I was hoping to gain some insights for myself.

"It depends on who accepts her." Sari hit the walk button at the corner, but didn't bother waiting for the light to turn before stepping into the road and making her way across, oncoming traffic be damned. I picked up my pace and followed in lockstep, eager not to miss a word.

"Abington would be my first choice," she went on. "Nobody is better than them when it comes to child development. They are on another level with all the additional support, the OT, the cog behavioral specialists, the tai chi and meditation classes, and that nut-free kitchen. It's like if Maria Montessori had a three-way with Julia Child and the Dalai Lama." She turned to me, as if expecting a laugh to come tumbling out. But I was too overwhelmed.

"Wow. I want that," I said wistfully.

"Who doesn't?" she practically snorted. "But you need a golden ticket to get into Abington! Every parent in the city is gunning for a spot."

Deflated, I looked down at the sidewalk.

"My husband went to Ellsworth, which is also respectable, but I already know that Waverly would be miserable there."

"Waverly," I repeated. "That's so different!"

"My husband and I met at the Waverly Inn. Good thing we didn't meet at the Spotted Pig." She laughed, then got back to business. "I have a whole list of places I'm going to tour, but we'll see." Sari stopped short, as if nervous that she'd given away too much information. "Which way are you going?" she asked, hopping on her bike.

"Umm, that way." I pointed in a random direction. "If you ever have time for a coffee, that would be great," I threw out. "I'd love to pick your brain and see your list of schools."

Sari nodded, feigning interest as she tucked a curl behind her ear and checked the time on her phone. "I'm late right now for an install, but let me get your number from the class list and I'll shoot you a text with some times."

"I'd love that." I smiled, wanting to believe that I'd hear from her.

The further away I got from Roman's school, the easier it became to breathe again. A weight was lifting. An unbearable blanket of guilt, love, and responsibility. I'd loved my parents, boyfriends, and of course my dog, Red,

but motherhood was different. This was a vomit-inducing kind of love. An infinite joy mixed with infinite terror that never seemed to go away. My postpartum depression lasted, well, postpartum. It wasn't just a phase; it was a new way of seeing the world after children. While I wouldn't have traded motherhood for the world, I felt like my life was bifurcated in two disparate halves: the Meg I'd been before my kids and the one I was after. As I hurtled toward my first job interview of the day, my worries about resuscitating my dead-end career were compounded by this new belief that maybe Roman had bigger issues that I was neglecting to see. He was my first, so I really didn't know what to compare him to. When I looked at other children walking with their parents, though, I felt envious. Nobody was bolting out into the street, tearing off their shoes because they detected a grain of sand, asking ten thousand times if they were going to be late to wherever they were headed.

When Roman wasn't spilling over with anxiety, he was spinning or daydreaming or bouncing up and down. It was terrifying. He was my kite and I was his string. Maybe I should have just let him soar, but tethering him to my wrist often felt like the only true way to protect him. My friends liked to tell me that I was overreacting, that he would outgrow whatever problems were revealing themselves at the time. I desperately wanted this to be true. But I couldn't be sure that it was.

I took a deep breath and tried to focus on the only thing I could control at present. I'd promised my son that it was going to be a good-luck day.

The second interview was the one that mattered. It was for Lippe Taylor, a big-time marketing and consulting agency. The first was more of a random opportunity that came up through a publicist I'd worked with on a cauliflower rice campaign several years back. It was for a start-up company that made matcha tea. She'd told me upfront that the brand didn't have much capital, which was publicist code for "They're going to pay you peanuts." I almost declined the opportunity to meet for a job that couldn't cover the cost of a babysitter. But I was rusty when it came to pitching myself and figured that I could use a practice run before the big interview.

As I waited for the light to change, I pulled out my compact and checked my teeth for mystery flecks. All clear. I reapplied my lip gloss and grinned at myself. I'd get through the interviews and google the fuck out of private schools later that evening.

CHAPTER FOUR

After crossing Broadway and a few more streets I'd never heard of, I realized I'd overshot the mark. Matcha Pitchu had a brick-and-mortar coffee shop on the corner of Lafayette and East Fourth. I was now on Second Avenue, and on track to be late if I didn't hightail it.

Berating myself for not taking a cab from school and opting to wear herbal deodorant on this sultry day, I finally swooshed into Matcha Pitchu. I was out of breath and even more out of sorts.

A man who appeared to be a fifty-year-old, caffeine-addled former punk rocker greeted me at the door and introduced himself as Seth. After offering me an iced tea and a beanie with his company logo, he led me up a flight of stairs. I trailed behind him, admiring his artificial sandy blond hair and neck full of sterling silver jewelry.

The corporate office was in an open space decorated in psychedelic colors and alien-themed tchotchkes that you'd buy at a roadside kiosk in Roswell, New Mexico. It reminded me of the dorm room of a guy I used to hang out with for free weed in college. A glass wall separated several rows of desks from the brightly lit conference room that also doubled as a test kitchen.

"We are still a tea brand, but I'd say forty percent of our current business is CBD, and I expect it to just keep growing," Seth said. As he talked, his overly dyed unibrow moved up and down his forehead. "We carry brownie bites, lotions, and all the kitsch shit like cock oils and mints, but what we've found is that there's still a hole in the market." He gave a lopsided smile that could have been the result of bad Botox or a mild stroke. "Nobody is targeting moms! And moms control eighty-three percent of household purchases.

That is just moronic!" he exclaimed, handing over a chalky sphere. The label told me that it was infused with 20mg of sustainably sourced CBD. "Do you know much about CBD?" he asked.

"A bit," I lied, still trying to figure out why anybody would purchase what I was holding.

"It's a bath bomb," Seth announced in the proud tone of somebody introducing me to the lightbulb.

"So did you always want to be a copywriter?" he asked, momentarily interested in somebody other than himself.

"Yes," I said. "I mean, it wasn't my childhood dream, but it's the thing I do well. And I like doing things well." I smiled. He seemed to like what he was hearing.

I could come up with snappy copy. But my real gift was an ability to read people. One look at a person and I knew exactly what they wanted. Just as I'd get a sense of a person, I could understand a brand and instantly be able to communicate on its behalf.

It began in college when my roommates started making me write their MySpace bios and Facebook status updates. After college, I moved to Los Angeles with the hopes of landing a staff job on a sitcom. I was a part-time hostess at Saddle Ranch on Sunset, with two shitty pilot scripts and three creative-writing credits from Santa Monica community college to my name, when I finally found my voice. I'd get jacked up on lattes from the adjacent Starbucks all morning then go back to my studio apartment on Martel, boot up my computer, and fire off jokes that nobody could hold against me.

I didn't know what copywriting was aside from the depiction of 1960s ad agencies I'd seen on *Mad Men*. But that was before a neighbor who worked at Brigman Stern, one of the most prestigious West Coast firms, came to me one night in a panic over a vegan bagel account she'd been assigned. The product Fagels (fake bagels) needed a catchphrase, and I offered up: "Once you go Fagel, you'll never go bagel." It was stupid and never in a million years did I expect it to leave the confines of our building courtyard. But the client did cartwheels, and my neighbor was promoted to senior copywriter shortly thereafter. She was so grateful that she rewarded me with freelance gigs whenever she could. I mostly worked in packaged goods, writing text for "alternative food brand" campaigns. I learned more than I ever wanted to about monk fruit sweeteners and sorghum flour, but with time, I found myself bored and wishing I were half as good at writing screenplays. A senior creative director at the company who worked on the Coca-Cola account picked up on my pessimism. "You might just be selling water with bubbles," he told me, "but if you don't believe in your product and think that you are changing the world, you're never going to be able to convince others to buy it." So I learned to believe — or pretend I did anyway.

Seth had me sit on a red velvet loveseat shaped like lips as he kept rambling on about how his products were going to "disrupt the space," though I was unclear what "space" he was referring to. He'd been tight-lipped over email, but now he was making up for lost time. While I was fairly certain the CBD market was already saturated and catered to everyone from moms to miniature schnauzers, I told Seth that his business sounded "very disruptive."

Seth's business partner, Vigo, a shorter, younger finance guy with spiky hair that had an electrocuted air, materialized and helped himself to the spot next to Seth. He offered no words, nor eye contact, but listened intently as Seth continued his rant. The pair sort of reminded me of a real-life Bert and Ernie. Part of me wanted to believe that they were lovers.

"Like instead of downing a bottle of white wine at night, pop one of our Mommy Bombs in the tub and take the edge off," Seth said with a clownish grin. Vigo sat there, straight-faced. It was getting harder to look at them seated next to each other and not picture them in shower caps singing "Rubber Duckie."

My personal opinion, not that it mattered, was that CBD was like lavender. Great in concept, but in no way capable of making a real dent on a person's stress level. At least not the kind of stress I had.

"Mommy Bombs?" I asked, hoping that the name was just a working title.

"You know I invented the matcha latte, right?" Seth said.

"I didn't," I said, looking at Vigo to see if he was going to dispute the claim.

"Before me, it was all chai all the time. Look it up, it's on my Wiki page."

I nodded politely, pretending not to know that anyone could edit his own Wikipedia page.

"CBD is a crowded market at the moment," I said, trying to influence them into feeling a bit less confident. I'd seen other copywriters do this in the past, in order to make a client feel extra services were needed. Once I saw an entire dried fruit campaign go to this moderately talented writer who convinced his clients that after the South Beach Diet, all women feared bananas and that the only way out was an entire rebrand on the fruit itself.

"There are plenty of similar wellness products already on the market, aren't there?" I said. "So I guess my first question would be: What makes this different? How are you better than the competition?"

Seth started revving up, excited to make a believer out of me. "Look, could these women use Epsom salts and add a couple drops of CBD oil to their tub for a similar result? Sure! But they aren't, because there is nothing exciting about that! People want a sexy miracle drug, not some depressing health food store remedy. The success of this project hinges on the way we market it. You know that better than anyone."

"Go on," I said.

"Take a basic necessity, throw some sans serif font on it, shoot it on a muted pink backdrop, and sell the idea of luxury at a price that is accessible to all. Now *that's* the name of the game, right Vig?" The straight man nodded, and Seth went on, "We are just taking things a step further because our bath bombs aren't shitty. They are actually pretty magical. They are handcrafted in small batches with high-end essential oils and top-grade CBD. Not to mention packaging that makes you want to nut."

'I'm sorry?" I asked, certain I must have misheard him.

"But I don't just want this to be a fake status symbol sitting on your bathroom sink next to your high-end soaps, I want this to be a movement! An inflection point in the industry!" Seth continued, like a charismatic funky-haired preacher at a rock and roll church. "Dirty Lemon dude figured out a way to make lemon water sexy. Do you know how cheap and easy it is to make lemon water?" He walked over to the sink and turned on the faucet. I watched as Seth grabbed a lemon out of a fruit basket and sliced it in half.

"There," he said, dramatically dropping the half lemon into a glass of tap water and slamming it down in front of me. "I just made it."

I granted him a smile and brought the drink to my lips. "It's delicious," I said.

He nodded and watched me take another sip. "We thought about hiring Black Reindeer for this... but they botched our nitro-infused chocolate milk launch by convincing us to put the ingredients from the back on the front. Do you know how much motherfucking sugar is in chocolate milk?! Nobody should see that info EVER!"

I looked over at Vigo, who'd picked up a laptop and started typing on it, madly. My spidey sense was that he was the true brains behind the operation but knew better than to interject when Seth was on a roll.

"Do you have a creative director?" I asked. "Art director? People I'd be collaborating with?"

"Nope. It's just us. We're doing this almost entirely in-house. Vigo is the strategy guy and I'm more of the creative force. I also have a bunch of interns and a web guy I like to use. But I need a killer copywriter and I've been told that you are stellar. Or at least the best in our price range."

"That's really nice to hear," I said, my voice ringing with disbelief. How was this guy at the helm of any company?

"We are very collaborative here. You got ideas, throw 'em out there and let's see what sticks. Bottom line is, we want this to be fresh but not young. We need someone your age to make it authentic."

"My age?" I laughed.

"Advertising is a bit like modeling. After thirty, you are past your prime. But so is our demo! And we want to come across as real but also aspirational."

Vigo nodded in agreement, then went back to taking notes as if he were a courtroom stenographer on amphetamines.

"Well, I think you're right about the authentic part," I said. "You need to reflect your consumer, not talk down to them."

"Right. Of course." Seth nodded, trying to understand.

"Instead of the 'This is how good your life would be if you had us' approach, consumers, especially moms, want to feel understood. They are too savvy. Especially millennials. They see through the other shit. You need to become the consumer. You need to talk like them, dress like them, and even joke like them. That's how you establish a bond."

Seth looked at Vigo. "I have goosebumps. Do you have goosebumps?"

Vigo shook his head. No goosebumps.

"So is this an offer?" I asked. Boldness wasn't my specialty, but I was feeling more self-confident than usual. This guy was a joke and I just wanted to go to the Lippe Taylor interview with a bird — or bath bomb — in hand.

Seth pressed his lips together. "Can you give us a minute?"

I watched Seth and Vigo huddle together on the other side of the glass wall like they were discussing a football play. I figured that when they came back in and begged me to come aboard, I would play it cool and tell them that I would give them an answer by the end of the week. People loved to get answers by the end of the week. When you asked for any more time, it was an obvious brush-off. But an "end of the week" answer always felt like a tentative yet not desperate "yes." It was the best way to close out a meeting and an even better way to enter another one.

I pulled out my phone, trying to look nonchalant, when I saw something that made my heart sink. Sitting in my inbox was an email from my contact at Lippe Taylor informing me that the interview had been canceled. "We're going with an internal candidate. We were so looking forward to meeting you and we will keep you abreast of any upcoming opportunities." Before I could respond, Seth burst back in, beads of sweat dripping down his cheeks. He looked like a peroxide blond beer that had been left out of the cooler.

"Okay. So… I wasn't sure over email, but now that we've met you, Vigo and I believe that you are the *only* person for this job. You can speak to this crowd in a way that we can't. And I think we share the same worldview."

"We do?" I looked at him, nonplussed.

"This bath bomb is every mom. You want to escape your kids, but you also don't want to be out at the nightclub. You want to have your cake, but you don't want the calories after nine p.m. You are part of that 'self-care isn't selfish' crowd. You're privileged, but still put upon; blessed, but batshit; fun, but functional —"

"Sorry," I stopped him. "Are we talking about me or the figurative 'me'?"

"You… But also the *figurative* you!" His eyes were bulging with excitement. "We don't have a ton of money so the retainer would be modest." He coughed and glanced down. "Twenty grand for six months. We're also open to offering points."

"How many points?" I asked with my best poker face. I'd never been offered a point in anything.

"We'd need to look at the math —" Vigo interjected. It was the first time I'd heard him speak. His voice was low and creaky.

"Look," Seth said. "You get this company up on its feet and we can talk about it."

I was blinking, my head swimming in confusion. I wanted a job. But did I want to hitch my wagon to these two? For what amounted to an annual salary of forty grand?

"Two skews are ready to go!" Seth jumped back in. "'C-section blues,' 'TGI-Monday,' you know, because Monday is when the nanny is back. That one was Vigo's idea!" Seth looked back at Vigo, who groaned. "We want to launch with a total of five," Seth told me. "But cute so far, right?"

"Yeah," I told them. "I totally see it."

I was nodding my head, unsure if I saw anything or I just really needed a job.

CHAPTER FIVE

No matter how many times I entered Chelsea House, I always felt like one of those imposter colognes they sell at big box stores. Not quite Georgio, not quite Calvin, but something that came in an aerosol can and potentially caused some sort of contact dermatitis. Maybe it was by design — the straight-faced hipsters holding open the front door, the Rasta-chic gatekeepers positioned behind the front desk, the waitstaff with their Pilates-toned bodies encased in perfectly asymmetrical Belgian-designer uniforms. Even though I knew most of the people working there by name, I could never shake the feeling that I was about to be thrown out for simply lacking whatever ephemeral quality everyone else possessed.

Chelsea House encouraged members to think of themselves as part of an elite cabal of artists and dreamers sent down to earth to exchange ideas and energies in a super chic setting that offered movie screenings, free Wi-Fi, swimming pool access, and endless plates of painstakingly massaged kale salad.

Originating in London, the club thrived on its reputation for excluding anyone whose job involved wearing a tie to work. Bankers from the Upper East Side all the way down to Battery Park City begged and pleaded their cases, but rarely made it past the membership committee, of which Iliya was now the head. He'd been an interesting choice considering that Iliya, who'd come of age under the Coney Island boardwalk, didn't have an elitist bone in his body. Off the record, he thought the whole concept of Chelsea House was bullshit. But the concept liked Iliya. He had a strong work ethic, and his looks didn't hurt either. Normally, the club liked to give all their membership director positions to people already living within the community from which they'd be picking and choosing, but with the opening of new clubs like the Wing, the Soho House, the Norwood, the Well, the Wonder, and the The (a nonbinary concern that insisted on being called a "collective" and not a "club"), Chelsea House was losing not only its edge, but its supremacy. And Saro Stark, the master of the Chelsea universe, believed that Iliya was the only person fit for the job. He wasn't entirely wrong.

When I walked into the sixth-floor clubroom, I found Iliya in a back booth. He appeared to be comforting a distraught waitress. Though he was merely listening to her as she sobbed, I felt the hairs on my neck go up as I called his name across the room. No matter how pure the waitress's intentions, she would eventually try to fuck him. They all did. Even the ones who liked women.

"Iliya," I said in as bright and calm a tone as I could muster. Iliya glanced up, totally unfazed. He wasn't worried. Maybe it was a sober thing, but giving in to temptation, whether it was a glass of whiskey or an eager hostess, was something he deemed the province of the weak. It was beneath him.

"Hey, Meg," Iliya said. He appeared surprised, but not unhappy to see me. The waitress adjusted her blouse as Iliya stood to hug me. "Logan, this is my wife, Meg," Iliya said, somewhat stiff.

Whenever he introduced me to new people, especially women, I always felt their eyes linger on my face a few moments too long. I could read their thoughts. They wanted to know how *he* was with *me*.

At thirty-five, I was neither young nor old. I was still able to rock jean shorts, but past the age where guys tried to communicate with me through music. I was a plain Jane with a black bob and boobs that didn't require a workout bra. In a place like France, where women could look like boys and still be sexy, my stock might have been higher. But where I grew up, most people wrote me off as a suicidal goth or militant lesbian because I owned

Doc Martens, listened to Ani DiFranco, and had hair that didn't reach my shoulders. Which was fine with me. I'd seen enough horror movies to know that girls like me had the best odds for survival. The cheerleaders and prom queens were always the ones who ended up slaughtered or electrocuted with their own blow dryers.

The buxom twenty-something smiled, extending her hand. All I could focus on was the large ink merwoman on her forearm.

"I like your mermaid," I said in a sugar-sweet tone, overcompensating for my insecurity.

"It's a siren," she corrected me.

"Even better." I laughed awkwardly and Iliya shot me a look. I was overdoing it. "What?" I gave him a playful hit on the shoulder. "I'm a big fan of using my feminine wiles to lure men to their deaths. You know that."

He sighed. "I do."

When I first met Iliya, I was twenty-five years old and bartending at Geiko, the Japanese steakhouse whose employee dress code had been put in place well before the #MeToo movement. I'd heard all about the brooding night manager from the other waitstaff before actually speaking to him and had already determined that I wanted nothing to do with him. Which of course meant that I wanted everything to do with him.

He made me nervous to look at, and I knew he wasn't the type of guy you could expect to call you back, let alone commit to something exclusive. He was dark and mysterious, with his faint Russian accent and all-black wardrobe. I was hired to work day shifts and he only worked nights, as I could only assume his daylight hours were spent sleeping in a sarcophagus.

For my first two months on the job, our paths never crossed. But when I switched to evenings, there he was, the vampire from every Anne Rice masturbation fantasy I'd ever had. He drove a motorcycle, smoked cigarillos, and wore a leather bomber with a mandarin collar. I fucking hated mandarin collars. But his fashion sense was one of the few things about him that allowed me to feel mildly superior. He might have been hot with his chiseled cheekbones, but he was still a dork in a fucking mandarin collar that nobody had the balls to inform him was hideous.

As a manager, Iliya wasn't allowed to involve himself with staff, even though I had full knowledge that before I'd worked there, he'd hooked up with more than his share of cocktail waitresses in the coat closet. This was before he stopped drinking and before he got promoted, but the rumors never died.

Aside from when he was using the same three Spanish phrases on whatever busboy he'd come across, pretending to be a laid-back man of the people, sober Iliya was intense. He was detail-oriented, not a little neurotic, and harder on me than the lunch-shift manager, whom I could control with flirting. Iliya tried to be delicate when he eventually fired me, calling me out on the fact that I spent half my time behind the bar gossiping with the busboys about his outfit choices and the other half eating maraschino cherries. In closing, he explained that it was obvious I didn't see myself in the restaurant business for the long term.

"Do you really think anybody working at this place sees themselves here long term?" I replied, wondering if now was a good time to give him my thoughts on mandarin collars.

"I do," he said plainly. The look he gave me told me I should be ashamed.

What I'd failed to realize then was that Iliya had worked his ass off to become a manager at Geiko. And my mocking the restaurant industry as a whole only seemed to make him more annoyed.

I left that afternoon burning with shame and hoping I'd never see him again, but also sort of hoping that I would do something with my life that would land me on the giant billboard outside his office window.

Two weeks later, while aimlessly drifting around Cost Plus World Market at the Grove, I bumped into him. Literally.

It was a gloomy Sunday afternoon and instead of channeling my depression into another screenplay about my parents' divorce that I'd waste 200 dollars to print at Kinko's, I decided to max out my last working credit card on redecorating my apartment. I was holding a basketful of tea lights, paper star lanterns, and a handful of summer sausages when I heard someone *pssst* in my direction. I half thought I was being accused of shoplifting and spun around nervously. Iliya looked less greasy under the fluorescent lights. His leather jacket was nowhere to be seen and he was wearing actual colors: blue jeans and a thin maroon V-neck that looked like it might belong to an ex-girlfriend. I jumped back and one of my sausages went flying down the aisle. Iliya promptly went after it. I tried to act cool, disinterested, and like I'd never tried to find his Facebook page when he walked back over. "What?" I said, as if he'd been nagging me for weeks.

"Why are you always so angry?" He grimaced and put his hands up in the air.

"Well, you did fire me," I said, snatching back my sausage and stuffing it into my basket.

"I'm sorry," he said softly. "If it makes you feel any better, upper management wanted me to do it three months ago."

I shrugged and pretended to organize the contents of my basket, trying my hardest not to let this new information wound me.

"You changed your hair," he said.

"No, I just brushed it," I corrected him, shocked that he noticed my hair now or ever. "How's your restaurant career going?" Condescension tinged my voice.

"Good." He nodded. "How are things going with you, work-wise?" I swallowed and pretended I didn't care what he thought. "I'm writing jingles and helping my friend from college cut demo reels. You have one? You should play a Dracula in something," I said dryly.

Iliya smirked. He started to say something, but then stopped. "Are the sausages really great here or something?" He scratched his head, staring at the multiple links of beef in my basket. "You sure have a lot of them."

I huffed, pulling my basket closer to my chest. "What are you here to buy? Were you looking for something?" I shot back.

"Just you," he said without flinching.

I felt my stomach drop the way it did on roller coasters.

"I saw you through the window and wanted to make sure there were no hard feelings between us," he said.

"There is nothing between us," I gulped, very much wishing that there was something between us.

"Okay." He nodded and moved to go, then hesitated. "Now that I'm here... maybe I need a new French press, a disposable table-cloth? Obviously, it seems like summer sausages are a must!"

I didn't want to laugh, but I couldn't help it. He was funnier than I'd realized. And perceptive, the way that only women usually were. I rolled my eyes, trying to stay strong. But I knew that I was screwed. Even if he walked away, never to be seen or heard from again, I was going to think about him, obsess over him, and probably spend the next three months reading his horoscope and replaying this exchange in my head.

"You always roll your eyes at me!" he mused as we walked toward the end of the aisle. "Is that all men or am I special?"

"I do it to all men," I said, turning into another aisle and praying that he followed me. He did.

I could only play it cool for so long. I watched him speak Russian to the elderly checkout woman and help her bag my groceries. Next thing I knew, I'd agreed to have dinner with him. We went to some stroganoff place in Glendale. I rode on the back of his sleazy motorcycle, drank two shots of vodka, and gave him permission to enter my apartment afterwards (something I knew better than to do with a potential vampire).

I started the evening proudly telling him that nothing was going to happen between us because he wasn't my type and ended the night begging him to fuck my brains out in his mandarin collar. We were married a year later.

"Aren't you supposed to be at your interview?" Iliya asked, discreetly kissing me on the cheek.

I pouted. "Lippe Taylor canceled."

"I'm sorry." Iliya grabbed my hand. "You okay?"

"Yeah, actually. I got the first one." I smiled, trying to seem excited.

"You got the first job." He perked up. "That's great."

I nodded. "They're making weed bath bombs for moms. Oh, excuse me, CBD."

"I thought it was a tea company." Iliya's eyes narrowed. "That seems like a weird fit for you, no?"

"You mean a weird fit for you," I corrected him. "I have no issues with CBD. And it's supposed to be for moms."

"Moms doing drugs? You really want to get involved with that?" Iliya probed, his judgment loud and clear.

"They aren't ingesting it. They're soaking in it. Who knows if it even does anything."

"Well, I don't want any," Iliya said. "Are they going to pay you decently?"

"Yeah," I lied. "I might even get a point in their company."

He scowled. "That means they *aren't* paying you."

"They *are* paying me! I just got a job offer! Can we be happy for a minute before picking the whole thing apart?"

"I'm sorry." Iliya gave me a slow smile. He was backing down. "That's great that you got something. I told you that you would."

"I know, you're always right." I was still annoyed.

"You want to eat lunch?" he asked, trying to defuse the tension.

"With you?" I cocked my head. I knew what he meant.

"I can't right now. It's crazy here." Iliya barely pressed the button for the elevator before he was back on his phone, shooting off more emails. "That mer-waitress was cute," I couldn't resist saying as we waited. Iliya rolled his eyes.

"Are you going to be home later or..."

"I doubt it." Iliya looked back down at his phone and shook his head, frustrated with whatever he was reading. He was still screwing up his face at the screen when the elevator doors opened.

"I got to take care of this," he said with a sigh that was meant to evoke pity. "Bubby is on the roof. She'll handle you."

"So glad I'll be handled," I said dryly, walking into the elevator before he could hug me goodbye.

The doors shut and I took a deep breath. *Don't cry, Meg,* I told myself. "UGGH! Don't you just wish everybody would just fuck off sometimes?" a voice behind me roared. Startled, I looked over my shoulder. I'd been so caught up in the waves of resentment that I hadn't noticed the blonde in oversized sunglasses

standing behind me. My fellow passenger had a faint accent that I couldn't quite pinpoint.

I wiped my eyes, mortified. "Yeah," I said, forcing a laugh. "I guess I do."

"Emotions are powerful. No need to hide them," she said, taking a tissue out of her oversized clutch and handing it to me. "He would have been lucky to handle you." She took off her sunglasses and gently squeezed my hand. With one blue eye and one green eye she was unquestionably striking. But it was her intensity that stopped me in my tracks. Her focus was practically invasive. I had to look away. "You are far too powerful to be fucked with," she told me as the doors opened. "Don't take any more shit, okay?"

"Thanks," I said watching her walk off in tall dark combat boots and a voluminous pink babydoll dress that made her seem at once a woman and a child.

Iliya's understudy, Bubby, spotted me and rushed over in her Gucci slides and a cashmere sweater embroidered with the sentiment *Think outside of my box.*

Her real name was Jami, but Iliya nicknamed her "Bubby" because she ate her bagels with the dough scooped out, drank only hot water with lemon in the morning, and was always complaining about her sciatica like she was a seventy-three-year-old widow from Boca, not a twenty-seven-year-old dictator of New York society. I looked across the rooftop for my elevator companion but was disappointed to see she had vanished.

"Meg," Bubby said brightly, taking me by the elbow. "Let me get you set up."

CHAPTER SIX

Bubby installed me in a corner spot. The rooftop pool was already packed with beefcakes in banana hammocks and lifestyle bloggers surreptitiously trying to snap pictures of their pedicures as they waded into the water.

Unauthorized photography was strictly forbidden at Chelsea House. If you were caught so much as taking a selfie, you were promptly asked to leave. The house was as rigid as a state legislature. Their latest policy, mandating that children have their own memberships in order to gain roof access, had members fuming. As Iliya had explained it, it was a measure against the place turning into a giant summer camp in the warmer months. While they were happy to accommodate hotel guests and certain families with pull, the club wasn't looking to turn into a day care facility. Only problem was, that's what it had been the previous summer, and members were up in arms.

"How are you?" Bubby inquired.

"Good. Better. I think I found a job. You know that tea shop, Matcha Pitchu?"

"Yeah, but no," Bubby said, displaying only slightly more interest than Seth had shown in my career trajectory. "Do those two dudes look like they're about to fuck?" I looked over to see two trainer types grinding in the hot tub passionately enough to rub off each other's spray tans. "Because there is absolutely no fucking allowed on the rooftop," Bubby reminded me, like I was the one considering it.

"I think they're just…" I started before she cut me off.

"I'm sure you're freaking out about schools."

"How did you know?" I asked.

"It's September. That's when all moms start freaking out about schools. Isn't Roman a kindergartener?"

"He will be soon." I nodded, impressed that she remembered.

"So you really are in the thick of it!" she laughed. "Don't worry, everybody is in the same boat. Going through this gauntlet is a New York rite of passage. The bar bill this month is going to be off the charts." She grinned.

"Don't look too pleased," I said.

"How could I not? I love it! The desperate frenzy. The cutthroat nature. The eventual reckoning with one's real status in the world. As a person without kids, it's deliciously satisfying to watch the unraveling."

"Well, I don't know if I can unravel any more than I already have."

"Oh, you *can*, believe me," Bubby said, encouragingly. "You're doing private, yeah?"

"To be honest, I really don't think we can afford it. Tuition at these places is outrageous."

"You find a way. I used to commute two hours roundtrip every day to go to Spence, and it changed my life."

"It's *that* different from public school?" I asked.

"The education is great, sure, but it's all about the connections and relationships. In New York, when people ask where you went to school, they're talking about high school. Not to scare you."

"It's fine. I've been scared my whole life."

I started to say something else then stopped. The blonde from the elevator was back on the scene. Now shoeless, she was dangling her feet into the pool.

"Do you know her?" The words almost slipped out of me.

"Do you *not*?" Bubby tried to swallow her laugh.

I looked at the woman again, "No...Who is she?"

"Aren't you supposed to be in advertising?" Bubby shook her head in disbelief. "You really *are* new to town. That's Daphne Cole — or as she's better known on Instagram, Sweaterweather365."

"I don't really deal with fashion," I said. "That's more of a New York thing."

"Fashion is a New York thing?" Bubby snickered. "I'm pretty sure there's fashion in LA too." Daphne's and my eyes met. I felt a prick of embarrassment, then glanced away.

"She was a fashion influencer, but then she had kids and now she's more of a mom-fluencer but with killer fashion," Bubby explained. "She's mega."

I'd worked with a good amount of wellness gurus, DIY crafters and smoothie artists, but this was new ground. "What exactly *is* a mom-fluencer?"

"It's its own subgenre. Like, she is still a super high-end fashion chick but now she also does deals for diapers and those little whistles you stick up baby's asses to make them fart... the Windy?" Bubby looked over at

Daphne, cocking her head and furrowing her brow. Daphne's hair was falling out of its topknot in waves and her boots were cast aside as she delicately traced shapes in the water with her toes. She wasn't overly skinny; she had hips and curves, cracks and crevices. What was most striking was a quality I couldn't put a finger on. She was gorgeous, magnetically so. It was almost blinding.

"Her style is siiick, right? Those Bottega boots are sold out everywhere. And the Cecilie Bahnsen dress? I can't! So many *Killing Eve* vibes. Apparently, her closet looks like Hirshfield's." Bubby added, sotto voce, "When you are that rich you can take fashion risks. You don't need to mess around with basic black."

"Where did she come from?" It was all I could think to say.

"I think she's like first-generation Albanian or Bosnian or one of those Balkan countries. Her accent sort of ebbs and flows. Her mom was a housekeeper, or groundskeeper, or what are those people who have, like, a skeleton key to every room?"

"A female butler?" I asked incredulously.

Bubby shook her head. "Story is she worked for a few high-profile old-money families uptown. Daphne used to help organize closets before she was old enough to work retail. You know how Paris Hilton treated Kim Kardashian like her closet bitch? That was basically Daphne. Came from nothing, worked her way up, and now she's crushing it. Can build an Eiffel Tower out of French toast, gets gifted Chanel bags, never seems to have a bad fucking hair day, and just announced that she's designing a capsule collection for Revolve. With her kids."

I laughed nervously, baffled by how somebody with kids could possibly be that productive. "How many kids does she have?"

"Two. Twins. Vivienne and Hudson," Bubby said. "I'm embarrassed that I know that, but I do. The kids are part of her whole schtick. The husband gets dragged into it sometimes too. Kip? He's like a finance dude. Of course. Sort of a frat boy type... Cute, but in, like, a dorm room non-consensual hook-up kind of way."

I squinted, trying to picture what she meant.

"Anyway, yeah... I hate when people are so perfect, don't you?" Bubby was staring at Daphne's back. It wasn't tan, but it glowed.

"Jesus, yes." I smiled, trying to mask my growing feelings of inadequacy.

When Bubby bopped off to do her job, I pulled out my phone and wrote to Seth and Vigo to accept their offer. I had planned on waiting until the end of the week, but I was bad at waiting and too nervous that they might

change their minds by then. I needed to know that I had a job even if it was a dodgy one that wasn't going to cover the cost of a New York City education. I needed my family and the people around me to know that I had a purpose. Maybe I wasn't some self-made fashionista crushing the

motherhood game, but I was still somebody. I was the person who needed to know that most of all.

When I finished my lunch, I took the long way toward the elevators, passing the spot where Daphne had been sitting. The ice cubes in her otherwise empty glass were precariously balanced on top of each other like discarded toys wedged into Roman's closet. I felt a strange stirring, regret mixed with happiness. Even if Daphne was long gone, she'd still seen me at my most vulnerable. We'd shared a moment, and that was never going to become untrue. I bit down the smile that was forming on my lips and headed home.

CHAPTER SEVEN

Marina left our apartment at three-fifteen, not a second later. I made dinner, cleaned the kitchen, fed and walked Red, washed two kids, killed three roaches, and sent four bitter texts to Iliya. Taking matters into my own hands, I researched home extermination remedies online and applied a mixture of sugar and borax along our baseboards, under the cabinets, and around the sinks.

"I just can't get comfortable!" Roman tossed and turned, restless well past eight p.m. I'd been in his room for almost an hour. Sweet Felix was catatonic in the crib beside us.

I placed his weighted blanket back over his body and once more tried to extricate myself from the room. "Okay, I'm gonna go for real now—"

"Mommy?" Roman grabbed me, his grip tightening around my waist.

"Yes?" I whispered.

"I'm scared."

"Of what?" I asked, looking at his glowing purple night-light that made me feel like I was on mushrooms.

"Are you gonna die before me?" He blinked, ever so seriously.

My heart dropped. "No. Nobody is dying," I lied, finding myself moving closer toward him when I was supposed to be creeping away. "No, but I mean, like, someday you are going to die, and Daddy is going to die, and Felix is going to die —"

"That isn't happening ever!" I stopped him. "I love you, and you are healthy, and Mommy is healthy, and Daddy is—"

"Dying first because he is older than Mommy," Roman informed me, wrapping his fingers around my wrist. "I love you so much. I'm going to be sad when you go to Kevin's."

"Kevin's?" I looked at him, confused.

"That's where you go when you die, up to Kevin's," he informed me stoically. It hit me that in the game of telephone that is being four years old, he'd understood "heaven" to be "Kevin's."

"Who is telling you all this? Marina? Your school?"

"Oh Mommy...." He didn't answer. "Don't get old...." He was starting to drift off.

"You are completely safe, and Mommy is going to be with you forever," I assured him in a whisper.

"Can you just brush me?" Roman flopped over and pulled up his pajama shirt, presenting me with his back like an overindulged house cat. I used a skin brush on him twice a day to help keep him focused, but the brush was stimulating, and I didn't like using it before bed.

"How about a little massage?" I offered.

"A big one," he said, and I couldn't bring myself to refuse him. "Down. More back. More. Stop. Front. Sides. Face."

"Face?" I laughed.

"Daddy does face and ears," he groggily informed me.

I missed the daddy that shared bedtime massage duty with me, the co-parent that lightened the emotional load. I tried my hardest to remind myself that Iliya was working for all of our benefits, and that overseeing an army of attitudinal servers wasn't how he wished to be spending his night.

Once Roman was basically asleep, I scooped Red up in my arms and placed him on top of Roman's comforter. I wanted him to sleep there, at the foot of the bed, like those movie dogs that forge a special bond with a troubled teen and change their lives forever. Red wasn't going for it, though. He came right over to my feet.

I'd always believed that having a dog and then having a child was like falling in love with somebody new while still living with your ex. And I had a feeling Red shared this view. Sure, he'd seen enough of Roman's acrobatics on the couch to know that closing his eyes anywhere near Roman was enough to land him in one of those canine wheelchairs. But it was more than that. He saw himself as my dog, and my dog only. The kids were simply interlopers.

The second I started my Seal Team 6 crawl out of the boys' bedroom, Red followed me. At last, I got in my own bed with Red in one arm and my laptop in the other.

I had work to do. Both Bubby and my new mom acquaintance, Sari, had made it sound like child protective services would come for me if I didn't at least look into Abington.

According to the school's website, tours were already underway. Financial aid was awarded to a select number of kids, and the school itself was barely a mile from Ken's roach motel. If for no other reason than to be able to tell myself that I had tried, I submitted a request for a tour. Then I reached for my phone in a sort of mindless haze and found myself staring at the explore page on my Instagram.

I typed the letters slowly. "S-W-E…" Before I finished the word, Daphne's face appeared, right under the Sweetgreen account.

I felt a prick of excitement as her feed sprung to life: private beaches, presidential suites, and room-service trays spilling over with exotic fruits. There were charcuterie boards and paper mâché castles as tall as the ceiling and children's bento boxes filled with gourmet desserts. There were carousels and costume balls, cold Champagne bottles, tricked-out cars, and oh, the clothing — capes and dresses and shoes and handbags. It was retail porn, lifestyle porn, vacation porn, and food porn with the occasional bathroom bikini selfie that teetered into the realm of porn-porn.

Daphne's body looked smaller in the photos than it had on the roof. The pores on her face were nonexistent, as if she'd been attacked by a giant eraser. I tried not to think too much about her captions, most of which sounded like they'd been lifted straight out of a "Quote of the Day" desk calendar.

But just when I wanted to cringe, I'd stumble upon a post where she would pour her heart out with a rawness that was rare to find among influencers of her caliber. She talked about things that women didn't often talk about — her struggles with depression, her dissatisfaction with her body, her thyroid autoimmune disease, her screwups with her kids, and her guilt about preferring Netflix over fucking her husband.

I wasn't unfamiliar with the world of influencers by any means. I'd ghostwritten captions for quite a few of them, when they were working with brands that had hired me. But perhaps because I understood the machinations behind the posts, I'd never found any of it all that interesting. There was something different about Daphne. Something that was impossible to ignore. It didn't matter if you cared about her Balenciaga bag or botched Botox or brown-bag lunch challenge. She sucked you in. The commentators seemed to agree. "Where are the other honest portrayals of motherhood?" one follower wrote. "Sending love and light your way, my queen," somebody else chimed in. "You are saving my life," added another.

Mixed in with the autobiographical content and sponsored brand posts with everyone from Prada to Pampers were pictures of her fraternal twins, a boy and a girl who appeared to be slightly older than Roman. Wide eyed and moon faced, they were photographed from all angles in high resolution and with such frequency that after only five minutes of looking, I was certain I'd be able to pick them out of a crowd. While I never could have felt comfortable sharing my kids the way that she did, from a brand perspective they were what grounded the whole thing in reality. For as fancy as some of her content tended to be (she wasn't afraid to post a Birkin riding in a chopper), she was still a mom with all the same struggles.

Scrolling back through her feed, it seemed as if she was the originator of nearly every offbeat trend. She wore oversized eighties-looking suits with giant shoulder pads, nylon body suits that had built-in feet, patent leather trench coats with see-through mesh T-shirts, top hats, bowler hats, boater hats, and sombreros — and that was all years ago.

Having met Daphne in real life, it was hard to look at her page objectively. I kept trying to find the woman I'd encountered in person, but aside from the over-the-top-fashion, she wasn't quite there. This was someone different.

In person she'd been sarcastic and mischievous, almost aggressive. Online she was softer and more feminine. Something about her posts told me she was in on the joke, which made me like her even more. She was playing to the crowd, without apology. She'd determined who they were and fed it back to them with a glamorous twist. She was doing the same thing I did. Only she wasn't working for a brand. She *was* the brand.

After scrolling through roughly four thousand posts, I still wanted more. And so I opened my email and started to type. "You guys need a face for your product," I wrote to Vigo and Seth. "And I think I found it."

CHAPTER EIGHT

"Sweaterweather365? That's her *name*?" Seth asked the following week. He presented me with the elaborate tea that he'd been crafting for the past twenty minutes. "But what about when it's hot outside?"

"I hope it didn't seem like an overstep, but I really think this woman would be —" I stopped talking and gasped when I caught sight of the calico cat made solely out of foam and chocolate powder looking up at me from the mug.

"That's Hot Tea," Seth said with a smile.

"Yeah, but the cat. It's practically a photograph!" I shook my head in disbelief.

"No, that's his name. Hot Tea," Vigo explained, breaking his silence to clarify.

"I'm a cat daddy," Seth confessed. "I have Ankimo, Bowie, and Rachel Meowdow. But Hot Tea is the prettiest. Bowie only has one eye and the other two are Cornish Rexes, so they basically just look like raw chicken breasts with whiskers."

"Right," I said, looking over at Vigo and wondering how in the hell these two had ever got together.

It was a little after nine a.m., still early at Matcha Pitchu headquarters. Aside from the two baristas downstairs preparing to open, the place was empty. Seth had been there all night working on new formulas and had demanded that we meet as soon as possible to discuss "next steps." Dressed in flannel pajama bottoms and red Elmo house slippers and with hair that looked as if it had been used as a youth league soccer field, Seth seemed to look more on the verge of a breakdown every time I saw him.

Vigo pulled up Daphne's Instagram on his laptop and showed

it to Seth. I'd been working on them for over a week, and this was the first time I'd managed to hold their attention. He'd stopped on a photo of Daphne kneeling on the bow of a yacht in the South of France with a caption that read, "Feeling a bit Nauti and not giving a ship."

"I love these captions!" Seth exclaimed.

"The captions are terrible," Vigo baritoned.

"I thought the same thing.... at first." I pressed my lips together. "But it's a bit. She's making fun of herself. And what's more, she's the most influential mom in the city. There's a self-awareness under there. That's her secret sauce."

Seth hummed and continued to peruse Daphne's page while Vigo typed some things into his phone. "I'm running her through StarShoot," he grumbled. "It's a platform that does the math for marketers. There's an influencer engagement calculator. It's basically 'likes,' plus comments, plus reposts, divided by the total number of followers and then divided by the total number of posts," Vigo explained slowly, as if he were speaking to a couple of foreign exchange students. His face brightened. "Not bad. She has an average ER of 1.97, which is high considering she isn't a celebrity and I had never heard of her before."

"You aren't her demo," I said. "Moms are!"

"One problem." Vigo set his heavy-lidded eyes on me. "We don't have the kind of money that a chick like this would require. Her rates are probably something like thirty grand for a post. Maybe two to three hundred thousand for a full-blown campaign."

Seth's mouth dropped open. "For real? Should I be an influencer?"

"I'd follow you," I said.

It always seemed crazy to me that the act of posing in front of bubblegum pink walls and boomeranging into marshmallow-filled bathtubs was a legitimate twenty-first century career. But I had watched regular people build small empires, frame by frame, avocado toast by avocado toast. I had been in the room when big companies committed to compensating online personalities who'd agreed to a single post more than they paid me for a year's worth of work.

"Those twins hers?" Vigo checked.

I laughed. "I don't think they're child actors."

"Twins scare me," Seth said.

"Okay. I get it." Vigo capitulated. "But some of these captions. Oy vey," he groaned.

"I can fix the captions for our purposes if we can get her," I promised.

Vigo looked to Seth, then back to me, still processing. Finally, a slow smile played across his mouth. "Let's bag her."

It took a week of going around and around with Daphne's agents before we learned that she might be interested. As luck would have it, she didn't have any conflicts or exclusivity in the bath bomb or CBD space. But for a half-day photo shoot, two press interviews, one static post in her feed and a single three-frame story, the agency was requesting 150k. After consulting with Matcha Pitchu's investors and throwing in another 10k he'd squeezed out of his parents, Vigo countered at 50k with five percent of total back-end revenue. It was the best he could do.

Daphne respectfully passed on the offer.

CHAPTER NINE

Corralling Roman across the threshold of Abington School, my adrenaline kicked in. I'd killed myself to get a time to bring him in, but now confronted with the perfect moms streaming through the doors of the Harry Potteresque building, I knew I was in over my head.

My heart rate started to settle as we made our way inside. Beyond the austere exterior, Abington was colorful and warm, with hallways that smelled of buttered toast and freshly purchased books. Large picture windows looked into each classroom. I couldn't help fantasizing about what kind of life I'd have had if my parents had actually invested in my education.

"Greetings and salutations!" The words came from a small woman wearing Iris Apfel reading glasses. She stood in front of a large banner that bore the words: "Don't Dream It, Be It."

"*Rocky Horror Picture Show*?" I exclaimed, giddy.

"Pretty sure it was Eleanor Roosevelt," she countered.

I was pretty sure that it was Tim Curry but chose not to argue.

"This is Roman Chernoff," I said. "He's here for a playdate and I'm here for the parent tour."

"Well, as we tell prospective parents, it's not exactly a *playdate*." She delivered her scolding in a cheery tone. "We like to think of it as a *child visit*."

"Oh, of course." I blushed, remembering the jargon the Abington admissions worker had used on our phone call.

"What time was your appointment for?" she asked, eye level with my waist. Discreet as she tried to be, I could tell she was sizing me up to see if I wore a Rolex or any other status symbol that might in-dicate that I was capable of contributing generously to the school's annual fund.

"I'm Marilyn, the dean of the lower school." She smiled, twisting the simple strand of pearls she wore under her checkered button-down shirt and cashmere cardigan.

"If you wouldn't mind, leave your contact info with Norma." She motioned to a gray-haired woman seated and looking forlorn in the corner. "And then head on over to the Mandela room." She pointed down the hallway with her tiny doll-like fingers. She reminded me of that little woman from *NCIS: Los Angeles* who was always telling the team what to do.

"I don't want to go on a playdate!" Roman shrieked as we entered the wood-paneled conference room filled with stoic-faced parents in folding chairs. "It's a *child's visit*." I corrected him calmly, looking to the other parents for approval.

"Who am I visiting?" he rebutted.

"You know... I really don't know." I laughed, hoping someone would come to my rescue.

The crowd remained quiet, avoiding eye contact like a bunch of fifteen-year-old girls in a Planned Parenthood waiting room. Coordinated in gray sweaters, navy suits, and Marilynesque pearl necklaces, each parent looked more uptight and stressed out than the next.

With fewer than twelve spots available for incoming kindergarteners and a sibling policy that gave preference to kids who already had an older brother or sister at the school, they were ready for war. And so was I, to a lesser degree.

"Meg?" a familiar voice called out. I turned around to see Sari sitting in the corner. Her tote had been traded in for a sophisticated black Chanel bag. And her curly hair was now styled into a Heather Locklear bouffant. She looked as though she'd woken up early to get a Cosmo from Dry Bar. She motioned for me to join her.

"I woke up early to get a Cosmo from Dry Bar. Is it over the top?" she asked under her breath, touching her head.

"You look great," I reassured her.

She smiled. "I wanted Waverly to get one too, but her hair is just too thin to hold anything," she confessed, glancing at her daughter. "Say hi, honey," Sari instructed the kid. Waverly looked at me stone cold, then pretended to shoot me with a finger gun. As the imaginary bullet grazed my ear, I instantly felt better about Roman's chances.

"Are you nervous?" Sari asked. "I'm crawling out of my skin." Before I could respond, she leaned in closer and whispered to me.

"You know the price doubles when they go to the upper school, right? And they also want a donation each year." She scanned the room, sizing up the competition. "Did you know that they hire outside investigators to advise on what your value is? It's crazy. Where else are you guys looking?"

I managed a flat smile. "This is it so far," I said, and immediately understood that I'd provided the wrong answer.

"GIRL! What did I tell you last time we spoke? You need to cast a wide net. You won't get in everywhere. Nobody does, unless you are a crazy billionaire or something. You aren't a crazy billionaire, are you?" She stopped short, more interested in me than she'd ever been.

I laughed. "Just crazy."

"Oh, thank god. We need more normal people around here." She paused. "And by normal I obviously mean, like, normal rich. I'm not saying you're *poor*. Look, I live in *Brooklyn*," she reminded me, pronouncing the borough as if it were a venereal disease.

Just then Marilyn poked her head in the doorway. She was

flanked by two younger women holding clipboards.

"Okay parents, time to bid your little scholars farewell while we take our tour and they have their visits. We're going to split the kids up into groups of three and…" I watched her lose track of her thought as she clocked Roman, who was now wearing his nametag across his eyes like he'd been censored in a photo. My heart quickened and she resumed her spiel. "And we will meet back up in about thirty minutes."

Marilyn had her sales pitch memorized and perfected as she led the gaggle of slobbering parents through each of the building's five floors, strategically stopping in front of all the portraits, plaques and trophies. "So, this is where we have the kindergarteners through fifth graders, and then at our uptown campus, we have sixth through twelfth," she said, escorting us up a grandiose staircase. "This building is obviously more modest than our uptown location, but we still have two gyms, one pool, and our own nut-free cafeteria that provides all meals. We don't allow outside food because of allergies, but we do make everything on premises from scratch using as much produce from our organic rooftop garden as possible. We'll be visiting the garden momentarily."

Sari whispered in my ear as we continued to ascend the marble stairs. "This is such a tease," she went on. "I have friends — two gay dads, biracial, Ivy League educations, the grandma has a wing named after her at Lenox Hill — and they didn't even get an interview because their flight back from Nairobi was delayed and they applied on October first. In the end, they were waitlisted at every school." Before she could give the appropriately mournful shake of the head, she let off a horrified gasp. I followed her gaze, expecting to see blood. It was Daphne Cole, talking to a group of friends.

Daphne was dressed in knee-high snakeskin boots with jeans

and some sort of bondage-type spine harness over a plain white tee that most definitely didn't come from the Gap. Her hair was longer than I remembered with a darkened root that blended into a caramel blond. I could feel the sudden quickening of my breath.

"I can't. I literally cannot," Sari said. "That's Daphne Cole." Our tour group was moving ahead but the two of us stood frozen in place like two unfortunate citizens of Pompeii.

Daphne was talking to a shorter woman with dark hair and skin that was probably allergic to the sun. She looked familiar in that vague way people do when maybe you'd gone to high school together. Or perhaps she was in one of those United Airlines seat belt videos. She wasn't memorable enough to be the lead, but maybe she could have been the second or third flight attendant who got to wear an oxygen mask and sit next to a real-life kangaroo.

"That's her cousin Lauren," Sari whispered. I could tell by her tone she wasn't a big fan.

"I think maybe I've seen her before," I said, trying to make sense of my *deja-vu.*

"Probably. MommybearTribeca? She pays to get her pics promoted on the gram." Sari rolled her eyes.

Paid-promo Lauren looked rigid, and like she was desperately trying to exude a youthfulness that was just out of reach. I could picture her straining to learn TikTok dances and wearing Minnie Mouse ears to Disneyland.

"Come on," Sari said, and we hustled to catch up with Marilyn and company. They were winding their way down a hallway toward the woodworking studio. Kids wearing matching Kevlar aprons sanded and sawed pieces of plywood that were to eventually become part of the end-of-semester project, a sculpturally innovative, freestanding residence for the school's potbelly pig, Tofu. Roman was going to flip out when he learned that the school had its very own pig.

"So they're related?" I asked Sari. It had been minutes since Lauren and Daphne were within our view, but she knew who I was talking about.

"By marriage. They were roommates who married cousins. Lauren moved to New York when she was, like, twenty-two. She met Daphne when they were both interns at *Teen Vogue*. And when Lauren met her husband, Sheldon, she introduced Daphne to his cousin Kip."

"Sounds incestuous," I whispered.

"They didn't get together right away. Daphne was too busy dating some married banker with a burner apartment in Gramercy."

Our group rounded another corner. This hallway was filled with science projects and abstract seascapes made out of kidney beans glued to construction paper. It was all the tactile stimulation that my son's busy brain needed. God, this place would be so perfect for him.

"So how did the whole Instagram thing start? How did she get so huge?" I asked, finding my mind wandering back to Daphne as I followed after Marilyn, who was moving at a surprisingly fast clip for somebody with such small legs.

"Lauren was actually doing it before any of those girls," Sari supplied. "Posting pictures of herself running on the beach in ball gowns. It just never became anything because she has nothing to say. She also has a horrendous sense of style. I was brought in on a remodel she was doing to her Amagansett house, and I swear to god, the whole place was so Miami it made my head spin." Our group had come to a stop. Marilyn had us line up and wait for our turn to peek into the Science Lab. "I'm not talking mid-century

Miami — I mean marble bathtubs and Serge Roche palm frond mirrors on every wall," Sari said.

I nodded, as if I could picture exactly what she was talking about.

Our line inched forward, and Sari resumed her lecture in a whisper. "If you did an anthropological study on Manhattan moms, Lauren would rank at the top for most out of touch," she said. "A friend of mine has one of her old nannies working for her; Lauren has a fleet. Not only did she pay shit and never make direct eye contact, she also insisted that all the children's clothing be air-dried and ironed. Can you imagine asking your nanny to do that?" Sari looked at me.

"Definitely not." I shook my head, pretending to have access to both a nanny and an iron.

The tour ended unceremoniously with Marilyn walking us back to the Mandela room to reunite with our kids.

"So that's it," she smiled, bidding us farewell. "I wish every one of you the best of luck," she said. It sounded as if she'd already made up her mind that nobody in our group was worthy of moving forward in the application process.

Roman ran toward me, all smiles. "I got gummy bears!" he announced. I'd never seen him look so jazzed after having been separated from me for over thirty minutes.

"We're done?" I muttered to Sari. I'd missed my opportunity to take Marilyn aside and inquire more about financial aid.

Sari gave a dejected shrug. "It's not like any of us had a chance."

Jacked on high-fructose corn syrup, Roman bounded off ahead of me. "Roman, wait!" I called after him, worried he would do something that might further seal his fate.

"Wait for your mom, little guy," a voice warned.

I gulped when I looked up. Daphne was standing by the front of the school, blocking Roman from barreling headfirst through the exit.

"You again," she said. "How's your life going?" A slight smile crept across her face.

"Better!" I chirped. "Just… you know, doing the school thing!"

"Do you guys know each other?" Sari looked confused, then mad at me for not having said anything earlier.

"Not really. I mean, sort of. I..." I wasn't sure how to explain.

Daphne held up her hand and proceeded to set the record straight. "I tried to pick her up on an elevator."

CHAPTER TEN

Daphne was with Lauren and a delicately featured woman with artfully spiraled hair and arms who looked like she slept in plank position. Lauren squinted and reached out her hand. "We haven't met," she said, clearly trying to decide if I was anyone worth knowing. "I'm Lauren."

"Tanya." The other woman gave a wave.

"And this is... I never got your name." Daphne aimed a smile at me.

"Meg Chernoff," I told her.

"Daphne Cole," she said, extending her hand.

"I know," I blurted out.

Lauren's eyes widened. She let off a cough that escalated into a choking sound.

"Lauren! Are you okay?" Tanya started walloping Lauren's back aggressively, as if she'd been waiting for an excuse to hit her for the entire duration of their friendship.

I turned back to Daphne, whose multicolored eyes were still focused on me. "I know who you are because I work for a company that was trying to get you for a campaign," I said, trying to recover. "A bath bomb thing."

"Oh yeah. That sounded cool." Daphne tucked a piece of hair behind her ear, revealing a constellation of diamonds crawling up her lobe.

"Hey Lauren, I'm Sari," my companion jumped in. "I helped on your Amagansett reno. The place turned out stunning. I really hope AD takes it!"

Lauren made a look of confusion.

"*Architectural Digest!*" Sari said.

"I know what AD is." Lauren's smile said she was disinterested in Sari on every level. "My kids have already destroyed the place. We'll see."

"You're new to town?" Daphne looked at me, one eyebrow raised.

"Is it that obvious?" I asked.

Tanya laughed and Daphne shut her up with one withering look. There was no question that Daphne was the Heather With The Red Scrunchie of their group.

"My husband runs membership for Chelsea House, so we moved out from LA about a month ago," I said. "He's from here. Or well, he grew up near... ROMAN!"

My son was submerging both of his arms into a small aquarium by the window as Waverly looked on in disgust. "I'm freeing him!" Roman said ardently, scooping the water like an animal rights renegade air-evaccing an orca from SeaWorld.

I redirected my gaze to the group of women, embarrassed.

"Speaking of fish," Lauren jumped in. "Can you get our kids hooked up with Chelsea House pool memberships?" She glanced at her gang. "Did you guys know that starting next month kids are going to need their own memberships to be allowed at the pool?"

"I heard about that," I responded. "Crazy, right? I can inquire..."

"Daphne doesn't think kids should be allowed up there," Lauren shared.

"I said that one time, about one kid!" Daphne scoffed.

"Yeah, mine!" Tanya clarified.

Daphne spared a quick glance for me, then looked around at the group. "Tramp Stamp starts in ten minutes. What are we still doing here?"

"How is it? I've been dying to try it," Sari interjected. I'd forgotten she was still by my side. "I've heard that it totally changes your body," she continued. Nobody responded.

Daphne's eyes were set on me. "Is your company on Instagram?"

"Yeah. The parent company is called Matcha Pitchu," I told her. "This new thing hasn't launched yet."

"How about you?"

I gulped. "Me?"

Daphne pulled out her phone. "Meg Chernoff, right?" I watched as she typed my name slowly. "You're private." She looked up at me, perplexed.

A ticklish sensation spread up through my knees. "I have kids. It can be scary. Child of the eighties, too many afterschool specials." My laughter sounded demented.

"I hear you," Daphne said. "Well, let us know if we can help you with anything."

I smiled, unsure if she meant help with the school or New York in general.

"It takes a village," she said.

"Or a vineyard!" I blurted out.

This time everyone erupted in laughter. Even Lauren was amused.

"You're funny." Daphne cocked her head to the side and looked at me again. "See you soon, I hope."

Sari turned to me, slack-jawed, once they'd left. "That was *huge*. You know that, right?"

Still unsure of what to make of the exchange, and a little embarrassed, I called out to Roman.

"Lauren is on the board here," Sari told me. "I'm sure she's the only reason Tanya's kid got in. He got kicked out of Avenues for breaking his math teacher's nose with an abacus. Tanya's husband is also one of the best plastic surgeons in the city," Sari said. "It was sort of a win for the teacher. Her old nose? It wasn't great." She grimaced. "Anyway, forget about how today's tour went! If those women want you in, you are getting in!" I could tell she was on the verge of tears. "I'm so happy for you!"

CHAPTER ELEVEN

Later that night, Roman picked at a plate of chicken tenders that had taken me two hours to heat in Ken's janky electric oven. Felix was over on the floor, fussing in his bouncer.

Iliya had texted that he wouldn't be home until eleven, which I knew meant midnight. The new normal. I wanted to be annoyed that he was always coming home later than he promised, but I was simply too tired to care.

Instead of fixating on Iliya, I thought again about Daphne and what she had said. Was she really offering to help me get my son into the perfect private school, the one with a fleet of therapists and a vegan potbelly pig? I would have been a fool to assume so. And yet, I couldn't help but daydream about my new fairy godmother and all the walnut-paneled doors she might open.

"So, what did they ask you in the interview?" I looked over at Roman, who was now scribbling on a piece of construction paper next to his plate.

"I don't remember." He gave a preoccupied grunt.

"Well, was it good or bad? How did you feel overall?" I pushed my notepad covered in potential bath bomb names to the side and gave him my full attention. "Could you see yourself happy at a school like that?"

Roman blinked up at me. "How do you spell the word *kill*?"

"What? Why?" I craned my neck trying to get a glimpse at what he was drawing.

"When is RiRi coming back? It's no fair Felix gets to play with her all the time." His little brother wedged his entire hand into his mouth and let off a whelp. "Why is he SO LOUD?" Roman covered his ears.

"He's getting teeth. Which means he's in pain. And you were this loud too," I informed him, grabbing a frozen toothbrush from the freezer. Red followed close behind, hoping that whatever I was holding was made of ham.

Felix was teething and, according to Marina, he'd been "super annoying" all day. He had a low-grade fever but nothing severe enough to warrant a trip to the doctor. I was afraid of those chemical teething gels, and sadly all the chamomile drops just didn't work.

"I can schedule a playdate for you and RiRi. I'm sure she'd love some alone time with you," I said, sitting down beside Felix to massage his gums with one hand. I picked up my phone with the other hand and banged out the words "teething baby."

"Can you get me a cookie?" Roman called out, batting his enormous eyelashes.

"A cookie? You still haven't eaten your dinner." I motioned to his plate.

"I will eat. For a cookie," he negotiated.

Before I could decide whether to laugh or just give in, my phone started ringing.

"Teething baby. Genius!" Seth exclaimed. "Hashtag I love it, hashtag no-pants dance!"

God, "mom brain" really was a thing. In this case, though, it was working in my favor.

"Mom! Cookie!" Roman proudly waved his empty plate in the air.

"What he's trying to say is that he's excited." Now Vigo was commandeering the phone. "Also, he's not wearing pants." This was more than I wanted to know.

"So, what's the last one?" Seth asked eagerly.

"COOOOOKIE!" Roman's demand grew louder.

I gave Roman a signal with my hand, then put on my headphones and continued the conversation as I rummaged through the fridge. "The last bomb? I'm not sure yet," I said, glancing at Felix, who was drooling in his docking station.

I unwrapped a tube of premade cookie dough and absently threw a few discs onto a half-greased pan. "But I have been thinking about the brand as a whole and I still hate *Mommy Bombs*," I said. "It's not sexy enough." I was starting to feel more comfortable in my role, however undefined it was. "So here's my pitch: I think you should call it NBD."

"Is that like an NDA?" Seth wasn't following.

"It means No Big Deal."

"Oh, I like." This was Vigo.

"Right?" I was excited. Or I was excited that they were excited. "And for the final bath bomb…" I racked my brain, frustrated that I was still racking my brain.

"Magic," Seth said. "I think having the word 'magic' in the title is good." He started to spitball. "Magic woman, magic juice… magic woman juice…"

My phone was glowing with a notification. "Daphne Cole has sent you a follow request." I felt a spike of adrenaline. And then it hit me. "Guys— It's Trophy Mom." The minute I said the words, I knew that they were the right ones.

Seth howled. "That's fucking brilliant!"

"That works," Vigo agreed.

I hung up the phone feeling high on something far more intoxicating than CBD. Throwing the cookie sheet into the mini oven, I sashayed back into the living room. Once I'd transported my slumbering baby to his crib, I sat down next to Roman, careful to shield my phone with a throw pillow as I opened Instagram and pressed on my profile picture. Before I accepted Daphne's request, I wanted to take a quick inventory. I deleted a handful of sunset pics and a couple of close-ups where my chin looked a tad too Jay Leno.

"What are you doing, Mommy?" Roman asked.

"Nothing," I assured him, massaging the back of his neck. Just then, a DM appeared in my inbox. "Are you going to accept my friend request or what?"

Both taken aback and excited by her forthright method of communication, I put on an episode of *Paw Patrol* for Roman, then slipped off to the bathroom.

"The thing is. I don't have any followers. As you might have noticed," I wrote back.

"I did. That's why I want in. I like the idea of being part of a club that won't have me." I could picture her lips curling into a smile. Her next message was much longer. "Speaking of… I wanted to invite you to this ridiculous, and pretentious supper club my friend Lauren does. It's totally awful but I keep coming back. It's like a car accident or super obvious facelift that I can't look away from."

"You're really selling me." I laughed as I wrote back.

"We're doing it at my place this month." Daphne attached a picture of the invite along with her cell. "If you don't come, I'll never forgive you." She added a winky face emoji. After sending back my number along with a "thumbs up" emoji, I took a deep breath. There was no going back.

"So, what are you doing right now?" She wanted to continue our conversation.

"Watching *Paw Patrol* with a four-year-old. You?" I settled onto the raggedy Turkish bathmat on the tile floor.

"Hiding from my kids in my closet and drinking." I couldn't tell if she was joking.

"I wish I could hide in my closet but it's not big enough," I lamented.

She shot back a laughing emoji. "Welcome to New York."

"I'd try the fire escape but my eldest is sort of like Kathy Bates from *Misery*. If I try to hide, he'll break my legs and never let me out of his sight again."

"You are really funny!" she replied, then started writing something else. My anxiety mounted as I watched the three little dots dance across my screen. "Remind me, what do you do for the CBD company?"

"I am writing their copy and helping with the brand development." I tried to sound somewhat important.

"So you're a writer."

I had to stop myself from replying no. I had imposter syndrome as a writer and felt no right to actually identify as one. Even seeing the word spelled out made me uncomfortable. I had a highly specific skill set. But I was no Nora Ephron, and to suggest otherwise would be far too brazen.

"Copywriter." I included the uncomfortable emoji that looked like Felix when he was passing gas. "Just accepted you," I added, eager to steer us away from the topic of my not-quite career.

The conversation moved from DM to text almost without my realizing it. I stood up to splash some water in my face and turned to go check on Roman. Another vibration. "Going through your pictures. You are an absolute knockout." I almost dropped the phone into the sink. "I don't care if that is creep status," Daphne added, "I just had to say it."

"Are you sure you're looking at the right account?" I replied. "The one with all the stock photography of Croatia?"

"Pixies reunion concert looked fun," she shot back.

Oh my god. She'd seen the picture of me kissing one of my girl-friends outside the Greek Theatre in Hollywood in '07. I cracked the bathroom door open, checking that Roman was still in the same place I'd left him. "I miss my old life," I wrote.

"How was it better?" she probed.

"It was just different," I replied. "Now there are no concerts. Just a kid I have to convince to sleep and a closet that is body-shaming me."

"LOL your body looks great to me," she wrote. "Okay so you miss concerts. What else?" I could tell Daphne was having fun, and truth be told, so was I. While I realized I should have inquired more about Abington and the possibility of her writing me a letter of recommendation, I just wanted to keep things light and playful.

"What else do I miss? Hmm…. Concerts, cocaine, cult sta-tus movies, the usual pre-kid life unencumbered by fear or consequences."

"You had me at cult."

I bit down a smile. I hadn't bantered back and forth with some-one in years. It was fun, and it felt good to know that I was still capable of it. Red wedged his way through the door to see what I was up to. After giving me a once over, he shot me a judgmental stare and walked out.

"You are the first person I've met in a long time who truly doesn't give a fuck," Daphne continued.

"That's not true. I give so many fucks," I confessed, closing the door so that Red couldn't come back and guilt me with his all-knowing eyes.

"Seeing you at Abington was a breath of fresh air. You aren't like those other women."

"Neither are YOU." I smiled as I typed. "But I admire how you play to them."

"Oh? Go on."

"Not just the moms at school. All the moms. You give them what they want. They think that you are them when you are just serving up what they asked for, with a side of sarcasm and a whole lot of oversharing. It's very smart."

Daphne didn't write anything for a good minute. A minute that felt like an eternity. I hoped that I hadn't been too presumptuous. "So what do you think?" she said at last. "Should we run away together?"

"I don't have a car," I typed, trying to play it cool. "Would you settle for a Citi Bike?"

"Baby." She stopped typing, allowing the word to sit on the screen all by itself. She was flirting with me. And I liked it. "So are you gonna follow me back?"

"I really only use the app for work. I don't follow anyone."

"And to catalog vacations, and ex-girlfriends," she teased.

"I wish those were my vacations! I've never even been to Europe." I said, dodging the comment about the ex-girlfriends.

"Make you a deal: If you follow me, I'll unfollow everyone else. That's four hundred people I'm willing to leave out in the cold just because I want your attention."

"Deal." I was smiling so hard it made my cheeks hurt. I could have stayed there grinning all night if it weren't for the sudden blaring of our smoke detector, snapping me out of my trance.

I raced out of my hiding hole. "Jesus Christ!" I cried. The cookies were in ruins. The whole apartment was engulfed in bitter smoke.

"Mommy! We're going to die! We're all going to die!" Roman cupped his ears and closed his eyes, preparing for certain death.

I opened the oven to retrieve the charred pieces of dough. "It's fine, honey! We're fine!" I assured him, opening the windows and jumping up and down, trying to knock the batteries out of the bleating contraption. If this caused permanent damage to Roman's eardrums, I'd never forgive myself.

When the room finally went quiet, I turned to Roman, out of breath and not a little embarrassed. "Honey," I said loudly, just in case I had actually damaged his ears. "I think it's time for bed." I meant it less for him than myself.

CHAPTER TWELVE

"Mommy? What's Jesus Cries?" Roman asked as I tucked him under his weighted blanket.

"What?" I was still frazzled and shaken by the night's events.

"You said it when you came out of the bathroom. When the house was on fire," he reminded me.

"The house was never on fire," I quickly clarified, making a mental U-turn back into mom mode. "I said... jeans... and... fries." I prayed he was too tired to continue the conversation.

"I love you, Mommy," he said in a drowsy whisper.

"I love you so much, Roman. More than anything in the entire world." I stopped for a moment, marveling at his beauty.

"More than Felix?" he probed.

"Not more; different," I explained.

Having a second child had proven to me that I could simultaneously love two people without one relationship taking something from the other. My heart had expanded when I had Felix the way I'd promised Red it would when I had Roman. The only one who lost in this magical equation was Red. My having an actual child had turned him into an actual dog.

"I love you because you are you and I love Felix because he's Felix," I said. "But I love you both more than anything else there ever was and ever will be." I finished the thought more for myself. My tiny captor had already fallen asleep.

The second I got out of the room, I shot Red a how-could-you look. The apartment had nearly burned down, and he hadn't so much as lifted a paw. Then I went to find my phone and text Daphne. I apologized for going dark on her. "Sorry, my kitchen was on fire." She didn't reply. I started rereading what I wrote over and over as if to be sure it sounded okay and not too insane. *Maybe she went to bed. Maybe she is judging me.* Thoughts spun in my head as I brushed my teeth. *Maybe she is calling Marilyn from Abington. Maybe she is calling the police.* I worried, gargling my mouthwash. *Maybe we weren't supposed to be friends. Maybe I crossed a line by endangering my children that I can never come back from.* I paced into the living room, checking my phone. She still hadn't written. *I guess I should forget about that invite she sent me. Maybe the people who dislike her will hear about her disliking me and take me in. Maybe someday years from now somebody will bring up her name and I will finally be secure enough to admit that we had this weird texting flirtation that lasted roughly fifteen minutes and ended in me almost burning down the carpenter from* The Oregon Trail's *apartment.* Half an hour later, I heard the jostling of keys in the hallway. Iliya walked in, looking dazed and spent.

"What's burning?" He sniffed around.

"The apartment is trying to kill us," I announced dramatically. "It took two hours to heat up the mini oven for the chicken tenders and then two minutes for it to burn the fuck out of the chocolate chip cookies. It makes no sense." I might have been chatting with Daphne slightly longer than two minutes, but I chose to omit that minor detail.

He frowned. "You should have put a timer on."

"A timer wouldn't have helped," I defended myself.

"You could have set off the sprinklers." Iliya shook his head as he clambered onto the kitchen counter to reinstall the batteries in the smoke detector. "Has Red been out?"

"No, not yet. I couldn't with both kids." I surreptitiously glanced back down. No notifications on my phone. That was it. She hated me.

"Can you hand me that plastic piece?" Iliya pointed to the top of the smoke detector, now sitting on the sink. I reached for it and passed it to him just as my phone pinged with a notification. It was Daphne. All she sent was a single kissy face emoji, but it was enough. I could breathe again.

"I can't believe you're still awake," Iliya said as he climbed back down from the counter. He was giving me his look. I knew where this was going.

"I thought you were going to walk Red," I said, watching him move closer.

"I am," he said quietly. He took my phone from my hands and tossed it onto the couch. "Hey." He gave me a glassy-eyed smile. "I'm proud of you."

"For what?" I asked, wishing that I could catch a glimpse of the screen from where we were standing to make sure he hadn't accidentally called her.

"You're working again. It's what you wanted." Iliya started kissing my neck.

"I..." I began, but he stopped me with his mouth. His hands slowly worked their way down my body. He backed me into the mini fridge and dropped to his knees, burying his head between my thighs. I unclenched my jaw and let my eyes flutter closed.

His hands dug into my ass as he picked me up and sat me on the kitchen island. Mumbling under his breath in Russian, he took his time entering me. Pictures and sounds rushed through my mind as I let myself go. I was thinking about him, but I was also thinking about her.

CHAPTER THIRTEEN

We woke up later than usual. Red had spitefully peed on the rug and my phone was still on the couch, at four percent charge.

I rushed to get Roman out the door. As we raced toward school, I apologized about burning the cookies and promised to make it up to him. Roman was in a forgiving mood. He squeezed my hand and gave me extra hugs at the school door.

I was standing at the crosswalk in a pair of vintage boots I'd dug out of a still packed suitcase and a white T-shirt that sadly didn't include one of Daphne's crazy looking bondage belts when Seth called, frantic.

"You're never going to fucking believe this," he started.

"You're bankrupt," I guessed, already surfing around on LinkedIn in my head.

"No, dummy. Daphne Cole is gonna do our campaign."

According to her agents, Daphne had a change of heart and decided that NBD sounded "like a lot of fun." She "believed in the product" (that she'd never tried) and "took a shine to the overall brand aesthetic" (that she'd never seen). It was obvious that this had nothing to do with NBD and everything to do with me. I felt like I was flying.

Her schedule was tight as she had Fashion Week obligations, a capsule collection she was designing, and a trip to Paris for a Zoe campaign in mid-December. But she was excited to "collab," and willing to reduce her rate as long as we covered glam and her agent's ten percent commission. Though she didn't want to do any interviews or appearances, she agreed to a three-hour photo shoot. Two pictures would be approved for promotional usage on the company's website and on her personal Instagram. After that she'd syndicate to her Facebook account in order to amplify reach. The latter was my suggestion. I had enough experience in this world to know that without the paid amplification, sponsored posts ended up as good as dead. I normally didn't concern myself with back-end minutiae, but I didn't trust Seth and Vigo to handle it alone.

It took a week to cobble together the funds, the crew, and the equipment before Seth and Vigo invited Daphne and her team over to Matcha Pitchu HQ for the shoot. If we'd had actual money, I would have forced them to rent a real space. But between the cost of paying employees, the cost of manufacturing the product, and Daphne's fee, they were already strapped. They were so strapped, in fact, that I agreed to let them pay me at the end of the quarter, whenever that was.

"We didn't expect the Daphne thing to actually work out," Seth said. He was wandering around the conference room barefoot, wearing a kimono that easily could have doubled as a hospital gown. "I know it isn't much for her, but that is a big check for us to have to write. If I paid you today, I'd have to shut down the whole operation, you dig?"

I wasn't shocked. I knew the company's financials, and how much the shoot was costing. But I didn't care. Daphne was worth it.

Seth's face lit up. "How is this for a jingle: A soak a day keeps your children at bay." He delivered this in a singsong voice, mean-while sprinkling the contents of a Splenda package in a line across the conference table. I watched him remove a small straw from his pocket and snort the long line of sweetener in one inhale. I didn't know whether I was impressed or horrified. "I'm getting kind of nervous," he said.

I couldn't think straight. It had been over a week since I'd ban-tered with Daphne from my bathroom. And I had no clue what it was going to be like to see her in person. Maybe I'd read too much into her flirtations, and it was going to be a cordial working relationship just like any other. Or maybe she'd act like she had no idea who I was. I'd resisted the urge to text when her deal closed for fear that she might not reply. I had no good reason to think that she would ignore me. I just wasn't comfortable giving my power away and risking potential rejection. I'll admit it. I had a girl crush. Or a crush-crush. It didn't matter that Daphne was a woman, or that I was happily married with two kids. I wanted this feeling to last forever.

Daphne was due to arrive in less than an hour and things were far from ready. A phalanx of interns practiced filling a large porcelain tub with bubbles and foam while two grips argued over where to hang an enormous piece of paper that we planned to use as our backdrop. I helped set up a tripod for light, securing it with sandbags made out of bulk beans that Vigo picked up at Costco and rice plundered from Seth's doomsday stash in the basement.

The photographer, Zed, looked like Terry Richardson if he'd eaten Terry Richardson. He'd showed up with a twenty-year-old assistant wearing a cropped babydoll T-shirt that said, "Fuck the Pain Away." Vigo had sourced the guy off Craigslist and offered him two hundred bucks in cash and a hundred-dollar Matcha gift card for the half-day's shoot. I hadn't seen his body of work, but had a strong feeling it featured plenty of shots of his assistant.

"So what's the plan?" Seth looked at me blankly, as if we hadn't gone over it countless times.

I stared at him. "We are going to get Daphne in that tub and get as many shots of her as we can before noon. She has a hard out." I looked at Zed and Vigo, both of whom had drifted over to us. "Is that not the plan?"

Seth raised his arms in the air. "I'm totally open to just vibing off whatever..."

Zed started nodding slowly. "Let's get her in the tub. I like that... Or is in the tub too on the nose?" Zed backtracked. "Draped on the tub? Under the tub?"

"Guys," I said, trying to keep my cool. "We have a tub so let's use the tub. Let's not overthink this." I was only supposed to be their copywriter but for some reason I now found myself wearing every hat there was.

I sat down in a club chair and checked Daphne's page to see if she'd posted anything new. I couldn't help myself. I just couldn't stop. Even though I knew she was being paid to say half the things she was saying, I still found myself wanting more. I wanted to know about the new "sponge concealer" she was buying, what she packed her kids for lunch and how much of it they ended up eating. I wanted to know what style pants she thought were the most flattering and what children's books she felt promoted self-esteem and helped young readers locate their North Star. I wanted the scripted answers and I wanted the real ones. I stopped on a picture of her leaning against a graffitied wall, wearing a studded skirt and designer fanny pack. I began to ponder if maybe I needed a designer fanny pack of my own when I heard Vigo call out my name.

He gestured at a small entourage of people coming toward me. There she was. Daphne had on a Metallica T-shirt with beat-up jeans and was holding a tan lapdog with a smashed-in face. Daphne's eyes were set on me. "Hi, stranger," she said, her indeterminate accent stronger than ever. She moved toward me, kissing my cheek. "This is Cha Cha, my favorite child," she continued.

The dog looked at me with palpable disinterest and then burrowed her head into her own butt.

"She's adorable." It was all I could think to say. "What is she?"

"Pekingese, according to the breeder. But who knows? He was arrested and his mill got shut down, so I never got her papers," Daphne said.

"Are you serious?"

"Meg. I'm messing with you. I thought you knew me better than that." She smiled coyly.

Lauren humored Daphne with an obligatory laugh then turned to me. "I sent my kids' applications into Chelsea House," she informed me.

"Great. I'll tell my husband to keep an eye out," I said. Daphne introduced me to the rest of her team. Michael, her hairdresser, was a feisty blond with balayage locks just like Daphne's. From behind, he could have played her stunt double. There was Nicky, Daphne's malnourished makeup artist, and her agent, Susan, who was in the corner screaming into her phone. The introductions hadn't been necessary on my end. These people were all staples on Daphne's Insta feed.

Michael and Nicky stared at me. "Where should we set up?" Michael asked, still not removing his sunglasses.

Vigo corralled everyone toward a foggy full-length mirror and wardrobe rack he'd set up in the back of the room.

I gave them a good hour before I started stressing. Eventually, I had no choice but to approach and check on her ETA.

"France will be fun!" I heard Nicky gush. "Especially around Christmas! I've always wanted to go to a Paris show."

"The fall shows are better," Daphne said. "But after New York Fashion Week, I'm too spent to fly seven hours and run around Europe with ten thousand suitcases. It's always so crowded and none of the good restaurants have space. December will be far more chill."

I peered around the rack. Daphne's head hung down and she was staring at her phone while Nicky swabbed at her eye. "How are we doing?" I asked nervously.

"THINGS ARE GOING," Michael hissed into his blow-dryer like it was a microphone.

"Okay, great." I smiled.

"She just needs lashes," Nicky said.

"Sorry." Daphne reached out to squeeze my hand. "I was hoping you'd come find us."

I smiled back, embarrassed by the attention but also in disbelief that we were touching. Michael pretended not to notice but clearly had an opinion, which he expressed by "accidentally" aiming the blow-dryer at my face. Susan reappeared holding Cha Cha and looking flustered.

She had a compact gymnast's build and an arched back, making her look like she'd just dismounted the uneven bars. I knew she had to be at least twenty-five but if she told me that she was only fifteen, I would have believed her.

Daphne stood up and wiped her hands together. "So how long do we have here?"

"Two hours," Susan replied crisply.

"So… yeah, if you are good to go," I said. "We want this to be an easy day. I promise to get you guys out of here as quickly as possible." I tried to sound professional as I inhaled Daphne's perfume. There were notes of amber, vanilla, and other things you'd be inclined to set on fire. I felt my skin getting warmer and my neck starting to itch. But it wasn't just the scent I was responding to.

To simply call Daphne gorgeous would be an understatement. Like standing too close to a mural that stretched a city block and only seeing the square foot that was immediately in front of you, you wouldn't get the full picture; you'd be missing out on the masterpiece. Daphne was so much more than gorgeous. Her beauty was raw and complex and just the slightest bit tortured. She was like nobody I'd ever known before, and yet she felt like someone I'd known forever.

"I have too much curl on this side," she said, playing with her hair in the mirror. "We need to bring it down a bit. I look like a fucking homecoming queen." Daphne turned to me. "Meg, you weren't a homecoming queen, were you?"

I shook my head. "Musical theater geek."

A sly smile appeared on Daphne's face. "I almost believe you."

She was right. I'd been exaggerating. I was a latchkey loner who listened to Portishead and Tori Amos and cut out clippings of models from fashion magazines to glue to my bedroom ceiling. I barely had the courage to sing in the shower let alone in my high school's production of *Mame*.

I used to fantasize about what it would feel like to be one of those popular girls, to have two parents who were married and could afford to buy me a car. I wanted to have family dinners and game nights with brownies made from scratch. To own a wardrobe that came from Banana Republic and a Princess Diana commemorative Beanie Baby that watched over me while I slept. It would have been fun. But even with those luxuries, I don't know if I would have truly fit the part. Because in order to be popular you have to be a bit naïve, like a toddler still unaware of its own mortality. If you've experienced disappointment, if you understand how ephemeral everything is, you'll never feel popular. You'll just feel lonely.

"Let's get this show on the road! I want to make our lunch

rezzie," Susan demanded.

At the mention of food, Lauren looked up from her phone. She claimed she was tracking one of her son's Lyft trips but from where I was standing, I could see her scrolling through a BuzzFeed article titled "23 Dogs Who Totally Nailed Wearing Socks."

"Does anybody know the Wi-Fi password here?" she asked.

"Yeah, Hide your kids hide yo Wi-Fi," I said, mortified.

Lauren made a face of disgust. "With a y-o ?"

"Do you have dogs?" I asked, motioning to her device.

"No," she said curtly, stuffing her phone back into her pocket.

Daphne disappeared behind a folding screen, then reappeared in a tie-dyed silk robe. "What do you guys think?"

"LOVE it." Susan swooned.

"It's cute." Lauren shrugged, barely looking up.

"Can I be honest?" I said. Daphne's entourage went silent. I looked down at my shoes for no other reason than I needed to look somewhere. "I really don't think we need all that..." I trailed off.

"All what? It's just a robe." Daphne shook her head confused.

"I mean the tie-dye," I explained. "I think it might be a bit too Cherry Garcia when paired with the CBD." Michael bit his lip. Susan's eyes widened, nervous. Daphne swallowed, clearly not used to hearing that her fashion sense was off.

"It's still a great piece!" Susan assured her.

"I love it," Michael agreed. "Maybe not for this, but it's great."

"Did she just compare you to a Ben & Jerry's ice cream flavor?" Lauren snickered. "Who is the designer?"

"Nobody," Daphne said curtly. "Just some art student off Etsy. I thought the big pearl buttons were sort of fun." She tugged at the neckline, slightly wounded.

Her entourage kept supplying compliments. Daphne responded

by stripping off the robe. It fell to the floor. All she had on under-neath was a white lace bra and underwear set. "Well, it's Meg's cam-paign and she hates it, so I hate it. So what do you want me in?" she asked. "I didn't bring a lot of options."

I took a gulp and tried not to stare at her cleavage. Before I real-ized what I was saying, I asked, "Are you comfortable in just that?"

"This?" she asked, letting out a small laugh.

"Minus the bra." I doubled down, serious. "Who takes a bath in a bra?"

Daphne looked at me and cocked her head to the side. I could tell she was impressed by my boldness. Frankly, so was I. "Not me." Daphne shrugged as she approached the bathtub in her underwear, covering her breasts with her arms. Vigo and Seth stared, slack jawed, as she submerged into the bubbles.

Seth looked at me. "Are we not doing a top?"

"She's in the tub," I said. "What kind of top did you want?"

Zed turned to Vigo and shrugged. "I'm digging it," he said, and started shooting. The moment the camera snapped, Daphne's confidence seemed to disappear. Suddenly, she seemed skittish, awkward even. Daphne gave Zed her no-joke-required laugh and moved so quickly for the camera that you'd think the tub was filled with ice. Her movements were jerky, her expression slightly panicked. I didn't want to say anything, but I could tell she was growing more and more uncomfortable.

"She seems a little jumpy," Vigo worried, looking at Seth. "Should we pull her out of the water?"

"That's the thing with influencers," Vigo said in an undertone. "They aren't real models."

"It doesn't help that your photographer looks like a convicted sex offender," Susan shot back. "He's probably freaking her out."

While Zed was easily an eight on the most likely to kidnap you at a truck stop bathroom scale, he wasn't the issue. Daphne was freezing up for other reasons, I was certain. I thought about all the pictures I'd seen of her in the past and realized that they were mostly selfies. "Would it help if you could see the monitor?" I called out to her.

"YES! PLEASE!" she said through a clenched smile.

I pulled the monitor closer to the tub and sat down next to her.

"Do they think I look chubby?" She sounded so vulnerable. "You can tell me. I can take it."

"What?" I said. "Not at all. It's all good. Breathe." She wasn't relaxing.

"Let's take a ten-minute break everyone," I called out. "Would you feel better in the robe?" I asked her as the crew dispersed.

"You hate the robe." She laughed nervously. "I was a fat kid. My sister and I weighed in twice a day, naked, on two different scales. One digital and one old fashioned. And if we weighed more during our evening weigh-in, Mom made us ride the exercise bike in the basement before dinner. Instead of saying grace before a meal, we would hold hands as she said, 'Over the lips and onto the hips.' She used to refer to my body as 'bodacious'...The word still haunts me."

"Okay. Stop. Get all that out of your head. I am promising you on my life that you are a total smokeshow. These are gonna be some of the hottest photos you've ever taken. And I've seen almost every photo you've ever taken," I confessed.

Daphne smiled and brushed a piece of hair from my face. I could feel the peach fuzz on my cheeks stand up straight. "You have such great hair," she said. "I love how shiny and dark it is."

I smiled, flattered, then mentally smacked myself across the face. Time was running out and we needed these shots. "What kind of music do you like? Do you have a playlist?"

"On my phone," Daphne said, looking over to Susan.

Susan handed Daphne's phone to Zed's assistant, who scrambled to hook up the Bluetooth. Beyoncé's voice filled the room.

"Formation," I said, nodding in approval.

"The only album of hers I ever liked."

"The best Beyoncé was the scorned, vegan Beyoncé," I agreed.

"She's only relatable when she's starving and hates her husband," Daphne said, laughing.

Zed started shooting before I even had a chance to leave the frame.

"The giggly girl stuff is working!" Vigo called out from behind the monitor.

"Meg, stay put," Seth demanded.

"I don't normally do professional shoots," Daphne confided.

"Don't worry," I said. "These guys are so not professional."

She laughed. "I have a photographer I shoot with all the time but he's just a dude from Craigslist."

"So is this guy," I whispered.

Daphne smirked. "You know, I thought he seemed a little dodgy. Like he's definitely shot at least one porno in his life."

"And he thinks he's shooting one right now." I looked to the group for encouragement. "She's got this, right everybody?"

"Yes! Fuck yeah!" They cheered.

"Meg, can you splash her up a bit?" Seth asked. "Throw some suds back and for—" Before Seth could finish the sentence, Daphne tugged on my shirt and pulled me into the tub with her, clothing and all. I fought back viciously, splashing her face as she tried to dunk me under the surface. The room burst into hysterics as we struggled like fools.

"We got it!" Zed finally declared. "That's a wrap!"

Michael and Nicky didn't hesitate before grabbing their kits and fleeing the scene. "That was FIRE!" Susan declared, handing Daphne back her phone. The second the device touched her fingertips, her eyes widened, and her face contorted into a delirious grin. She held her phone high above her head and made a face I'd memorized from hours of scrolling through her page.

She turned and flashed me the photo she'd just taken. "What should I caption this?" Daphne began reading off a list she'd saved in her email drafts.

"Can I see it again?" I asked.

In the picture, Daphne looked sultry with wet hair, smoky eyes and wearing nothing but a bathrobe.

"What about, something like *Is this a good look for drop-off?*"

"I'm dead!" Daphne looked back down at the photo and shrieked diabolically. "Do I dare?"

Even Lauren couldn't help but let out a chortle from across the room.

"Well, you look too hot," I said. "And when you don't call it out, you just seem like an asshole." I was starting to understand that the more blunt I was with Daphne, the more she seemed to respect me.

She laughed as she typed. "I'm going with your caption." When she was done, she looked back up at me. "Hey, are you coming to that dinner? Say yes. I need to see you drunk."

I clocked Lauren looking slightly shocked.

"Maybe!" I said. "I just have to check with... my family." For some reason, I didn't want to say the word "husband."

Daphne didn't seem to register any of it. "What do you do for workouts?"

I shrugged. "Stress. That's my primary cardio."

"What do you have tomorrow at nine-thirty?"

"I'm technically supposed to be working." I glanced over at Seth and Vigo, remembering that they still hadn't given me a dime.

"Have you ever heard of Tramp Stamp?"

I shook my head, pretending not to already know everything there was to know about Amy, pronounced Ah-Mee, the former Tracy Anderson instructor who'd gone rogue and created her own method of movement, a dance and trampoline hybrid that, according to the website, gave women the ultimate "booty-pop."

"Give me an hour and I'm going to change your life," Daphne promised.

As if she hadn't already done just that.

CHAPTER FOURTEEN

The following morning, I tried to tamp down the anticipation coursing through me as I entered Tramp Stamp's Tribeca studio. Daphne was nowhere to be seen. A currant-scented candle burned next to bowls of complimentary apples and hair ties on the white lacquer counter. Behind it sat a dewy pixie of indeterminate age wearing a name tag that said "Swae." I told her which class I was there for.

"Nine-thirty is for members only. Are you a member?"

"No... but I'm friends with Daphne Cole."

"Megan?" Swae looked me up and down again.

"That's me." I smiled.

She didn't crack one in return. "Wait over there."

I walked to a white sofa and pulled out my phone, my go-to move whenever I was feeling out of place or uncomfortable. In the few moments since I'd last checked, Daphne had managed to make her third post that morning. This one was of her kids having a pillow fight on her bed while she sat on the edge doing her make-up. "Just winging it. My motto for life and eyeliner." I laughed to myself. She really did have the most corny captions.

"Morning, sunshine!" I glanced up to see Daphne beaming at me. She was wearing shiny purple leggings and a tank top that looked small enough to belong to one of her twins.

"The caption." I laughed, flashing her the post.

"Do you approve this time? Or still too cheesy for your taste?" she asked coyly.

I gave her a look.

"Hey, make for the masses, take Tramp Stamp classes," she joked, rubbing her fingers together as if she were a strip club patron doling out one-dollar bills to the entire room.

Daphne led me down a corridor and waved at someone through a window that overlooked a studio filled with women jumping up and down on mini trampolines. Tanya dripped in sweat as she bounced on the lone trampoline on the raised platform in the front of the studio. Ever the Tramp teacher's pet, Tanya had been chosen to lead the rest of her classmates as an instructor paced around the room, calling out moves on her headset. When Tanya saw us, she threw up a peace sign, then stuck her tongue through the middle of her raised fingers.

"I can't believe that bitch! She said she was only taking the nine-thirty but now she's in the eight-fifteen too," Daphne scoffed. "Such a workout whore."

Before I could think of a witty response, Swae appeared behind us.

"We have to do an intake for you if you're going to take class today," she said with zero enthusiasm.

Daphne wished me luck and disappeared into the depths of the locker room. I followed Swae into a tiny office that smelled of lemon disinfectant and half-eaten Sakara salads.

"One class isn't really gonna do anything," she said plainly. "It takes time to learn the routine, sculpt your skin into a shape we think would look best on you. We'll see how today goes."

After filling out an endless digital form that asked everything from my marital status to when I last ovulated, I passed Swae back her iPad.

"Great, great," she said, reading over my answers. "Now take off your clothes and tell me everything you hate about yourself."

I hesitated for a moment, unconvinced that she was serious. Swae picked up a digital camera and waited for me to reply.

She was dead serious. Standing in front of a blue wall and posing awkwardly, I felt the need to make excuses for my body. "I just had a baby, so everything is a little saggy."

"Turn around. Arms out to the side." Swae sounded like a bored TSA agent. "Do you like your ass currently?"

I knew that if she was mentioning a body part, it was obviously one that she wasn't into.

"I never see my ass, so I don't really think about it," I replied. "It probably sucks, though." I was eager to find some common ground.

"It's not optimal," she agreed. "Don't worry. Amy is a pro at eradicating math teacher ass. You know her story, right?"

"She was a math teacher?"

"Very funny," Swae said, not laughing. "When Amy created the method, she drew inspiration from a lot of different places. Obviously, Tracy Anderson, Body by Simone, The Class." Swae clasped her hands together and leaned forward. "She was a backup dancer for Justin Timberlake for years. So the technique is rooted in hip-hop cardio. But Amy isn't just interested in achieving that long and lean muscle look. She believes in booty."

"Just not math teacher booty."

Swae couldn't spare a smile. "That's why we bounce. Okay, let's see the numbers." She pointed to a state-of-the-art digital scale. I gingerly stepped on and held still while Swae affixed a panoply of wires to various parts of my body. "OH MY GOD!"

"What?!" I asked.

"You are like thirty-five percent fat! How are you even standing up? Average body fat for a woman is typically between twenty-five to thirty-one percent. It's like you have rickets."

"You know I just had a baby, right?" I reminded her, still hoping for a little leniency.

"So did Amy." Swae pointed at a picture of Amy taped to a bulletin board. Her curly hair was tamped down with a Rosie the Riveter-style bandana, and she looked chiseled as could be in her jean shorts and cropped tank. "That was, like, two weeks after the baby," Swae intoned. "She's bounced back now... Literally!" It was the first time I'd heard Swae laugh. She reeled herself back in and effected a humorless expression. "So, the deal we usually offer influencers is unlimited classes in exchange for one video story per class and an in-feed static post monthly."

"I'm not an influencer," I clarified.

"Daphne said that you were." The lines on Swae's forehead grew more pronounced. "Well, then it's fifteen hundred."

"Dollars?"

"No, pesos," Swae joked. "I just need a card number and we can put you on a monthly renewal." She was growing angry. "Do you need to think about it?"

"Yeah... I should probably think about it."

"First class is complimentary." After handing me a bottle of water that retailed for thirty dollars, Swae pushed me through a heavy soundproof door and into the studio. Rap music was blasting through two large subwoofers and the instructor, Bambi, a smolderingly sexy woman with fire engine red lips and a fishnet bodysuit, bent over as she did some sort of ass smack move.

"Thirsty thot! Thirsty thot! *Thiiirsty*! YAS, ladies!" she cried, dropping to her knees. "You're hot. You're smoking!" She screamed into the sea of middle-aged white women flailing in the air like so many aerodynamic rag dolls.

With sweat glistening on her chest and arms, Daphne mouthed every lyric of the NSFW Azealia Banks song, as she kicked her legs high above her head. *I guess that cunt getting eaten, I guess that cunt getting eaten, I guess that cunt getting eaten."* There was something so primal about her, so aggressive and intense. I focused on bouncing. Anything to keep myself from staring at Daphne.

Within three minutes, I was sopping wet and could hardly breathe. After the class, Daphne and her friends infiltrated a corner of the locker room that they claimed had the best selfie lighting. Lauren took a gulp of lemon water from her jug, toweled herself off, and then began crawling around on the floor like a dying seal.

"What are you doing?" Tanya stopped snapping photos of her ass. She looked at Lauren, horrified.

"What does it look like? Stretching out my sacrum!" Lauren shot back. Various unfazed Tramp Stampers stepped over her on their way to the showers.

"So? How did you like it?" Daphne locked eyes with me. "I told Swae that you were an influencer. Did you go along with it?"

"Um, no. It was pretty obvious I'm a member of the *influenced* class."

Daphne scoffed. "I was trying to hook you up. Think faster next time."

"Haven't you hooked her up with enough?" Lauren said from her spot on the floor.

"What are you talking about?" Daphne shot back.

Lauren stood up and took another swig of lemon water. "Never thought it would be harder to get Silas a kid's pool membership than it would be for a complete rando to score an invite to Daphne's house."

That was enough to make Daphne snap. "If I hear one more comment out of you about who I invite anywhere, I'm gonna shove that jug down your fucking throat."

Nobody in the entire locker room dared move.

"I didn't mean it like that," Lauren tried backpedaling, but it was no use.

"APOLOGIZE," Daphne demanded. I'd never seen this side of her. It was scary. It was also a little hot.

"I'm sorry," Lauren stammered. "Geez, it was a joke." As Lauren gathered her belongings and slinked out of the room, Tanya couldn't help but comment, "That was pretty intense, Daph. I probably would have gone with something more casual, like carving 'slut' into her locker —"

"Careful," Daphne warned.

Tanya tried to lighten the situation. "I should do doubles more often. The nine-thirty is clearly where the action is!"

Daphne turned to me, her eyes filling with tenderness. "I'm sorry about her. You okay?"

I nodded, hurt but also touched. Daphne Cole was my protector.

"Lauren will chill out," she promised.

"I'll work on the pool thing," I said, knowing that Lauren wasn't going to make my life any easier until I helped her with hers.

"Who cares about whether Silas gets to swim," Daphne said, still peeved by Lauren's poor form. "You're coming to that damn dinner."

CHAPTER FIFTEEN

When a high-profile fashion influencer capable of impaling someone with a jug of lemon water tells you to do something, you do it. When that thing happens to be attending an exclusive all-women supper club at her fancy Tribeca apartment, you buy yourself an outfit for the occasion. Unfortunately, I couldn't afford a new outfit. I still hadn't been paid and even if I had, that money needed to go toward more important things, like cobbling enough cash together for my children's exorbitantly priced lives.

If I mentioned any of this to Iliya he would have given me shit about working for free and followed up with more shit about my need to impress a bunch of vapid strangers. Under normal circumstances, I might have agreed. The supper club was the last thing I should have been thinking about. It was also the only thing I could think about.

I managed to convince Marina to stay late on Thursday night while I attended a "work function" by promising her an extra fifty bucks and a spicy tuna roll with tempura flakes from Blue Ribbon. "I'm literally sabotaging my relationship with Lastrelle over this and all I'm getting is one spicy tuna roll?" Marina kvetched as I gave myself a final once-over in the mirror by the door. "I should at *least* be getting the sashimi platter."

When she wasn't driving her wing mobile, babysitting for us, sexting on Tinder, or lying to her mother that she was still enrolled in nursing school, Marina was hustling. Her most ingenious way of obtaining extra cash was by scheming her way into focus groups for anything from pharmaceuticals to breakfast cereals. She was registered on some lists as a female between the ages of 18 and 25 and others as a female between the ages of 35 and 45. Over the years, she'd pretended to have cats, be allergic to wheat, and even suffer incontinence — whatever it took to make it to the final round. While she signed up for the money, Iliya and I suspected she stayed for the validation. If she wasn't going to be America's Next Top Model, she was at least going to be America's Next Top Survey Taker.

"Lastrelle was only going to give you another twenty-five bucks," I said, evening out my under-eye concealer with my pinky finger. "This is a better deal — even without the sushi."

"You're missing the point, Meg. I was supposed to show up. My reputation is at stake." As she spoke, she took a shot of her cleavage and uploaded it to her Snapchat.

"Fine. You can get two rolls. But not the sashimi!" I backed away from the mirror and ran my hand down my outfit in an effort to banish any creases.

After hours of rummaging around my closet, I'd settled on my black maternity trousers that I belted high on my waist. On top I wore one of Iliya's nicest dress shirts and a vintage cropped blazer that I'd originally bought for an eighties-themed birthday party back in LA. Using one of Ken's dull bread knives, I unceremoniously tore out the cartoonish shoulder pads.

"Why do you have to leave? I don't want to go to bed without you!" Roman whined from the couch. He was distraught, but not enough to take his eyes off the TV. Marina had made her way to the kitchen, where she was searching for pre-sushi snacks.

"I'm not going to be gone that long," I said, carrying Red out from my bedroom and setting him down next to Felix's bouncer. Red waited all of two seconds before shooting me a "fuck you" look and scurrying away.

"I'm really feeling this dentist by the way," Marina said as she followed me toward the door with a mouthful of peanut butter Puffins. "He's playing games, which you know I love."

While she was desperate for a relationship, Marina never seemed to like guys who liked her back. If they were too nice or too normal, she was immediately turned off. It was only the guys with emotional baggage and unexplained eye patches that seemed to hold her attention.

"I think he might be the one. Won't send me a photo." She wistfully shook her head and leaned against the deadbolt. Crumbs were trickling down her shirt.

"Wait. You've never *seen* him?" It suddenly occurred to me that she might be talking to some kind of child predator who could be endangering my kids.

"He's not divorced yet so he's cagey about posting online."

"Can't he just privately text you a pic?" I inquired as I moved into the hall. I was running late and could not afford to let Marina lure me deeper into the conversation.

She shrugged. "It's more fun this way."

"We'll talk more later!" I assured her as I scurried out of the apartment, toward the elevator.

I heard the door slam shut and then I heard her exclaim, "Who wants to build a fort?" It sounded like Roman cheered in response, and I wondered how much of his anxiety was his own and how much of it was mine that I'd managed to project onto him.

It was still warm outside, and the slightest breeze was coming off the Hudson. The trees were in full autumnal glory, shades of aubergine and blood orange blazing overhead.

Daphne lived in an apartment building on the corner of Vestry and Greenwich Street. It was one of those addresses that always had fresh floral arrangements and no fewer than three doormen standing vigil at all times. The men on duty watched me as if they'd made an unspoken pact to mace me if I dared wander anywhere past the front desk. A concierge wearing a tightly tailored black suit did a bad job concealing his surprise when he heard that I was heading to Daphne's apartment.

The elevator delivered me to a foyer whose walls were covered with black and white wedding portraits. I keyed into the sounds of the party and took a deep inhale.

"Welcome!" A plump woman in navy slacks and a white polo materialized and asked if she could take my jacket.

"I'm fine," I said hesitantly, not wanting to reveal the surgery marks on my jerry-rigged outfit.

"I'm Rosamie," she said sweetly. "Do you want anything? There's a beauty closet for guests."

Trying not to be offended, I shook my head. "I'm not really a big makeup person," I told her. I followed Rosamie past a seven-foot-tall sculpture of a weeping woman I recognized from art history class as a Lichtenstein, and into a living room grander than any I'd ever seen. A pair of all-white leather sofas wrapped around the room like snow-covered train tracks. In the center, a marbled coffee table groaned with silver towers of exotic fruits and cheeses. The shelves held art books and small precious objects that could serve as instruments of violence if wielded the wrong way. The room was warm and noisy, as the assembled women competed to be heard over the surround sound's sultry jazz.

Walking out onto the terrace, I could see clear from the Brooklyn Bridge to the Empire State Building. I tried to maintain my composure as I gawked at the sweeping view.

"I was standing behind this weirdly hot guy at Sweetgreen today," I overheard somebody say. "He was half my age but *still*, I felt like we had this cosmic sex connection. Then he just took his blackened chicken salad and left. Barely ever looked at me." The woman telling this story was a Barbie-bodied brunette wearing a sweater whose embroidery let the world know that it was Balenciaga. "If I had been ten years younger, a guy like that would have been begging to drizzle his cashew dressing all over me," Barbie lamented. "I know as women we're not supposed to want to be objectified anymore, but don't you feel like being invisible is even worse than the alternative?"

A slightly older woman wearing silk pajamas with feathered fringe was nodding in fervent agreement. "I face-tuned a photo of myself so much yesterday that when my daughter saw it, she asked if it was her."

Stifling a giggle, I rounded a corner to see Lauren sitting on a lounge chair, wearing a floral smock dress and smoking a cigarette. I'd take Barbie over her any day, and I turned back around. "Oh, come on, we are still hot!" Barbie reminded the group. "We've got at least ten more years before facelifts."

"They say that 40 is actually the best time to get a facelift," the older woman countered. "I'm having this vaginal rejuvenation procedure done in Midtown that is supposed to increase libido. Apparently, you go in and get banged by this metal probe that rebuilds your collagen. My friend Dina had an orgasm the last time she was getting it done and the nurse told her to just let go and embrace it." She drained her drink. "I don't know if I'd be able to have an orgasm with some nurse staring at me."

Now Lauren came over and took a seat between the two. She tugged on her necklace that read Mommy in diamond pave and stared through me. I didn't know how to enter the conversation, so I just pretended to be busy studying the view like I planned on painting it.

"Are you talking about Dina Sarcoski? The six-sentence poet? I'm really good friends with her!" Lauren said. "She told me about her magical doctor's appointment. I'll have what she was having any day."

"Dina? You're kidding. She's never mentioned you." The older woman cocked her head.

"I mean, we've never met in real life but yeah, I consider her a *pretty* close friend. We've had some late-night DMs that get deep. I actually think we're profiling her on the blog next month." Lauren shifted her tone and looked straight at me. "Meg, can I help you with something?"

All three women turned my eavesdropping way, and my stomach did a twist. "Is Daphne out here?" I asked, unable to think of something better.

"No." The woman in the pjs was staring at my outfit like it was a math problem she couldn't solve.

"This is Meg, Daphne's new Alek," Lauren supplied. I had no idea who Alek was, but it was clear from Lauren's tone that she was being disparaging. "Her husband is head of membership at Chelsea House," Lauren added.

The women with Lauren brightened. "Love Chelsea House," the woman in pjs said. "I'm Tabitha."

"And I'm Karla." Balenciaga Barbie waved and smiled at me, until she was distracted by Tabitha's micro purse. "Le Sac Chicito? What actually fits in it?"

"Nothing. It's empty," Tabitha replied giddily. "I've heard next season they are going even smaller! I can't wait until it's practically invisible."

"Daphne is upstairs with Tanya," Lauren informed me. "Bitch

has been here less than fifteen minutes and already lost her phone. They're combing the place trying to listen for a vibration." She rolled her eyes. "Hey, any movement on those pool memberships? I'm getting nervous that we aren't going to have them in time for summer."

"It's still October," I reminded her. "I think that they are just making their way through all the applications before they sit down for a proper powwow. Sort of like at private schools. Speaking of..." Lauren hated me, it was obvious, but I wasn't going to let that get in the way of my trying to secure an amazing opportunity for Roman. "I heard that you are on the board of Abington. I'm getting ready to send in my son's application."

It was Tabitha's turn to weigh in. "My sons went to Collegiate but if we'd gone co-ed, it would have been Abington, hands down," she said. "That rooftop garden!" Tabitha trailed off and stared at her empty glass in confusion, as if trying to recall if she was the one who'd drunk the contents.

"It's pretty impressive," I beamed.

"Well, for that price tag it should be," Tabitha murmured.

"Collegiate is the same price," Lauren reminded her.

"Is it? I don't remember. It's been a minute." Tabitha signaled to a waiter for another cocktail.

"Yeah, the finances are still something we need to figure out," I said, forgetting my audience.

"She can't afford it. Or can you?" Lauren aimed a venomous smile at me.

"Can I what?" I stammered, taken aback.

"Afford it?" she stopped. "I just assumed. Based on... you know... All of it." She waved her hand down my body, dismissive. "It doesn't matter to me either way. I'm still happy to help. There are a handful of families there on scholarship." Her smile widened. "But it's gonna cost you pool memberships."

"You can't be serious!" It appeared that Karla was getting off on Lauren's cattiness.

"Of course not." Lauren laughed. "Or am I?" She winked at me.

A waiter who was probably two seasons away from being the next Bachelor appeared beside us with a silver tray full of Michelin-starred maki. Half tempted to dump the entire tray into my purse to bring home to Marina, I took a single toro roll and ate it.

Tabitha looked at her watch and made a sad face. "I'm intermittent fasting," she said. "I can't start eating until nine."

"There she is! The queen bee herself." Lauren pretended to bow as Daphne descended an outdoor staircase. She looked majestic in her tight-fitting black sweater dress that had open crocheting down both hips. Tanya was close behind her in red leather leggings and a cropped tartan blazer. "We found it!" she declared proudly, waving a phone in the air.

I wanted to go join Daphne but a bald guy in a tight suit covered in Gucci logos and snakes got to her first. "Hell-o GORGEOUS!" he squealed. I was left to read the words on the patch across his shoulders: "I'm super famous."

Daphne gave him a few minutes of attention, then got lost in the sea of people, exchanging kisses and pleasantries. At last, she raised her voice. "Shall we eat?" she asked, motioning toward her dining room.

When I entered the fabric-walled room, I was relieved to see name tags discreetly folded into the linen napkins on top of each place setting. I didn't want the pressure of choosing where to go or the awkwardness of being asked to scoot so far down the table that I ended up in the kitchen.

"Meg, you're next to me," Daphne called out.

"Love it," I said stupidly, feeling dizzy and a little scared.

I was next to her! OMG, yes. But also, OMG, NO! Sitting next to Daphne meant that I couldn't slink into a corner and hide. It meant that I needed to be on, and that I had to be funny, and that I couldn't slip out early in order to relieve my impatient, sushi-mongering sister-in-law. Sucking in my stomach, I sat down beside Daphne.

"Thank god you made it," she said sweetly. "You look beautiful, by the way."

"I had nothing to wear." I shook my head, embarrassed. "I knew trying to keep up with this crowd would be impossible but... wow. These women are next-level."

"Meg, you could be in a paper bag and you'd still be the hottest one here."

"Said the woman who was literally the hottest woman in all of Manhattan," I replied.

"You aren't vegan, are you?" Daphne asked as a waiter interrupted us, placing a small plate in front of her.

"Oh, no! I love meat!" I said, wanting to seem as low-maintenance as possible.

"I don't eat meat," Daphne replied. "Just fish."

"Me too," I faltered. "I mean, if I have the choice, I *always* choose the fish."

"Fish is always a good choice." She smiled a wry smile. I averted my eyes, glancing down at the smoked salmon that had been placed in front of me. The sliver of fish was folded in a way that made it look like a tiny vulva. As if reading my thoughts, Daphne looked at the amuse-bouche and started giggling.

"This is a female empowerment dinner. But I thought we were

going for a Georgia O'Keeffe vibe, not Penthouse Pets." Daphne cast a look at the waiter.

"I'll let the chef know," the waiter said.

"No need," she told him. "It's funny."

"What's wrong, Daphne? I thought you ate vagina," Gucci dude teased.

"I thought you didn't," she shot back.

Ever the hostess, Daphne leaned in close and provided bios of my dining companions. If they weren't CEOs of real companies, then they were CEOs of fake companies that still managed to afford brick-and-mortar storefronts up and down Bleecker Street.

"You see, it's no longer cool to just have a jewelry line or be an interior decorator," she said. "*Ladies who lunch* was our parents' generation. These are ladies who *launch*." Daphne regaled me with tales of when all these women were just girls, when they were interns and styling assistants living in studio apartments in Bushwick and Murray Hill and playing musical chairs with their career paths and romantic partners.

"Before Lauren was with her husband, she and this girl, Harley, once serviced Kip under the table at Florent. It was a dare, and they were on coke but like, how tacky? I always bring it up whenever we go on double dates because it makes her husband furious," Daphne cackled. "Oh, and Karla was a bottle service girl at Tao before she met her husband and built that palace south of the highway in Bridgehampton. She was always such a founder hounder. I think at one point she was dating a Winklevoss. Oh, and for her fortieth birthday, her husband rented out the Ziegfeld and she entered the party from the ceiling suspended by wires."

I looked over at Karla and tried to picture her flying. "That sounds absolutely amazing," I said.

"Oh right, you're the purported theater geek!" Daphne said in a teasing tone. "Maybe you guys could do some wire work together? Sing some Pippin to the group?"

Before I could respond, Lauren started tapping her Champagne flute. "EVERYONE, *shhhh*!" Lauren continued clinking. "Ladies, goddesses, welcome to Mompire, our third power mama supper club of what I hope will be many! I will have you know that this table was meticulously curated by Daphne and myself, and each of you is here because we consider you a BOSS BITCH. I hope tonight will be filled with inspiring conversations and ideas that we can apply to our daily hustles. So first, I wanna do a little trust exercise. If that is cool with you girls?"

Everyone in the room nodded trepidatiously.

"Pull out your phones," Lauren said. "Now open your text messages and pass your device to the woman on your right." Lauren's eyes were growing big, like a cartoon cat that had swallowed a canary. An uncomfortable energy fell over the room. Guests turned to each other, preparing one another for what they might be about to learn. "Ladies! We have to promise not to be offended. No matter wh—" Lauren's instructions were interrupted by Tabitha, who was already seething with anger. She'd seen something unfortunate.

"Karla!" Tabitha wailed. "You bendy little bitch!"

"I wasn't body-shaming you!" Karla gasped. "I just meant that you looked fuller... in a good way... weight makes your face look younger!"

"Oh, so I'm old now too?" Tabitha threw her hands in the air.

Daphne tutted and turned to me, offering up her phone. She extended her palm, ready to receive mine. Wracking my brain trying to think of what or who I'd texted last, I had no choice but to let her take my sacred device.

I watched as Daphne read through a panicked conversation I had with Iliya about Roman's obsession with me dying, then a half-baked rant from Seth that was mainly turkey emojis, and finally a brief exchange with my mom where she pretended to be curious about how we were adjusting to New York and then never responded to my answer. I was so relieved that Daphne's name hadn't been featured in any of the threads that I almost forgot I was holding her phone too.

"Go ahead." She motioned to her device.

The first message was from Lauren bitching about where I was seated. Apparently, there were "way bigger people" that Daphne was slighting by switching the seating chart at the last minute. The second was a back and forth with Susan about a Target deal falling apart because the client wanted an "actual celebrity like Chrissy Teigen's mom." The third stopped me in my tracks. It was a fight between Daphne and Kip. She accused him of being indiscreet with his extramarital affairs and he called her a total fraud.

My stomach bottomed out. "Thank you for sharing," I said at last. I couldn't think of anything else to say.

"For the record, next to me was the only place I would have ever seated you," she said, as if the other texts didn't exist.

"So, what did Daphne's texts say?" Lauren called across the table, eager to embarrass Daphne in front of the guests.

"Yeah! I wanna know that too!" Gucci guy slurred. His shirt was suddenly unbuttoned down to his navel like he was my dad in the seventies.

I looked at Daphne, who looked at me, aware of what I'd seen on her phone but not betraying any worry. It almost felt like it was a test.

"Just a text from you about me…" My tone was all syrupy

innocence. "Want me to read it?"

"That's okay," Lauren backed down, knowing she was busted.

"BORING!" Gucci man groaned. "Go to the next thread."

"All right, everyone. Forget that exercise!" Lauren said. "It's time to go around the room and introduce ourselves. But look, instead of talking about our triumphs, let's talk about something we are struggling with. I want to remind you that this is a totally safe space. Feel free to open up. I guess I'll go first." Holding up her butter knife in lieu of a microphone, Lauren dropped her head and took a deep breath like she was Barbra Streisand giving a farewell concert. "So, most of you already know me. I'm Lauren. I run MommybearTribeca." She paused, waiting for applause that didn't come. "I don't need to tell you guys that multitasking isn't easy, running back and forth between fittings and shoots and soccer practice," she continued. "But we make it work. Sometimes with chipped gels and only a half hour of cardio— but we get by... I guess what I'm struggling with right now, as I watch my business grow and all these AMAZING opportunities come my way, is balance. Yes, that's right, balance." Lauren repeated herself like she'd said something worthy of being etched on a slab of limestone.

Daphne pretended to listen to Lauren while glancing back at me every now and then.

"Bread?" A waiter appeared beside me holding a basket of brioche.

It smelled delicious. Trying not to salivate, I shook my head no. Not indulging in the breadbasket was one of the cardinal rules of being a woman, right up there with wearing flats to a concert and always carrying a backup tampon.

Lauren was only getting started with her woes. "Last weekend we were out at the Amagansett house," she continued. "I was on the phone arguing with Harry over at Mecox about the turkey I reserved for Thanksgiving when the boys started fighting. I got off the phone expecting to see one of my Rogan Gregory sconces shattered on the floor, or one of their iPads floating in the swimming pool, but there was nothing. When I asked what the problem was, they said that they were upset because they both want to marry me when they grow up." She let off peals of laughter. "I tried explaining that I was already married to Daddy and that it wasn't really an option. Which maybe I shouldn't have said, because it only seemed to make them want me more. They are just like their father. They refuse to take no for an answer." She snorted. "So eventually, after my blowout, we set up a mini ceremony on the tennis court. I gave them both flower bouquets and had Jehan take the train back to the city to pick up my wedding dress. It gave me a good excuse to see if I still fit into it." She paused for dramatic effect. "Which I do!" Color rose to her already-rouged cheeks. "We took so many pictures and had so much fun. Silas got one shot of me, silhouetted on the bluff and was like, 'Mommy, this is too good not to post!' There's gonna be a whole story about it on the blog next week. It was really sweet, and well," she smiled coyly, "I guess I'm a polygamist now."

The point of Lauren's story might have evaded the entire room, but it didn't stop them from applauding. Lauren was the co-host, after all.

My nervousness grew as the knife slowly made the rounds. There were so many things I could have said, so many ways I was feeling inadequate, both as a woman and as a mother. But it was doubtful the crowd would have understood.

As the tales piled up, with their ample mentions of designer clothes, private schools, big city apartments, second homes out

East, weekday nannies, weekend nannies, interior designers and exterior groundskeepers, I burned with shame. I hated that I didn't have any of these things, and I hated myself even more for wanting them.

My feelings of inadequacy didn't stop at all the things I didn't have. What hurt most was the person who I wasn't. Coming on five years into having kids, I was only getting worse at the juggle. I still hadn't figured out how to be the woman who I dreamed of becoming and the mother I never had. I was forever trapped, a slave to two masters.

The knife was in the hands of the woman across from me, Heidi Glick. Buttoned up with a slicked-back bun, Heidi looked like she belonged at a law office rather than a swanky New York dinner party.

"I have to have a D and C tomorrow," she started slowly. "I was pregnant, or am pregnant, sort of... hence why I've been back and forth to the bathroom all night. Anyway, my OB says there is nothing inside the sack so technically I'm not pregnant, but my body thinks it is..." Tears ran down her face and Mr. Gucci rubbed her back. "It's a blighted ovum, which I guess is quite common, but this is my second miscarriage. And my hopes of having a third child are really starting to dwindle." She paused to wipe her eyes. "Back to the drawing board, I guess." Heidi nodded stoically as people began chiming in with recommendations on acupuncture and IVF clinics.

Her story was more moving than any that had come before it. There was no way I was going to follow Heidi. *How, after a series of vapid shares, did I happen to be sitting across from the one woman in the room who just brought everyone to tears?* Before Heidi could pass me the knife, Daphne leaned over and asked if I wanted to sneak out.

"Please!" I looked at her, desperate.

"We'll be right back, small emergency," Daphne told our end of the table as we slipped out of the room. "You want to meet my roommates?" she asked in a conspiratorial tone as she led me upstairs.

"Sure," I said, assuming we were going to check on her kids.

I followed Daphne down a hallway lined with vintage Italian sconces and a giant art photograph of bathers on a European beach.

"Heidi really sucked the air out of the room, didn't she?" Daphne shook her head. "I mean, don't get me wrong. It's great content and she does need to have another baby if she's so determined to keep up with the Joneses. Three is the new two, after all." She said this in the tonal equivalent of an eyeroll. "But talk about a heavy drop. Made me want to stab myself with that butter knife."

"It was heavy," I concurred.

We made our way upstairs and rounded the corner past a spotless playroom and an all-white office, finally arriving at her bedroom. An epic four-poster bed draped in camel-colored cashmere stood tall in the center of the room. There were no stray containers of Pirate's Booty, no striped pajamas piled up on the floor. "I don't get it," I marveled. "It's like you don't even have kids."

"The maids were just here," she explained as she shut the door. She seemed more relaxed now that we were away from the party. "Lauren always insists on doing these weird activities instead of letting people just enjoy their meals." Daphne kicked off her heels. "Last month she hired the Medical Medium to come and tell us who at the table had Epstein-Barr. She thinks it's bonding, but it always just ends up getting weird. Next time, we'll do a normal dinner. Maybe a double date? I'm so curious to meet your husband..."

"Iliya," I said, hoping I didn't sound as awkward as I felt. "He wants to meet you too."

"Let me show you my favorite room," Daphne said, leading me through a door at the far end of her bedroom. We found ourselves in a massive walk-in closet that had been converted into one of those beautiful French fashion house-type sitting rooms, filled to the brim with taffeta, tulle, and silk. With powder pink walls and a matching mohair lounge chair, the space was a shrine to some otherworldly fashion god, a temple graced with the wisdom of Anna Wintour and the strength of a thousand Hermes horses. I tried counting the Birkins but kept losing track.

"These are my closest friends," she said with a light laugh.

It suddenly dawned on me that the roommates she'd referred to weren't her kids but the clothes.

"It's a lot," Daphne admitted, sounding mildly embarrassed. "But it's not like I bought it all."

"Is that supposed to make you more relatable?" I teased her.

"Organizing closets was one of my first jobs. That might explain why this is my little retreat."

"Little?" I looked around, still mesmerized. This was a candy shop of cashmere sweaters and denim, shoes in every heel height and color imaginable.

"I'll tell you a secret. It starts to lose its excitement when it's free."

This made sense. "A friend of mine actually did his dissertation on the religion of luxury," I told her. "His central thesis was that when you sacrifice an exorbitant amount of money on something it's sort of an offering to the gods, and the item is instilled with this religious importance."

"So I guess that explains how I've lost my religion." Daphne let off a rueful laugh. "The truth is, it's hard for me to spend a cent on anything. I come from nothing. I'm not from this world, Meg." Daphne met my eyes and paused. "I'm more like you than you realize."

"It's impressive," I told her. "What you've built."

"Thank you. Everything I have is because I busted my ass." Her accent was starting to warble. It did that when she was overcome with emotion. "Kip does fine. But this life that we are living? This is my creation. You know, I didn't even go to college."

"College isn't everything," I said.

"True. I just tell everyone I graduated from Bronx Science." She paused. "I mean, I *did* go to school in the Bronx. And I took science." She gave a wicked smile. "You need a good story if you ever plan on getting anywhere. This town treats you how it meets you."

I wasn't sure what surprised me more: That she'd lied about such a trivial part of her backstory, or that she was confiding in me about it.

"You look like you just saw a dead body. Do you hate me?"

"Not at all," I stammered. "I just can't believe you're...." I tried to think of a nice way to put it. "You're basically the Great Gatsby. I love the way you're writing your own story."

"Oh my god, Meg. I think I love you," Daphne shrieked. "Speaking of stories. Did you write your Abington essay yet?"

"I started and stopped about three times," I confessed.

"Just be creative. That's my unsolicited advice." Daphne walked closer toward me, and my palms began to sweat. I cut through the awkwardness the only way I knew how: by asking more questions.

"What is going on with all these clothes? Do they just magically show up on your doorstep?"

She laughed. "You want to know how that all works? You worked in advertising, I'm sure you have some idea." She bent over to pick up a Dior bag. "There's no real money in the luxury brands because they don't need to pay for publicity. But I end up getting deals with the Kate Spades and Reeboks of the world. And they pay a ton. I got a hundred thousand dollars to announce my pregnancy with Clearblue Easy. The trick is to mix it up, high and low. I show you all this stuff you can't afford," Daphne said, playfully pulling things off their hangers and throwing them at me. "Then I post a pair of New Balance shorts that are verified cute but also within your budget and you don't think. You just add to cart!"

"I hope you weren't totally insulted by the NBD offer," I said, suddenly self-conscious. "I know you took less than your quote."

"I wanted to do it," Daphne said. "How else was I going to see you again? She stopped for a second, staring at me. "Have you ever considered doing your own account? You would kill at this."

I laughed. "I don't think I have anything anybody wants to see."

"You have the commentary. And you're adorable."

Oh my god. She was serious. And calling me adorable.

Daphne handed me a gown that weighed roughly fifteen pounds. "Try it on."

I looked at her in confusion. "Now?"

"It's going to be big on you. I'm like twice your size. And your age."

"No you aren't."

Daphne touched the dress. "I wore it to the royal wedding. Not to the church but one of the parties. There were so many parties and after-parties, I couldn't keep count. They took our phones so that we couldn't document. Shame." She laughed as she walked over to the bar and poured two glasses of brown liquid from an Art

Deco decanter. She waited while I climbed into the dress. It was basically a giant trench coat and five inches too long on me.

"Wow. Fire." Daphne pulled out her phone and snapped a pic. "Okay now what would you caption this?" she asked, flashing me the image and taking a swig of her drink.

I tilted my head to the side, thinking. I looked absurd. But cute-absurd. "I'd probably go with, *Hamburglar but make it fashion?*"

Daphne spit out her drink. "Why is nobody funnier than you?"

"I'd like to thank the competition," I said, pointing to the floor. "I can only imagine who's holding Lauren's knife now."

"Good point," she said, rolling her eyes. "I mean it, though. You would be such a breath of fresh air. You actually have talent. You're a real artist."

I'd never been called an artist in my life and tried to savor the words for as long as possible.

"Look at Lauren," Daphne said. "I guess she's sort of a micro-influencer at this point, with like forty or so thousand followers. I would kill for you to have more than her. God, that would be so satisfying. Let me just get you to fifty?"

I imagined what Iliya would say if he could see any of this. "You're crazy."

"Actually, that would be you. For not taking me seriously." Daphne helped me onto a pedestal in front of the full-length three-way mirror. She took a step backwards. "Jesus Christ."

"What?"

"You're fucking beautiful."

I felt a prick of sadness. It had been so long since anyone other than Iliya had made me feel attractive. I shouldn't have cared about that sort of thing, I knew. A mother's mind was supposed to be on more pressing matters. But I couldn't help mourning the days when I felt more seen.

I turned to look in the mirror. The ball gown was supposed to be snug around my breasts but ended up gaping with a low-cut V-neck that dove straight down to my navel. And yet, it was gorgeous.

"The piece was a one-off, made originally for the Met Gala and then never put into production," she said. "It's Zoe. That's who I'm flying to Paris for in December. Ever since Salvatore Firenze took over as creative director, their vision has gotten so good. I think he drops a lot of acid. Enjoy the dress. It's yours."

"I'm not taking your things!" I protested.

"I've already been paparazzied in it so I can't wear it again."

"Daphne, there's no way. The sentimental value alone. You wore it to the royal wedding after-party."

"The *after*-after-party," she corrected me. "Take the gown or I'm never letting you out of my closet. All it needs is a little tailoring. I have a woman you can call."

She turned me back toward the mirror, holding the dress in place with her hands. Our eyes connected in the reflection when I suddenly heard a man's voice. "Looks like I found the real party."

I turned around. It was Kip, looking past me the way men do when they meet women they don't want to fuck. He was shorter than he looked in pictures, with bluish eyes and a Keebler Elf nose. His workout shirt was dripping with sweat.

"Meg, meet ball and chain," Daphne said, turning to her husband. "Soul Cycle?"

Kip grunted. He never really smiled in the pictures that I'd seen on Daphne's feed. I'd always assumed that was his resting bitch face, but now it was clear that he just hated his wife. "Playing dress up?" he asked disinterestedly as he opened a drawer and pulled out a large Ziploc bag packed with weed. "Don't you have guests downstairs?"

"I do," Daphne replied. "Maybe you should go say hi."

He glared at her as he lit a joint. Kip finally looked at me for a moment, taking a long drag. "Careful," he said. "You're her type." He blew a ring of smoke into the room as he walked out.

"It's getting late," I told Daphne. "And I need to be up early with the kids. And you have your fans who must be missing you."

"You're not staying for dessert?"

"I really can't." Things had gotten weird enough for one night.

"You're a good girl." Daphne smiled, visibly disappointed. "You almost make me want to be better."

I tried not to make too much noise as I crept into the apartment lugging my gargantuan party favor.

"So how was it?" Iliya was sitting up in bed, still working on his phone.

"Good. Yeah, I think it was really good that I went," I said, trying to make my way toward the garment rack in the corner of the room before he questioned what I was carrying. "Everyone there wanted pool memberships for their kids."

"So does everybody everywhere." Iliya looked up. "What is that?"

"What is what?" I played dumb.

"Meg, you have a dead body in your arms. Did you kill someone?"

"It's just a dress," I said airily.

"That's a dress?" Iliya gave me an incredulous look. "For what? Your coronation?"

"My second marriage," I shot back.

"Very funny. Where I come from, women who try and leave their husbands get stoned to death."

"So you've told me." I laughed.

"I hope you can stuff that in a drawer because we don't have enough space to hang it."

"How about you go to sleep and let me worry about the dress."

"I will. But first, we need to talk," he croaked. "Something happened."

I tensed, preparing to run straight back to Daphne's if he said that he was having an affair.

"Ken's dead," He said, pulling his hair the way he did when he was stressed.

"He's dead?" I stared at Iliya in disbelief.

"Not Ken. The character. He got killed off." He was barely able to get the words out.

I looked at him, still in shock. "Dysentery?"

He shook his head. "Typhoid."

"So when will he come back?" My head started to spin.

"December... or... I don't know. Sometime soon after Christmas. He met a girl. They're going to Kona-"

I cut him off. "Iliya, it's October. What are we going to do?"

"We're going to try and find another place. Is your start-up compensating you for your time yet? Because it really makes no sense to keep paying my sister if you aren't actually working."

"I AM actually working," I barked back, years of resentment rising in me. "I was just at a WORK DINNER!"

Furious, I walked into the bathroom and closed the door behind me. After brushing my teeth and washing my face, I checked Daphne's feed to calm myself down. She'd posted another photo, a close-up selfie. I recognized the closet in the background, and the vulnerability in her eyes made me fairly certain the picture had been taken soon after I'd left her. "The *after*-after-party misses you," she captioned the picture. It was a message for me. I couldn't help but blush.

I got into the shower, letting the hot water run down my back. I leaned against the tile wall and took some calming breaths. I closed my eyes and tried to relax by thinking of nice things. A purple flower. A beach. Daphne's face when we'd locked eyes in the mirror. That's when I reached between my legs, rubbing myself slowly until I climaxed into the steam.

NAME: ROMAN CHERNOFF
GRADE: KINDERGARTEN
PERSONAL STATEMENT

My son Roman has always had a noticeably high EQ. He is asser-tive, enthusiastic, social, and more than a little persuasive. He is being raised bilingual, speaking both Russian and English in the home, has been playing piano since before he could walk and seems to under-stand the game of chess without ever having had formal instruction. As his mother, I would never be so bold as to call him a genius *but his pediatrician has thrown the word around once or twice.*

We recently moved across the country from Los Angeles, and Roman's ability to adapt to his new environment has been seamless. While he isn't keen on the fact that his parents both work full-time, he is grateful for the access and opportunity that our high-powered jobs have afforded him.

Even at his young age, Roman is ambitious. We have only been in the city for a few months and he already has a monopoly on apple cider stands at Pier 25. Originally he wanted to sell lemonade, but I told him that he was off season. Roman accepted the information and wasn't afraid to pivot. The cider is only lukewarm as Roman is acutely aware of the liability that comes with serving hot beverages to tots.

Aside from being an entrepreneur, Roman is also a lover of music and a young patron of the Met, the Whitney, and the Museum of Natural History. This year he hopes to start attending more theater as well as joining the Junior Fencing Society at Chelsea Piers.

I graduated from college summa cum laude and was blessed with a plethora of options for my master's. Wanting to stay on the West Coast because of a sick grandmother, I passed on the opportunity to attend Harvard and resigned myself to staying in-state. While I am satisfied with my education and am immensely proud of the work I do, I will always wonder where I would be if I had taken a different path.

As my Olympic track coach used to say, "A man is only as good as the people he surrounds himself with." We want to surround Roman with the very best, and we want to give him all of the opportunity he deserves.

Where I feel my son is the weakest is when it comes to creating his own boundaries. Roman has a need to be liked and often compromises his own needs in order to put others first. Roman wants to save the world and his idealism is infectious. He reminds me so much of our close family friends Tom Hanks and Rita Wilson. He is a true humanitarian with a selflessness that I lack the eloquence to articulate. He has a deep need to do the right thing. Fifty percent of the proceeds from his cider stands go to Jessica Seinfeld's Good+ foundation.

I am excited about the opportunities Abington offers not only in the way of scholastics, but also in its understanding that the world is getting smaller and smaller and participation in a global community is imperative. Being alive now requires a curiosity about others, a *willingness to see things from a different point of view, an ability to be flexible, and a generosity with knowledge that can extend beyond country lines. (If this generosity could also find a way to extend into our apartment — more specifically, Roman's toy box, which is still off-limits to his baby brother, Felix — that would be the icing on the cake!)*

With great thanks and warm wishes,
Megan and Iliya Chernoff

CHAPTER SIXTEEN

One week after I submitted Roman's personal statement, Abington invited Iliya and me for a highly sought-after applicant meeting with Marilyn. Not every applicant lucky enough to be invited into the school got to sit down with the queen bee. Some parents were relegated to various guidance counselors or even the school nurse, Chickie, as Sari had told me.

A meeting with Marilyn meant one of two things: We were either of great interest to the school and actually in contention, or Daphne had pulled some strings and Marilyn was simply humoring her. Either way, I was thrilled. I spent too long getting dressed for the appointment, and finally settled on my black jeans and a boatneck sweater that was presentable, if a tad too small thanks to a dryer mishap.

"I must say, your essay was impressive. Quite impressive indeed." Marilyn flipped through her notes as I held my breath, praying to God that she wouldn't read what I'd written aloud. I glanced at Iliya. He was clueless about the creative license I'd taken with our application, and I desperately hoped to keep it that way.

"Do you two have any questions for me?" This was the moment of truth. I'd read enough message boards to know that what we asked at this precise moment would define us and cast Roman's fate, for better or for worse. I tried to think fast but Iliya was faster and had started talking before I could open my mouth.

"I work in the private club business, which isn't dissimilar to what you have going on here," he said with a chuckle. "I'm curious; how are you making sure you aren't raising a bunch of — I won't mince words — privileged douchebags?"

Marilyn blinked up at Iliya, taken aback by his candor and

crudeness. "Douchebags?"

"Iliya went to public school," I jumped in, my heart pounding. "And so did I and we just want to be sure that if we were to get this opportunity, which would be beyond amazing, we will still be raising a good person with the right kind of values. I know values are very important to the administration here." I smiled, trying my hardest to undo the damage Iliya had done.

Marilyn cleared her throat and folded her tiny hands on the desk. "Let me start by assuring you that this is a different kind of education than what you are going to get at any of the public schools in our area. We are on a different level in terms of academics, cultural exposure, and teacher-student ratio. I'm not going to lie and tell you that our demographic is outrageously diverse. Roman would be one of several kids here on scholarship, were he to matriculate, but we also have children who spend their winters in Aspen and summers aboard yachts and whatnot. But we treat everyone the same. Our entire ethos is based on raising well-rounded, open-minded citizens of tomorrow."

I did a fist pump in my mind. "That is so good to hear, right honey?" I turned to Iliya, hoping he was swayed. I could tell he wasn't. But he smiled anyway.

"What really speaks to us is how much support you are able to offer the children emotionally," I said to Marilyn. "Not that Roman has any serious emotional issues," I was quick to add, "but so many kids his age are still working on sensory development and self-regulation. Your school feels like a place that really knows how to give each kid the individualized attention that they deserve."

Marilyn nodded. "That's true. That's what we do best. All kids have their strengths and weaknesses and believe me, we have dealt with them all. I have no worries about Roman on that level."

"Neither do we." I squeezed Iliya's hand.

When our meeting wrapped up, Marilyn escorted us through the halls, which were now fully decked out for Halloween, and led us to the front entrance where I'd originally seen Daphne and her posse.

"This is fun!" Iliya smiled, touching a fake cobweb stapled to a mahogany door frame. It was always the most random shit that impressed him.

"Oh, by the way," Marilyn said, reinserting herself into our conversation. "We still need your payment for the application fee."

"Of course." I turned to Iliya. "Do you have any cash? Or can we pay with a card?" I asked Marilyn.

"We accept any and all forms of payment." Marilyn pressed her lips shut.

Iliya pulled out his credit card and handed it to Marilyn. She smiled, clocking the wallet's frayed edges and missing stitching, then walked off to run the card.

"Great! Now she thinks we can't afford this!" I hissed under my breath, watching Marilyn disappear behind a door draped in fake caution tape.

"We can't afford it," Iliya calmly reminded me. "And why don't you have any cash on you?" Iliya hated when I wasn't carrying cash almost as much as I hated it when he walked into our bedroom wearing his outside shoes.

"I just need to go to the bank," I said, eager to move on. "By the way, what should we go as for Halloween? I'm thinking we should dress up as *The Incredibles* now that we have a baby Jack Ja—" Iliya took me by the arm and stopped me again.

"Is this because of your job? Tell me the truth. Are they not paying you?"

"I just don't have cash on me! Can we not do this here?" I looked around, embarrassed.

What I still hadn't told Iliya was that not only had Vigo and Seth failed to pay me a penny of my retainer fee, they also managed to max out my Mastercard buying the entire crew pizza the day of the shoot. The bill was around three hundred and fifty dollars, which put me over my thousand-dollar limit. Vigo had promised to pay me back as soon as possible, and I took him at his word. Besides, I was invested in NBD. I believed in the product, as much as anyone can "believe" in a bath bomb. More than that, I believed in Daphne.

"I really hate that you are walking around without cash." Iliya couldn't let it go, emptying out the fifty dollars remaining in his wallet and stuffing it into my purse like I was his teenage daughter.

It was early afternoon, and we were closer to Chelsea House than Matcha Pitchu's office. I had my laptop on me, so I decided to join Iliya and work remotely for the rest of the day. What were they going to do, dock my pay?

"So, what did you think?" I probed as we walked away from the school.

"I liked it more than I thought I would."

"And not just because you liked all the decorations?" I teased.

"If they could offer Roman a scholarship, I think it would be worth considering."

"Right?" I said, excited by his moderate enthusiasm. "Did you feel like she was into us?" I was replaying the interview in my mind.

"Sure. She seemed to like our essay."

The minute Iliya brought up the essay, my stomach dropped. He was staunch in his belief that one should never come across as too braggy or arrogant. His only advice to me before writing the essay was to keep things humble and real. Which probably precluded my lying about being besties with Tom Hanks.

But Daphne had advised me in her closet that being real wasn't what these people actually wanted — even if they claimed that they did. The truth was boring. At this age, all kids were pretty much equal. So I did with Roman what I would have done with any other product I was trying to sell: I hyped the shit out of him.

A gust of wind passed over us. The weather was finally starting to turn chilly.

"You need to start wearing a real coat." Iliya wrapped his arm around me.

"I'm fine," I lied. Trying to savor the occasional pockets of sunlight, I hurried along the streets, stopping when I noticed the Zoe flagship store. The mannequins in the window were wearing skimpy zipper dresses and cradling headless baby dolls.

"Nobody does the whole Madonna/whore complex better than this guy," I said, parroting what Daphne had told me. "I hear he drops a lot of acid."

"That's great," Iliya said. "Do they have coats?"

"Sure, for like five thousand dollars." I shrugged, still drooling over the display.

"I haven't seen you look at clothes in years." Iliya smiled.

I shrugged. "Check out those totes!" I pointed at a row of bags rotating the space on a giant conveyor belt. The bag leading the charge was a large carry-all embroidered with a serpent eating an apple.

"That's cool," Iliya said. "I could see you with that. You could probably fit your laptop inside it."

"In my dreams." I shook my head thinking about how Daphne walked into places like this like they were her local drugstore. I, on the other hand, would be afraid to pick something up for fear of being mistaken for a shoplifter.

Iliya checked his watch. "Do you want to go in?" he asked sweetly.

"No," I said wistfully. "It's just fun to look."

CHAPTER SEVENTEEN

Chelsea House was buzzing with activity when we arrived. Every table in the cafe was filled with a member accompanied by either a latte or a laptop. Most had both.

"Take one of the bar seats," Iliya told me. "I can't sit with you anyway. We have a special meeting."

"A *special* meeting? Sounds romantic." I scanned the room looking for a hot waitress to be jealous of.

"Super romantic. Founding members are here. We're finally going through the kids pool memberships."

My eyes lit up. "Oh, are you?"

"What?" He clenched his jaw. I could tell he was already on to me.

"Nothing… it's just, I know this mom who happens to be on the board at Abington and she *really* wants to get her kid up to the pool."

"Yeah, I think you've mentioned." Iliya seemed annoyed.

"Well, if we could help her… maybe she could help us."

"You know I don't do that." This was the Iliya who would shame me for letting our four-year-old son cheat at Uno.

"Not officially," I countered. He loved to play prim when it concerned others, but I knew that he bent the rules on occasion, accepting Lakers tickets in exchange for fast-tracking a friend off the waitlist at the Malibu property or upgrading someone's hotel suite if that someone happened to be Russian. "Please," I said quietly. "For Roman."

Iliya frowned. If I had said any word besides *Roman*, the conversation would have already been over.

"Can I just come along and offer a verbal recommendation?"

Iliya looked aghast. "Not happening."

"I'm a member. I'm allowed to recommend someone." I turned around and saw that my seat at the bar was gone.

"In writing," he reminded me. "And you aren't a founding member of this house, so you aren't allowed to sit in on meetings."

"Well now there's nowhere to sit so it looks like you have to let me come."

"You're not coming in," he protested.

"I'll behave," I said, the smugness rising.

The conference room was dark, save for a projection screen flashing faces of Chelsea House pool applicants. A trio of founders sat around a long table with notepads and mini bottles of sparkling water. Bubby walked in and insisted that I join them.

"Meg has work to do," Iliya said. "She just wanted to pop in and say, hello."

"Do it here," Bubby said. "There's literally nowhere to sit in the dining room and it's too cold on the roof."

I shot Iliya an I-told-you-so smile. Allowing me to sit in on the meeting was completely in character for a group of people who adored breaking their own rules. It was a way of flexing their power.

I took a seat near a man-bunned founder and checked my Instagram under the table. At the top of my timeline was a paid post from Daphne. She'd just built the most perfect gingerbread haunted house. It had three levels, a pool, stained glass windows, and even a two-car garage. "Halloween is my favorite time of year. And nothing is scarier than SUGAR!" her caption read. "Impress all of your little ghouls and boys with this wacky activity that the whole family can enjoy! Building these babies is a family tradition over at our place. Pair yours with a cauldron of hot cider or a super spooky snack board and you've got yourself a KILLER night in! Link in stories to purchase all the fun!"

I took another look at the gingerbread house. It belonged in a Harvard Design School graduate's portfolio. I didn't understand how Daphne had the time or patience to pull off all of the crafty projects she shared with her followers. She was a skilled chef, floral arranger, calligrapher, balloon twister, origami expert, and even a face painter. I thought about her kids, and how lucky they were to have a mom who could do everything.

"Where are all the cute kids?" Bubby was saying as she flipped through a facebook on a projection screen. This snapped me back into the moment. A few more members of leadership had dribbled into the room.

"Sorry to be so blunt," Bubby said, "but how did the tank get filled with so many bottom feeders?"

"What, you want models? These are the only kids we got. If their parents aren't members, they can't apply." This was Mona, an artsy forty-something with neon green nails and hair that looked like it was cut by her cats.

Bubby clicked past several more underaged applicants. "I get that, but if the kid isn't cool, we aren't letting it in."

"It?" Iliya furrowed his brow.

"You know what I mean! This isn't coming from me. It's coming from corporate," Bubby insisted.

"I thought *we* were corporate," Iliya said. "Why are we gathered here if not to make the decisions?"

"I don't even have health insurance," Bubby fumed. "Not to be a bitch but just because they're minors doesn't mean that our entire aesthetic goes out the window. We need to curate a specific look and vibe that's on par with the caliber of adults we have in the house. We can't just have a bunch of brace faces floating by on inner tubes and trying to kill each other with water guns. This isn't the goddamn YMCA."

"I hate to say that I agree but… I do," Nir, a soft-spoken man with wire-rimmed glasses, chimed in. "We need the right kind of kids."

"These are kids. Let's not lose sight of that." Iliya was shaking his head in disbelief.

"Easy for you to say," Bubby said. "I bet you were a hot child." She glanced at me, and I shrugged in agreement. I detected Iliya cursing in Russian under his breath. Bubby continued going through photos. I spotted Lauren's son, Silas. He was dressed in a Vineyard Vines-style bow tie standing next to what must have been his grandfather's yacht.

"Yes!" I blurted.

Iliya shot me a look.

"Ew! Noooo!" Bubby made a cringe face. "He's a total Chadtuck-et. He looks like the kind of prick who accidentally roofies himself and then wraps his dad's Porsche around a telephone pole."

"Wow. So visual." Mona widened her eyes.

"It's a hard picture," Man Bun shared.

"I have a nonbinary sort of punk-rock-looking teen from the East Village. The dad is the bassist for the Sunday Sauce, and he's a member," suggested Emmanuel, a portly Frenchman who went by his DJ nickname, La Poubelle.

"What does the mom do?" probed Mona.

"Not a member," Emmanuel replied. "But she's a wellness influ-encer. She's into cauliflower smoothies."

"You know why we don't serve cauliflower smoothies on our breakfast menu anymore? Because people were complaining that they tasted like fucking cauliflower." Bubby shook her head.

"You hid cruciferous vegetables in the smoothies? No wonder I was always getting gas," Mona said, as if she'd just discovered the Fibonacci sequence.

If I planned to act, this was my moment. I looked at Iliya nervously. He was pretending I didn't exist. "Can I just say one thing?" My voice cracked.

"By all means," Bubby said.

"Okay, so I know this kid's mom and she's...nice." I lied.

"*This* kid?" Man Bun asked in disbelief, gesturing at Silas.

Bubby looked down at her stack of applications, reading. "MommybearTribeca? She sucks balls. You know how I know that she sucks balls?" Bubby asked.

"How?" I tried to tamp down my nervousness.

"Because she literally signed her application "MommybearTribeca!" Lauren wasn't making this easy for me, but I refused to give up.

Iliya looked at me and I took a deep breath. "I thought that she sucked at first too." I racked my head for a moment, remembering the universal defense for all assholes the world over. "She's just painfully shy."

"She doesn't seem shy to me." Man Bun was onto me.

"She's in therapy," I told him. "She's been working through a lot of... trauma. And she's actually been really helpful to me, with all the mom stuff. She's different once you get to know her privately." The lying got easier as I kept talking. It wasn't like I was hurting anybody. It was a stupid social-club pool. "I've met this boy and he was lovely. He's much edgier and more creative in person. He knows everything about nineties hip-hop and he's really into... freestyling." I'd never actually met either of Lauren's sons, but now I was the one freestyling.

"Meg isn't on the committee," Iliya reminded the room. "So I don't want us making decisions that we are going to be blaming her for later."

Bubby looked around the table. "Are we accepting the kid or waitlisting him? And by waitlisting I obviously mean never letting him in ever."

"To be honest, I don't really care. I just want to get through this meeting. Anyone opposed to giving him a shot?" Emmanuel asked the room.

"And his brother," I added, sheepishly. "I mean, you can't just take one."

"Fine." Bubby slammed her fist on the table like an auctioneer's gavel. "They're in."

Feeling flush with victory, I turned to Iliya and grinned. He barely blinked.

My spirits soaring, I shot Daphne a text from under the table. "Guess who just got their pool memberships?"

CHAPTER EIGHTEEN

"We're moving *again*?" Roman asked at school pickup the following day. There was never a good time to break bad news to Roman, so I'd kept it to myself, but he'd overheard Iliya bitching while surfing apartment listings the night prior. Roman was impossible with transitions. He'd just gotten used to living at Ken's, and we were already getting the boot. "But will Santa know where I went?"

"First Santa is gonna come. *Then* we're going to move," I explained. "But it's going to be great. Everything is working out." I held onto his backpack, trying to keep him from darting into the road.

"Can we get ice cream?" he asked at the sight of a passing food truck.

"Honey, that's a kebab truck." I shook my head. "Besides, it's too cold for ice cream."

"Okay, then what isn't it too cold for?" He gave me a look to let me know that whatever I suggested better be equally decadent.

"I have an idea," I said, suddenly inspired. "You want to make an enormous gingerbread house?"

Fifteen minutes later, Roman sat in my Whole Foods shopping cart as I wove in between professional grocery shoppers on scavenger hunts for other people's pantries and depressed housewives looking for Chardonnay. I typically didn't shop at places where a pint of strawberries cost over seven dollars, but it was the closest grocery store around. Standing in the dairy aisle and scanning the egg cartons, trying to determine which illustration of a farm looked the most like a Club Med, I heard someone call my name.

I spun around to see Sari, her basket heaving with probiotics and melatonin gummies. "Girl, you're everywhere I turn!" she exclaimed.

I grabbed a random carton covered in hens wearing red bikinis and smiled at her. "Hey!"

Sari's expression shifted to something a little darker. "Congratulations," she said. "So how did you do it?"

"Do what? Are you talking about my interview with Marilyn?"

"I'm talking about Daphne Cole." Her eyes bore into me. "The post."

My head was swimming with confusion. "What post?"

"Can I set this here while I run and grab some It Chardonnay?" Sari smiled at Roman, who accepted her basket. "Check your phone."

Once Sari disappeared, I reached into my bag and pulled out my phone. What I read made me gasp. "What happened?" Roman asked. "Is it from Santa?"

Daphne hadn't just tagged me on her page. The post was a picture of me. Just me. In her closet. Wearing her clothes. She even used my caption, "Hamburglar but make it fashion." The picture had over four thousand "likes" and the comment section was too long to scroll through. I felt dizzy.

"Who is that?" wrote @PriceisnoSnobject, Vogue's accessories editor. "What designer is that?" wrote @Bagsforally, a well-known handbag consigner. "Are you able to share deets on who designed your closet?" another follower commented. It went on and on.

"Next level, right?" Sari said, reappearing with two armfuls of Chardonnay. "And when are we having drinks, by the way?"

I cocked my head ever so slightly. Sari had never initiated drinks before now. She still hadn't gotten back to me about coffee.

"Is now a bad time?" she asked, resting her bottles in her basket.

"I could also do it later this evening." She sounded hopeful, almost desperate.

"I'm supposed to be decorating a gingerbread house tonight," I said. "But soon?"

"I'm going to hold you to that. I know I'm small potatoes compared to Daphne Cole, but I'm still fun." She smiled, grabbing two bottles and pretending to chug them simultaneously.

When Roman and I got back to Ken's building, the grocery bags hanging from my wrists were cutting off my circulation and turning my hands a cyanotic shade of blue. Fingers still tingling, I pushed open the front door and I saw a stack of packages blocking my mailbox.

"Did you order me something?" Roman sounded excited.

Assuming that there was either a mistake with the post office or that Marina was shopping on Ambien again, I picked up a box and examined it. It was addressed to me.

After two elevator trips, I'd managed to bring everything upstairs. Roman sat at the bar peering over me as I opened the first box with a pair of scissors. "Is it a new Ben 10? Is it a Kevin 11?"

Marina, who'd come out of the boys' bedroom holding Felix, was equally transfixed.

"Is it a LuMee light? Is it something from Kim Kardashian?"

Tuning them out, I tore through an inordinate amount of tissue paper to find a note from Susan, Daphne's agent. "Daphne thought you'd enjoy! Xo Susan and the team at SLAY!"

"It's a beach ball," I announced, confused.

Typed on a postcard taped to the inside of the box were instructions. "Hey Meg, wanted you to be the first to hear about @PlantainBaby, the all-natural sunscreen for little ones that now comes in a variety of bright fun colors. Paint on your face, get into a bikini, and use this beach ball in a quirky yet sexy pic you share with your followers. Don't forget to tag @PlantainBaby so we can see your silly style."

The next package contained seven boxes of chickpea crackers and a note that read: "Toot your heart out with these gluten-free, nut-free, dairy-free, sugar-free, vegan, organic, paleo, Tootchips. Show your love by tagging @TootChipsUSA."

I ripped open a bag. "Not terrible," I said as I tasted a chip.

"These aren't yummy!" Roman exclaimed, spitting a mixture of chickpea powder and vegan cheese all over the hardwood floor.

Marina dove into another box filled with Styrofoam noodles and branded water bottles. "This is what happens when you're an influencer," she told me excitedly. "You just get sent free swag all day long."

"I'm not an influencer!" I assured her. "Daphne just had this stuff sent here." I was baffled yet amused.

Marina snorted. "My brother is going to kill you, you know…"

"Why?" I asked even though I already knew the answer.

"Because he hates this stuff." Felix was getting buried under all the wrapping paper on the floor, and Marina picked him up.

"What stuff? Chickpea chips?" I watched as Roman chased Red around the couch with the Plantain Baby beach ball.

"Strings-attached stuff." Marina took a flat stone from my hand and started running it over her forehead. "It's called a gua sha, it's a beauty contouring tool. They're like thirty bucks at Sephora. Consider this part of my payment for today."

I stared at her, still not satisfied with her response. "What strings are attached exactly?"

"These companies want you to post this stuff. And if you want more, which you will, you'll have to post more. That's how it works.

How am *I* the one telling *you* this?"

"Yeah, I get it but I'm not even public!" I reminded her.

"Duh! That's the first thing you have to do," she said, rolling her eyes. "Fix that shit."

It was past ten o'clock when Iliya finally got home. He smelled like booze and perfume, which was not uncommon but never failed to stress me out. He headed into the bathroom to wash off.

When he was fresh out of the shower, Iliya stood in front of me wearing nothing but his towel. He gestured toward the boxes in the kitchen. "So..."

"My friend Daphne. You know, the influencer I told you about."

"Who?" he asked.

I glanced away, then back at him. God, his abs were so annoying. "The woman I met at Chelsea House," I said. "I've told you all about Daphne, no?" I'd managed to avoid saying her actual name aloud to my husband for nearly three months. I was too afraid that if it slipped off my tongue, he'd be able to read every thought I'd ever had about her. "She has kids at Abington," I added.

"The pool membership lady?" he asked, still not following.

"No! That's Lauren, her cousin. I've been working with her on the NBD campaign," I continued, trying to seem nonchalant and professional as I rummaged through a drawer for nothing that I actually needed.

"NBD?" he looked at me perplexed.

"The mommy bath bombs? I told you that I made them change their name."

"No, I don't think you did. Just like you didn't tell me they hadn't paid you yet."

"I told you everything," I insisted. "You probably just weren't listening." I'd had enough petty fights with Iliya to know that if I stuck to my story long enough, he would eventually give up and agree with me.

"Okay, maybe you did. I have a billion things on my mind at the moment."

"It's fine. Anyway, she had her agent send a bunch of products over," I said. "It's just random junk they send influencers. They probably had extra," I added nervously. "Don't worry, it was free."

"Nothing is free," Iliya mumbled. "So are *you* an influencer now?"

"No, but it would pay a hell of a lot better than copywriting," I said with a sigh. "Marina said that I should make my account public." I waited for him to reply.

"She also said you have over ten thousand friend requests," Iliya said, two steps ahead of me. I was a fool to think that my sister-in-law could keep a secret. She'd probably called her brother the minute she'd left our home.

"I'm not really sure how the whole thing works," I said, knowing that I was at exactly eleven thousand two hundred and twenty requests the last time I checked. Five minutes ago.

"If you are seriously considering accepting all those people, you need to delete the kids," he said firmly.

"I'll delete them," I agreed. "That's your only thought on the subject?"

Iliya shrugged. "So you're really going to do it? You're going to put yourself out there for all the criticism... all the judgment..."

"All the Toot Chips," I said, trying to make light of it.

"It doesn't seem very *you*." He looked at me, skeptical.

"What does that mean? I already do it for other people."

"Yeah, for other people. But for yourself? I don't see it. You're not the kind of girl who needs all that attention. And I mean that as a compliment." His phone vibrated on the dresser. The name Anna popped up. I'd never heard him mention anyone named Anna.

"Actually, a little more attention would be nice." I motioned to the phone. "Do you need to take that?"

"No, I'm off work. They can survive without me."

"Can Anna?" I asked archly.

Iliya was getting flustered. "You know what? Go for it. Maybe it will make you more secure with yourself and you won't sit here accusing me of nonsense."

"Really?" I was too elated to be jealous.

"Sure," he said. "But no pics of me and no pics of the kids."

"That's fine." I watched him pull a clean T-shirt over his head. "We might make some money. The kind that could help pay for wherever we are moving in January, money that could help with private school. Money that could help pay for a lot of things."

"What the fuck am I wearing?" Iliya cut me off, looking down at his chest. The front of his shirt was printed with "How Do You Toot?"

"Oh that," I said, trying not to laugh. "It came in the mail."

I could tell Iliya was annoyed but also a little amused. "It's actually pretty comfortable."

I looked at him and smiled. "I know how to get you more."

CHAPTER NINETEEN

I woke up early the next morning trying to recall if I'd actually pulled the trigger on going public or if it was just a dream. The text from Daphne set me straight: "Proud of you, baby." As I digested her words, I felt a heat building within. And not just because she'd called me baby. This was exciting. It was also quite scary. While I had wanted all the perks that came with shrugging off my private status, I didn't know if I wanted all the attention. Especially this early in the morning.

I glanced across the bed and contemplated waking Iliya up and making my anxiety his problem. But I knew that if I actually admitted why I was freaking out he would say, "I told you so."

I remained tight-lipped about what was going on until I showed up at work. Seth spun in his swivel chair like a child who'd never sat in a swivel chair before. "With those kinds of numbers, we have our own in-house influencer."

"I wouldn't go that far. Twelve thousand is a random college kid with a podcast," I said, brushing off his claim. "I'm by no means an influencer."

"Yet." Seth's eyes widened. "But you will be. And it just so happens that we have a perfect post for you." Seth pointed at Vigo, who was looking at the shots from Daphne's shoot on his laptop. "Hit it, Vigs."

"So, you are going to think we are crazy but..." Vigo looked at Seth, a devilish smile creeping across his face. "The shots with you and Daphne. You're like the yin to her yang."

"We like that," Seth told me as he began nervously braiding his bangs.

"For the campaign," Vigo clarified.

I felt a pit in my stomach. "I was just there to make her comfortable," I said. "I'm not going to *be* in the campaign."

Vigo flashed me a picture from the shoot. My body was halfway submerged in the tub, a leg hanging off the side of the basin. My hair was wet, and my shirt utterly soaked. Daphne, covered in suds, appeared to be completely nude. We were both laughing as she held me by my wrists, trying to dunk me.

I shifted uncomfortably. "This looks like softcore porn."

"I know, right?" Seth nodded in excitement. "It's perfect. She's the trophy mom and you are the..."

"Teething baby?" I offered.

Vigo cocked his head. The vibe is more C-section Blues here."

"Look, Meg," Seth said, softening his tone. "This was a happy accident that none of us could have seen coming. But that's how these things usually work."

"Daphne is never going to go for this." I shook my head and started to worry about how Iliya would react to seeing my nipples standing at attention on a poster.

"If we want to take this campaign national, we can't just have some New York socialite as our spokesperson," Vigo explained. "We need someone approachable."

"You mean poor?" I laughed in disbelief. "Speaking of which... maybe if I were actually getting paid for the work I'm doing here, the class divide wouldn't be so big."

"It's coming," Vigo promised.

"For real, when am I getting paid?"

"Let's not make this contentious." Seth used his hands to call for a time out. His braid now looked like a broken unicorn horn flopping back and forth on his forehead, which made it even harder than normal to take him seriously. "The money is coming. And tell us how we can help you, Meg. We want you to be happy."

I raised an eyebrow. "First of all," I said, pulling my credit card statement from my purse and slapping it down on the table. "You need to pay this off before my husband sees it and has a fit. Second, where is my retainer fee? And third, *Daphne* is your brand ambassador. Not me. She signed a contract to be *the* face of this campaign. Singular. We are launching at the beginning of November. To start changing things now is just —"

"For what it's worth, she looks way thinner in the shot with you than the rest of the shots, and that seemed to be an issue," Vigo said.

"That's ridiculous," I retorted. "You sound sexist and body-shaming."

"I'm just saying what she said." He shrugged. "I'm a good listener."

I clenched my teeth. I didn't want to be in the NBD campaign with Daphne. I was meant to be the Cyrano de Bergerac of the operation, putting words in other people's mouths, lubricating the wheels for the talent to shine.

Just then, my phone started vibrating. I glared at it, annoyed that the day was blowing up and I still hadn't even helped myself to a free hot beverage. I had made it a goal to drink as many as possible on the job, at least until my payment came through. When I saw Daphne's name light up the screen, I motioned for the other two to pipe down.

"Hello?" I answered nervously.

"Hi, stranger." Her voice sounded almost sweet. "The world's looking at you. So when are you going to post something?"

"Soon. I'm still trying to think of what it should be."

"Hurry up," she said. "Lauren says thank you for the pool

hook-up, by the way. That was really cool of you."

"Oh, of course. No problem," I said, pretending it had not required my bursting into a private meeting and risking all my credibility with Iliya's co-workers. I signaled to Seth and Vigo that I'd be back, and I brought the phone into the hallway.

"So this is going to sound crazy, but Susan's favorite image — and mine too," Daphne said, "happens to be of the two of us. Have you seen them? They're hot. What are the odds of you agreeing to let us use one of them for the campaign?"

"I don't know if that's necessary," I replied. "There are so many great shots of you alone."

"I still just really like the ones of the two of us the best," she whined Veruca Saltishly. "I look skinnier. And happier." It was clear that Vigo had already spoken to Susan. Before I could deflect with another joke, Daphne continued laying it on. "I know that you are afraid to put yourself out there, but you are a total smokeshow. And these are the hottest pics you've ever taken. And I've seen every pic ever taken," she said, throwing my words back at me.

"You're too much," I laughed.

"I just know how talented you are. Not to knock the Matcha Pitchu guys but you're too good for them. You could be big time. You took the first step. You can't spend your life just taking care of other people. It's time to be the hero of your own story."

I glanced back at my purported bosses. They were playing a violent game of thumb war. To each his own foreplay.

"I'll think it over," I told her.

"Think about it," Daphne replied. "But just so you know, there's only one right answer."

CHAPTER TWENTY

The following weekend, Daphne invited the kids and me to join her at the Museum of Cookies for a "content shoot." The museum was an interactive art exhibit with themed rooms that celebrated the invention of the cookie. Maybe it wasn't the hottest ticket among the Guggenheim Museum crowd, but in Daphne's world it was. Even Roman had heard about it somehow. When I told him I'd be taking him, he went berserk.

We showed up a few minutes before the doors opened. The line to get in already stretched around the block. Daphne had told me to text her when we arrived. A young woman wearing an apron and a pink lab coat scurried outside the building and introduced herself to the kids and me. Helping me with Felix's stroller, she led the three of us to the front of the line, pushing people out of the way as if I were Lady Gaga.

Inside, she affixed nametags on our shirts and opened a sliding door that brought us into a room covered in pink wallpaper with giant fake clouds hanging from the ceiling. A sulky teen boy who could have been a stand-in for Claire Danes stood behind a counter pulling small sugar cookies out of an electric oven. His nametag read Simon Snickerdoodle.

"Welcome to the other side of the rainbow," he said in a rehearsed and unenthusiastic mumble. "Would you like a super sugary sugar cookie? Heads up: They were made in a facility that uses nuts."

"YES!" Roman screamed like he'd just won a game show.

Just then, another door slid open to reveal Daphne. In full hair and makeup, she was wearing a crisp color-blocked suit that appeared to be made of taffeta.

"Meg!" She waved me over. "Thank fucking god that you're here because I'm at a total loss for captions."

"You're so dressed up," I said, flooding with insecurity over my disheveled appearance.

"I should have had something sent over for you," she replied, taking in my cropped sweatpants and Nirvana T-shirt.

"I was on my own this morning. Iliya had to go to work. And I lost track of time," I said.

"Iliya," she repeated. I detected a tinge of prickliness in her voice. "We still need to do that double date. Otherwise I'm going to start feeling like your side piece."

"Totally," I said, looking around the room. "Where are your kids?"

"Oh, they got a better offer." she said, rolling her eyes. "But I'm so glad you brought yours."

Daphne awkwardly knelt down and patted Felix on the head like he was a macaque on a chain in the Marrakesh Medina. She rose back to her feet and introduced me to her photographer, Rodrigo, an NYU film student rocking a faux hawk. Then Daphne turned to me with puppy dog eyes. "Can I trouble you for one itsy bitsy caption? Please? You'll figure out something good." Before I could ask what picture, she dove into a fake swimming pool filled with chocolate chips.

"This one," Rodrigo said, flashing me a shot of Daphne luxuriating in the pool with her eyes half closed.

I thought it over for a moment, then waited for Daphne to return to my side. "How about, *My muscle relaxant just kicked in*?"

Daphne looked at the image on Rodrigo's camera and snorted. "Oh my god. Earmark that."

She was far more in her element with Rodrigo than she'd been with Zed, and it wasn't just because her clothes were on. The pair had a rapport. She trusted him. I watched Daphne work her angles, all the while lecturing me as people trickled into the room. "I look at the world in terms of backdrops," she said somewhat grandly from her corner of the chocolate-chip pool. "Everywhere I go I think to myself: Would that make a hot photo on my grid or is that just some throwaway for my stories? What did I post last? What is getting the most traction? It's all a rather complex equation, and sometimes you have to let your instinct take over."

I nodded and listened like I was James Lipton listening to Sir Anthony Hopkins break down his craft on *Inside the Actors Studio*. She was sexy and confident when she talked shop. There was a method to the madness. And she'd chosen me, of all people, to mentor.

"There are tons of copycats out there, so in a week every Becky With The Long Hair is going to have this exact shot," she said. "That's why it's important to act fast. You always want to be the first 'grammer to capture whatever the next cultural phenomenon is."

"And this week it's cookies?" I smiled unsurely.

"Along with PopSockets, plant-based eggs, and shackets."

"Shackets?" I repeated.

She fixed me with a stare. "Shirts that are also jackets."

"Aren't those just shirts?"

"Not exactly. You'll know when you see one."

Daphne and Rodrigo both looked at me with equal parts patience and pity, as if I were a foreign exchange student who'd just been introduced to her first pumpkin spice latte. Daphne resumed cavorting in the pool, alternately blowing kisses and throwing chocolate chips into the air, while Rodrigo captured every moment.

A lifeguard perched on a graham cracker diving board informed us that we should try and finish up. As Rodrigo snapped his final shots, influencers of varying ilk wandered into the room and took turns diving into the chocolate-chip pool. They, too, wanted their money shot.

There were prematurely sexualized TikTok tweens, a twenty-something Rock-a-Billy who wore head-to-toe magenta, a K-pop princess, and a German dude with a selfie stick.

Roman was enjoying himself but mainly because he was being plied with sweets at every turn. I pushed Felix through the crowd as I followed Daphne and Rodrigo into a darker room that had been designed to look like a subway car.

I told Daphne the place reminded me of an article I'd once read about underground sex clubs in Japan, where perverted businessmen could go into fake subway stations and feel up all the actors posing as passengers.

Daphne looked at me. "Are you coming on to me?"

I laughed, trying to think of how to respond when Daphne's attention abruptly shifted to the top of my head. "So what are you thinking about your hair?"

"Umm... I wasn't really thinking about it," I said, confused.

"I love it. But did you notice it photographs a bit harsh?"

"Really?" I asked, trying to swallow the blow.

"It makes you seem slightly unapproachable, and you are anything but that," she assured me. "I'm just thinking ... should you lighten it?"

"I mean, I could," I said, feeling completely destroyed by the criticism.

"I think you'd look stunning. Not a huge change. Tiny. Maybe even let it grow out a bit. Get your bangs looking a little less *Amelie*. It's cute and all, it's just a little 2001." She slowed down when she spotted a woman on the opposite side of our car taking photos with a gaggle of kids. "The Mormons kill it on the 'gram," Daphne said. "I guess it's mostly through affiliate programs, but that chick is making a million bucks a year just from swipe-ups. It's all about the kids." Daphne turned to Rodrigo, concerned. "Should we get some kid shots? Where's Roman?"

My son was waiting for his turn at the top of the slide.

"I think you are fine without kid shots," I offered, suddenly worried she might try to pick up Felix and use his body as a prop.

Luckily, Daphne seemed to forget about kids. She was distracted by a knapsack attached to a stroller in the corner of the room. "That's a dope Chanel backpack," she told me. "It's from their pre-fall collection! You should take a picture with that. They don't come around often."

"Don't you think that would be weird? Considering it's not mine..."

Daphne rolled her eyes, then looked at Rodrigo, who shook his head and chuckled. "Meg, you have to fake it till you make it, remember?" she reminded me. "If it makes you feel any better, the bag I'm carrying doesn't belong to me either." She held up her rhinestone-encrusted Oreo cookie-shaped clutch. "This is borrowed from the Judith Lieber showroom. And this suit is a sample too. It's getting picked up by Alice + Olivia later this afternoon."

I guessed it made sense. Daphne changed at least three times a day and never repeated pieces, aside from her Max Mara Teddy coat. I'd seen her closet, which was already bursting at the seams. She couldn't possibly keep everything, and why would she when more was always coming?

Her eyes held mine. "People don't follow you for the truth, they follow you for the fantasy. They want to believe that if they just owned a pair of Celine sunglasses and a two-toned Rolex Daytona, their lattes would taste sweeter, their Sunday scaries would evaporate, and their personal life would come together like the last fifteen minutes of any Nancy Meyers movie. I mean, who doesn't want that?" Daphne walked up to the unattended stroller and lifted the Chanel off the handlebar. "These women who follow us, they might not ever make it to New York City or the Museum of Cookies." She was referring to the Museum of Cookies as a bucket-list destination. I tried to keep a straight face.

"It's our job to take them there, Meg!" she went on. "Our followers rely on us for all that is missing in their lives. They need us to break them out of their monotonous, thankless jobs, their fucked-up marriages, their dysfunctional families, and all the depression that comes with age and mounting responsibility." Daphne gazed into the distance like a Union soldier who'd just won the Civil War surveying the Great American Plain. "I take what I do seriously because I know that I'm not just selling cookies or handbags. I'm helping women all around the world live their best lives. I'm a humanitarian, for god's sake."

"They would love you at Coca-Cola," I said under my breath.

Daphne held the knapsack in front of her and dangled it like a hypnosis pendulum. I tried to be discreet as I made my approach and swung the bag over my shoulder. As soon as Rodrigo started snapping shots of me and "my" Chanel, Roman came bounding toward me with another small boy with bright blue fingers and lips.

"They have a cotton candy cookie!" Roman exclaimed. He was jumping up and down.

"We have to get you out of here." I shook my head, already dreading bedtime.

"Hey, that's my mom's purse!" The little boy was pointing his

154 ~ Jenny Mollen

sticky fingers at me.

"Oh my god!" the woman accompanying Roman's new friend exclaimed, and my stomach bottomed out. She was going to call security on me. Then I realized she was staring at the back of Daphne's head, her eyes growing bigger and bigger. "I knew it!" she gushed when Daphne turned around. "Wow. Such a fan." The woman did not seem to be remotely worried about her purse. "I have a whole text thread with my girlfriends simply titled *Daphne Cole's post-baby abs*," she told Daphne. "Speaking of, where are Vivienne and Hudson?"

"Oh, you know, probably off with the woman who actually carried them." Daphne laughed and took the knapsack from my hands.

"You crack me up!" the woman howled.

"Your bag is phenomenal," Daphne said, touching the shearling before returning it to its rightful owner. "It's so hard to get a sense of the scale of these things in pictures."

The woman nodded. "I love it because it's just so easy with my city lifestyle. I mean don't get me wrong, I loved cruise collection but where am I wearing that see-through life preserver bag? Even the vanity cases just don't work when you're a mom."

Daphne erupted into hysterics, then masterfully tied up the exchange by offering the woman something even more desirable than another Chanel bag. "Hey, how about a selfie!"

CHAPTER TWENTY-ONE

I posted the picture of myself holding up the Chanel backpack and captioned it: "Chanels like teen spirit." Not everyone got the joke, which led to hours of insecurity and self-doubt. And I wasn't just kicking myself for making a Kurt Cobain reference in a Coco Chanel world. The picture was so basic and bougie that no matter how witty the caption, I felt like a douche.

Daphne assured me that the post was funny even though I'm not entirely sure she was telling the truth. She tended toward captions like "when life gives you lemons, put them in your vodka." But she warned that if I spent too much time thinking about a post it could be paralyzing. It was far more important that I commit to churning out content at regular, ideally constant, intervals. I was up to 16,000 followers. And I did start to post more. Stupid signs I'd see around the city. Pictures of my bra on the floor. My overflowing Diaper Genie. Things that I found funny and that I felt other moms might relate to.

I didn't want to mimic Daphne, who shared photos of herself hanging from the side of the Brooklyn Bridge in a Balenciaga bodysuit or waltzing down Times Square in plastic pants and eight-inch platform high tops. I didn't want to present my life like it was somehow perfect or easy. Because it was anything but easy. I still didn't even know where I was going to live by the end of year.

"I am the mom your kids warned you about," I wrote on a post of myself holding up a botched pancake that looked like Gene Simmons from KISS. "Like for Like" @Sheshootsforthemoon replied. "OMG MOM FAIL!" @Victorialovespolo exclaimed. "Been there!" @Apple234 assured me. "Are those gluten-free?" "Where do you buy your dish towels?" "Where do you buy your dishes?" "Where do you buy your pancake mix?"

I didn't know these people, but I felt obligated to answer them like I was their primary-care physician. They asked questions about everything, from organic toothpaste and eco-friendly cleaning products to ski resorts and breast implants. I didn't know why they wanted my opinion, or why they trusted me as an authority on any of these subjects. They just did. So I went with it. And just like that, I was up to 20,000 followers.

As my career started to veer in two separate directions, so did my daily life. There was the path that I was on with my family. And then there was the path that I was on with Daphne. They both required so much time and maintenance. It was nearly impossible to keep everyone happy.

Busy as she was, Daphne was hyper-invested in my success. "What is going on with your outfit?" "Did you call my hair guy yet?" "Why aren't you posting more?" she'd write to me. Despite how much she had going on, she responded to my every move. She never missed a thing, which meant that I couldn't let go of the wheel either.

On Halloween, Iliya was losing patience with me. "Can we put our phones away for a bit?" he asked, taking off his Mr. Incredible mask to do a safety search through Roman's Halloween bucket.

"Sorry, it's NBD stuff," I lied. "These guys need so much hand-holding," I said, answering a message from Daphne about a "sick" sample sale she wanted me to attend with her.

"Daddy is trying to steal my candy!" Roman cried, fending off Iliya like he was some kind of Grendel figure attacking his village.

We were all dressed as the Incredibles with a sexy pirate cat in tow (Marina), making our rounds through Tribeca and up into the West Village. Daphne was in Midtown dressed as the Tin Man at some Wizard of Oz-themed Heidi Klum event she'd been paid to attend. She was clearly bored out of her mind.

"Do you and your husband want to go to this new restaurant in Chelsea where we have to fish for our own dinner?" "I'm considering getting the bags under my eyes removed. Do you think I have bags under my eyes?" "Can you tell that I'm bored here and hate my husband?"

Her texts kept coming. Every few blocks, I pretended that I needed to pee so that I could sneak off to a restaurant restroom and answer them.

We were ambling down Barrow Street when Iliya sprung something on me. "I think I might have found us a place," he said. We were at the foot of a brownstone stoop while Marina led Roman up a flight of stairs.

"Really?" I said, filling with guilt that I hadn't so much as clicked on a single link to aid in our apartment search. I justified this by telling myself that I didn't know the first thing about the city, and I was handling everything else. "Where is it?"

"Long Island City," Iliya said. "It's not a terrible commute."

"Where is Long Island City?" It sounded more than a couple blocks away.

He pointed his finger in the direction of the health food store on the corner. "Queens," he said.

"But what if we get Roman into Abington?"

"That would also be a commute," he admitted.

"Are you sure this makes sense?" I was starting to panic, knowing that Daphne would find my moving so far away from her wholly unacceptable. "I thought we wanted to try and stay in the area," I added. "For your work, too."

"Meg, look around you. We can't afford this area." I scanned the block we were on. It was all Land Rovers, twelve-million-dollar townhouses, and an overpriced soap store.

Before I could come up with a retort, I noticed Marina snapping a picture of us.

"Sorry to interrupt your little spat," she said from the top of the stairs. "But with your costumes on, it was too good. I'm sending it to you both."

Iliya would not let me post pictures of him online. But since we were both wearing masks, and also because I was so frustrated with him, I took it upon myself to upload the picture to my feed. The caption was: "Great shot of my husband and me communicating. #HappyHalloween." Before I could stuff my phone back in my jacket, Daphne fired off a text. "SHOW YOUR GODDAMN FACE. Don't be an amateur."

"Don't you have a party to be focusing on?" I wrote back, obstinate. But she was right. The majority of the photos I was posting were just random things I snapped without much thought. If I really wanted to legitimize myself, I needed to make more of an effort. I needed to become the main character of my feed, not just the narrator. And to do that, I needed a freaking photographer.

Later that night, I approached a promising candidate as we waited for Roman to finish brushing his teeth.

"So what exactly would I have to do?" Marina asked.

"Just help me take the pictures," I explained.

Iliya popped his head back into the bathroom. "Just checking to see if I'm hearing what I think I'm hearing. Because if so, it sounds pretty warped."

"This is hard for me to ask! Please don't make it any worse," I said. "You said you would support me," I reminded Iliya, annoyed.

"I never said that I wouldn't make fun of you." He waggled his eyebrows.

Ignoring him, I turned back to Marina. "It will be a creative project! Daphne said that she has tons of props that I can use. And clothes. Things that she's already shot in. Last season Gucci, Prada, and even a couple Marni pieces that she claims actually have a shape."

"Who *are* you?" Marina stared at me, turned on by my growing lexicon of high-end designers and the perks of being my sister-in-law.

"Thank you," I said, giving her an arm squeeze. "You won't regret this."

CHAPTER TWENTY-TWO

Marina's virgin white Mercedes GLA 250 peeled out of its tight parking space on Watts Street like it was being commandeered by a band of Muppets. I checked that my seat belt was securely fastened. "This thing is a fucking stick shift?" I looked out the window, making sure the car parked in front of us still had its bumper. How were you ever an Uber driver?"

"A Wing Woman," she corrected me for the gazillionth time, flipping a U-turn in a street thronged with pedestrians. "And my clients were all drinkers, so they were much more relaxed than you'll ever be." She was having fun teasing me, but not as much fun as she was having zipping through streetlights like they were mere suggestions.

"How's the dentist?" I inquired, reaching into the back seat and resting my hand on my sleeping baby's lap. Felix felt so tiny and warm.

"I finally got a photo. He's a little bald, but doesn't that mean he's well-endowed?" Marina said as if there wasn't a baby in the back seat.

"I think it just means he has an excess amount of testosterone."

"Whatever, that's not what I care about. We've been getting super hot and heavy over text. I told him that I wanted a mold of my mouth made by next week."

"Mouth mold," I said. "Sounds hot."

"It's always good to throw out a couple ultimatums to see how serious someone actually is."

Before I could respond, I glanced out my window and saw a cluster of NBD posters plastered down the side of a building on Canal. My stomach dropped.

Just then, my phone started vibrating. It was Daphne.

"THEY ARE UP," she wrote. "Do I look old?" "Why am I older than you?" "Do I look fat?" "Why am I fatter than you?" "Don't let me eat again." "BTW I booked our double date at the fish restaurant." "Fuck, I guess I'm eating again." "You better start typing back or I'm coming to find you."

"CHILL! I'm literally on my way to your house, bitch!" I wrote back, accidentally talking to Daphne the way that I talked to Marina.

"I'm not home," she finally responded, leaving me wondering if she was telling the truth or just pissed that I'd called her a bitch. "Wynne is bringing stuff down." I'd never heard of Wynne but told her that sounded great.

"Jesus Christ, I hope Iliya is happy to have his wife's nipples plastered all over downtown!" Marina exclaimed, snapping me back to attention.

"I'm building a career," I said, gritting my teeth. "And now you're my right hand. You're supposed to tell me that it's art and he will understand and it's going to be all good."

Marina threw the car in park and turned to me. "It's art and he will understand and it's going to be all good."

"Do you mean that?"

"Not even a little bit."

When we arrived at Daphne's address, a preppy woman in her early thirties was waiting outside the building. She introduced herself as Wynne as she barreled toward me, her arms full of boxes. "Daphne said you were taking all this?" she asked.

"If that's okay," I said, getting out of the car to help her.

"Fine by me." Wynne laughed as she loaded the boxes into the trunk.

Marina looked at Wynne and did a double take. "I know you!"

Wynne looked at Marina. "Lastrelle!" they said in tandem.

"Oh my god!" Marina said. "Are you still in the study?" I detected a smidge of jealousy in her voice.

Wynne shrugged. "I have rosacea, so I sort of had an advantage. They wanted to make sure it worked for sensitive skin."

"And does it?" Marina inquired.

"Not really," Wynne admitted. "But I made an extra hundred bucks for saying so in a testimonial video."

"Congrats." Marina nodded solemnly as if she was an actress who'd just learned that she'd been beaten out for the lead role in a new Warner Brothers franchise.

"I hate lying," Wynne confessed. "My boyfriend is in law school studying to be a public defender, but you know how it is. They get you in there and next thing you know you're telling them what they want to hear simply because you want that money." Marina nodded along. "Anyway, they were stupid to cut you. You are so pretty, you would have made an amazing spokesperson."

Marina smiled, and then looked at me. "You ready to unbox these fuckers?"

I glanced at the trunk of the car, which we'd barely been able to close. "Let's ride."

From the second we opened up the first box of Daphne's belongings, Marina no longer cared about surveys or sexting. I'd never seen her so focused on anything that wasn't her horoscope. She had a new purpose: to make me over. "The best years of your life were wasted in sweatpants and Mavi jeans!" she told me. "If you don't wear the shit out of this stuff, you are doing a disservice to women everywhere."

I learned quickly that in order to build my following, I had to feed it. Every one of them — a number edging close to 25,000 — wanted to feel heard, and I needed to take the time to let them know that I was listening and that I cared. That was what made Daphne so successful. She wasn't just a pretty picture or silly video to swipe past. She was your friend.

The pictures I took with Marina's assistance weren't as serious as Daphne's. And the captions I threw up were mostly nonsense that happened to make me laugh. I couldn't keep a straight face sipping coffee at Sant Ambroeus or looking lost and lonely as I crossed the cobblestone street. Instead I played in the produce section at Trader Joes, climbed trees in Battery Park, and rented paddle boats down by Pier 26. Marina and I were just two girls playing dress up. And I had to admit, it was kind of fun.

By the time I had 30,000 followers, Seth and Vigo finally ponied up and gave me half the money they owed me. They were probably scared that I was going to post about their cavalier attitude toward labor laws. They promised me that the rest of what I was owed would be in my bank account by the new year. The posters were up, and the bath bombs were online. My work was ostensibly complete. But Seth wanted me to stay on past the holiday push to help them develop a line of adaptogen-infused shower gels for the "trophy mom on the go," whatever that meant. There was only one issue. Vigo was looking for investors for their second round of funding, and until he had a better sense of where the company was going to land, he couldn't renegotiate my contract. This was more than annoying. If I didn't start pulling in more cash, we were going to end up living with Iliya's mom and her fake Faberge egg collection.

My part in the NBD campaign gave a bit of a boost to my Instagram account, but Daphne was the real reason it kept growing. She kept tagging me and reposting my shots on her stories with little stickers and thumbs up emojis. For all intents and purposes, she had made me, and she wanted to show me off.

I wasn't seeing dollars, but the products kept rolling in. Boxes of everything from veggie-flavored ice cream to serums made out of pig placentas started showing up at my door. I switched from almond milk to tigernut milk because Daphne claimed it was better for gut health. I started eating collagen gummies from some company called Goo and put Red on a grain-free diet that showed up monthly on dry ice. My nightly beauty routine grew from ten minutes long to an hour and a half once I factored in the glycolic peels, vitamin C drops, hydration pellets, and the red-light mask. These things were mine for free as long as I posted them.

I was already up to 40,000 followers when I met up with Daphne at her hair salon. The space was wide open with poured concrete floors and steel-framed windows. Styling assistants scurried back and forth, mixing colors and fetching diet sodas for the thirsty clientele.

Daphne stood over my chair, scrutinizing my tresses. "So I don't want you to mess with the length," she told the stylist, Javier. "We're letting it grow. And for the color..." Daphne cocked her head, pretending to think even though it was obvious she already knew exactly what she wanted. "Just softer. More like mine." She looked up at Javier, who nodded.

"I know what you like," he told her.

"Of course. This isn't your first rodeo." Daphne picked up her phone so she could film us. "Javi. Sorry... Can you start your bit again? Tell me what you want to do and then I'll come in with my thoughts?"

"And what should I do?" I laughed awkwardly.

Daphne smiled from behind her phone. "Just sit still and look pretty."

CHAPTER TWENTY-THREE

Shoppers had started lining up in the middle of the night. Some of them brought folding chairs, and I even spotted a couple of tents. It was ten a.m., and the queue snaked around the block, teeming with women waiting to ravage the L'Orangerie sample sale once it opened to the public. Daphne, Marina and I were already past the warehouse gates, since Daphne got early access. Not only did she get to assess the wares before they were picked over by the hoi polloi, but she could take whatever she wanted, free of charge. So, for that matter, could her entourage.

Marina could barely contain her excitement. "We can just help ourselves to *anything*?" she confirmed.

"Pretty much," Daphne said. "This is all last season's inventory. There's nothing they can do with it besides take the hit and sell it off to Nordstrom Rack. We're doing them a favor if you think about it."

"Does every designer do this?" I asked.

"Except for the top ones. The Guccis and Louis Vuittons of the world set their shit on fire in Piscataway." She sounded nonchalant.

"NO! You're kidding!" Marina gasped. "But… Why?" Marina's face took on the expression of a child who had just been told that Santa Claus wasn't real.

"Two reasons," Daphne said, sauntering down the aisle. "One, they don't want to flood the market and mess up the exclusivity of their brand and two, they are imported products, which means that they paid an import tax to get each piece into the United States. So if they destroy their product and then report it to customs, they get some money back. Kind of brilliant if you ask me."

"Louis Vuitton bags… burning in New Jersey," Marina said, her voice quivering. It sounded like she might cry.

This was the first time Marina had been around Daphne. And aside from their shared love of European luxury cars and liposuction videos, the two women couldn't be more unalike. Daphne had ascended to an enchanted place where everything was handed to her, whereas Marina made it her life's work to shamelessly scheme and haggle and grab as much as she could take. They were both beasts, but from wildly different animal kingdoms.

"I think I'm going to have a panic attack," Marina said.

"Relax, this should be fun." Daphne smiled. "What are you in the market for? Going-out looks? Vacation? Work clothes?"

Marina puckered her lips. "All of the above?"

We followed Daphne over to a rack and stood back as she loaded a shopping cart with leather bombers. It felt like a fever dream or some sort of hallucination, watching Daphne fill our cart with garments that she had no intention of paying for. It was a Vegas buffet where we could consume as much as we wanted. Daphne rattled off commentary as she went. "This is great!" "Take it!" "You don't need it, but with the right top…" And while she didn't pay Marina much mind, she was never dismissive, as I had feared she might be. "Meg!" Daphne held up a turquoise mohair sweater. "I've been wanting to see you in more blue. How good does she look in blue?" she asked Marina, who was too busy sniffing a buttery leather pant leg to register that she'd been called on.

After our two-hour bender, a PR rep checked us out, if you could call it that. The receipt stapled to the side of my shopping bag was at least two feet long. At the bottom, the subtotal was zero.

Marina was on cloud nine as we made our way back home.

"I should really start influencing too," she said as she sped down the FDR.

"Would you want to?" I asked. "You totally could."

"Not yet," she said. "I wouldn't attract the same demo as you. I'm too young and hot. I'd just have an inbox full of dongs."

Her delivery could have been more tactful, but she wasn't wrong. "Scantily clad sexpot" was its own Instagram subgenre. And while those sexy accounts bolstered big followings, they rarely made any money. They didn't get the big deals because they had the wrong demographics. Their followers were creepy men, not women who were in the market for skinny teas or diaper bags. It was the moms who had the buying power. And Marina was right. The moms would hate her.

"Maybe once I have a baby..." she said dreamily, gunning her car over a nasty pothole.

CHAPTER TWENTY-FOUR

My adventures in influencing didn't trouble Iliya as much as I'd thought they would. He was more freaked out about my new hair, which he said glowed in the dark. He was also troubled by the fact that it was hard to walk around our apartment now that it was filled with cardboard boxes.

Or maybe he was too distracted with the apartment search to notice just how consumed I'd become with my life in pictures. He was still angling for the Long Island City apartment that was more affordable than anything he'd seen in Manhattan. Iliya showed me a video, and while it looked lovely, I had my reservations. Moving to another borough wasn't ideal. I certainly didn't mention the possibility to Daphne, who saw anything further than Bergdorf's as another country she'd only travel to for a CO2 laser.

I hoped Iliya wouldn't bring it up on our double date. The long overdue outing was finally happening. We'd made plans to meet Daphne and Kip at PESCE, a new "concept" from the guys behind Matador, one of Daphne's favorite restaurants. Iliya didn't have time to come home after work, so we agreed to meet at Chelsea House and walk to the restaurant from there.

I could feel the tension between us as we started down the street. It was one of those nights where a fight was imminent. It was just a question of when. We'd already gotten into it that morning, bickering over where we were going to spend the winter holidays. I wanted to get away and go somewhere pretty. He wanted to stay close to his mother and sister, now that they were finally in the same city.

"But you guys are Jews! I don't know why we have to spend Christmas with your mom when she doesn't even celebrate it."

"Where we grew up it was illegal to be Jewish," Iliya said. "So yeah, we do Christmas even if we don't do Jesus."

"I just feel like everybody is going somewhere but us!" I said, none too proudly.

"Stop looking at your phone and maybe you won't feel that way." It was a low blow, and I was still smarting twelve hours later.

"I'm freezing," I muttered, trying to keep up with Iliya in a pair of Daphne's old knife mules.

"I told you to wear socks. It's winter."

"Technically it's still fall. And I'm suffering for fashion." I tried to make it sound like I was joking.

Iliya stopped and cocked his head. "Those shoes are fashionable?" He was trying not to laugh.

"Yes, they are."

"They're also way too big for you," he noted. It was true, Daphne's feet were a size bigger than mine, but I was usually able to cheat it in pics. Before I could respond, Iliya picked me up and flung me over his shoulder.

"Put me down!" I was kicking and screaming. He paid me no mind and lugged me like a disgruntled sack of potatoes the rest of the way to our destination.

The restaurant was behind a nondescript door. Iliya rang a bell and smacked my ass while we waited. "Ow!" I shrieked, fighting my way to the ground.

When a man in a gondolier hat opened the door, I rushed inside, trying to shake off the chill.

"I think we have a reservation," Iliya told him.

"Do you have a password?" the man asked.

"I'm sorry?" Iliya's eyes narrowed.

"We text all our patrons a password an hour before their reservation. If you want to check your cell?" He motioned to Iliya's pocket, but Iliya didn't budge.

"We aren't using our cells," Iliya said plainly. "It's date night. The last name is Chernoff. Iliya Chernoff."

Hearing Iliya's name, the man snapped into hospitality mode. "Mr. Chernoff! Of course. I'm Serge. Danny mentioned you were coming in and to take good care of you. Can I take your jackets?"

"This is my wife, Meg," Iliya said, handing Serge his jacket.

"We are actually meeting Daphne Cole," I added.

"Yes, of course. She hasn't arrived yet but let me show you around."

"Meg was just on the verge of shoeicide, so if there is a booth she can kick her legs up in," Iliya started.

"A booth? Didn't Danny tell you?" Serge looked at us, surprised. "You're in boats tonight."

"I'm sorry?" Iliya coughed.

We followed Serge past a bar filled with bankers out for their monthly bro-makases down a long hall covered in sea grass and vertical veggie gardens.

"Up front we have our crudo bar where we do more casual dining," Serge said, leading us into what looked like a man-made grotto with a giant pool of water in the center. "And this is where we have the main event." Serge motioned toward the gondolas filled with foodies fishing for their dinners. The boats floated past in every direction. "All you need to do is catch a fish. Chefs are floating by and ready to clean, grill, and garnish," Serge said.

"This is wild!" I said.

"Actually, all the fish is farm-raised," he whispered under his breath.

"Your secret is safe with me." I nodded as the bellowing voice of a baritone singing Pavarotti echoed through the cave.

Iliya held his tongue as we stepped into our boat. Once Serge was out of earshot, Iliya turned to me. "You've got to be fucking kidding me, Meg. What is this, Disneyland for douchebags?"

"This isn't my fault. She picked the place. And you spoke with Danny beforehand. Did he not mention anything?"

Iliya struggled with an oar and pushed us away from shore. "Do you think I asked him if we were riding in bumper boats? And how are we expected to eat with anybody? We're in a two-seater," he pointed out, flustered.

Just then a small dude covered in neck tattoos rowed his way up beside us. He poured Iliya a kombucha and delivered me a glass of prosecco, then handed us both fishing rods and a tackle box filled with bait and bibs.

"At least you're getting the vacation you wanted," Iliya said a moment later. "If you squint your eyes almost shut, you could tell yourself you're in Italy."

"Are you going to be making fun of me all night?"

"Meg!" A voice came from across the grotto. It was Daphne, dressed in a bustier and spray-painted jeans. Kip stood next to her, talking on his phone. They were still on land.

"Come here!" She waved us over, like a Siren beckoning a ship of sailors to their death.

"You've got to be kidding me. You guys have matching hair," Iliya said under his breath as he rowed.

"Hiiii," Daphne cooed, instantly sizing up Iliya. I could tell she was impressed by his good looks. "So I finally get to meet my competition," she said. "I feel like we should arm wrestle or something."

"You might be stronger than me," Iliya said. "I've seen the videos of your trampoline workouts." This was news to me. I wondered what else of Daphne's he'd seen.

Daphne laughed. "Hey, I like your shirt. It looks better on your wife, though."

I looked at Iliya again, realizing that he was in his favorite button up. The same one I'd worn to the Mompire dinner. Iliya shot me a look.

"Hey, man. Nice to formally meet you." Kip looked at Iliya. I clocked that they recognized each other from somewhere.

"Nice to meet you," Iliya said, playing along. A dock worker helped Daphne and Kit into their gondola, then tied our two boats together.

I was waiting to see how long it would take for Kip to acknowledge me this time.

"So!" Iliya said, placing his hand on my knee. "Should we fish?"

"This place is so crazy!" I smiled at Daphne. I wanted to let her know that she still had my undivided attention.

"What? Sorry, I'm a little distracted," she said. "I'm getting emails from Instagram telling me that my pictures go against the platform's guidelines. And that if I continue, they are going to shut me down!"

By the look of Kip's face, this was a topic he was sick of hearing about.

"That's impossible," I said. "You haven't posted anything inappropriate."

"Well I must have because certain posts of mine are missing. They took them down!" Daphne pulled out her phone and scrolled through her grid, trying to remember which shots had vanished. "You know what? Fuck that! Let's make some more inappropriate content," she said, changing her tone. Daphne held her phone in my face and motioned for me to smile as Kip engaged Iliya in the kind of ritualistic small talk that men reserve for other men. "I think if I get another notice telling me that they really are deleting me," Daphne said, "the move is to just post a full nude saying, 'bye bitch!' " Daphne cackled.

"Give 'em what they want," I laughed.

"Speaking of posting, I was thinking that you should talk to Susan," Daphne said, now aiming her camera lens at her tackle box.

"About what?" I took out a gummy squid and attached it to my pole.

"About her repping you. She's expressed interest. That dog food company has money and Cha Cha hates their food so I'm out. If you had someone in there who could negotiate on your behalf, I know that they'd pay you."

"But Red is like a thousand years old. He's not exactly a cover model," I reminded her.

It wasn't my dog Daphne wanted to talk about. "You're already posting for them anyway. You should be getting something more than just free food. You're at what? Fifty-five thousand followers now?" she said, pretending not to know.

"Something like that," I said.

"You are no longer micro, Meg. You passed the 50k mark. You can start demanding a fee. Especially with that hair."

I blushed, watching Daphne struggle with her pole. Eventually she gave up and took Kip's.

"Hey!" Kip protested. "I was getting a nibble!"

"You have the following, but you need an agent if you want to make any money." Daphne glanced at Iliya to see if he was listening. "Oh shit! I think I have something!" Daphne yanked so hard on her pole that our boats disconnected.

"Slow it down!" Daphne kept yelling.

"I'm trying!" Kip shot back, annoyed.

I watched as Kip and Daphne floated away. There was something strangely cute about them. They were similar in a certain way, like siblings who spent too much time together or two actors who hated each other but were stuck playing love interests on a hit TV in its seventeenth season.

"Well, this is fun," Iliya said facetiously.

"We have to go get them."

"Do we?" Iliya looked at me. "I can't spend another minute talking about Ben Roethlisberger. You know I hate American sports."

"I know. But we still haven't even eaten anything," I reminded him.

Iliya continued to bitch as we rowed our boat back to the other side of the grotto. We found Daphne and Kip tied up to another gondola. I was taken aback to see Tanya and her husband riding in it. I thought this was supposed to be a double date, not a party.

"Long lifeline," Tanya said, hanging off the side of her boat reading Kip's palm as we approached. In the boat beside them, a chef tended to sea bass cooking on a Roboto-style grill.

"That's not the only thing that's long," chimed in Tanya's husband, Howie. He was a super tan, well-preserved man of about fifty-five with curly salt and pepper hair and a wrist full of kabbalah bracelets. Tanya gave her husband a for-shame look. "What?" he said. "I've stood at a urinal next to this guy. I know you aren't supposed to peek but I'm a doctor so I'm just looking out. Kip, free scrotox when you're ready, bud."

"I'm going to vomit," Tanya said.

Daphne must have sensed my discomfort. "Meg!" she cried out. "Kip caught a bass! And look, I caught a crab!" she pointed to Tanya and laughed.

"I'm not a crab, I just don't want to talk about nut sacks while I eat."

Howie shook Iliya's hand like they'd just pledged the same fraternity. "Who is this handsome Dan?" Howie slurred, drunkenly.

"Howie!" Tanya hit her husband on his non-braceleted hand.

"Easy, princess. That's my injecting finger!" Howie pointed his crooked finger into his wife's face, scolding her. "And I'm secure enough in my heterosexuality to be able to appreciate an attractive man when I see one. Let me ask you something," Howie said, scrutinizing Iliya. "Your nose, made by the knife? Or life?"

"This is why I didn't want to do the wine pairing." Tanya looked at Daphne, frustrated.

I could feel Iliya's judgments flying. There was nothing he hated more than a sloppy drunk. Actually, there was: a whole sea of them.

"You don't mind if they join us, do you?" Daphne batted her eyelashes.

"Of course not," I said, elbowing Iliya.

"I'm so glad we bumped into each other! Literally!" Tanya laughed then turned to Iliya. "So, what do you think about your wife becoming an influencer?"

"I have a lot of new visors and sleep shirts." Iliya said, clearly fading out. He was done with these people.

"Kip, why don't you ever sleep in any of the swag I get?" Daphne picked up her phone, seizing the moment to film.

"Why would I wear anything to sleep when I'm next to you?" Kip was cranking up the charm. They were a different couple when the camera was on. It was almost sociopathic.

"Oh Kippy! I love you!" Daphne said. They kissed for the camera, then went back to eating in silence.

"What do you do, Iliya?" Howie asked.

"I'm in the private club business," Iliya said, trying to stay vague.

"Like strip clubs? I put tits on half the dancers in this town. You ever been to Happy Endings in the Financial District? They've got some very talented young ladies."

"Howie!" Tanya shouted.

"What!? They do! They're excellent dancers. Very flexible."

"I'm so sorry about him." Tanya shook her head, mortified. "He doesn't get out much."

"It's fine." I smiled.

Before there was time to order tiramisu, Iliya was asking for the check.

"Oh, don't be silly," Daphne said to him. "It's comped. Because we posted."

Iliya nodded, then steered our boat over to the dock and helped me back onto land. I was embarrassed that we were rushing out, but I knew that if we didn't, Iliya was going to lose it. He gave zero fucks what Daphne or any of the people floating around us thought. And he would have no qualms sharing that information with them if given the opportunity.

After tipping the waitstaff, we hopped in a cab, damp and smelling of fish viscera. The second the taxi meter started running, the fight I'd been anticipating all evening finally broke out.

"*That* is who you got pool memberships for?" Iliya shook his head, disgusted.

"No! That girl wasn't even there!"

"Are you claiming that the woman who you hooked up is any different from the sampling of people I just met?" He gave me a long, hard look. Now was not the time to tell Iliya that Lauren was actually worse than the people we'd just dined with.

"You're just annoyed because they were tipsy," I said. "You don't even know them."

"I know enough. Did you see how they were sizing me up? Wanted to know what I did for a living? I'm sorry but I refuse to associate with a bunch of arrogant, status-obsessed, drunk douchebags."

"Um, sorry but there is no difference between these people and all your drunk Russian friends except for the fact that my friends can actually afford the Hermes belts they're wearing!"

Iliya ignored me. "And that Kip guy? Do you know how many times I've seen him in the club with other women? Does your friend not know, or does it not count in your world if there aren't any pictures to post?" This took the wind out of me. I couldn't cobble together a response fast enough. "Seriously, Meg. I'm asking. Tell me how it works. Now that you're such an expert."

"Wow, Iliya. I take you out to meet my new friends — something you sure haven't done since we came to New York — and this is the way you want to act? I'm glad you're so superior to everyone else on earth. It must feel pretty awesome. You know what else would be awesome?" Tears were pricking my eyes and I could hardly see anything. "If you would kindly fuck off."

CHAPTER TWENTY-FIVE

There was no exercise on earth more annoying than bouncing. It hurt my knees and every time I jumped, a little bit of pee seemed to escape me. But Tramp Stamp was where Daphne went. And that's where I found her two days after our dinner. Before I could talk to her at the end of our session, Lauren cornered me.

"Meg, I keep seeing your face all over my walk to school. Congrats on the NBD launch. It's a pretty BD!" she laughed. "We should do a feature with you on my blog. Maybe we could shoot you at home with the kids and husband? I heard he's hot. At some point I should properly thank him for getting me those pool memberships." She was being nicer to me than she had ever been. Daphne and Tanya came over to join us.

"I don't show the kids' faces on social media," I said almost apologetically. "And Iliya is pretty private."

Lauren buried her sweaty head in a towel. When she looked back up, half of her face had smeared off on the terrycloth. "Well maybe we could do something just you and me," Lauren said, looking to Daphne for her approval.

"You and Meg?" Daphne cocked her head to the side. She seemed dubious.

"Yeah, like a fireside chat for mom-trepreneurs. Maybe even stream it….," Lauren spitballed. Before she could continue, I felt a tapping on my shoulder.

A glistening twenty-something in a spandex hot pink workout bra was standing inches away. "Knew it! From behind I could have sworn that you were Daphne."

"It's the hair!" Lauren and Tanya said in unison.

"I'm right here!" Daphne waved her hand.

"Duh. I know. I'm just saying that you guys are like twinning," the spandex girl said, then turned back to me. "You're Meg Chernoff, right?" She sounded nervous. "My friends and I are obsessed with your feed. *Chanels like teen spirit*? I died laughing!" she gushed. "Would you mind if we took a selfie?"

"Sure," I said, feeling anything but sure.

"Sorry I'm so sweaty." I could feel the girl shaking as I wrapped my hand around her waist and smiled. I knew that people were following my account, but this was the first time I was face to face with a "fan." It felt surreal.

"Thanks so much!" she said. "Keep doing what you are doing. And Daphne, you know I love you too, obvi!"

"Thanks, girl." Daphne waved as the girl pranced off.

Lauren's eyes widened, unable to hold back her shock at my ascent. Having 60,000 followers was one thing. But IRL fan girls bum-rushing me after gym class?

"So, about our fireside chat," Lauren continued, talking faster than before. "I'm out east for Thanksgiving and then I have a couple of non-negotiables, but how about mid-December?"

"Meg can't do it," Daphne interjected as she led us out of the muggy studio and over toward the juice bar. "She'll be with me in Paris."

"What?" I stopped and looked at Daphne.

"You're going to Paris with me in two weeks. Did I forget to tell you?"

Lauren looked at me, clearly seething with jealousy.

"This is the first I'm hearing of it," I told Daphne.

"I asked Susan to try and get you a fee!" Daphne announced.

"A FEE? For WHAT?" Lauren couldn't help herself. Her face was growing redder by the second.

"For her time. You should really be offering her something too if you're gonna use her to promote your blog, Lauren. Even her dog is commanding fees these days. Right, Meg?"

Daphne handed us each a pea green wellness shot. Lauren looked like she was going to be sick, and not because of the wheatgrass.

CHAPTER TWENTY-SIX

Thanksgiving in Tribeca was quiet. According to my feed, most people were either cuddling under cashmere blankets in the Hamptons or flouncing around in flannel upstate. Iliya insisted on hosting dinner at our place even though we barely had a functioning kitchen. We ordered in and invited my mother-in-law, Dasha, whom I'd successfully avoided since our move back east.

Dinner had been ready for a half hour, but we were still waiting on Marina. She was supposedly on her way but not picking up her phone.

"We can't keep Red on that disgusting food," Iliya said. "He's had blood in his stool for the past two days."

"I know, but we need to pretend he's on it because they just started paying us," I said, watching Iliya cut up a scrap of turkey and toss it into Red's bowl. "And why are you giving him more meat? He's clearly reacting to the protein. We need to just have him on a pumpkin and rice diet for a few days." I snatched the meat out of Red's bowl and excused myself to go to the bathroom. There was a frantic text from Daphne waiting for me.

"THEY ARE GETTING RID OF LIKES!" she wrote. "Do I still have them? Will you check my page?"

Before I could reply, she continued typing. "Some accounts have already lost them. ARGH!! And I have a weird feeling that I'm being targeted."

I'd read about Instagram removing "likes" and as a parent, I felt that it made sense. Kids were killing themselves based on how many people hearted their photos. But Daphne didn't see it that way. "Kids have no place being on Instagram to begin with!" she'd proselytize, then post a picture of her twins doing an ASMR video or wearing matching pajamas.

"Your likes are still there," I assured her.

"Thank god," she replied. A second later, a video of Kip and his buddies doing a cheer pyramid on the beach with the caption, "Get a load of these turkeys! #HappyTurkeyDay" appeared on her feed.

Before returning to the living room, I freshened up in the mirror. Then I pulled my old bottle of half-eaten placenta pills out of the cabinet. "I was in charge of the stuffing," I wrote, followed by Daphne's hashtag, #HappyTurkeyDay

I laughed out loud at my own joke but then instantly worried that Daphne might think that I was spoofing her and quickly deleted the hashtag.

"Mommy! Are you pooping? Come OUT!" Roman screamed. "I have presents!"

"Is Marina here yet?" I inquired, secretly hoping that her tardiness would buy me a few more minutes alone with my phone.

I knew that my family was on the other side of the door, and that it was a holiday and that these moments with my kids were limited. They wouldn't be this young forever. I would eventually regret not savoring every second of their youth. But I just couldn't stop scrolling, pulling down on my screen to refresh the content like it was a slot machine.

Finally, I came out to find Iliya's legally blind mother sitting on a hemorrhoid pillow on the couch and pulling age-inappropriate gifts out of a Rite Aid bag. "There is no Kevin's," she grunted to Roman. "When you die, you die."

"What are we talking about?" I looked at Iliya, who clearly wasn't keeping an eye on his mother in my absence. "Nobody is dying. These are adult topics that we don't need to be discussing with a preschooler."

"Mama, *perestan' govorit' o!*" Iliya called out from the kitchen.

"No death talk, fine. I'm gonna die first, you know," Dasha added in the same breath. "And what is happening to your wife's body?"

"What do you mean?" I asked timidly.

"You're getting too thin!" she scowled.

"Can she even see me?" I asked Iliya under my breath, scattering pecans on a salad.

"Of course, she can," he insisted, his hands covered in butter.

"From this far away?" I squinted at Dasha from across the kitchen island.

"I can hear you, too!"

It was true, I had been losing a bit of weight. It was a side effect of following along with whatever fad diet Daphne was on. Some days it was no dairy, some days no gluten, some days it was something called a GG cracker, which was basically just a high-fiber crispbread that tasted like tree bark.

"Yeah! A gun!" Roman exclaimed. "Thank you so much, Nana!" he said, pointing the pistol straight at his little brother.

"Hang on! No guns!" I stopped him. "We aren't a gun household."

"It's not a gun! It's a water gun," Dasha clarified, annoyed. "You people are so uptight. Live a little. Jesus."

"Jesus?" Roman said, having his eureka moment. "Mommy was saying that when the house was on fire!"

"When was the house on fire?" Dasha asked, picking Felix up from his playmat and placing him on her lap.

Iliya shook his head, pleading for me to disengage. "We don't have to do Christmas, okay?" he negotiated under his breath.

Even before kids, my relationship with Dasha had been a struggle. I respected all that she'd been through and all that she'd sacrificed for her children. But she was difficult to be around. She was a master at finding a way to make herself the victim in any circumstance. She simpered and pouted and glared like nobody else. I'd once been to a restaurant with her where she pulled out her Weight Watchers scale to weigh an eight-ounce petit filet. When the steak came in at two grams under, she complained until her meal was comped. And she wasn't even the one buying.

She was bitter about her life and lonely living alone the past few years since Marina had moved out. There was nothing any of us could do to make her happy. Sometimes she'd laugh or smile at the boys, then catch herself and retreat back into her gloom, disappearing into her bedroom to sneak a cigarette and contemplate how her husband died of lung cancer when he never smoked a day in his life.

"It's time to eat!" Iliya called out.

"But what about Marina—" Roman reminded him.

"It's time to eat anyway." Iliya took Felix from his mother and brought him to the table.

Just then Daphne texted: "So are you coming to France or what?" She hadn't mentioned Paris since Tramp Stamp and I hadn't brought it up. It was almost as if she telepathically felt my attention shift toward my family and needed something to reel me back in.

"You're not serious, are you?" I wrote.

Iliya shot me a look. "Honey?"

"I get two tickets and you know I don't want to take Kip. His French is abominable. He pronounces the T in Merlot."

"Honey?" Iliya intoned again, this time less softly.

"Can I think about it?" I asked, typing as quickly as I could.

"THINK about what? It's fucking ZOE!"

As far as Daphne was concerned, there was no greater honor

than being invited to a Zoe anything. And I understood enough to know it would put me in a different echelon of influencers. I wouldn't just be part of the downtown mommy 'grammer scene, I'd be part of the global luxury market.

"MEGAN! We are about to eat dinner. Can you put the damn phone down?" Iliya snapped.

I looked up at my family seated around the table. Roman blinked at me. Dasha looked at me with an air of superiority and judgment. Felix just babbled to himself in his high chair and Red slowly crept out of the room to go post a want ad for a new family.

"Sorry," I said sheepishly.

My phone vibrated again, and it took every ounce of self-discipline I had not to look down.

Later that night, once the kids were asleep, I walked into the kitchen to find Iliya still tidying up.

"Daphne invited me to Paris," I told him.

"Okay." He didn't sound surprised. "Are you going to go?" He didn't look up.

"Can I?" I was waiting for him to make eye contact.

"You can do whatever you want," Iliya said, grabbing a loaf of black bread and making a turkey and pickle sandwich. "How many days?"

"Like, three!" I said.

"I didn't ask *like* how many days. I asked *how* many days."

"I'd fly out late next Thursday night and be back Sunday.

"I have the Chelsea House holiday party next Friday. It's all the investors. There is no way I can get out of it."

"Well, maybe your sister —," I started.

"Maybe." He shrugged. "But those things go late..."

"If it's too much right now I understand. Red is going to need to go to the vet if this rice doesn't help him. And you'd have both kids...." I trailed off, feeling guilty. While I wanted to go more than anything, I knew that it would be a logistical nightmare.

Iliya stared at me. I could tell he was trying his hardest to stay even-tempered. "Do you want to go with her?"

"I mean, it's Paris!" I said. "You know I've always wanted to go to Europe. And when are we going to be able to afford a trip like that?"

"Just you and her?" I could see him grit his teeth. He reached for a stack of mail.

"I don't know why you don't like her. She's been so good to me."

"I don't not like her. I just don't like what she does to you."

"What does she do to me? She thinks I'm talented. I don't know where I'd be right now if it weren't for her." I shook my head.

"You'd be here," he said bluntly, then passed me an envelope with my name on it. It was my credit card statement. I steadied my breath as I ripped it open. Of course, Vigo hadn't paid my balance. Those guys didn't give a shit about me. I was just a cog in a wheel, useful but replaceable. If I wanted my life to change, I needed to do it myself.

"Thank you," I said to Iliya. "I'm gonna go."

CHAPTER TWENTY-SEVEN

The Air France A380 departed JFK for Charles de Gaulle at 9:55 p.m. I questioned my decision to board up until the minute I took my first sip of complimentary Champagne. I knew that I wasn't leaving Iliya in the best position but opportunities like this one only came around once in a lifetime, if that. I'd arranged for Marina to watch the kids Saturday night so that Iliya could make his big work event. And I'd made them both promise to contact the vet if Red's condition worsened.

Vigo had assured me that his assistant had sorted out my outstanding pay and promised that he'd settled my credit card bill. He even swore that he'd gotten the late fee waived. Unfortunately, I could only check on my account from my laptop, so I had to hope I was in the clear to score a few small gifts to bring home to the boys.

With muted shades of palomino leather and warm pink lighting, the first-class cabin was a capsule of serenity. Daphne sat to my right wearing Gucci sweatpants and gigantic designer dad sneakers. Her Birkin was filled to the brim with rose water facial mist, digestive enzymes, satin eye masks, fashion magazines, iPhone chargers, and collagen protein bars. Aside from a cashmere hoodie that used to be Daphne's, I looked like an imposter cocooned in my pod with a hiking backpack and Ziploc bag full of raw almonds.

Thankfully, a dividing wall separated our seats, relieving me of the anxiety that had been building up all day long. I had no idea how I was going to be my chattiest and funniest self for seven hours straight. I was browsing the movie options on the TV in front of me when Daphne's head popped over the privacy divider. She was taking my picture, I realized after the fact.

"Look natural," she said, sounding disappointed.

"Okay," I said, resituating myself into a position that she approved of.

"Your hair looks so good. Did I tell you that already?"

"Yeah, I'm getting used to it now. Javier did a great job." I smiled.

"He's the best!" she cooed. "I think next time we can even go lighter."

Daphne reached her arm over the divider. A bottle of Ambien was in her palm. "Want one? I like to take mine before the meal comes."

I tensed up. "I don't like to take anything just in case something happens to the captain and I have to land the plane."

"Do you have a lot of experience landing planes?" She cocked her head, amused.

"If my life depended on it, I'm pretty sure that I could figure it out."

"Take half." She bit a pill in two and fed one half-moon to herself, handing its mate to me. I inhaled deeply and swallowed the medicine.

After a dinner of foie gras and brioche (Daphne passed on the toast) followed by filet mignon and risotto (Daphne passed on the risotto), I tried to stay coherent by making small talk about how cute I found the mini bottles of olive oil and balsamic vinegar.

"These would have been perfect in your Feast of San Gennaro-themed lunch," I said.

"Which lunch?" Daphne asked groggily. "Can you pull it up?"

"I don't think I have service." I checked my phone for bars.

She looked at me, half-smiling. "Babe, you know I don't actually make any of that food, right?"

"You don't?" I stared at her, confused and fading.

"Do I *look* like I can cook? I'm afraid of food!" She laughed. "I have a chef who does all those meals. It's not even my kitchen! Haven't you ever zoomed in on the marble? It's so obvious."

I looked at her in disbelief.

"Do you think I'm a bad person now?" she whispered, leaning closer to me.

"What? Of course not," I said, trying to seem unfazed. I felt like an honor-roll student being offered a blunt under the bleachers.

"You're so innocent, Meg. I'm a curator. I'm not sitting in the kitchen making my own sourdough and shit. When would I have the time? *You* don't even have the time."

I forced a smile, trying not to take offense. Instead, I asked about her epic gingerbread house, even though I already knew the answer.

"Did you see that thing? It wasn't even edible. It had running water and electricity. Who do you think I am, Bob fucking Vila?"

"And… The cardboard Paw Patrol vehicles that the kids drove trick or treating around Tribeca?"

"Meg!" She leveled her eyes at me. "That was a sponsored deal with Michaels. It *said* #sponsored in the post. Have I taught you nothing?" Daphne shook her head with mock disappointment. "You are my favorite person, you know…"

"Don't forget your kids," I reminded her.

Daphne continued as if she hadn't heard me. "This trip is going to be so good for you. You are going to meet so many people, and they're all going to love you." She smiled. "Aside from the fall show, this is Zoe's biggest event of the year. Being a part of this is going to get you everything you want. Do you even know what you want?"

"I guess I want to be able to keep living in Manhattan. To get my kids into great schools… maybe write something real one day." I flinched at my own honesty.

"Like a book or something? You could totally do that." Daphne squeezed my hand, and a wave of warmth rolled over me.

"And you? What do you want?" I asked, curious if she had a master plan.

"I want what everybody wants..." She smirked, reclining deeper into her seat as her eyelids grew heavier.

I looked at her lying there in her three-thousand-dollar track suit with her perfectly highlighted hair. In this soft lighting, I could almost tune out the metal bead extensions peeking out between each strand.

Daphne closed her eyes and her lips parted into a dreamy smile. "More followers."

CHAPTER TWENTY-EIGHT

It was morning when we landed in Paris. My heart skipped as the plane made its descent. I stared out the window at the Eiffel Tower, almost unable to believe it wasn't an Epcot Center reproduction. Daphne's Ambien had worn off and she was back to her more coherent self. She'd managed to expertly apply a full face of makeup in the lavatory before landing, if only to cover it up with a large hat and oversized shades.

After an Air France liaison escorted us through customs and helped us get our bags, a Mercedes S-Class ferried us from the airport to our hotel. I gawked out the window the entire ride. I'd always wanted to come to Paris. I had to keep pinching myself. It was all too good to be real.

Daphne was giddy as she led me by the hand into the lobby of the Plaza Athenée. A white-gloved bellhop whisked away my fifteen-year-old duffel bag along with Daphne's custom-painted Louis Vuitton trunks.

"Madame Cole! So lovely to see you again!" an immaculately coiffed woman with a name tag that read *Cosette* said. "We have a gorgeous suite waiting for you."

"Merci. *Je ne peux pas attendre.*" Daphne smiled, reminding Cosette that she spoke French.

After pointing out the courtyard with its red window awnings and equally red geraniums, Colette walked us past the Alain Ducasse dining room, insisting we order the patisserie tower for brunch.

On the elevator up to our room, Daphne switched into work mode, ignoring Cosette and walking me through the next forty-eight hours.

"Okay, so this morning we shoot content in the room, then I go to my product shoot with a few other bloggers. I'll get into which ones to avoid later — there are some doozies. Tomorrow is the actual show. Oh, and *tonight* we have the welcome dinner. The dinner will be fun."

"What are you promoting by the way?" I asked.

"Hiking sandals. They're like Tevas, but twelve hundred dollars," she said, straight-faced.

"Diva Tevas!" I joked.

"Exactly!" Daphne nearly spit in amusement.

Long-legged Cosette led us down a carpeted hallway that smelled of vanilla and cigarettes.

"No way! You guys are giving us 361?" Daphne gushed. "This is my favorite suite in the entire hotel."

Cosette suppressed a smile and opened the door, revealing the most breathtaking room I'd ever seen. Just beyond the grand piano and chandelier decorated in black tassels was the kind of view of the Eiffel Tower that compels people to drop down to their knees and propose marriage. A ring of velvet sofas and upholstered Louis XIV chairs surrounded an antique coffee table laid out with fresh fruit, a chocolate cake, a bottle of Champagne and the Zoe tote that I'd seen in the store window with Iliya. Daphne's name was embroidered on the side of it.

"Oh my—," I gasped, collapsing into a plush loveseat.

"Don't get too comfortable," Daphne said under her breath. "This isn't the room we are sleeping in. This is just where I'm shooting all my hotel content. Check out this view. And the bathrooms...," Daphne said, trailing off as she walked into the large marble bathroom. "I hope they still have the Bulgari soaps."

"If there is anything else you need, please don't hesitate to call,"

Cosette said, standing by the door.

"You got the tote!" I marveled.

"Yeah, but I already have one in red." Daphne sounded bored. "Why don't you take it?"

"It has your name on it!"

"All the better." She laughed. "It's like the new letterman jacket."

"You're insane." I smiled, picking up the tote and walking toward an antique full-length mirror. "I never thought I'd hold one of these bags in real life."

"It's a great tote. You can fit your laptop in it," Daphne said with a fraction of the enthusiasm I had for it.

"Honestly, I couldn't. They want you to have it." I handed the bag back over.

"No, they want me to *post* it," she corrected me. "After that, I think they could give two fucks. No more discussing. It's yours." Daphne dove onto the king-size bed like a six-year-old girl at a slumber party. Apparently the don't-get-too-comfortable rule only applied to me. "I'm already having the best time ever! Are you?"

Before I could figure out a way to gracefully fall down onto the bed beside her, there was a knock at the door.

Daphne looked up. "That's probably the clothes,"

With my new tote on my shoulder, I walked to the door with confidence. A bellhop stood next to a rolling rack filled with standout pieces from Zoe's upcoming spring collection. Two stacks of shoeboxes teetered on either side of the trolley. The attendant wheeled it into the room and vanished before I could tip him.

"I thought you meant *our* luggage," I called out to Daphne.

"Yeah no, those bags are going straight to our real room. Although I might need to run down there for a belt or two." Daphne took her time moving from the bed to the trolley, sifting through the deliveries with laser-like focus. "No. No. This was way cuter in the look book." She held up a pink suit with matching gaucho pants. "I really had no idea what it would look like in person." She sighed. "I still don't know how they expect me to pair this stuff with hiking sandals." Daphne opened a shoebox and pulled out a pair of bedazzled hiking sandals with large white rubber soles and two-toned snakeskin straps. Aside from the flashy rhinestones and the word "Zoe" printed all over the heels, the shoes looked like something one of my mom's ex-husbands would have bought at a camping store and paired with cargo shorts and a Cliff bar.

"These are trending?" I asked incredulously.

"They will be," Daphne assured me. "And apparently they're edible. Made out of sugarcane and coffee. Smell."

I did as I was told. They did smell delicious, like breakfast in bed.

Daphne examined the clothes, arranging and rearranging them next to various pairs of shoes. "THIS! Now this is chic. You should wear this to the dinner," she said, walking toward me with a green sequined dress. She held my gaze, and I felt a blissful weightlessness. Maybe it was the jet lag, but I doubted it.

Three hours later, I woke up dry mouthed and groggy in our much smaller hotel room. Daphne was gone. My nerves settled when I saw the note she had written on the hotel stationery. "Please don't make other plans. I want you to come to my "Teva Diva" shoot at the Eiffel Tower. P.S. I have exciting news." Checking her stories, I saw that Daphne was already there. She looked beautiful and dewy as she posted about her *#nonstop* day.

Wearing one of Daphne's full-length sheepskin coats and one of Iliya's old soccer scarves, I headed to the Eiffel Tower, the place I'd nurtured dreams of going my entire life.

The city was already decked out for Christmas with fairy lights and poinsettias lining every block. The sky was pink, and the air smelled of roasting chestnuts and mulled wine. Cheesemongers sucked cigarettes outside their fromageries, and young couples canoodled at cafe tables on every corner. Each building I passed was more charming and historic than the last, and every passerby looked like an extra from one of the Jean-Luc Godard films I'd studied in college.

From the crosswalk at Avenue Gustave Eiffel, I could already see the flashing of cameras. The shoot was well underway as Daphne and a couple of fellow influencers walked arm in arm toward a photographer and steadicam operator. Here, in the shadow of the Eiffel Tower, Daphne looked a million times more confident than she had in Seth and Vigo's bubble bath.

"Meg!" Daphne called out, looking ready for spring in a floral sundress and denim jacket.

"Hi!" I waved. "You must be cold!" I said, noting her bare legs.

As I made my approach, I recognized two of the other women from Instagram. In a tank top and painted mom jeans was Rebecca Silva, a former Brazilian model who went by the handle @FashionTravelPancakes. She always showed up on my explore page chowing down on a lamb skewer in Chefchaouen or eating crickets at a night market in Bangkok. Wearing a long pleated black skirt paired with a cropped neoprene vest was Kiki Chu, a pint-sized heiress from Hong Kong who went by the handle @Kikachu.

"Come over here!" Daphne demanded during a break. "Guys, this is Meg, one of my most favorite people ever!" Daphne exclaimed. "Meg, this is Kiki, Rebecca, and Dagmar." Now I noticed another member of their pack, ridiculously tall and dressed in head-to-toe camouflage like she'd just returned from Operation Desert Storm.

"Hi," Dagmar said. "You're pretty. Are you a fashion girl?" She spoke in a thick German accent, like a villain from a James Bond movie. Dagmar continued to fire off questions while the photographer resumed taking pictures. "How do you guys know each other?" "Are you on Instagram?" "How many followers do you have?" "Are you going to the dinner?" "How old are you?" "I'm at the George V but I hate it and want to move. The turn-down service is a joke and the honeymooners in the suite next to me won't stop bonking." "Where are you staying?"

Daphne shook her head "no" behind Dagmar's shoulder, implying that I shouldn't answer Dagmar's question.

"You're with us at Athenée, aren't you guys?" Kiki turned to Daphne, oblivious.

"Yeah, but it's also not great," Daphne lied. "The Dorchester group really needs to step up their shit. It's also not a good look, considering the Sultan of Brunei isn't exactly a fan favorite. But Le Bristol was all booked sooo…"

"I might be joining you later," Dagmar informed her.

Daphne shot me a look just as a stylist stepped in front of her to take her jacket and adjust her shoes. I looked down and noticed all four women had on the same atrocious sandals, each in a different color.

At the next break, when the others dispersed, I stole a minute with Daphne. "So what's the exciting news?" I asked.

"Oh!" Daphne plopped down in a director's chair with her handle painted on the back. "Can you hear the wedding bells? Susan wants to know if you would be willing to let your dog get married."

"Red can get married?" I looked at her in confusion.

"It's a whole collab with this new doggy detangler brush and they want two dogs to 'tie the knot.'"

"But aren't they anti-knots?" I was struggling to follow.

"Yeah, the pitch is that they get married, then they get groomed during the reception, and at the very end, the whole thing is annulled. It's a cute publicity stunt. *The New York Post* is going to cover it. Cha Cha is the bride, but they need another dog and I asked Susan if it could be yours. Anyway, we'd be doggie in-laws!" She smiled. "You'll only get twenty grand, but it should be easy for you. The dogs do all the work."

I coughed. That was a semester of private school. "Are you serious?"

Before Daphne could respond, the director, an older Frenchman with salt and pepper hair and enough ego to land a girlfriend far out of his league, screamed that he was ready. "Think about it," Daphne said.

Twenty thousand dollars. That was what Seth and Vigo had offered, and I still had only seen half of it. There was nothing to think about. "Red's in," I told her.

"Goody!" Daphne clapped her hands and smiled. "I'll get Susan to email you all the deets." And with that, she rushed to join the other girls.

I stood in place, watching the foursome laugh and pose as if the best of friends. Zoe brand reps swarmed the talent the moment the director yelled "Cut!" While Daphne said her goodbyes, I crept off to a private area where I could FaceTime with my family.

I was waiting for Iliya to pick up, aiming my phone at the Eiffel Tower, when Daphne slithered up from behind and rested her chin on my shoulder. "Let's go get a drink!" she said. "I need something strong if I'm going to get through tonight!"

"Yeah, sure," I said shakily. "I was just checking in with the boys. I wanted to catch Roman before he went to school," I explained, distracted by her head and wondering if she was going to move it before Iliya appeared on my phone.

"Did you do the math? It's already ten there," she informed me. "I've learned not to check in when I'm away. It's too easy to get sucked into whatever drama is going on at home."

There was still no answer on the tenth ring, so I hung up. I'd try again later.

"You haven't posted anything since we landed," Daphne informed me. "Zoe is expecting you to. They are hosting us, after all."

"Of course!" I said, caught off guard. How naive of me to think they were just operating out of the kindness of their hearts.

I held my phone up to the Eiffel Tower and took a shot. I posted the pic with the caption, "I was starting to worry that there weren't enough pictures of this tower on the internet," followed by all the Zoe hashtags I could think of.

Seeming pleased, Daphne wrapped her arm around me. She was in a chatty mood as we walked back to the hotel. "See what I mean about Dagmar! If you give her an inch... And what the fuck with asking how old you were? She's so weird. We can't let her wind up at our hotel because we will never be able to get rid of her." Daphne sighed. "How did I look in the shoot?"

"It was great. You looked gorgeous," I gushed. "The shoes are going to take a while to grow on me but —" A flock of young schoolgirls was heading toward us, with matching blazers and bobs straight out of a Madeline book. Daphne was too distracted to take note.

"Did I seem comfortable?" she asked. I told her she'd been in her element. "Good, I thought it went well too. Now at least you know that I'm not always a disaster." She went on, "I know there's room for improvement. I'm shooting my capsule collection for Revolve in February, so I really need to figure my shit out before then. The pieces look so good. I can't wait to get them on you." She paused to raise her finger. "And you will not forget to post them."

"I'm planning my rollout already," I told her.

Back at the hotel bar we ran into Kiki, the tiny heiress, and her entourage. Along with her personal makeup artist, a square-jawed blue-haired girl who looked like a Minecraft character, were a nerdy web designer who ran her blog and three gay BFFs she paid to keep her company.

The two of us sat at a nearby table sipping martinis as Daphne scrolled through her phone. A post Kiki had just uploaded revealed that she had suffered a seizure.

"It's so fucked up of her," Daphne said. "She gets everything. There isn't an issue this girl hasn't revealed. She's been ADD, OCD… had a UTI, a DUI… and even an SUI… although I suspect that one was a sponsored deal."

"SUI?"

"Stress urinary incontinence. She pees when she laughs. WHO CARES!"

"And now she ticks seizure off her list!" Daphne popped an olive in her mouth. "I suppose I'm just being jealous," she finally admitted. "I just don't get her appeal. Her style isn't even that original!" I glanced back at Kiki again, who I saw was wearing a unitard made entirely out of bottle caps. "Her grandfather is like the Sumner Redstone of Singapore, so visibility for her is easy. She hosted this show called *The Fake* where five strangers are thrown into a dinner party and have to pick out whose handbag is real and whose is a knock-off. It ran for sixteen seasons!" Daphne rolled her eyes. "I'm just internet famous. Not even… I'm app famous." Daphne sulked. "I need to get a third kid. It's really the only way to stay in the game."

"I still haven't met the two you *do* have," I said, trying to lighten the mood. "And you don't need more children to stay in the game. You *are* the game!" I protested. "What you've already done, most women only dream about. You didn't have any of this given to you. You built it with your own two Photoshopped hands," I said, swigging what remained of my overpriced cocktail.

Daphne laughed. "How do you know I Photoshop my hands?"

"Because you're a perfectionist. You don't let anything slip."

Daphne smiled at me like a guru pleased with her disciple's spiritual progress. "You're really learning how all this works."

I felt two large hands pressing down on my shoulders. For a second, I thought it was Iliya. "Meee again!" Dagmar's Teutonic singsong caused me to jump. "What are you guys going to do before dinner? Should we all go somewhere for drinks?"

Daphne looked up and smiled a fake smile. "I have to do an interview. There's a reporter coming from *Marie Claire*."

"Online or for the actual magazine?" I could hear the competitive streak in Dagmar's voice.

"They said both," Daphne replied.

"That usually means just online." Dagmar pressed her mouth into a frown. "*Argh*, they were giving me such a hard time up front about Helmut." She looked down at her purse and I realized the fluffy lining was actually a terrier. Helmut had milky eyes and a *Hedwig and the Angry Inch* bouffant.

"They thought he was a possum! Can you believe it? This guy who has three hundred thousand followers was mistaken for a rodent!" Dagmar announced loudly. "He could tell they were giving him no love and he was NOT happy. And you know how Helmut gets when he isn't happy."

As Daphne and I walked toward the elevator, she told me about Helmut's better days. In his younger years, back when he didn't look like a rat pumped full of formaldehyde, Helmut had been quite an Instagram sensation. At one point he even had a sister that looked just like him, but she was killed in an unspeakable gender-reveal accident.

"Now he's just scary to look at," Daphne said with a shudder. "That's why they didn't approach Dagmar for the doggy detangler deal. She is going to shit a brick when she finds out that we're doing it." She clasped her hands diabolically. "I can't wait for dinner!"

"Please don't bring it up," I said. "She scares me!"

"Oh, she's harmless. She's just weird."

We entered our room to find a bouquet of flowers sitting on the desk in the corner. There was a note. "Thank you for a successful day!" Daphne read out loud. "Can't wait to see you tonight. Love, Your Zoe Family."

Daphne uncorked her gifted bottle of Champagne and poured us each a generous glass. "They are so classy." Daphne mused, setting down her drink and snapping a pic with her phone. "I have to post these." She stalled. "What would you write?"

I pretended to be thinking, too buzzed to be of any real use.

"I already know that this post is going to underperform. If you've seen one bouquet of flowers you've seen them all." Daphne walked around the bed and came toward me slowly. My neck went warm, and I gulped.

"Why not write something ridiculous like, "My husband is too cheap to ever spring for bouquets this fancy. Thanks for always raising the bar @Zoe!" I said, looking out the window, scared she might be able to detect my nerves. She was standing so close to me.

A bright smile broke across her face. "You're just fucking

brilliant." She shook her head typing.

"I'm just awkward, is the truth," I corrected her. "I'm terrible with sentimentality." I could hear my voice catching. "Maybe I'm just scared of vulnerability."

"Or maybe you're just fucking funny."

Our faces were now so close that I could see the congested pores on Daphne's chin and the slight creases around her eyes. I wanted to kiss her and be her all at once.

"I..." I hesitated, as if standing on the ledge of a building deciding whether or not to jump. Before I could say anything else, my phone started ringing. My stomach lurched when I saw who it was: Marina.

I immediately answered.

"Meg." Marina coughed. "I have food poisoning. I've been vomiting my brains out all morning. Bodega sushi. My body is rejecting these toxins."

I was screwed. Iliya had his Chelsea House holiday party that night. Investors were going to be there, Saro was going to be there, everyone was going to be there. This wasn't just bad. This was really fucking bad.

"Where are you now?" I asked.

"I'm at my place," she replied.

"Wait, then who is with Felix? I double-checked the time.

"Iliya. I told him that I had a survey thing I had to go to because I was hoping that with enough fluids I could beat this thing, but it's not happening," she continued. "You have to tell my brother."

"Me? But you're the one who's sick!"

"If I do it, he's gonna think I'm lying," she countered.

"*Are* you lying?" I was pacing around the room, trying to sober up.

"I'm really sorry, Meg. I have to go hurl."

I stood there for a moment thinking about my options. It was six-thirty in Paris, so that meant that it was twelve-thirty in New York, still early enough to find someone. But who? Iliya's mother could barely see, Seth and Vigo knew nothing about children, and Bubby had the same obligation as Iliya. "Fuck." I let off a long exhale.

"What?" Daphne asked from the other side of the room, finishing the last of her Champagne.

"My sister-in-law is sick and Iliya has to be at this event he can't miss. We have no sitter." I started running through different scenarios in my mind. "He could put the kids down before he goes at eight. But that's if Roman actually goes to bed at eight. And even if he does go to bed at eight, who the hell is going to stay with them after? I have nobody."

"There's no nanny?" Daphne looked at me confused.

I shook my head.

"No weekend babysitter?" she asked.

"Nope." I tried to take a deep breath.

"A housekeeper? An intern? An au pair that you pay under the table?"

Daphne ran down the list as she started shooting off texts. Moments later, she looked up. "Okay, I got you someone. Wynne can do it."

"Wynne! The girl who gave us the clothes at your building that day?" I remembered liking her. I hoped I did anyway. "Can I trust her? Can she stay late? He's not going to be able to leave until his boss does."

"She's outstanding," Daphne said. "I've known her for at least ten years. Super trustworthy. And yes, she's a big girl, she can stay up late." I tried not to watch as Daphne changed into a tailored two-piece suit, ditching her bra and buttoning the jacket at her navel. "You can trust her, trust me. I just shared her number with you." Daphne pulled her locks into a clip, then dropped to the floor. "Where are my Manolos?" Daphne giggled. "Where the fuck are they? Did they walk away?"

I looked over at the bar and saw the Champagne bottle was empty. I'd only had half a glass.

Just then, the phone rang. The interviewer from *Marie Claire* was waiting in the lobby. Daphne was in no condition to be talking to anyone with a recording device, but I knew better than to stand in her way.

"Be downstairs in an hour," Daphne said, grabbing her bag. As she stumbled into the hall, she had more instructions for me. "Do the sequined dress. And wear your hair up."

"At your service," I called after her.

As soon as I was alone, I texted with Wynne and explained my situation. If she could drop whatever her plans for the night were and watch my kids while I cavorted with Instagram stars halfway across the world, she'd be saving my life (I didn't get into the cavorting part). The second she agreed, I called Iliya, who was too frazzled to put up a fight.

"And you know her?" he double-checked.

"Of *course*, I know her, Iliya. And your sister loves her," I said, stress-eating all the Jordan almonds in the mini bar.

"And what about the kids?"

"The kids aren't even going to see her. This is Daphne's nanny of over ten years. She's practically part of their family. Just order her a pizza and tell her to make herself at home." I was now standing in front of the wardrobe rack, deep in a staring contest with the incredible sequined dress.

"How is everything else?" I said, thumbing through the other dresses on the rack. I stopped to process a not-so-classic LBD with a built-in bustier for three breasts.

Iliya was still unloading about the stress of single parenting when I tuned back into the conversation. "He doesn't want to wear clothes and if he does, he wants them to be matching but what is the problem with mixing navy and gray? I'm no fashion icon but what the fuck?"

"And Red?" I asked.

"RED? He won't even wear black!"

"Not the color, our dog!"

Iliya grunted. "Same as when you left. I called the vet and she said to bring him in but I was waiting for you to schedule."

"Is it urgent? Because if it's urgent, Iliya, just take him. I have a deal where he is going to make us twenty-grand, so I need him healthy."

"You want me to take him to the vet for one of your *deals*?"

Shame churned through me. "No, he's clearly sick and I want him to get better. But that's a lot of money," I pointed out. "Can you just call the vet and see what options are available?"

"Can *you* call? I'm trying to do a lot of things here, Meg. I didn't even go to work today!"

"I get it, you're a big deal. But it's not my fault that your sister ate shitty tuna rolls. I'm trying to help. And I'm halfway around the world."

"I'm well aware of that," he said, his resentment oozing through the phone.

I took a deep breath. "Look, I don't want to fight. I appreciate you letting me take a weekend trip."

"Thursday's not really the weekend," Iliya pointed out, then changed gears. "So how is it?"

I walked to the window and drew back the curtain. The view of a brick wall wasn't exactly on par with the one offered by our first room, but it was still a brick wall in *Paris*. "It's been flying by," I told him. "We've been so busy I haven't really seen the sights. But it's magical here and the city looks so gorgeous with all the likes."

"Stop," Iliya said. "Did you just say, 'with all the *likes*'?"

"No. I said *lights*. It looks gorgeous with all the lights. For the holidays."

"What time is it there? Have you been drinking?" he asked judgmentally.

"Not really…. A bit," I admitted.

Iliya didn't say anything for a moment. The silence was worse than hearing whatever thought about me was running through his mind.

After we got off, I looked at the clock and realized that I needed to get down to the lobby. Daphne was a stickler about time, at least when it pertained to the punctuality of other people.

CHAPTER TWENTY-NINE

The green sequined Zoe dress had a giant slit that ran from the bottom left hem all the way up to my right hip, as I discovered once I'd slipped into it. I'd never shown so much leg in my life. Not even back in the day when my body was nothing but legs. Stepping into a pair of heels, I looked at the woman in the mirror and felt a surge of confidence. The buzz helped, sure, but I felt like a million bucks. Or whatever the Zoe dress retailed for.

When I came downstairs, Daphne was sitting at the bar whispering into a brunette woman's ear. The moment she saw me, she jerked back and stopped speaking. A group of French businessmen turned their heads to ogle me as I walked past them.

"Meg." Daphne smiled, unable to stop staring at the slit up my leg. "What a dress!" She stared a moment longer, then remembered the person to her left.

"This is Alek, she's one of my most favorite people ever."

So she had multiple "most favorite people ever," perhaps one in every port. I tried not to grimace at "Alek," the mystery woman Lauren had compared me to in that unmistakably worrisome tone once upon a rooftop dinner party. Now that I was standing closer to "Alek" (I still couldn't think about her without the quotes), I saw that she looked just like me, only about ten years younger. Same brown eyes, same pretty enough face, same bushy eyebrows. Only difference was her dark hair. I felt a little queasy.

"Nice to meet you," Alek said, clearly having the same thought I was but playing things far more cool. "Love that look. It's a killer."

"*She's* a killer," Daphne corrected. "Anyway, we should get going. It was really good to see you, A."

"You too," Alek said wistfully. "Do you know when you'll be

back to town?"

"Not for a while, baby." The second the word came out of her mouth, I felt something inside me burst.

Daphne kissed Alek on both cheeks while clocking my reaction out of the corner of her eye. Alek looked at me too. "I used to have that hair color," Alek said.

"You did… It looked great on you." Daphne smiled. Alek gave a sigh and watched us head out.

Once we were in the car on the way to dinner, I couldn't resist asking Daphne about her friend. "How do you know Alek?"

"We met a few years back. She used to live in Dumbo. Good girl. Super talented writer. But young. Too young for me."

Overcome with jealousy, I turned to the window and gazed at the Seine.

"She brought us party favors." Daphne opened her clutch and pulled out a bag of white powder. She dipped her pinky nail into the bag, shoveling up a bump that promptly disappeared up her nose. "I can't wait for you to see this dinner. Salvatore is a fucking trip. Have some?"

"I… I should probably eat something."

Daphne playfully shoved my shoulder. "Come on, you love it. Cocaine, concerts, and what was the third one?"

"Cult status movies." I softened slightly. She remembered our first text exchange.

"That's it," Daphne said, sliding closer. She excavated more white powder and held her nail up to my nose. I inhaled and could almost immediately feel my heart speeding up.

The car stopped in front of a wide stone stairway leading down to the water. A white riverboat waited at the dock below, with tuxedo-clad men ready to help us aboard. In the boat's lavishly decorated parlor, fashion influencers, VIP shoppers, and a smattering of corporate types bantered, waiting to take their seats at a long table that stretched the length of the ship. Dagmar and Kiki were among the few attendees I recognized.

Daphne pointed to a beautiful man in red leather pants and chain-link shirt holding court in the corner. "That is Salvatore. Isn't he hot?"

With long curly hair, exaggerated cheekbones and kohl-rimmed Jared Leto eyes, Salvatore *was* sexy in an androg kind of way. He seemed like the kind of guy who might try to suck your blood one night and then make you watch him suck himself off the next. Salvatore smiled lasciviously as we approached. He then pointed at me and kissed his fingers. "*Très magnifique.*"

"I think he likes your dress." Daphne laughed.

"Thank god," I said, my heart still pumping faster than I was used to. "He definitely seems like someone who wouldn't hold back if he didn't."

"You okay?" Daphne asked. "You seem a little off."

Before I could respond, a waiter rang a bell signaling for everyone to be seated. As soon as we sat down, large towers filled with oysters, shrimp, and tuna tartare materialized on the table. In front of each plate was a gift box, neatly wrapped in white paper with a sterling-colored bow. Several photographers circled the table like fish swimming in and out of a coral reef, documenting the proceedings from every angle.

Sitting across from me was a wacky-looking designer chick from Silver Lake named Jane who went by the handle @JanesAddictions. She had aqua hair and wore a necklace that informed people she was bipolar.

"I hope it's the Chinese handcuff bracelet! I've been coveting one since last year." Jane tore into her box and pulled out a keychain. "Really?" She turned to Dagmar, waving the gift in her face. "Is he kidding with these? What are my kids going to say?" Hanging from the sterling silver key loop was what looked like a tiny mold of somebody's cock and balls.

"I wanted to share a piece of my heart with you but found the 'heart' thing a bit of a cliché so instead decided to give you an organ I liked better," Salvatore shared with a glint in his eyes. "They are my body!" He paused for effect. "We did a limited number, and these will NEVER be available for purchase! Only for my most beloved."

Daphne looked at me. "I told you we'd need drugs for this."

The Champagne continued to flow as a sixteen-course meal unfolded before us, each plate more decadent than the next.

"The service sucks here." Dagmar stared at me like it was my fault. "And I was in the middle of fishing." She went on to explain what she meant. Fishing, it turned out, was sending messages to the Instagram accounts of random companies in the hopes that they might send products in exchange for a post. "Sometimes they don't even respond, they just leave you as 'seen.'" She sighed. "But that's half the fun. It's strangely therapeutic. Like biting your toenails."

After several vodka shots, Jane started waving her new keychain in the air. "So seriously, whose keychain do I need to suck to get seated front row at the show tomorrow?"

Daphne did a spit take, Champagne spraying everywhere. She couldn't contain her laughter. I pretended to think Jane's joke was just as funny as Daphne did. But I wasn't a good enough actress.

I had to give it to her. Jane was quick. And I was feeling slow. I tried to look for openings where I could and remind Daphne that I was the funny one, but I was too off my face. I could feel myself spinning out of conversational relevance as Daphne slipped through my fingers.

Salvatore clinked his glass and gave a toast. "Each of you is here because of your dedication to fashion. I am honored that you have supported Zoe for all these years and stand with me as we revolutionize the hiking sandal. You are all — how do you say? My little cabbages."

I looked down at my keychain again. "These are cabbages? I thought they were supposed to be testicles."

I was louder than I'd realized. Salvatore shot me a look. He wasn't amused. "I love your guyliner!" I squeaked.

I scurried off to the bathroom as soon as Salvatore's remarks had concluded. Trying to get a hold of myself, I splashed cold water on my face. A knock came at the door. At first I didn't answer, but there was another one, this time more urgent.

I cracked open the door and Daphne pushed her way in. I thought she was going to berate me or slap me back to my senses. But instead, she grabbed my body and began kissing me. Her tongue pressed into my mouth as she pushed me up against the mirror. She pinned one arm against the wall as she moved her hand up my dress, groping between my thighs. I'd envisioned this moment so many times, yet I was paralyzed with fear. Did I want to do this? Before I could practice restraint and tell her that I loved my husband or join her in her passion, she stopped and pulled away. "That's better. Now you look a little more relaxed." I stared at her, out of breath. "Do you want another bump?" she asked casually, cutting up a line and snorting it straight off the sink.

I was shaking. "I'm fine."

Daphne smiled, as if nothing had just transpired between us. "You feel better? You okay?" She patted me softly on the cheek.

"That was hot. Let's do that again sometime." And then she vanished.

I stood there for a good five minutes trying to understand what had just happened. Part of me wanted her to fuck my brains out while the other part of me wanted never to see her again. What game was she playing? Whatever the answer, I was losing.

When I returned to the table, I found that Daphne had helped herself to my seat so that she could be closer to Jane. She was regaling her with the exact same stories she'd told when we first met. Daphne finally acknowledged me, all bubbly. "Meg, you have to keep Jane company at the show tomorrow. You guys are going to be seated together!"

"You and I are the low-level influencers who didn't make the front-row cut." Jane laughed.

"That's not true!" Daphne insisted. "You guys are still in Paris at the Zoe show! Think of how many girls wish they were in your shoes right now."

"You mean our hiking sandals," Jane said. She couldn't keep the annoyance from her tone. "You know only the front row gets photographed. We are just tagalongs. There is a big difference between sitting next to Cardi B and the guy who does her makeup."

Jane was upset but Daphne was cracking up. "You are so funny!" She was squealing. "I can't believe we've never hung out before!"

Daphne was over me. I could see it in her eyes. I knew her better than she knew herself. She'd found a new favorite. Or a new "most favorite" as she was prone to calling us.

The dinner refused to end. And all I wanted to do was to go back to the hotel. But Daphne was still too high to turn in after the boat docked. "We're gonna go to a club by the Bastille," Daphne informed me.

"Who is we?" I already knew the answer.

"Oh, me and Jane and a few of the other girls. But you seem tired. You should go get some rest. Show starts at nine a.m. tomorrow."

Blinking back tears, I looked at Daphne. She was scanning the crowd, trying to find Jane. What point was there in trying to fix things? I just nodded along and told her that I'd see her in the morning.

The hotel phone woke me up. Well, that and a pounding headache.

"Hello?" I answered.

The voice on the other end was speaking French. All I could make out was something about "le glam team."

"Okay," I said, groggily reaching for the lights and looking around the room for Daphne. There was a knock at the door. I rushed to get it and almost tripped over the body splayed out on the floor. It was Daphne's. Her phone was still secured tightly in her hand and one of her shoes was on.

"One second!" I called out as I tried shaking her awake.

"Daphne. DAPHNE!" I slapped her face, but she still didn't budge. With no other option, I opened the door.

"What are you going to do?" Marie, a nicotine-stained makeup artist, asked when she took in the situation.

"She's not going anywhere," said Chuckie, a towering man with dreadlocks and a duffle bag full of hair pieces.

"She has to," Marie said, panicking. "If she isn't there, she will be blacklisted. Nobody will work with her again. Us, too. You know how Salvatore gets. This is going to come back on us. She's in the front row and he's expecting us to deliver her!"

Chuckie hummed ominously as the three of us carried Daphne

to the bed.

"Daphne?" I called her name one more time. Daphne suddenly sat up and looked at me, a glint of recognition in her eyes.

"Hi, baby." She smiled, then turned her head in the other direction and vomited all over a pillow. Before I could react, she rolled over and passed out again.

"*Dégueulasse!*" Marie shuddered. "You know what's going to happen. It will all be my fault. I'm good as sacked." She picked up the cordless phone on the bedside table and threw it at Chuckie's shoulder. "We both are."

"*Merde!*" Chuckie exclaimed.

It was already almost eight o'clock. The show started at nine and there was no way in hell Daphne was going to make it.

"You look enough like her. Why don't you just go?" Chuckie suggested. "I have her hair pieces here. We can match the length exactly."

"Are you kidding?" I cried.

Chuckie looked at me. "It's not like she's famous. She's internet famous."

"Worse! She's app famous," Marie added.

"And it's not like these girls look like their posts in real life anyway," Chuckie said, growing excited.

"*C'est genial!*" Marie exclaimed, lighting up a Gauloise.

"This is utterly batshit," I said.

"You have a better idea?" Marie stared at me.

I didn't. I was furious with Daphne, but I wasn't going to let her piss her career away over one drunken night. Thank god Iliya was fast asleep and half a world away. I could only imagine what his advice would be.

"Do you know which look she's supposed to wear?" Marie

flipped through the wardrobe rack like she was searching for a misplaced record.

"No idea." I shook my head.

"The Zoe publicist has certain pieces already reserved for bigger celebs," Marie explained, picking Daphne's phone up off the floor and handing it to me. "Well, go through her messages and find out."

I glanced at the clock.

"*Allez-y!*" Marie exclaimed. "We're running out of time."

I pulled Daphne's head toward her phone, using the face recognition feature to unlock it. Scrolling through her most recent emails, I found an update from the Zoe team. I had my choice between the boiled wool tube dress with cut-out nipples or the mustard silk culottes and raincoat made out of what looked like used condoms. I opted for the latter.

I grabbed Marie's cigarette out of her hand and took a drag, psyching myself up. "Okay," I said. "Let's do this."

CHAPTER THIRTY

The Zoe show was held inside a former Yiddish theater in Northern Paris that had been transformed into the Garden of Eden. I was beset with a case of nerves, but the paparazzi lining the streets seemed untroubled by the sight of me disembarking the car. I'd already disabled the lock on Daphne's phone, so it was with ease that I could post "her" updates in the moments leading up to the big event. While Daphne and I had similar hair, especially now thanks to the seven pounds of extensions weighing my head down, we still didn't look alike. She was model-gorgeous, with ample cleavage. I was plain and ordinary, with no boobs and a math teacher ass. But the glam team had done one hell of a job. The people that I needed to dupe — aka the people who didn't really know Daphne — would be none the wiser.

An assistant checked Daphne's name off a list, then escorted me and Daphne's oversized sunglasses to her front-row seat. Every time a camera snapped, I tried to pull my hair over my face or glance down at my sandals.

Kiki scurried in and helped herself to the seat next to me. Dressed in a fur-collared shirt and leather pants with a detachable zebra tail, she looked like some kind of dominatrix-minotaur crossbreed.

"Can you believe Tony, Jhoni, and Tao weren't even allowed to sit on the balcony?" she said distractedly. She was busy on her phone, refreshing the Zoe hashtag.

"That's wild," I said.

Another moment passed before Kiki looked up at me. She gasped. "What the fuck? Where's Daphne?"

My heart pounded and my eyes flared. The lights were starting to dim. "She's still at the hotel sick. Please just go with it." I picked up Daphne's phone and started shooting.

"You even know what you're doing with that thing?" Kiki asked like I was holding a buzz saw.

"I have a pretty good idea." I nodded, adding a filter to the video and tagging both Daphne and Kiki.

The room was pitch black, silent but for the sound of a heartbeat. Gradually, the noise built into a screeching cacophony of animals mating or dying, I wasn't entirely sure. Models strutted down the runway in their Diva Tevas looking hungry and like they wanted to fight. The mud on the catwalk splashed onto the front row with each intentional stomp. The music got louder and more intense. I felt a dollop of mud hit my cheek. And then — no models, no lights, no sound. The whole thing lasted under five minutes.

"That's *it*?" I turned to Kiki, confused.

"Yeah, it's always shorter than you think." She nodded. "That was brilliant though." The lights came back up and all of the models returned to the stage for a victory lap. They were covered head to toe in muck, making it impossible to see any of the outfits. Finally, Salvatore stepped out, in a simple and immaculately clean sweatsuit.

He waved and blew kisses to the audience. It wasn't until he turned to walk off stage that I noticed that his sweats were assless. I snapped a pic and gave it a very Daphne caption. "Suns out Buns out," I wrote, followed by several beach umbrella emojis and Zoe hashtags. Kiki looked over my shoulder. I could tell she was impressed by my work.

By eleven I was back at the hotel, giddy as a cat burglar who'd just cleaned out the Isabella Stewart Gardner Museum. I was eager to tell Daphne all about my success, but when I entered our room, it was empty. I reached for the phone in my bag and tried to call

Daphne, only to remember I was calling her on her own device. I then tried my own number. The ringing came from under the bed. I pulled my phone out to see that I had twenty-six missed calls and fifteen text messages.

"Oh my god." My stomach dropped. Why hadn't I brought both phones with me?

The first message was from Wynne. "Your dog is super sick and is having diarrhea. I have to take him downstairs. I texted your husband but haven't heard back. Hope it's okay."

The next text was from Iliya and came almost twenty minutes later. "Meg, pick up the PHONE. The fire department is at our apartment and the babysitter isn't answering."

The third text simply read: "MEGAN!"

I stopped reading the rest and called Iliya. He'd been trying to reach me since nine a.m. Which was three a.m. his time.

"Iliya!" I was relieved to hear his voice, but terrified of what he might tell me. He was seething. "Where the fuck were you?"

"I was… at a fashion show." As the words came out of my mouth I was flooded with guilt.

"That girl you hired." He was so furious that he could barely finish his sentences without stopping to catch his breath. "She isn't a nanny. She barely knows your friend. How could you be so insanely irresponsible!?"

"Stop, Iliya. Just tell me, are the kids okay?" My entire body was shaking.

"The kids are fine." He paused. "The apartment… isn't. The fire department had to break down the front door."

"What are you talking about?" I exclaimed.

"She was reheating pizza in the oven when she locked herself out."

"Why was she out of the apartment?"

"Red was having diarrhea all over the floor," he grunted. "She ran out with him and left her phone inside. The neighbors called Ken and he called me."

"Oh my god." I was crying.

"Roman was scared to death, Meg. I don't know what we are doing to that kid, but it isn't good."

"I'm so sorry." I was slobber-crying. "Can I talk to him?"

"Not right now." His voice was cold. "I just got him back to sleep. I'll see you tomorrow. You're still coming home, right?"

"Of course." I sniffled as I got off the phone.

"What the fuck is wrong with you?" Daphne seethed, bursting through the door.

"What the fuck is wrong with *me*?" I screamed. "Are you kidding? I thought you said that Wynne was trustworthy. She nearly killed my sons!"

"What kind of weird *Single White Female* game are you playing?" Daphne walked straight up to me, ripping a clip-in extension off my head. She was not concerned about the welfare of my family.

"You told me that Wynne was your nanny." Anger flooded my voice.

"I never said that," Daphne scoffed.

"Yes you did. You told me that she'd worked for you for ten years. That I could trust her with my children!" I shot back.

"Meg, you just hijacked my phone and went to the fucking Zoe show in my place! Is that what this has been all about? Do you think that you are me? Because you're not. And you never will be."

"Daphne, you were drunk and passed out in your own vomit. I went to save your ass!"

"Save me!? You wore the mustard silk culottes and that was the same look that Cardi B was in. That's all anybody is talking about!" She snatched her phone out of my hand. "I need some air." The door slammed behind her.

I sat there, paralyzed and scared of all that I was on the brink of losing, if I hadn't lost it already. Instead of giving in to my desire to start throwing furniture around the room like a member of Mötley Crüe, I washed off my war paint and ripped out the rest of my fake hair. I'd get on an earlier flight.

CHAPTER THIRTY-ONE

Twelve hours later, I slipped through the busted-up door to our apartment. It was nine p.m. New York time and Iliya was sitting in the living room waiting for me.

"Hey," I said cautiously. I couldn't read Iliya's expression. "Are the boys asleep?" I put down my things and walked over to Red. He was on his side. He let off the faintest of whimpers. "Maybe I should take him in tonight," I said, worried.

"Maybe," Iliya replied. "Or maybe you should just call Tom and Rita and see if they have any thoughts."

I was speechless.

"Tell me something." He got up to hand me a printed copy of my school statement. "Did you even read this thing through?"

"Apparently *you* did," I replied. "Is there a problem?"

"Do you even recall what you wrote? Because it's fucking insane!"

I glared at him. "You just don't like playing the game, but this is what everybody does."

"Claim to be Olympic athletes?"

"I was writing ad copy. And ads always overpromise!" I insisted.

Iliya shook his head in disbelief. "Do you hear yourself? Listen to how frantic you sound."

"I'm not frantic! I'm trying to keep our son from falling through the cracks!"

"How about you just work on keeping him safe in his own home! Do you understand what we could have been dealing with here? I thought the police were going to arrest me for child endangerment." Iliya's voice was getting froggy, the way it did when he was about to cry.

Before he could continue, we heard a thud from the kitchen. I turned to check on Red. The spot on the floor where he'd been resting was empty. I felt all the blood drain from my face.

It's weird when an animal drops dead. You just don't hear about it happening all too often, but that's what happens. Or happened to Red, anyway. One minute he was there, the next he'd toppled over and was gone. When I saw his sweet body on the kitchen floor, I let out a shriek. I threw myself on top of him, sobbing.

I'd had Red since he was a baby. Since I was baby. I was twenty-one years old when I got him. He'd known me longer than Iliya had. Our relationship changed when I moved in with Iliya and kept changing when I had Roman and then Felix, but he'd remained my faithful sidekick. I'd often pictured him dying, sometimes because of his age and other times because I didn't feel like walking him. But I always expected his passing to be more theoretical and gradual.

I would never get over what had just happened. I'd hardly petted him when I'd walked through the smashed-in door. I'd spent the last moments of his life screaming at my husband, and the last six months of his life staring at my phone. No wonder he'd collapsed. Who wouldn't have?

Iliya stayed home with the boys while I took Red's body to the 24-hour vet. The doctor explained that heart attacks in dogs were extremely rare and that any vet telling someone that their pet had a heart attack was in fact just lying out of sheer laziness. Maybe he had an aneurysm, maybe there had been internal bleeding. She couldn't really say without sending pieces of him to a lab. I wished that she would have just lied to me and said that it was a heart attack.

I left her office that night with nothing but a receipt and a small

Ziploc bag filled with a mound of his hair for remembrance. When I returned, Iliya was sitting on the couch with Roman curled between his legs, fast asleep.

"I paid the extra hundred to have him cremated," I said. I walked toward Iliya and collapsed into his arms.

"Good." He enveloped me in a hug as I soaked his shirt with tears. Even if he was still angry, Iliya put that aside and was there for me in my moment of grief. Which only made me cry harder. I didn't deserve him. I kept crying as I mourned my former dog and my former self.

My sobbing eventually woke Roman. From the look on his face, I could tell that Iliya had already tried explaining what had happened. "Mommy, where is he? Where did you take him?"

"I..." As much as I wanted to shield my son from the harsh realities of human existence, I was not going to win a war against the world. "Red went to Kevin's, honey."

"Forever?" he asked.

"For now," I answered. I squeezed his body tightly, as if by applying pressure I could somehow stop his aching.

I waited until the next morning to text Daphne and tell her what had happened. I knew that I shouldn't reach out, but a part of me was still hoping she'd be the friend I thought she was.

"Oh, no. So sorry, babe!" she replied casually. "I'll tell Susan. I'm sure she can find another dog. They wanted to do it on New Year's Eve, which is just annoying. Who wants to spend their New Year's Eve working? It's for the best."

I was trembling. *What* was for the best... *My dog's death?* I wanted to shake her and make her see how hurtful she was being. But I didn't want to risk more rejection. So I let it go.

Two weeks after Red's passing, I found myself still reaching to fill his water bowl and searching for his torso in my bed. I was sleeping alone, since Iliya had co-opted the couch. He needed space and was still unable to speak with me about anything that didn't concern the kids. In other words, he was pissed. And he didn't even know the half of it.

In an effort to assuage Iliya's anger, I invited his family for Christmas Eve. Iliya seemed appreciative, though he could barely meet my eye. While the turkey cooked in our god-awful oven, Iliya caught up with his mother, sister, and her dentist date. I hid out in the bathroom.

From my perch on the toilet seat, I stared at a picture of Daphne and Kip in Saint Barts. Tanya and Howie were there, too, and Lauren and her husband appeared to be staying nearby, on someone's yacht. I assumed all the kids were in tow but hadn't yet seen them posted. All of the Insta stories were videos of sweaty women spraying each other with magnums of Champagne, claiming that they were "100 percent THAT BITCH."

I hadn't seen Daphne since Paris. It almost felt like it had all been a dream. In a picture that she captioned, "I've got 99 problems but a beach ain't one!" Daphne looked happy, without a care in the world. I missed her, but I also saw through her smile. She used to make my stomach do somersaults. Now she just made me nauseous.

I left her page but didn't get up. Instead, I posted a picture of myself sitting on the toilet and captioned it, "Somehow my mother-in-law managed to get herself re-invited to Christmas. If anybody needs me, I'll be in my office." I now had over 75,000 followers who were all waiting to hear what I'd done for the holidays. My bathroom selfie would likely disappoint them. But not posting anything would disappoint them more.

"Meg?" Iliya knocked on the door. "Everything okay?" He knew I hadn't so much as unbuttoned my pants. He knew I was sitting there staring at my screen, snorting up content.

"Yeah. One sec!" I said, deleting the picture and opening the door.

"This arrived." He held up an envelope. "Some weird dude."

Inside was a Christmas card along with the remainder of my NBD retainer fee. I looked at Iliya. "Did Vigo drop this off?"

"Does he braid his bangs?" Iliya asked.

"No, that's Seth." I smiled softly. "That was cool of him."

I stepped into the living room feeling guilty for ever having doubted them. Seth and Vigo may have been nuts, but they were good nuts.

Roman burrowed into the pile of presents like a pig rooting around for truffles.

Dasha was grilling Irving, Marina's divorced dentist boyfriend. "So, what exactly is your intention with my Marina?"

Irving wasn't as old as I'd pictured. Whenever Marina had spoken about him or his kids, I'd envisioned him with an oxygen tank like that little man in the wheelchair who married Anna Nicole Smith. But Irving seemed youthful and sweet. He also clearly liked Marina a lot. I could tell he was the kind of guy who made plans and actually followed through. The kind of person who sent flowers and sat Shiva with you after you lost your dog. A memory of Red floated to mind, and I tried to push it back where it came from. Roman was simultaneously ripping into two presents. "Hey, kiddo!" I called out. "Save some for the morning."

Marina was telling her mother about her and Irving's plans for New Year's. "We're going to Boca!" Marina sounded giddy.

"I have a small condo there and a little time off," Irving said, modestly.

"Do you make a good living?" Dasha asked. "My Marina drives a Mercedes." I caught Iliya's eye, and we shook our heads at each other.

"He knows, Ma," Marina said.

Evidently mortified, Iliya announced he was taking Felix to bed.

"And you know she's studying to be a nurse." Dasha brought a game of Yahtzee and a small box over to Roman, then sat back down on her ever-present inflatable pillow on the couch.

"A nurse?" Irving shot Marina a look of confusion. "I didn't know that."

Marina hadn't been in nursing school in over a year, but still hadn't worked up the courage to tell her mother she'd dropped out.

"I'm a woman of many masks," she said.

I was pretty sure she meant "many talents" but Irving didn't seem to care. He placed a hand on her knee and smiled at her like a lovestruck teen.

"Open it," Dasha instructed Roman.

"Wow! A knife! Thank you!" Roman exclaimed.

"No knives!" I said, snatching the weapon out of Roman's clutches.

My objections were lost on Dasha, who was back to grilling Irving.

"How many kids do you have?" Dasha asked. "Where's the mother? She's probably feeling quite intimidated seeing my Marina on your arm."

"Well, I have two and they haven't met. I really don't want the kids knowing that I'm dating quite yet. This all happened so suddenly." Irving smiled.

"You don't want the kids knowing about her? Why not? She's

perfect! She's a ten! No, she's a twelve!"

Iliya interrupted the interrogation as he returned to the room, presenting his mother with a gift.

Dasha opened the small box to find a pair of gold hoop earrings I'd picked out in the jewelry district and a larger box filled with a bunch of free face products that I'd been asked to post about.

"You shouldn't have!" she said, when I was pretty sure what she actually meant was, "You should have a long time ago!"

Marina explained some of the more cutting-edge creams to her mom while Irving pulled me aside. "How am I doing?"

"Good. I think she really likes you," I whispered. "Did you make her a night guard?"

"A great one."

"Cool. I know she's into that." I smiled, then looked over at Roman, who was chomping on a candy cane he'd pulled off the tree.

"Think he'll need braces?"

"Hard to tell." Irving shrugged. "Most kids do."

Our eyes met, and it took every ounce of restraint not to suggest that he and I do a "collab."

CHAPTER THIRTY-TWO

Our move was scheduled for January 2. Our bags were already packed, and there wasn't much to do but wait. Every time I looked on Instagram, I fell deeper into a depression. People's holiday vacations and adventures unfolded before me with up-to-the-moment footage from Grand Cayman, Whistler, Hawaii, Switzerland, Cabo, Aspen, and even the Maldives. Everyone but me was #livingtheirbestlife somewhere wildly romantic, sporting either Brazilian bikinis or brightly colored puffer jackets.

As luck would have it, NBD was shaping up to be one of the biggest earning products of the holiday season. Our campaign didn't just work — it *rocked*. Every time I logged into my account, a sponsored post popped up with Daphne's face. She was going to haunt me forever, and it was nobody's fault but my own.

Iliya had New Year's Eve off, but we had no real plans. Marina was in Boca with her darling dentist. Tanya and Lauren were still in the islands, and Daphne was now somewhere over New Jersey. I only knew because she posted a picture of her legs on a private jet heading into Teterboro.

We were free to pop by Chelsea House but going to a big party was the last thing Iliya was in the mood for. He went to pick up takeout from one of his favorite spots in Chinatown while I stayed back with the boys.

I was bathing Felix when my phone pinged. I couldn't resist checking to see if it was her. The notification was a message from Susan. "It could be you next time!" She'd attached a picture of Daphne standing next to none other than @JanesAddictions at the Doggy Detangler event. When I canceled, I didn't get into the details. I didn't want to relive the experience again or deal with any more condolence texts or flowers. I simply said that Red was unavail.

Daphne's caption talked about how a portion of the proceeds from each detangler would go to the ASPCA, and how she was honored to be involved with a company whose ethos and regard for pet welfare mirrored her own. I snarled at "ethos." Daphne didn't even know what that word meant. Not only did she not care that I was going through a personal tragedy, she was also selfish enough to take the twenty grand and do the detangling deal without me. I was trembling. People threw offers at Daphne all the time. She could have passed on this. She *should* have passed on this.

I scooped Felix out of the water, wrapping his body in a towel. After I wrangled him into his pjs, I caved and went to Daphne's feed to see what else she'd posted. I watched a clip of Cha Cha walking down a makeshift aisle toward Dagmar's dog, Helmut. He was wearing a tuxedo and looked like the canine version of Bernie from *Weekend at Bernie's*. "Red would have hated Cha Cha anyway," I told myself. She was too basic and purebred. It would have been over from the first butt sniff.

Feeling betrayed, I wrote a comment under the picture of the happy couple. "Cherish these moments," I typed. "They grow up so fast." I couldn't help myself. I had to say something just to let her know that she wasn't getting away with anything and that her dog would die someday too.

CHAPTER THIRTY-THREE

New York in January was all slush and drudgery, which was actually fine by me. There was comfort to be found in the joylessness permeating the entire city. I wasn't the only one having a rough go of it.

After dropping Roman off at school, I stopped in at a coffee shop to do some journaling before heading to work. I'd been trying to get my head back on straight and writing about it was cheaper than seeing a therapist. Seated at a table in the back corner, I wrote about my efforts to get acquainted with my new neighborhood via exploring every single corner market ("good deli cats, meh produce") and my search for a local gym ("nowhere where you have to learn a routine or sweat in the dark"). I wrote about how I still wondered if Iliya would ever stop hating me (he wouldn't), and I promised that I would not reach out to Daphne, nor would I comment on her posts "NO MATTER WHAT, pinky swear, dear diary." I made it to half a page of jottings before I gave in to the temptation to look at my phone. When I opened Instagram, I almost sprayed my espresso across the table as one of Daphne's posts appeared on my screen. She was holding a pregnancy test and frowning.

"It was a blighted ovum, which I guess is quite common, but this is my second miscarriage. And my hopes of having a third child are really starting to dwindle," Daphne wrote, followed by an announcement in all caps that she would be taking a hiatus from social media in order to give herself "TIME TO HEAL."

I clicked on her account, noting that her hiatus had lasted all of twenty-five minutes before she posted again with a video of her face trying not to move or blink, like she was one of those living statues you find in Washington Square Park. "I love you like Kanye loves Kanye," she wrote. The Visine that she'd clearly squirted into her eyes pooled in both tear ducts instead of falling down her cheeks, as I'm sure she would have preferred.

The blighted ovum story was a direct rip-off of Heidi Glick's share from the Mompire dinner. It was now clear that there was no boundary she wouldn't cross. No secret too sacred to share with the free world. Predictably, Daphne's follower count jumped by the hundreds each time I refreshed the page. Just then, a blocked number appeared on my phone. The only person I knew with a blocked number was Susan, who'd been angling to get me to sign with her ever since the doggy deal fell apart.

In a haze of disillusionment, I picked up. "Susan?"

"No, dear. It's Marilyn. I wanted to call because I was truly moved by your application and well, I just feel terrible that we aren't going to be able to accommodate your son Roman next year at Abington. Emails are going out today. I'm not sure if you've received yours yet."

I gulped. "I haven't." I tried to hear her out, but my mind had gone numb.

"We just had so many worthy candidates this season," she went on. "And the board can only offer so many scholarships."

I wanted to believe Marilyn, but I just couldn't. It didn't add up. Or rather, it did. I was paying the price for my misadventure. Daphne was still pissed and wanted to punish me.

"Is this because of Daphne?" I blurted out.

"I'm sorry?"

"Did Daphne Cole say something to you?" I asked, my head spinning. "Did she tell you not to accept my son?"

"I'm sorry, I still don't follow," Marilyn said. "Why would Daphne Cole weigh in when she doesn't even have children at this school?"

"What?" I could hardly see straight. I thought she was a school mom. Was there validity in anything I believed? Was Daphne even a real person? Was she even a *mom*?

I managed a meek "thank you" as I got off the phone with Marilyn and immediately started looking back through Daphne's page at the pictures of her pregnancy. She never showed her actual belly. She'd bounced back after a month. When I was at her place, there were no signs of children. It was all sinking in: The look of discomfort on her face when she'd held Felix, the fact that her alleged kids weren't with her at the goddamn cookie museum. My stomach was in knots.

Daphne didn't have kids. Of course she didn't. She didn't even have a real marriage. All of it was fabricated for financial gain. Being a mom not only opened new doors, it kept her relevant and relatable. OH. MY. GOD. This woman was nuts. She was a complete fucking sociopath and I'd let her commandeer my life.

Weeks went by before I finally heard from her.

"Hey," her text said. "We should talk…"

The message was short and direct. I wondered if she'd spoken with Marilyn.

"We should," I replied, trying to keep my emotions in check.

"I'll be near your place tomorrow, doing my Revolve shoot. Do you want to swing by?" I didn't bother to tell her that I'd moved to a far-off outer borough, to a basic two-bedroom apartment that was nowhere near swinging distance. I simply made the plan.

CHAPTER THIRTY-FOUR

It was bitingly cold when I took a cab to Daphne's Revolve shoot, the kind of weather that makes you wish you still lived in California.

A mighty gust pushed hard against my back as I thanked the driver and attempted to slam the car door behind me. The wind didn't want the door to close. It was a cosmic urging to simply get back in the vehicle and leave Daphne alone. But I couldn't leave her alone. She was like a pack of cigarettes in my glove compartment. I didn't trust that in a moment of weakness I wouldn't reach for her unless she was completely banished from my life.

The set was only three blocks from Ken's place and I could see my old apartment building from where I stood. A gaggle of crew members dressed in down jackets scurried up and down the sidewalk, trying to look busy. Daphne was huddled under a tent next to a heat lamp. She was scrolling on her phone and having her lipstick reapplied by a makeup artist.

"Meg!" she called out in a tone that was impossible to interpret. Was she happy? Was she sad? Was she even capable of any feeling at all?

Her eyes bore into mine as she walked toward me. Her coat was unbuttoned, and I noticed that she was wearing the exact same tie-dyed robe from the NBD shoot. She must have been freezing. She stopped just shy of hugging me, waiting for some kind of cue that it was okay. But I stood still.

"You finally found somewhere to wear the Etsy robe." I could see my breath in the air as I spoke.

"This is actually my design," Daphne said without flinching. It was as if she'd never told me about the art student online who'd originally designed it. "It's part of my capsule collection. I love the big pearl buttons," she said, not realizing — or not caring — that she said the exact same thing before.

"Right." I nodded. Daphne hadn't changed a bit. She started fidgeting from side to side, eager for me to follow her back under the heat lamp. But I didn't move.

"I thought you said you hated copycats." I couldn't hold back my irritation any longer.

Daphne laughed. "I don't know what you're talking about." She pulled her coat closed and folded her arms.

"I got a call from Marilyn at Abington," I told her. "She said your kids aren't even enrolled there." I looked at Daphne, waiting for an explanation. "Your *alleged* kids."

"You seem mad." Daphne spoke in a sickly sweet tone, the way I imagined people did to 1950s housewives who were being shipped off to mental asylums.

"Oh really? I seem mad?" I laughed. "Of course, I'm mad, Daphne! I trusted you. I…" Now tears started to well up in my eyes. "I cared about you. And I thought that you cared about me."

"I do care about you!" She reached out for my arm, and I pulled back. "But I care about a lot of people. And you were getting a little intense. I think you might be putting too much weight on what happened between us on the boat."

"This is not about the boat," I scoffed, trying to cover up my sense of hurt.

"I was just having a bit of fun," Daphne said casually. "Some girls just don't know how to separate that stuff. Why do you think I never took things further and fucked you? You would have been a total head case." Her words pierced my heart. "But babe, you are still my Galentine!" Daphne's tone suddenly turned cheery. She pulled a red box out of her coat pocket and handed it to me.

"I'm your what?" I looked at her in confusion.

"My *Gal*-entine," she said, lowering her voice to a whisper. "I know we're still a few weeks out, but Valentine's Day isn't just for lovers anymore. Open it." I took the lid off the box. It was filled to the brim with red-foil-wrapped chocolate lips.

"We got it!" a photographer called out from behind me, giving Daphne a thumbs up.

I could feel my knees buckling. "Is this..." I stared at Daphne in disbelief and loosened my grip on the box. The chocolate lips fell to the sidewalk. "Did you ask me here so you could use me for a paid post?"

"Oh come on, Meg, I wanted to see you! And I was planning on sending them to you anyway. What's the difference?"

"You're absolutely insane."

Her lips curled. "*I'm* the one who's insane? I'm who I've always been, Meg. You're the one who has no idea who she is."

"Say you're sorry," I told her.

"For what? Those are Jacques Torres chocolates." She cast her eyes down on the sidewalk. "They *were*."

I shook my head, almost pleading with her to just fess up. "Maybe you can fool other people with your fake miscarriage, your fake gingerbread mansions, and your fake children, but you can't fool me. Not anymore."

"I was never fooling you," she said in a harsh whisper. "*You* were fooling yourself. You wanted a distraction from your boring life and an escape from your lonely marriage."

"I like my husband," I shot back. "I wanted a friend."

Daphne shook her head. Her eyes filled with pity. "You wanted a mommy. Someone to tell you what a pretty, talented girl you were."

I was burning with hurt. "You endangered my children's lives, Daphne. You let me leave them with someone that you BARELY KNEW!"

"That was a misunderstanding. And you might want to keep your voice down." I saw that members of the crew were starting to drift closer to us, clearly trying to eavesdrop. What did I care, though?

"You didn't give a shit when my dog died. All you cared about was that stupid doggy detangler deal. The deal that you went out of your way to do anyway."

"It's not like I —"

"It's almost like you wanted to hurt me. You could have sat this one out. Instead, you took the twenty thousand dollars when you specifically told me that Susan doesn't let you leave your house for under seventy-five. You can lie about who you are to other people, but don't do it to me."

"*You* were going to make twenty thousand. *I* made eighty-five," she said coolly.

Every cell in my body was vibrating with rage. "Nice." I shook my head.

A PA interrupted, asking Daphne if he should call security. "I'm fine," she said, stepping away from me. "Good luck, Megan. I hope you get everything you want."

I watched as she tore off her coat and walked across the street, toward her mark on the corner of Canal and Mercer. Traffic whizzed by behind her as she glanced back at me with her saucer-like eyes and the chin dimple she always Facetuned out of photos. For a brief moment I was almost able to forget how crazy she was, how crazy *I* was, and just appreciate the beauty of the woman who had broken my heart.

"I'm sorry!" she called out to me. "For real." This was her last-ditch attempt to charm me into submission.

"Don't use that word, Daphne," I replied. "Nothing about you is real."

"Who said anything about real?" She looked at her crew and chuckled. "I'm selling fantasies out here."

"Maybe to other people," I said, playing the one card I knew she couldn't beat. "I unfollowed you."

Daphne reared back and stopped in the middle of the street, frozen. With the click of a button, I had erased her from my life. Not once in our six months together, not in any of the 4,892 photos of her that I had pored over online, had I ever seen her look so speechless. I was the one walking away. People didn't do that to Daphne. Passersby started to shout, but it was just noise. Neither of us saw what was coming next. An Uber X rounded the corner and barreled straight into her. And with that, Daphne Cole was gone.

CHAPTER THIRTY-FIVE

Everybody wanted the gory details, even Iliya, who never wanted to talk about Daphne. The truth was, I hardly remembered a thing. Moments after the accident, I passed out, and when I came to, I was lying on the sidewalk, looking up at the wintry sky and the heads of people hovering over me. I heard offers of water. I heard sirens. There was a blur of movement in the background. It was paramedics carrying Daphne's body away, I realized later.

Daphne had once given an interview to *Hamptons* magazine in which she said that she wanted her ashes spread around the coast of Manhattan, starting at East Sixty-Fifth Street (where the city's biggest Chanel store was) and then all the way down and around the island, past the Statue of Liberty and up to the Chelsea water-front. So that's what she got.

The farewell ceremony took place on a chartered motor yacht at sunset. Iliya offered to come, but I didn't want him to. I said I was sparing him the hell of being stuck on a boat yet again with some of the worst people he'd ever met. But I wasn't only operating out of kindness. I wanted a moment alone with Daphne. While I now understood that everything about her was fake, there was still something between us that had been real. At least on my end.

"Hey, baby." The words sent chills up my spine as I turned around to see Lauren standing behind me, wearing a full-length puffer coat and holding out a glass of Champagne. "Come have a drink with us?"

I followed her up to the top deck, passing familiar faces clustered around heat lamps. There was Christo, Daphne's personal shop-per from Barney's; Javier, who had lightened my hair; superagent Susan; Mia from Tramp Stamp; and a smattering of women who all looked eerily like me.

Near the bow I spied an older woman who was a dead ringer for Daphne. They had the exact same face, give or take twenty years. The woman looked monied and refined. She was wearing a navy wool coat and a dark pencil skirt.

"Not exactly how Daphne described her," I mumbled to nobody in particular.

Lauren turned to give me a quizzical look.

"That's the 'housekeeper mom from the Bronx'?" I asked.

"Connie, third-generation Sicilian from Summit, New Jersey. She works in real estate." Lauren rolled her eyes. "Daphne loved feeding people that bullshit story. Made her sound like the American Dream."

"I bought it," I said, shrugging.

"Didn't her accent ever tip you off? Like what was it even?" Lauren laughed.

I was too knotted up to speak. Daphne had told me that night in her closet that her entire life was a fabrication. She'd been clear. She hadn't hidden her red flags. I was just the fool who kept painting them white.

Lauren squeezed into a table next to Tanya and grimaced. Off in the corner, Kip was talking a little too cozily to Kiki. "And there goes the merry widower," Lauren said with a sigh. "The last thing Daphne's ashes need is another article in Page Six."

"Another article?" I didn't follow.

"They're running a piece about how he's been fucking Mia since the Tramp Stamp pop-up in East Hampton last year.

"That's old news." Tanya yawned. "The only person who didn't know that was Daphne."

"And you guys never bothered to tell her?" I looked at them.

"Hell no! Mia is the best trainer at Tramp Stamp. The real losers in that situation would have been our abs. You know she always had that rule, "Don't fuck where you sweat." She would have been furious!" Tanya turned to Lauren. "Speaking of workouts, did I tell you I found a new spot? Pump and Dump!"

"Oh, I've heard of them!" Lauren lit up. "Dance cardio, right?"

"It's more sculpty. You basically lift weights in a heated room for fifty minutes and then you get a colonic." Tanya smiled, then turned to me. "I'm really sorry about your dog."

"Thanks." I was genuinely shocked she'd remembered.

"Me too." Lauren feigned sympathy. "But you seem to be holding up. Your numbers must be jumping because of all this drama! How many followers do you have now?"

"I— I actually haven't looked in a few days," I lied. My count was now well past 90,000.

"Even Howie is getting work out of all of this," Tanya admitted. "Three women scheduled nose jobs this morning! Oh, and Daphne's numbers are through the roof!"

"Yeah, I'm thinking we'll make it into a tribute page for a bit. Gonna post a bunch of her best stuff, the greatest hits if you will, then maybe move into funny outtakes before I merge it with my own," Lauren added.

"You're taking over Daphne's account?" I looked at her.

"More like carrying the torch," she told me. "Can you watch my things for a second? I need to go say hi to Susan."

I sat there, soaking it all in. The likelihood of Lauren being able to pull off what Daphne had achieved was slim to none. But even Daphne's fiction was quietly falling apart, according to her "friends." Daphne's body had barely cooled before Kip was being asked to move out of the apartment. Half their rent was paid in trade and contingent upon Daphne talking on her feed about how the building was the best place to live.

Kip now stood at the center of the deck, calling out for everyone's attention. "Hi, everyone. Thank you so much for coming. It means so much to our family."

What family? I wondered.

"Before we do this," he went on, "I thought it would be great to get one last epic selfie with the queen of selfies herself." Kip held up a brass urn and my stomach recoiled as he gave it an Eskimo kiss with his Keebler elf nose. "Everybody, let's all squeeze in. And if you don't mind, tag the picture #WomanCrushWednesday. We'd also love it if you could kindly tag Triton Yachts, Krunktown Gin, and Ashes2Ashes, who did the most beautiful cremation I've ever seen."

I stood back and watched as Daphne's mother poured her daughter's remains into the river, each dusty particle delicately sinking into the abyss. Some onlookers cried, but most of the people on the boat just gossiped and chatted with friends as if they were on a sunset booze cruise.

Not in the mood for talking, I disappeared into a corner and stared out at the Manhattan skyline. I wondered if I'd made the right decision in coming here. In LA everybody was trying to find themselves, while in New York everybody was trying to become someone else. Where did I belong? Tears ran down my cheeks and I didn't even know who I was crying for.

I was done with trying to sell myself to strangers as somebody who they should aspire to be. I was done exploiting my children's childhood for bullshit chickpea puffs and organic sunscreen. Here I was, quite literally, lost at sea.

"Cigarette?" I looked up to see Tabitha Rose taking off her

shearling-lined gloves and opening up her pack of American Spirits.

"Thanks," I said. "I don't smoke." The breeze sprayed cold water against my cheeks.

"Me neither." She smiled coyly. Tabitha lit two cigarettes, handing one to me. "Such a shame, isn't it? An Uber X whose driver only had like a three-star rating. Thank god Daphne will never know what pancaked her."

It was my turn to feign amusement, but I felt heavy inside. I held my unsmoked cigarette over the ledge and watched as it disintegrated to ash, meeting Daphne in the brackish water below. "I'll miss her," I finally said.

"Will you?" She paused, lost in thought. "I'll just miss her clothes." Tabitha tossed her butt over the railing and walked off as if our conversation had never happened.

A moment later, Susan came around the corner holding a plateful of crab cakes and a glass of Champagne. "Meg! It's just so sad."

Her eyes were red, and her nose was puffy. I could tell that she was genuinely upset, which made me like her more than I ever had. "I don't know how I'm going to spin this," she said, biting into a crab cake. "Can you describe the driver to me? I'm so glad it was a man. If it had been a woman, this would be *so* much less relatable."

"It's all sort of a blur," I told her.

Susan drew a deep breath. "I'm already over this year."

"Only, what, eleven months to go?" I said.

Susan inched closer to me and raised her eyebrows. "I sort of have a small ask. *The Today Show* wants to do a piece about Daphne's death and influencers and has this all gone too far, yada, yada. Not to be morbid or anything, but you watched it happen. Would you be interested in talking to Jenna and Hoda?"

I gave a slow shake of the head. "I don't think I should."

"Come on! It's national television. You'd for sure get a few thousand more followers."

"I'm really not in the market for any more followers."

I saw that Susan was distracted, pulling a dark curly hair out of her crab cake. She shuddered.

"Nice," I deadpanned. "Comes with its own floss."

She snorted. "Daphne was right. You *are* funny! Look, I just need you to say a few things. Keep people believing in the art of influencing." Desperation filled her eyes. "A lot of people's livelihoods depend on this, Meg. If Lauren goes on the air, we're in trouble." I was unable to argue with her point. Susan looked at me imploringly. "Daphne would have wanted it to be you."

CHAPTER THIRTY-SIX

Two days later, I sat in a makeup chair in *The Today Show* green-room as a disinterested makeup artist slapped concealer under my eyes.

"I can't thank you enough for doing this," Susan said. She was standing beside me wearing a bright pink sweater and eating a stale bagel.

"We're going to move you guys up to set at the next break," a production assistant whispered to Susan.

I heard a familiar voice coming from behind and looked into the dressing room. There sat Marilyn from Abington, drinking a Dunkin Donuts coffee and talking on the phone. A young woman was at her side.

"Next!" the makeup artist called out.

"Ready for me?" Marilyn popped her head out. Her glasses sat crooked on her nose. She pushed them up, then did a double take when she saw me. "Megan!" she cried, then introduced me to her companion. Her name was Justine, and she was a reporter from the *New York Times*.

"So tragic what happened," Justine said. "I'd love to speak with you at some point. Maybe I can get your number before you go?"

I was too confused to give her an answer. "Are you also going on air?" I asked Marilyn. "I thought Daphne *wasn't* an Abington mom."

"Lauren and a few of the other parents are setting up a scholarship in her honor," Marilyn informed me. "She wasn't a part of the school per se, but she was a big part of the community." Marilyn looked down. "A new scholarship will mean a new opportunity. I know we weren't able to accommodate Roman initially, but that was before these unforeseen events… I can't imagine anyone who Daphne would have wanted to help more."

Before I could respond, the production assistant flew over to move us along. "Sorry, guys. We gotta scoot you up to set. We have Tom Hanks coming in to promote his new movie and he has an entourage of about ten people."

My stomach bottomed out. "Tom Hanks? He's here right now?"

The assistant went back to a conversation that was happening on his walkie-talkie. He then turned to me and nodded silently.

"I'd love to meet him if you'd feel comfortable introducing me, Meg," Marilyn said with an eager smile. "*Green Mile* is my favorite movie of all time."

Susan's ears perked up. "You know Tom Hanks?"

Blood rushed to my temples. My stupid application essay. "Like they say on Facebook: It's complicated." I smiled meekly.

Once I was on set, the sound guy clipped on my microphone, then handed me over to the AD. I was then led out onto the stage, where I took my seat next to Jenna and Hoda. They were just like I'd expected, only tinier.

"Now, don't look directly into the camera, and remember we are live. No cursing," the AD instructed before disappearing into a sea of light.

I smiled quickly and mouthed an awkward "hi" to Jenna before a red light indicated that we were rolling. Hoda turned to the camera, introducing our segment. "The Age of Influence," she said in an ominous *Dateline*-esque tone. "Has it gone too far?"

I tried not to look like I was on the verge of a panic attack as she caught the audience up to speed on what had happened. "Today we have one of Daphne's close friends, Megan Chernoff, here to share some insights," she started. "So, Meg, first of all I want to say I'm so sorry for your loss." I mumbled a thank you and shifted uncomfortably in my seat. Luckily for me, she didn't want to dwell on the condolences. "A hundred thousand followers, two kids, a husband, and a full-time career. I don't get it. It seems so exhausting. How do women like you and Daphne do it all?

"Well…" I started. The bright lights made me feel like I was under interrogation. I could feel my head throbbing and my knees shaking as I looked over at Marilyn, who stood next to Susan. My old friend Tom Hanks was across the studio, getting his mic checked. It was all too much.

"But seriously, what's the secret to keeping it so real?" Jenna chimed in.

My secret… I thought about Iliya, who I'd been keeping so much from, then I thought about my kids, who deserved better than what I was giving them. I owed it to all of them to tell the truth. And the truth was that I wasn't showing up in the way that I should have been. I was ignoring my real life in favor of a fucking app. I was no better than Daphne.

"I've been thinking about what I was going to tell you guys all morning," I started. "I don't keep it so real." I let off an awkward laugh. "The truth, Jenna and Hoda, is that nothing that's documented is real when you think about it. Once the cameras are on, it's all subjective. I'm lying all the time. We all are. And Daphne was no exception. She wasn't some superhero. She was a curator. She created a fantasy for women, for moms like you and me who desperately want to believe that motherhood can be summed up in a hashtag, that you can have it all if only you just own the right lunchbox or use the right face roller."

My hosts were nodding fervently.

"Stop!" Hoda said to me with a jokey smile. "I *love* my filters. I'm not sure I want to see the real me, or anyone else to see it, for that matter."

"But Daphne was in a league of her own," Jenna said, getting us back on track.

"She was," I agreed. "She knew how to take what people wanted and feed it back to them. She was a master marketer, but she certainly wasn't mom goals." I took a deep inhale. "In fact, she wasn't even a mom."

I saw Susan's eyes go wide.

Jenna gasped.

Hoda stared at me in disbelief.

Before either of them could formulate a question, I continued. "But I'm not here to tear down someone who can't defend herself. I'm here to clean up my own mess. My platform made me feel like the master of my own universe. I got to choose what people saw and what they didn't see. But that ability to play God started to permeate my real life. I've spent the last six months lying to everyone I know... I tried to get my son into private school by claiming that he was some sort of genius and that I was close friends with Tom Hanks." I peered into the studio and saw America's favorite actor look up at the sound of his name. "Hi, Tom Hanks, I'm Meg Chernoff. We've never met. I loved you in *Forrest Gump*. *The 'Burbs* was probably my favorite. *Splash* was great too!"

Tom gave one of his humble Tom Hanks waves. There was a kindness to the gesture that encouraged me to keep going. I turned back to Hoda and Jenna, trying to block out Marilyn, who was twitching with rage in the opposite corner. "Sure," I went on, "the outfits and captions were fun. But it was all a show. And it erased anything that actually mattered. I was so busy trying to prove what a good parent I was that I stopped being a good parent."

"Then why do it?" Jenna probed.

"I was addicted to the praise. To the external validation. To the free stuff," I admitted.

"But like my husband says, nothing is ever free. And it's never enough. It was never enough for Daphne either. 'More is more.' That's what she used to say. And I guess the biggest thing I've learned since her passing is that more is just more. It's not better. It doesn't fill the hole. It is the hole."

The studio was silent, and I could hear the buzzing from the lights overhead. Finally, Jenna came to her senses and called for a commercial break. "I'm sorry if that wasn't what you were expecting," I told her when I stood to leave.

She shook her head and embraced me. "Thank you for your honesty. It's refreshing."

I walked past Marilyn, who refused to make eye contact. She was really bummed that I didn't know Tom Hanks. Susan didn't seem too happy either.

"You realize you just brought down half my clientele, so I should hate your guts. But that whole bit about mom guilt? Genius," Susan said when we were alone. "You've probably blown it with most mainstream brands; they like their influencers a bit less Machiavellian. But what you're doing is different. It's fresh. If you ever want to talk about representation... my offer stands."

"Thanks, but I was serious up there, Susan. It wasn't a bit. I'm done."

We walked out an exit where a row of black SUVs waited next to a cluster of autograph hunters holding Tom Hanks headshots. My phone was blowing up with messages, some from Iliya and others from friends I hadn't spoken to in years. I turned to go, then stopped. "Hey, Susan? Out of curiosity, were there others? I mean, more than a couple?"

Susan shot me a look that said nothing and everything all at once.

"You were one of her most favorites."

CHAPTER THIRTY-SEVEN

After watching *The Today Show*, Marina agreed to postpone her date with Irving and stay to watch the boys. At Iliya's behest, I met him after work for a much-needed chat.

We went to Veselka, the Ukrainian diner on Second Avenue that Iliya had managed in his youth and still talked about in rhapsodic tones. We were seated in a booth up front. A knot of Russian men congregated at the counter, along with a smattering of aging East Village punks. The hipster foodies one booth over were asking the grumpy waitress which menu items were on the Infatuation's current top-ten list.

"I haven't been back here in ages," Iliya said, biting into a piping hot pierogi. "You have to have one of these." He gave me a fork, but I was still too sick to my stomach to eat.

I chugged some ice water and took a deep breath. "I owe you an apology."

"Maybe," he said. His eyes twinkled in a way that gave me a modicum of hope.

"I fucked up." He nodded and motioned for me to keep going. "And I don't know if you'll ever forgive me, but I really want you to because I love you and I need you and I'm never going to be that person again. I let this whole thing control me. I let it take priority over everything — you, the kids, us. I don't know if you can hear this and believe it, but I want you to know that I'm sorry and I'm going to work every day to show you that you and the boys are all that matter."

"Thank you." He got started on another pierogi.

"I can't have you thinking that I'm a bad mom. That I'd ever intentionally—" I was on the verge of weeping.

He stopped chewing and looked at me. "I don't think that you are a bad mom. If I did, we wouldn't be sitting here." He put down his fork and paused. "And I should have supported you more."

I sat up straighter. "What do you mean?"

"I should have seen that you were struggling. I was just trying to push through. When what you needed, or at least what I think you needed, was just someone to listen."

Tears spilled down my face. I was overwhelmed with gratitude and remorse.

"Did you love her?" Iliya looked down, his voice cracking ever so slightly.

"Not like I love you…" I shook my head. "Nothing like I love you," I said, more certain than ever.

"Glad to hear it. So, what do we do now?" He resumed eating.

"We go back to normal?" I was digging my fingernails into my thighs under the table. "I stop with the influencing."

"No more toot puffs?" He rubbed his eyelids and gave me a smile.

I shook my head and laughed. "No more," I told him. "No more private school applications, no more silly trampoline classes, no more cardboard boxes blocking our front door."

Iliya pursed his lips and let off a slow exhale. "That sounds like a good place to start."

I felt an unclenching within. "I want to be with you, Iliya. I want to make this work."

"Me too." A smile came to his face. We were going to be okay. "Let's start with you trying a pierogi before I eat 'em all."

CHAPTER THIRTY-EIGHT

It had been an unseasonably warm winter, according to lifelong New Yorkers. We were only halfway through March and cherry blossoms were already starting to bloom.

I was almost hot in my parka when I arrived at the playground. It was 4:40 p.m. Felix's first birthday party was due to start in twenty minutes. I'd taken the day off work to run party errands. The subway from Long Island City had been slower than I'd hoped, and I had a ton of setting up to do. The party was downtown to make it easier for Iliya to join us after work.

Marina and the kids had gone directly to the park after school pickup. She waved to me from on top of the slide, where Felix was straining to touch his big brother, who was hanging from the monkey bars. I dropped my copious belongings on a long wooden bench and started preparing the picnic table. I was only halfway done separating the towers of party hats when my phone rang. It was Vigo, calling to ask if he and Seth could bring anything.

"No! Just come."

"Tell her that we didn't know what he was into," Seth said in the background.

"Tell Seth he's turning *one*," I reminded Vigo. "He's not into anything."

"Turn left!" Vigo said, presumably to the driver. "No, left. LEFT!"

"I'll see you guys soon." I smiled and hung up. Then I looked at my messages and saw that Bubby had texted to say that she was en route but stopping at Magnolia for the cupcakes. I took a short inhale when I saw there was only fifteen minutes to go.

Dasha's sciatica was acting up, so she wasn't going to make it, but Irving was coming with both his kids. This would be the first time they were meeting Marina, and we were all instructed to be on our best behavior.

Ken was back in New York and planning to stop by. He was coming solo. His girlfriend was working on a zombie movie in Budapest and was rumored to be hooking up with Wesley Snipes. Ken was a wreck, and Iliya made me promise not to bring up anything to do with zombies when Ken arrived. "That's going to be hard," I'd told him. "What else does anyone talk about at a one-year-old's birthday party where the theme is *Bubble Guppies*?"

Sari fumbled with the large iron gate at the entrance as Waverly effortlessly slipped through the bars and ran to join Roman on the swings. I went to help Sari unload goody bags from her car.

She lit up when she saw me. "Congrats, Meg! Is the deal officially closed?" Sari inquired, digging into her trunk for the candies to fill our piñata. I nodded, still unable to believe that it was real.

After the *Times* piece had come out, things changed rather quickly. I took two weeks off from launching Seth's shower gels to cobble together a book proposal based on my experience with Daphne and the world of influencing. It was pitched as a fairytale meets cautionary tale, and my agent had only been out with it for two days when three editors bid on the book. All that journaling had come in handy.

"I'm really proud of you," Sari said as we walked back into the park. "You've made me reevaluate how much weight I give this cursed thing." She waved her cellphone in the air. "I'm thinking I might go on one of those retreats where there's no Wi-Fi or Chardonnay."

As we put the finishing touches on the table, guests started to trickle in. There was Eszti, a mom friend I'd recently made in Queens, and her two boys. Then came Sylvia, one of Roman's favorite teachers, followed by Joanne, my new editor, with her wife, Laura.

Everyone was giddy over the signs of spring. Good weather was something we all took for granted in Los Angeles. But the changes in seasons seemed to bond New Yorkers, and I kind of liked it. It wasn't just a way to mark the passage of time, but a shared experience that we were all enduring, a common thread.

Our crew colonized the entire front corner of the park. Iliya was on the scene, entertaining a gaggle of guests with his boyhood tales of Coney Island mischief.

Sari nudged me. "Did you read that Daphne is being sued posthumously for that tie-dye robe she knocked off?"

"I missed that," I said, still figuring out how to hang a piñata from the leaning limb of a tree.

"Girl, there's a whole paper trail of her promising to post in exchange for free merch and then never following through. She was sending the stuff off to China and having it reproduced under her label for that Revolve collab. I can't believe you haven't heard. It's even on Diet Prada." Sari raised her eyebrows at me. "Do you not check your gram *at all* these days?"

"I have ten days under my belt," I said proudly.

"Well, when you have a moment of weakness, you really should peek, because they mentioned NBD."

"What did they say?" Apprehensive, I pulled my phone out of my back pocket. My finger hovered over the app's rainbow-colored icon.

"Mom! Mommy! Look how high I'm swinging!" I heard Roman screaming from the swings. "Mommy! Mommy! Look at me!" he called out again.

I looked up at my son, who was swinging his heart out. The

sunlight was refracting into thick segments and the sky was the truest blue I'd ever seen. It was so beautiful. Prettier than any filter. I asked Sari if she could finish rigging up the piñata and stuffed my phone back into my pocket.

"Roman!" I called out as I headed over to him. "I see you!"

ACKNOWLEDGEMENTS

Thank you to Lauren Mechling, who saw my vision from day one and elevated my work to levels I never dreamed possible.

And Haley Heidemann who championed this book through a literal pandemic and never stopped believing in its worthiness.

Thank you to my PR dream team Jami Kandel and Megan Beattie, who followed me fearlessly through the darkest of hours.

Thanks to Richard Pine, for convincing me to try fiction.

Thank you to Julia Bodner, Hilary Zaits Michael, Alicia Everett, Lauren Rogoff, at WME and my lawyer, Julian Zajfen.

Thank you to Ben Denzer and Aaron Bernstein for letting me micromanage the fuck out of this cover.

Thank you to Lauren Moffat, Lauren Stein, Christopher King and Jessica Casey at Sony and the incomparable Jamie Tarses, who I wish could have seen this one come to fruition.

Thank you to Brian Volk-Weiss, Rich Mayerik, and the entire Nacelle team.

And thank you to my friends, family and allies who have always helped propel me forward, Mom, Dad, Samantha, Mema, Poppi, and Chiara… Diablo Cody, Joe Veltre, Adrienne

Miller, Joanne Spataro, Charlotte Groeneveld, Stephanie Danler, Katie Sturino, Chelsea Handler, Stacey Bendet, Melody Young, Margret Riley King, Sophie Flack, Michael Kravit, Liz Vaccariello, Grant Ginder, Jessica Hartshorn, Jenny Hutt, Jill Kargman, Jess Glick, Curtis Rich, Victoria Gray, Breanna Schultz, Brent Neale, Shandiz Zandi, Beth Becker, Lauren Gershell, Emily Henry, Caitlin Mehner, Bethany D'Meza, Oren Tepper, Justin Bartha, Rebecca Serle, Jennifer Lancaster, Jennifer Eatz, Julia Chebotar, Olga Grinberg, Wynne Hamerman, Reid Rolls, Amber Mazzola, Miriam Tarver, Ashley Bellman, Ashlee Glazer, Dan Powers, Katie Taylor, Zibby Owens, Lauren Bochner, Jamie Rosenblit, Juan the lifeguard, Edsel the doorman, Lou, Max, Scottie, Nugget, Miguel, Rudy, Eszti, Jehan, Juju, Sylvia, Gina, Chad Gervich, and ALWAYS the ghost of MuthafuckingTeets.

Also to my sons, Sid and Lazlo who told me to quit writing and go back to being an out of work actor because then I could always pick them up from school.

And of course to my husband Jason… Jason, Jason, Jason. Only you know what writing this cost me, cost us emotionally. Thank you for being my cheerleader, my copyeditor and my confidant. You, are the only reason people think I know how to use a comma. I couldn't have done it without you. Or maybe I could have. It just wouldn't have been legible. I love you.

CPSIA information can be obtained
at www.ICGtesting.com
Printed in the USA
LVHW081132100522
717064LV00005BB/5/J